# CORPORATION
# AND SOCIETY RESEARCH

# CORPORATION AND SOCIETY RESEARCH:
## Studies in Theory and Measurement

Edited by

## LEE E. PRESTON
*University of Maryland, College Park*

 JAI PRESS INC.

Greenwich, Connecticut     London, England

**Library of Congress Cataloging-in-Publication Data**

Corporation and society research.

"Ten essays reprinted from Research in corporate social performance and policy, volumes 1–10, plus two new papers especially prepared for publication here"—Editor's introd.
    Includes bibliographical references.
    1. Industry—Social aspects. 2. Industry—Social aspects—United States.
I. Preston, Lee E.
HD60.C697      1990            306.3          90-4604
ISBN 1-55938-222-8

# CONTENTS

# LIST OF CONTRIBUTORS

Patti N. Andrews
*Boston University*

Kenneth E. Aupperle
*Kent State University*

Raymond A. Bauer
*Harvard University*

Max B. E. Clarkson
*University of Toronto*

Denis Collins
*University of Pittsburgh*

Robert J. DeFillippi
*Washington State University*

Kathleen Getz
*University of Pittsburgh*

Walter R. Holman
*Loyola College*

David Jacobs
*University of Maryland*

John F. Mahon
*Boston University*

J. Randolph New
*University of San Francisco*

William Oberman
*University of Pittsburgh*

James E. Post
*Boston University*

Lee E. Preston
*University of Maryland*

Lyman Reed
*University of Pittsburgh*

Daniel Singer
*Loyola College*

Robert Toy
*University of Pittsbugh*

# SERIES FOREWORD

This volume is one of five collections of essays reprinted from volumes 1-10 of the JAI Press series, *Research in Corporate Social Performance and Policy,* 1978-1988.

The five volumes being published simultaneously in 1990 are as follows:

*International and Comparative Corporation and Society Research* (Lee E. Preston, editor)

*Corporation and Society Research: International and Comparative Studies* (Lee E. Preston, editor)

*Business and Politics: Research Issues and Empirical Studies* (Lee E. Preston, editor)

*Government Regulation and Business Response: Research Issues and Empirical Studies* (Lee E. Preston, editor)

*Business Ethics: Research Issues and Empirical Studies* (William C. Frederick and Lee E. Preston, editors)

# EDITOR'S INTRODUCTION

This volume contains ten essays reprinted from *Research in Corporate Social Performance and Policy,* volumes 1-10, plus two new papers especially prepared for publication here. All of these pieces are concerned with the relationship between the corporation and its host society—particularly with the large and professionally managed corporation in contemporary, complex, postindustrial society. Most of them are also concerned with research methodology—that is, with finding ways to *study* corporation-society relationships so that one can discover what they actually are (as opposed to what may be intended or imagined to be), *why* they are as they are, and how they may be changing over time. In addition, some of these papers develop and apply sophisticated techniques of observation and measurement in order to describe particular features of firms and their environments, and to examine these relationships through statistical analysis.

The first essay in the volume, formally published here for the first time, surveys the evolution of corporation-society studies over the decades since World War II and identifies some important areas for future research. This analysis shows that the current level and focus of activity in this area evolved in response to widespread social change, and that new conceptions of corporation-society relations have now become institutionalized in both management practice and academic study. The second paper, also original in this volume, presents a comprehensive review and synthesis of the contents of volumes 1-10 of the JAI research series. The authors identify the main research themes pursued, the principal propositions investigated, and the main results obtained with respect to each. (They also identify many important research issues *not* investigated in *any* of the 112 studies published to date!) Since the body of work covered by their survey may be roughly estimated to constitute about half of all the significant empirical work published in this area over the past decade, their analysis should provide a useful framework for further integration and appraisal of this literature, including both past and future research contributions.

The following two papers, both reprinted from volume 1 of the series, present ideas that have had major impact on the evolution of this area of study over the past decade. My own essay attempts to establish a broad conceptual framework for the field. It was my hope that this framework—essentially the interpenetrating systems model—would be filled out with empirical studies in subsequent volumes of the series. (The analysis presented by Reed et al. in the preceding paper reveals the extent to which this goal was, in fact, accomplished in the first ten volumes.) Post's following paper further develops the interpenetrating systems perspective and illustrates its application in a specific research setting (the insurance industry). This essay also presents the typology of "corporate response patterns," which remains a prominent research theme in the field up to the present.

DeFillippi's essay from volume 4 follows up and expands on my own essay in volume 1, with greater emphasis on methodological issues. He explores in detail the differences among various research paradigms and emphasizes the types of choices that must be made as any substantial research study proceeds. Mahon reexamines the work of James M. Thompson, one of the most influential contributors to management theory, to discover its implications for corporation-society research, and summarizes the otherwise unavailable work of Thomas Page, who built upon and extended Thompson's ideas.

Jacobs' essay, reprinted from volume 7, presents an entirely different conception of the corporation-society relationship, derived from neo-Marxist analysis. (The short paper by Maurice Zeitlin in volume 1 of the series is also relevant in this connection.) The critical Marxist perspective contrasts sharply with the more benign paradigms characteristic of the management literature, but Jacobs' analysis shows that some of the same research problems, methodological approaches, and even empirical studies familiar to conventional researchers are also encountered and utilized by radical analysts.

Papers by Bauer, and by Post and Andrews, complete the broad theoretical-methodological portion of this volume. Bauer, a pioneer of social science research to whose memory the first volume of the research series is dedicated, describes the methodological considerations guiding a group of important field research studies carried out under his direction at the Harvard Business School. His paper, and the related Appendix A to volume 1 (not reprinted here), provides a step-by-step approach to this type of research. [Other papers published in the series, but not reprinted here, present the results of some of the studies using this method: e.g., Brenner (vol. 2), Taylor (vol. 3), Sonnenfeld (vol. 4).] The paper by Post and Andrews further refines the methodology of case research and shows how, in their phrase, "little steps" taken in the course of large and well-designed research projects can lead to important analytical results. (The corollary that "little steps," if poorly executed, can bring large projects to disaster is not emphasized by Post and Andrews, but is certainly worth noting here.)

The three other papers in this volume report on ambitious empirical research projects. Aupperle develops a method for quantifying the four-dimensional model of corporate social involvement suggested by Carroll, and applies it to several previously researched corporation-society issues; particularly the connection between corporate social orientation and financial performance. Although Aupperle's own empirical results are largely inconclusive, his analytical method and his survey of prior work on this specific issue have proved of continuing value. The empirical study by Holman et al. pursues the financial performance issue further, using more sophisticated techniques from the financial literature, and yields some significant results. Clarkson's essay reports on a study of major Canadian firms that was inspired by the Carroll-Aupperle approach and involved much more detailed scrutiny of individual firm activities and policies than most other large multifirm studies have been able to accomplish.

Since this volume contains papers published in the JAI series at various times over its initial decade, as well as a comprehensive analysis of the first ten volumes in their entirety, it seems appropriate to include some brief background on the development of the series from its beginnings. JAI editors approached the late Professor Raymond A. Bauer about the possibility of developing a research series in the "policy" area sometime in early 1976. He believed that the focus should be narrowed to corporate policies and impacts vis-à-vis the social environment, the theme of his own on-going research, rather than on either "business policy" or "public policy" in general.

When Bauer drew me into the project later in the year, we agreed that the series would emphasize empirical studies of the social impact, both intentional and inadvertent, of business operations, with particular emphasis on the efforts of firms to "manage" their relationships with the larger society. This decision reflected not only Bauer's current interests but also his lifelong emphasis on gathering and analyzing new kinds of social science data, an activity he referred to as "opening empirical windows." Selection of the phrase "social performance and policy" for the series title was intended to suggest that both the *intent* (i.e., "policy") and the *impact* (i.e., "performance") of corporate activity would be included. Bauer and I both wanted to avoid the phrase "social responsibility," which had acquired a wide variety of meanings—some of them quite controversial—over the previous decade. At the same time, we felt that the term "performance" (already widely used in economics and finance) carried the clear implication that the data gathered would be analyzed and evaluated—

but in terms of criteria specified and justified by the researchers involved, not according to any preconceptions of orthodoxy.

My own retrospective appraisal of the first ten volumes of the JAI series is that they have achieved their intended objectives to a considerably greater extent than might have been expected. I hope that readers who are introduced to the series by this selection of theoretical and methodological papers will want to consult the original volumes for additional examples of the type of work the series has stimulated. I hope and believe also that subsequent volumes in the series, under new editorial leadership, will continue to contribute to our understanding—and to the improvement—of this important sphere of managerial activity and social life.

LEE E. PRESTON

# CORPORATION-SOCIETY RESEARCH:
## RETROSPECT AND PROSPECT

Lee E. Preston

What is—and what *should be*—the nature of the large corporation? What is—and what *should be*—its relationship to the economy and the larger society? These questions have motivated a large and diverse body of research—as well as some heated debates—over the past half-century (Preston, 1975). And, although the answers could hardly be said to be "known" at this point, much has been learned in the process of exploration. This paper characterizes the recent evolution of corporation-society studies, and suggests some directions for future work. The analysis necessarily ranges back and forth between the groves of academe and the world of practical affairs and public policy, since changes in the environment alter the interests and activities of academics, and intellectual developments in turn affect managerial practice and public policy options.

# BACKGROUND

The points of contact between the large modern corporation and its social environment are many and diverse: human (quality of work life, standard of living), legal, environmental, systemic (competition, regulation). The classical concept of capitalism holds that these contacts should be mediated primarily through the market mechanism, with a secondary role for government maintenance of law and order, protection of property rights, and provision of a monetary system. According to Friedman's classic statement, "The role of government ... is to do something that the market cannot do for itself, namely, to determine, arbitrate and enforce the rules of the game" (Friedman, 1962, p. 27). In this perspective, managerial consideration of the social aspects of corporate activity outside of a market or regulatory framework is undesirable, and probably illegitimate. If the public will neither *pay* for something through the market nor *require* it through government, then managers *as managers* should not do it at all. (This dictum, of course, places no limitation on the freedom of managers as private citizens to exercise their tastes and resources in any way they see fit.)

Of course, there have always been benevolent business owners and managers who embraced early and paternalistic forms of what we now call "corporate social responsibility." The doctrine of capitalistic benevolence was formally proclaimed in Andrew Carnegie's *Gospel of Wealth* (1900), and many enlightened firms made long-term and costly commitments to the welfare of their employees and communities during the decades of industrialization between the Civil War and the Great Depression. (Heald, 1970, presents the best summary review of this experience; for an historic record of U.S. Steel's social program, see Hogner, 1982.) These activities, however, were of substantial scale only in a small number of cases, and during the Great Depression many corporate programs concerned with the welfare of employees were embraced by government regulation or taken over by the labor movement and addressed through collective bargaining.

Over roughly the same period—the pre-World War II decades—broader business concern with social problems ripened into the Community Chest movement (Heald, 1970). However, whatever its virtues, this movement focused primarily on problems and programs remote from the firm, rather than those closely associated with the impact of business activity on society. As a practical matter, management recognition of and response to the more direct human and social impact of business activity on employees, customers, surrounding communities, and others has been due primarily to legislative enactments and public programs brought about by political actors, labor groups, and dogged reformers. Little wonder that the relationship between business and public policy came to be seen as essentially adversarial, and that the study of this relationship became identified with the rubric "social control of business," with an emphasis on *control*. (J.M. Clark's 1926 volume of this title presents the classic treatment of the theme.)

Also during the same period, scattered expressions of a more contemporary viewpoint began to emerge. General Robert E. Wood, CEO of Sears, acknowledged "your management's stewardship ... of those general broad social responsibilities which cannot be presented mathematically and yet are of prime importance"in his 1936 Annual Report (Worthy, 1984, p. 173). Wood, along with Robert Wood Johnson (of Johnson & Johnson), was one of the first to acknowledge the multiple interests involved in what would now be known as the "stakeholder" model of the corporation, and to advocate managerial, rather than purely governmental, response to social concerns.

The views expressed by these pre-war "corporate social responsibility" advocates did not attract an immediate wave of followers. Nor did a contemporaneous effort of Stanford University Professor Theodore Kreps to develop a "corporate social audit" (Kreps, 1940; for more detail, see Carroll and Beiler, 1975). But popular conceptions about the social role of business began to change gradually during the 1950s. Many factors were at work, but the increasing role of government during the Great Depression and World War II laid the foundation for a changed perception, and continued business-government collaboration in the Cold War environment revealed the extent and importance of mutual interests. The prominent role taken by the Committee for Economic Development, an organization of enlightened business leaders aimed at continuing business-government cooperation through the postwar reconversion, reflected the more harmonious attitudes of the era (Neal, 1981).

The social revolution of the 1960s—expanding from the Civil Rights Movement to include opposition to the Vietnam War, women's liberation, environmentalism, consumerism and a host of other human and social issues—shattered this complacency. With cities in flames, corporate offices closed by demonstrations and bomb threats, and campuses under siege, it was apparent that some new understanding of the social environment, some new approach to dealing with pressing public concerns, was required, and not only in government, but in business and academe as well. When Votaw and Sethi (1969) asked "Do we need a new corporate response to a changing social environment?" it had already been obvious for some time that the answer was "yes." This was the setting for the new wave of corporation-society studies that continues up to the present.

## FOCUS OF STUDY

In both academic and applied settings, studies of the corporation-society relationship focus primarily on the *nonmarket* forces that form an integral part of the context of management. Although much of the writing in this area reveals a significant ideological base of some sort, corporation-society research—particularly research undertaken from a *management perspective*—does not involve commitment to any particular concept of "social responsibility" nor to any particular set of policy choices for citizens and governments. Instead, the focus is on the ways in which business, government, and other actors/forces in the social and political environment interact, and the kinds of policies and ultimate impacts that result. The practical purpose is to provide a basis for wise decision making and successful implementation by business managers.

The foundation principles of contemporary corporation-society research can be stated as follows:

1. The contemporary corporation is engaged in continuous interaction with nonmarket forces that vitally affect its operations and ultimate viability;
2. These nonmarket forces are frequently as important, and sometimes more important, than market forces in determining the long-run viability and success of the business enterprise;
3. Therefore, the nonmarket relationships of the firm require analysis and management comparable in quality and sophistication to the analysis and management of the market environment.

Corporation-society analysts generally believe that managerial organizations cannot operate successfully over the long run in conflict with their environments. Therefore, successful management involves some combination of (a) adaptation to environmental conditions, specifically those that arise from public policy, and (b) interaction with the environment, particularly through the public policy process, in an attempt to make it more hospitable to the organization.

The distinction between market and nonmarket forces affecting the firm, and the extent to which either is susceptible to managerial influence, is illustrated in Table 1. Both market and nonmarket environments contain substantial elements over which the firm has no discernable influence—the number and purchasing ability of the customer population, the social system, and structure of government, etc. By contrast, there are both market and nonmarket variables that are to some degree "manageable," i.e., within the firm's control. The familiar strategic marketing variables are joined here by the firm's involvement in and response to changes in its social environment and in public policy.

The "unmanageable" forces in the business environment are moderately familiar from general knowledge—although, as with the "unmanageable"

Table 1.   Focus of Corporation/Society Analysis

|  | Market | Nonmarket |
|---|---|---|
| Unmanageable | Population<br>Income<br>Tastes<br>Activities of other firms | Physical environment<br>Social system and culture<br>Government structure and<br>    fundamental policies |
| Manageable | Product/service offering<br>Market communication<br>Price<br>Location/investment | Public communication<br>Adaptation to external change<br>Participation in public policy<br>    process |

market variables, basic information must be continuously reviewed and updated, and new implications are often discovered. The action side of corporation-society analysis emphasizes the "manageable" nonmarket variables, and makes use of concepts and analytical techniques drawn from both management and the social sciences for this purpose. The varied content involved is suggested by some of the terms used to describe this type of activity:

*Environmental Analysis.* Encompasses the study of political, economic, market, and, sometimes, technological data in search of major developments and trends. In recent years, a number of people have tried to turn general trend-spotting for corporate clients into a commercial business. Prominent examples are SRI International and the Yankelovich and Naisbitt organizations; the latter was responsible for the popular bestseller, *Megatrends* (Naisbitt, 1983).

*Issues Management.* Applies techniques and information from environmental analysis to delineate the evolutionary path of critical public issues and to devise appropriate organizational strategies of intervention and/or adjustment. There is no implication that corporations will actually "manage" public issues; the idea is that they can and should try to "manage" their own involvement in such issues, rather than simply being overwhelmed by circumstances. The term "issues management" in this specific sense was coined by Howard W. Chase, publisher of the *Trend Report* and founder of the Issues Management Association.

*Public Affairs.* Now the standard corporate rubric covering the broad involvement and activity of the firm in relation to its external environment. The new public affairs function represents an evolution from the older "public relations" concept, with greater emphasis on information gathering and analysis and on internal corporate policy-making, including decisions about *business* involvement in the *public* policy process. The Public Affairs Council, founded in 1954 in response to a suggestion by President Eisenhower, has provided major stimulus for increasing professionalization of this activity.

Underlying these areas of practical application, the academic side of corporation-society research includes a broad intellectual interest in the processes of public policy formation and organizational adaptation that alter the business environment over the long term. An appreciation for the historical evolution of public concerns and governmental activities affecting business, and some comparative perspectives on other countries and cultures, are also included within the domain of the field. (See, for example, the coverage of some of the leading texts: Steiner and Steiner, 1988; Davis, Frederick, and Post, 1988; Buchholz, 1989.)

## THE EVOLUTIONARY PROCESS

Contemporary analysis of social change and policy development reveals that many different issues and concerns follow a common evolutionary pattern, "from social issues to public policy" (Eyestone, 1978) or "the issues life cycle" (Molitor, 1980). The schematic device used to describe this evolutionary pattern is a generalized growth curve, depicting an increasing level of activity over time up to some ceiling (Figure 1). The progress of development along the curve can be described in terms of three major phases—gestation and innovation, development and expansion, maturity and institutionalization. Issues and policies differ, of course, in the length of time involved in the various evolutionary phases and in the eventual level of development attained.

This section of the paper uses the "issues life cycle" concept to describe the evolution of contemporary corporation-society studies, in the worlds of academe and of practical affairs. Precise declination of the phases of evolution is, of course, somewhat arbitrary, but use of this model throws considerable light on the pattern of development—and particularly the interaction between external events and research contributions—over the recent decades. Highlights of each evolutionary phase are listed in Table 2.

### Precursors

Nothing, of course, happens without precedents. During the halcyon Fifties, thoughtful persons noted the new and apparently permanent importance of large scale organizations in economic and social life, and tried to explore its implications. Two important studies commissioned by the National Council of Churches—Howard R. Bowen's *The Social Responsibilities of the*

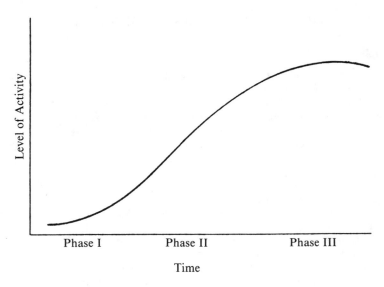

*Notes:*  Phase I: Gestation and Innovation (1960s)
Phase II: Development and Expansion (1970s)
Phase III: Maturity and Institutionalization (1980s)

*Figure 1.*   Evolution of contemporary corporation/society analysis.

*Businessman* (1953) and Kenneth Boulding's *The Organizational Revolution* (1954)—emphasized that the new role and power of large organizations, particularly business organizations, necessarily required a new level of social involvement and responsibility for management. A.A. Berle, analyst of the earlier managerial revolution involving the separation of ownership and control, argued that corporate management must now "take account of philosophical considerations. They must consider the kind of community which they intend to help to construct and maintain" (Berle, 1954, pp. 166-167).

## Gestation and Innovation

These prescient analyses appear to have passed almost unnoticed, but the times themselves were nevertheless a-changing. Expanding enrollments in business schools and a general impression that much of the education provided in them was of low quality stimulated the Ford and the Carnegie Foundations to commission study reports, both published in 1959, which recommended greater breadth in business education, including increased historical and social science background. A few institutions—Berkeley, Columbia, Washington— began to give the business environment prominent recognition in their

*Table 2.*    Highlights of the Evolutionary Process

---

*Precursors*

Committee for Economic Development, established 1942.
Public Affairs Council, established 1954.
Howard R. Bowen, *Social Responsibilities of the Businessman,* 1953.
Kenneth E. Boulding, *The Organizational Revolution,* 1954.
A.A. Berle, *The 20th Century Capitalist Revolution,* 1954.
Ford Foundation and Carnegie Foundation report on business education, recommending greater
    breadth, 1959.

*Phase I: Gestation and Innovation*

Joseph W. McGuire, *Business and Society,* 1963.
Keith Davis, "The Public Role of Management," Academy of Management Presidential Address,
    1964 (*Proceedings* 1965, pp. 3-9).
Keith Davis and Robert L. Blomstrom, *Business and Its Environment,* 1966.
AACSB Curriculum Standard IV(b), mandating "a background of the economic and legal
    environment ... social and political influences, effective 1967.
Dow Votaw and S.P. Sethi, "Do We Need a New Corporate Response to a Changing Social
    Environment?," *California Management Review,* 1969.
General Electric Company, Business Environment Group develops new and influential concepts
    and techniques; published as Dunckel et al., *The Business Environment of the Seventies,*
    1970.

*Phase II: Development and Expansion*

Academy of Management divisionalized; Social Issues in Management (SIM) Division established,
    1971.
General Electric Foundation conference grants to UCLA, Catholic University, Columbia, Berkeley
    and SUNY-Buffalo, 1971-79.
George A. Steiner, *Business and Society,* 1971.
Committee for Economic Development, *Social Responsibilities of Business Corporations,* 1971.
Abt Associates, Inc., Annual Report + Social Audit, 1971 (annual).
*Business and Society Review* established, 1972.
General Motors Corporation, "Progress in Areas of Social Concern," 1971 (annual).
Eastern Gas and Fuel Associates, "Toward Social Accounting," Annual Report Supplement, 1972.
Business Roundtable organized, 1972.
AACSB Annual Meeting on "Business and Society" theme, 1975.
Lee E. Preston and James E. Post, *Private- Management and Public Policy,* 1975.
William C. Frederick, "Business and Society Curriculum: Suggested Standards for Accreditation,"
    *AACSB Bulletin,* 1977.
AICPA, *The Measurement of Corporate Social Performance,* 1977.
U.S. Secretary of Commerce Juanita Kreps suggests development of a "Corporate Social
    Performance Index, 1977.
General Motors and others, Sullivan Principles for U.S. Companies Doing Business in South
    Africa, adopted 1977.
Lee E. Preston, editor, *Research in Corporate Social Performance and Policy,* Vol. 1, 1978.

---

(*continued*)

*Table 2.* (*continued*)

---

*Phase III: Maturity and Institutionalization*

AACSB, Business and Government Relations Committee Task Force, study of the business environment/public policy field, leading to (1) Buchholz Report, 1979; (2) AACSB BE/PP Conferences, 1979 and subsequent.

OECD, "Guidelines for Multinational Enterprise," 19791.

The Conference Board, *This Business of Issues* and *Guidelines for Managing Corporate Issues Programs* (Brown, 1979 and 1981).

Business Roundtable, "Statement on Corporate Responsibility," 1981.

WHO Code of Marketing of Breast Milk Substitutes adopted, 1980; Nestle Infant Formula Audit Commission established, 1981.

Issues Management Association formed by Howard W. Chase and others, 1982.

F.W. Steckmest, *Corporate Performance: The Key to Public Trust,* 1982.

*California Management Review* announces special focus on business and public policy field, 1984.

---

academic programs (Hanson, 1973). AACSB Curriculum standard IV(b) mandated coverage of the "economic and legal environment" and of "social and political influences" in all academic programs. And where students enroll in courses, textbook publishers will not be far behind. Keith Davis stimulated Joe McGuire to publish a short textbook based on a series of TV lectures, "Business and Society," he had given in Seattle (Davis, 1963). Davis subsequently introduced his own comprehensive text, which, with subsequent changes in title and authorship, remains a leader in the market today (Davis and Blomstrom, 1966; latest edition, Davis, Frederick, and Post, 1988).

At the same time, the nation was rocking with the impact of social change, and serious analysts were attempting to devise ways to analyze the external environment of organizations and integrate the results of that analysis with internal managerial decision- making on a continuing basis. Conceptualizations and techniques developed at General Electric (Dunkle et al., 1970) began to become widely known, and various organizations and groups began to call for and/or put forward statements about the proper role of business management in the new social environment.

Several aspects of this period of gestation and innovation are worth special emphasis:

1.  In spite of a good deal of inflammatory rhetoric, the social movements of the Sixties were for the most part not antibusiness. They essentially called on the old organizational structure, and particularly the large corporation, to respond to a new set of social concerns. They demanded that business use its power (and, indeed, its intrinsic roles) to deal with a greatly expanded agenda of human and social issues. As Keith Davis emphasized in his 1964 Academy of Management Presidential Address:

> [The] social powers of management today are much broader than the property rights which managers had 100 years ago ... More can be done with social powers because they involve a whole system far beyond a single organization ... The social role of management ... establishes certain responsibilities for maintaining a viable environment in which social progress may be defined and attained ... (Davis, 1965, p. 6)

2. Response to these expectations of greater managerial responsibility necessarily involved changes in management education as well as in business operations. New understandings were required, and new management methods would have to be developed, if new behaviors were to take place. Responsible managers and analysts recognized the need to alter their approaches to external issues and developments. In particular, they needed to shift from (a) making unrelated and often inconsistent ad hoc responses (whether acquiescent or resistant) to each individual issue and group, to (b) developing policies and methods of analysis that could deal in some coherent fashion with a constantly evolving array of concerns, problems, and interests. Obviously, some form of institutionalization within the corporation would ultimately be required, but at the dawn of the 1970s few could guess what that would be like.

3. By the end of this period, the scope of corporation-society study and practice had become defined as the *nonmarket* forces that have significant impact on the viability and success of the firm. The next evolutionary phase would involve several related developments: (a) narrowing and organizing a seemingly endless list of "forces" and "issues" into a coherent corporate social policy agenda, (b) moving away from an initial ideological or philosophical orientation and toward an analytical approach that would be widely applicable, and (c) developing methods and structures for introducing the results of social issues analysis into routine business decision making.

## Development and Expansion

A burst of activity in the academy and the corporate worlds occurred during the early 1970s. The first formal corporate social reports appeared (Bauer and Fenn, 1972; Corson and Steiner 1974), ultimately leading to the authoritative AICPA study *The Measurement of Corporate Social Performance* (AICPA, 1977). By the end of the decade the "public affairs function" had been established within most large firms (Post et al., 1983), and written codes of conduct had been developed and integrated into routine management training and operations (U.S. Department of Commerce, 1980). Top management gradually lost interest in debates about the appropriateness of corporate social involvement—indeed, the Business Roundtable eventually declared corporate social impact to be a primary responsibility of the CEO (Business Roundtable, 1981; see also Steiner, 1983)—and managerial attention shifted to questions of program structure, evaluation, and budgeting.

On the academic side, support of faculty development conferences by the General Electric Foundation, which took place annually 1971-1978 at UCLA under the direction of George Steiner, and at other locations as well, created a cadre of teachers capable of introducing new material into the curriculum. When the Academy of Management was divisionalized in 1971, the SIM Division was brought into being through the leadership of Sumner Marcus, Joe McGuire, Lynn Peters, and Walter Klein—and with strong support from Keith Davis and George Steiner. Membership rose rapidly to the 500-600 level, where it remains today. New and revised textbooks defined the subject matter of the field, there was a flow of research papers into Academy of Management publications, the *California Management Review,* and the new JAI research series began.

Looking back on the 1970s from the current vantage point, it appears that the revolution was both easier and more difficult than might have been anticipated. It proved to be quite easy to convince both corporate CEOs and business school deans that new staff positions and activities focusing on the external relations of the firm were required; indeed, demand for these innovations often originated with top management and advisory boards. It also proved relatively easy to distill and focus materials from history, political science, economics, and current events into courses that were interesting to both students and teachers, and that conveyed a perspective on the real world— and certainly on contemporary management conditions and problems—quite different from conventional micro-maximization courses that dominate the business school curriculum.

The difficult part came in demonstrating just how useful or successful all this activity really was in maintaining the viability and development of the corporation over the long term. The idea of a "corporate social audit" experienced a period of widespread interest and rapid development, peaked somewhere short of its initial target, and eventually became institutionalized in forms rather less ambitious than its more enthusiastic advocates had anticipated (U.S. Department of Commerce, 1979). The attempt to require greater legal accountability from the corporation, either through a federal incorporation law or through the SEC, met a similar fate (Nader et al., 1976). However, although the main proposals fell far short of their mark, SEC regulations were changed in modest, but not insignificant, respects (required disclosure of mandated environmental investments and legal liability exposure), and the Business Roundtable endorsed the principle that a majority of boards of directors should consist of outsiders, which was one of the reformers' major proposals (Business Roundtable, 1977).

## Maturity and Institutionalization

By the end of the 1970s the underlying principle of contemporary corporation-society analysis—that *the modern corporation is and should be permanently engaged in continuous and complex interactions with its social and political environment*—was permanently entrenched in both business and academe. The AACSB took over sponsorship of the faculty development conferences, giving them a certain "official" status; and the Buchholz Report (1979) revealed that required business environment courses had become almost universal in the nation's business schools. The GE approach to environmental analysis became enshrined in the textbooks (Buchholz, 1982, Chapter 22, and subsequent editions); and a specialized organization, the Issues Management Association, came into being to provide a forum for a new group of practitioners. Journals with a special emphasis on the managerial aspects of social issues/public policy topics increased in numbers and improved in quality. Commercial environmental scanning services—key elements in any serious and on-going issues management program—appeared to be thriving. The once-controversial corporate accountability/responsibility revolution evolved into the status quo (Post, 1983; Frederick, 1983).

And yet the world at the end of the 1980s does not seem quite as different as some of the 1960-1970s rhetoric might have led one to expect. The Business Roundtable's "Statement on Corporate Responsibility" (1981) and Fran Steckmest's formal codification of the corporate social agenda, which grew out of the work of a Roundtable Task Force (Steckmest, 1982) attest to the widespread acceptance of new perspectives, but by absorption and adaptation within the conventional framework. The wholesale replacement of classical individualist ideology by "communitarianism," widely predicted in the mid-1970s (Lodge, 1974), has clearly not occurred. Communitarian values are, indeed, widely recognized, but they have become integrated with individualistic values, not substituted for them. Contemporary managers are more aware of the impact of business activity on the physical and social environment and the quality of life, but production, marketing, and finance remain their primary concerns. In academe, corporation-society studies are well established as essential elements in a sophisticated and comprehensive management program—and popular themes in executive education—but their perspective does not pervade the entire curriculum in the way that some people once thought it might. (A similar conclusion, with respect to both the corporation and academe, is reached by Vogel, 1986.)

Returning to the original growth curve diagram, we may say that the curve did not continue to rise for quite as long a time, nor to as great a height, as some may have anticipated. On the other hand, there is no evidence that a declining phase can be observed or anticipated. Institutionalization implies stability; continuous managerial involvement with external social and political developments has become the norm. As Murray Weidenbaum has emphasized, for the contemporary manager public policy is "no longer a spectator sport" (1980).

# AGENDA FOR THE FUTURE

What are the critical areas of conflict, controversy and challenge in corporation-society research for the last decade of the century? An overwhelming agenda of specific policy issues—headed by tax policy, international trade relations, and environmental protection—dominates the headlines. Important as these individual topics are, however, they are essentially transient. Although developing analyses and policy alternatives relevant to a wide and ever-changing range of specific topics—and developing tools and concepts appropriate for this work, and methods of introducing its results into managerial decision making and behavior on a continuing basis— remain important tasks both in the corporation and in academe, a different and more fundamental research agenda demands attention. (Although independently developed, this list of research questions overlaps considerably with the one presented in Vogel, 1986.)

1. How shall the contemporary large corporation be governed?
2. How can an appropriate concern for organizational ethics be built into the teaching and practice of management?
3. What are the feasible and desirable relations between business firms and the political environment?
4. How can corporation-society analysis be integrated into the process of strategic management on a continuing and constructive basis?
5. How can this mode of analysis contribute more to the understanding and management of the corporation in the multinational business environment?

The remainder of this essay highlights current contributions, controversies, and research questions in each of these areas. One important point to note at the outset is that the questions themselves are intimately interrelated. The political role of business involves governance and ethical issues; strategic managerial decisions such as plant closings have wide-ranging implications (often including the multinational dimension), and so forth.

## Corporate Governance

Corporate governance is a subject quite unfamiliar to most laypersons and often badly misunderstood by people who are intimately involved. Even a half century after Berle and Means (1932), the myth persists that large corporations are in some meaningful sense "owned" (and possibly even "controlled") by their stockholders. The sources of this myth include the historical origins of the corporate form and the fact that hundreds of new, small firms that are, indeed, owned and controlled by their stockholders appear and disappear every year. However, neither the historical origins of the giants nor the ever-changing host of new small businesses—nor, indeed, even the current controversy about corporate take-overs—are particularly relevant to the fundamental issues.

The problems of corporate governance involve the giant firm with widely dispersed ownership, bureaucratic management, and continuing long-term relationships with employees, customers, communities, and governments in many locations and even nations. Critics such as Ralph Nader, liberal apologists such as J.K. Galbraith, and thoughtful analysts as conservative as Irving Kristol all agree that the contemporary giant corporation cannot be sensibly thought of as merely a "private" entity possessed by its stockholders. Nor is it formally an agency of the state. Instead, the large private firm is a servant of multiple interests, most of which have not only some plausible social claim to its attention, but also the power to pursue that claim through stockholder initiatives, collective bargaining, taxation, regulation, and private litigation, as well as in the marketplace. [A good overview of governance issues without legal detail is provided by Steckmest; see also the collection of legal perspectives in DeMott. The now standard "stakeholder" model of the corporation (Freeman, 1984) is discussed below.]

The fundamental question is: How shall the large corporation be governed so as to allow appropriate consideration of multiple interests without becoming converted into a "polity," a political entity in which governance is essentially an end in itself?

The most active critics advocate federal chartering, changes in the membership and role of boards of directors, and extensive new reporting requirements (Nader et al., 1976). Conservatives respond with powerful critiques (Hessen, 1979); and most analysts are inclined to think that extensive formal and legalistic modifications would be costly and ineffective. At the height of the debate the Business Roundtable (1977) issued a statement calling for the opening up of boards of directors to a wider range of influences, including a majority of outside members, although rejecting the notion of "constituency" directors representing specific interests.

Subsequent experience with Chrysler, Penn Central, midwestern banks, and, most recently, the savings and loan industry reveals that there are types of business enterprises that, for whatever reasons and whether rightly or wrongly, are generally believed to be serving important interests beyond those of their stockholders, and that attempts to protect those interests may lead to public policy interventions involving changes in modes of governance. The plain fact, clearly recognized since the New Deal securities legislation, if not before, is that there is a great "public" interest in the governance structures of large and influential "private" firms. Decisions of corporate boards of directors and managers do not have the same inherent legitimacy as decisions of a jury in a courtroom, nor as decisions of human persons with respect to their own lives and property, but corporate decisions may have far greater impact than either. Indeed, in our society, they are second in importance only to the actions of government itself.

Government regulation and court decisions have already gone a long way toward limiting the scope of business decision-making, and toward recognizing new rights for persons and interests that may be negatively impacted by business behavior. Some of these limitations have proved costly and time-consuming, some perhaps even ineffective. The contemporary challenge for the corporate sector is to increase the social legitimacy of the governance process, while avoiding the costs and rigidities of additional external controls. Appropriate changes probably involve various forms of participation and openness, although without creating formal constituencies or publicizing the *content* (as opposed to the *process*) of internal business decision making.

New research on corporate governance might involve detailed observation of the operation and impact of various governance structures already in place, both in the United States and abroad. Kohls (1985) found, for example, that the presence of outside and public policy or social responsibility committees had a statistically significant effect on one measure of corporate social performance. Imaginative development of new approaches that blend legal and behavioral considerations, and testing of these ideas in experimental or simulation settings, is another possibility. International comparisons of ownership and governance arrangements are also highly suggestive, but do not necessarily predict results that would appear in the United States setting.

## Organizational Ethics

Concern with business ethics is as old as the practice of business itself, but even in the most scandalous eras of the past interest in ethical issues has never been as great as it is today. The search for more effective responses to corporate ethical dilemmas runs from the boardroom to the classroom to the Congress, with the added stimulus of extensive coverage in the popular media. One of the nation's leading social scientists, Amitai Etzioni (1988), is currently assaulting the conventional rationalist paradigm by demanding recognition of a "moral dimension" in all of human behavior.

In contemporary analysis, a clear distinction is recognized between the ethical problems of the individual in various social settings (family, work, etc.) and those arising out of organizational structures and practices (Baumhart, 1968). For generations most business persons apparently believed that if they, as individuals, followed high ethical standards (i.e., did not lie, steal, or cheat; respected others in their personal contacts; etc.), all would be well. Now, everyone recognizes that even highly ethical individuals can become caught up in organizational policies that institutionalize racism and sexism, permanently damage the environment, and frustrate public and national objectives. Although endemic Ten Commandments violations—as well as questions about the appropriateness of constraints on individual behavior within organizational settings (e.g., When is whistle blowing acceptable?)—remain part of the overall ethics picture, contemporary analyses tend to emphasize organizational rather than individual ethical dilemmas. Conformity with broad social and public policy norms, as well as with the letter of the law, is now seen as an attribute of ethical management (Walton, 1977). [For contemporary surveys of issues and viewpoints, see DesJardins and McCall (1985); also Beauchamp and Bowie (1987).] The connection between corporate behavior and traditional religious values is examined in a group of extremely thoughtful papers edited by Williams and Houck (1982). Among the most useful recent publications are the research collection edited by Frederick (1987), and the short text by Buchholz (1989b).

The explosion of academic interest in business ethics is reflected in a host of new publications (Hanson, 1983), a new journal (the *Journal of Business Ethics*), the increasingly popular Bentley College Conference on Business Ethics held annually since 1977, and establishment of ethics research centers at several major universities (e.g., Delaware, Virginia). Developments on the action side of business ethics include continuing press coverage of scandals and catastrophes; thoughtful critiques such as the 1987 statement of the National Conference of Catholic Bishops (*Economic Justice for All;* see also Williams, 1985, and *Journal of Business Ethics,* Special Issue, June 1988); and the widespread publication and discussion of corporate "codes of conduct." The Ethics Resource Center has been a major stimulator of code development and works with individual corporations to design guidelines and programs appropriate for dealing with their specific ethical problems on an on-going basis (Ethics Resource Center, 1985).

The impact of all this academic and corporate interest in business ethics is difficult to assess. O'Toole recently hailed the accomplishments of some of the most conspicuously "responsible" corporations—ARCO, Control Data, Dayton-Hudson, etc.—as *Vanguard Management* (1985); Tuleja (1985) tells much the same story. A recent survey reveals that "maintaining a positive reputation" is seen as a key contribution to the central managerial goal of creating "an *effective* organization," and that "integrity is the personal characteristic or quality rated most highly by managers at all levels" (Posner and Schmidt, 1984). It is, however, quite difficult to find ways to institutionalize ethical precepts within organizational settings, and to discover how (if at all) such precepts influence actual behavior. Field studies and rather sophisticated role plays—as well as participation in actual corporate ethics programs, which are becoming more numerous—are probably going to provide the basis for the most interesting new research developments in this area.

## Business in Politics

A distinctive feature of the American Experiment over the past two centuries has been the attempt to draw a sharp distinction between economic and political life; overt business participation in electoral politics was severely restricted by both law and custom until the past decade. In spite of these restrictions, business involvement in politics was and is inevitable (Epstein, 1969). Since 1971, corporations—along with labor unions and other types of organizations—have been allowed to organize political action committees (PACs), raise funds, and make contributions to electoral candidates and expenditures for political purposes. Court decisions now protect corporate free speech on matters related to business activity, and prominent firms and organizations have adopted the regular practice of expressing a wide range of political and social views in the public press. A multimillion dollar "Influence Industry" (*National Journal,* 1985) flourishes in Washington and the state capitals, and accounts of business contributions to and pressures upon politicians fill the media.

Not surprisingly, the explosion of business political activity has produced an aftershock of criticism, much of it focusing on the scope and role of corporate PACs (Drew, 1983; Etzioni, 1984; Sethi & Namiki, 1983). For all the sound and fury about PACs, however, the important concerns actually involve not the electoral arena but the policy-making process. Although PAC contributions—and particularly concentrated and pyramided contributions— may have substantial impact on a few critical races, 80% of them go to incumbents, and thus serve to entrench already established political actors.

As noted above, the fundamental question is, once the politicians are in office, how do they vote? It is in the formation of policy, not the election of candidates, that the controversy over corporate influence becomes substantive. President Jimmy Carter declared that the political power of business was the greatest surprise he encountered in Washington, and experienced (and bloody) insiders such as Michael Pertschuk (1982) and Mark Green (Green and Buchsbaum, 1980) have published vivid critiques, the substance of which tends to be supported by less passionate analysts (Levitan and Cooper, 1984). The general view of most observers seems to be that business influence on U.S.

public policy is currently very great. This conclusion is underscored by the plethora of lobbyists eager to publicize their own effectiveness, the multiplication of forms of business political representation, and the popularity of handbooks of corporate political activity with such energizing titles as *Fighting to Win* (Grefe, 1981).

Business activity in the policy arena at both the federal and the state levels has certainly increased in recent decades, and this increase has been increasingly publicized. This activity is, however, by no means new, nor is its growth surprising. Historical analysis demonstrates the power of business influence as early as the Progressive Era (Wood, 1986). And it was predictable that increased government activity affecting business—taxation and expenditures, as well as regulation—has brought forth increased business activity attempting to influence government. The openness of the contemporary political process and the intensity of media coverage heighten public awareness of long-standing relationships.

The important question involves the effects (if any) of this high level of activity. Systematic review of multiple cases (Maitland, 1983; Marcus, 1985), as opposed to selective anecdotal evidence, suggests that business interests get their way in the political process only when (a) they present a united front (which turns out to be rare enough in itself), and (b) they succeed in enlisting a considerable group of voters (employees, customers, bank depositors, local community residents) in their causes. Even when business-labor coalitions are active, as in seeking international trade restrictions, careful research has shown that long-term government commitment to fundamental principles embodied in international agreements (in this instance, GATT) can offset conventional political pressures (Lenway, 1985). In spite of considerable analysis (and a great deal of rhetoric) the overall impact of business political activity remains largely unknown.

New research on business and politics should involve something more than the accumulation of additional case studies; these are the raw materials for serious analysis, but not the final product. Significant studies will try to specify more clearly the conditions under which political activity of different types and levels produces (or fails to produce) different kinds of effects. The regulatory arena, rather than the electoral or legislative process, may be the most important focus for attention.

## Strategic Management

The ultimate effectiveness of corporation-society analysis within the corporate world, and hence its ultimate status within academe, hinges on its integration into on-going, long-range managerial activity. Corporate behavior based on contemporary analysis should be fundamentally different from traditional public relations and lobbying efforts. The new "responsiveness" approach emphasizes internal change and anticipatory behavior, not simply post hoc reaction to external developments. In the jargon of the field, the shift is from "reactive" behaviors (whether resistant or merely adaptive) to "proactive" or "interactive" behaviors, involving appropriate changes in the firm's own structure and practices, as well as direct participation in the public policy process. In the ultimate case, the firm will change the way it makes decisions, not simply the decisions themselves.

The importance of external relations and public policy developments is now well recognized within the field of Strategic Management, as a survey of current texts clearly reveals. However, attempts to integrate the relevant analysis into the actual practice of strategic management in a substantial and continuing way are still in their initial stages. The Conference Board has been extremely active both in promoting and in reporting on these efforts as they may take place in individual corporations (Brown, 1979, 1981; Arrington and Sawaya, 1984). Three important books that attempt to address this problem in a serious way are:

> Tombari, *Business and Society* (1984). A comprehensive text with a strong strategic management focus.

> Freeman, *Strategic Management: A Stakeholder Approach* (1984). An ambitious effort to integrate detailed stakeholder analysis into the managerial process.

> Ansoff, *Implanting Corporate Strategy* (1984). A plea for the development of "societal strategies," alongside conventional business strategies, based on a continuous process of "issue management."

The close connection between strategic management concerns, which focus primarily on internal corporate structures and behaviors, and the external concerns emphasized in the earlier discussion of corporate governance issues should be obvious. This suggests that research studies linking broad concerns of organizational legitimacy and governance to more narrowly focused strategy choices may provide a fertile ground for research. Additional research studies require close observation of actual examples of strategic management systems that include substantial social and environmental dimensions (cf. Windsor and Greanias, 1982). Researchers could build on the GE model, or perhaps try out entirely different approaches, to strengthen the role of social and environmental variables in the design of strategic planning and management systems.

## Multinational Perspective

Both business *and* public policy are now significantly multinational in character, and the trend toward internationalization can only increase. Even firms that have no foreign operations encounter foreign competitors, customers, and suppliers; and even state and local government actions (e.g., product bans for environmental and consumer protection, unitary corporate taxation) give rise to substantial multinational impacts. The multinational environment, where external relationships are often the single most critical determinants of both decisions and outcomes, should provide unique scope for demonstrating the value of corporation-society analysis.

Unfortunately, in the international arena, even as is true domestically, the value of such analysis is often best illustrated by notorious examples of its absence. The widely discussed cases include Dresser Industries' production of equipment for the Soviet oil pipeline, the Union Carbide catastrophe at Bhopal, the international infant formula controversy, and U.S. economic involvement with South Africa. A common theme in these and many similar cases is the failure of corporations to analyze their own long-run and fundamental interests until powerful pressures for change have built up and the costs of conventional behavior or resistance become exorbitant. The fact that this same kind of behavior can occur in government as well as in business, and involve countries and cultures all over the world, makes it more, not less, important to deal with. The contribution of corporation-society studies in this context is to sensitize managers to complex multicultural situations and to assist them anticipating consequences—particularly adverse ones—while there is still room for innovative adaptation.

Attention to differences among social and cultural environments is the distinguishing feature of the international business field, and all books on international business contain extensive analyses of social, cultural, and public policy issues in a variety of settings. The leading text most clearly reflecting a broad approach is Vernon and Wells, *Manager in the International Environment,* now in its fifth edition (1986), which also contains an interesting collection of cases. A recent contribution from political science (Wilson, 1985) places the business-government relationship in a comparative perspective and offers brief nontechnical descriptions of several important examples—United States, Britain, Germany, France, and Japan. The new field of international risk assessment attempts to develop comparative summary analyses of multiple countries and these are used as guides to multinational corporate investment and management, as well as to foreign policy development by governments (Rogers, 1983, 1985). Current research questions encompass the entire field of international and multinational management, as a collection of recent studies reveals (Preston, 1988).

## CONCLUSION

In the corporation, and in academe, emphasis on corporation-society relationships—the business environment, public policy, social issues—has become routine. The importance of environmental trends and public policy developments for managerial decision making is now generally recognized; like it or not, the impact of social change in general, and government activity in particular, on business has become too prominent to be ignored. Analysts and practitioners have developed a set of basic concepts and analytical tools; and organizational structures necessary to implement and refine them have been put in place. In business and in the business schools, study of the nonmarket forces affecting business, in one form or another, appears to have won for itself a permanent place.

It remains to be seen, however, whether this new area of emphasis will be viewed primarily as a staff function, a source of specialized knowledge and expertise essential to effective management but outside the flow of line activity, or whether it can become—as Steiner, Ansoff and others advocate—a penetrating influence throughout the practice of management, an essential competence of line managers and particularly of higher level executives. Achievement of this latter goal requires the development of a comprehensive theoretical base that commands general acceptance, as well as demonstrated effectiveness in dealing with practical problems. If genuine progress can be made on the five analytical questions chosen for discussion here, the contributions may—along with the stakeholder concept—become foundation elements of an expanded conceptual and analytical framework, and of another wave of rapid evolution and growth. In the meantime, the new perspective is essential simply because it stresses that the nonmarket aspects of the business environment are *there,* that they are *important,* and that there are some better ways of understanding and responding to them than simply "muddling through."

## EDITOR'S NOTE

This paper adapts and updates material from two previously published papers (Preston, 1986a,b). An earlier draft, including a more personal "Foreword," was circulated under the title *Social Issues and Public Policy in Business and Management: Retrospect and Prospect* (Preston, 1986c).

## REFERENCES

American Institute of Certified Public Accountants (1977). *Measurement of Corporate Social Performance.* New York: AICPA.

Ansoff, H.I. (1984). *Implanting Corporate Strategy.* Englewood Cliffs, NJ: Prentice-Hall.

Arrington, C.B., & Sawaya, R.N. (1984). Issues management and corporate strategy. *California Management Review, 26,* 148-160.

Bauer, R.A., & Fenn, D.H. (1972). *The Corporate Social Audit.* New York: Russell Sage.

Baumhart, R. (1968). *An Honest Profit: What Businessmen Say About Ethics in Business.* New York: Holt, Rinehart and Winston.

Beauchamp, T., and Bowie, N.R. (1987) *Ethical Theory and Business,* Third ed. Englewood Cliffs, NJ: Prentice-Hall.

Berle, A.A. (1954). *The 20th Century Capitalist Revolution.* New York: Harcourt Brace.

Berle, A.A., & Means, G. (1932). *The Modern Corporation and Private Property.* New York: Macmillan.

Boulding, K.E. (1954). *The Organizational Revolution.* New York: Harper.

Bowen, H.R. (1953). *The Social Responsibilities of the Businessman.* New York: Harper.

Brown, J.K. (1979). *This Business of Issues: Coping with the Company's Environments.* New York: The Conference Board.

_____ (1981). *Guidelines for Managing Corporate Issues Programs.* New York: The Conference Board.

Buchholz, R.A. (1979). *Business Environment/Public Policy: A Study of Teaching and Research in Schools of Business and Management.* Washington, DC: American Assembly of Collegiate Schools of Business.

_____ (1982, 1989a). *Business Environment and Public Policy.* Englewood Cliffs, NJ: Prentice-Hall.

_____ (1989b). *Fundamental Concepts and Problems in Business Ethics.* Englewood Cliffs, NJ: Prentice-Hall.

Business Roundtable (1977). *The Role and Composition of the Board of Directors of the Large Publicly Owned Company.* New York: Business Roundtable.

_____ (1981). *Statement on Corporate Responsibility.* New York: Business Roundtable.

Carroll, A.B., & Beiler, G.W. (1975). Landmarks in the evolution of the social audit. *Academy of Management Journal, 18,* 589-599.

Carnegie, A. (1900). *The Gospel of Wealth.* Republished: Cambridge, MA: Harvard University (Belknap) Press, 1962.

Clark, J.M. (1926). *Social Control of Business.* Chicago: University of Chicago Press.

Corson, J.J., & Steiner, G.A. (1974). *Measuring Business Social Performance: The Corporate Social Audit.* New York: Committee for Economic Development.

Davis, K. (1965). "The public role of management," Presidential Address. *Evolving Concepts in Management,* Proceedings of 24th Annual Meeting, Academy of Management, December 28-30, 1964.

Davis, K., & Blomstrom, R.L. (1966). *Business and Society.* New York: McGraw-Hill.

Davis, K., Frederick, W.C., and Post, J.E. (1988) *Business and Society: Corporate Strategy, Public Policy, Ethics.* New York: McGraw-Hill.

DeMott, D.A., ed. (1980). *Corporations at the Crossroads: Governance and Reform.* New York: McGraw-Hill.

DesJardins, J.R., & McCall, J.J. (1985). *Contemporary Issues in Business Ethics.* Belmont: Wadsworth.

Drew, E. (1983). *Politics and Money: The New Road to Corruption.* New York: Macmillan.

Dunkel, E.B., Reed, W.K., & Wilson, I.H. (1970). *The Business Environment of the Seventies: A Trend Analysis for Business Planning.* New York: McGraw-Hill.

Epstein, E.M. (1969). *The Corporation in American Politics.* Englewood Cliffs, NJ: Prentice-Hall.

Ethics Resource Center (1985). *Creating a Workable Company Code of Ethics.* Washington, DC.

Etzioni, A. (1984). *Capital Corruption: An Assault on American Democracy.* New York: Harcourt Brace Jovanovich.

_____ (1988). *The Moral Dimension–Toward a New Economics.* New York: Free Press.

Eyestone, R. (1978). *From Social Issues to Public Policy.* New York: Wiley.

Frederick, W.C. (1983). Corporate social responsibility in the Reagan era and beyond. *California Management Review, 25,* 145-157.

_____ (1986). Toward CSR$_3$: Why Ethical Analysis is indispensable and unavoidable in corporate affairs. *California Management Review, 28,* 126-141.

_____ (1987). *Empirical Studies of Business Ethics and Values.* Greenwich, CT: JAI Press. (See also, W.C. Frederick and L.E. Preston, eds., *Business Ethics: Issues and Empirical Studies.* Greenwich, CT: JAI Press, 1989.)

Freeman, R.E. (1984). *Strategic Management: A Stakeholder Approach.* Boston: Pittman.

Freeman, R.E., & Reed, D.L. (1983). Stockholders and stakeholders: A new perspective on corporate governance. *California Management Review, 25,* 88-106.

Friedman, Milton. (1962). *Capitalism and Freedom.* Chicago: University of Chicago.

Green, M., & Buchsbaum, A. (1980). *The Corporate Lobbies.* Washington, DC: Public Citizen.

Grefe, E.A. (1981). *Fighting to Win.* New York: Harcourt Brace Jovanovich.

Hanson, K.O. (1973). Business schools make room for corporate social policy. *Business and Society Review,* Summer, 75-89.

_____ (1983). Business ethics. *California Management Review , 26,* 162-169.

Heald, M. (1970). *The Social Responsibilities of Business: Company and Community, 1900-1960.* Cleveland: Press of Case Western Reserve University.

Hessen, R. (1979). *In Defense of the Corporation.* Stanford, CA: Hoover Institution.

Hogner, R.H. (1982). Corporate social reporting: Eight decades of development at U.S. Steel. In L.E. Preston, ed., *Research in Corporate Social Performance and Policy,* Volume 4, pp. 243-250. Greenwich, CT: JAI Press.

Kohls, J. (1985). Corporate board structure, social reporting and social performance. In L.E. Preston, ed., *Research in Corporate Social Performance and Policy,* Volume 7, pp. 165-189. Greenwich, CT: JAI Press.

Kreps, T. (1940). *Measurement of the Social Performance of Business.* TNEC Monograph No. 7. Washington, DC: Government Printing Office.

Lenway, S.A. (1985). *The Politics of U.S. International Trade: Protection, Expansion and Escape.* Boston: Pittman.

Levitan, S.A., & Cooper, M.R. (1984). *The Business Lobbies.* Baltimore: Johns Hopkins.

Lodge, G.C. (1974). Business and the changing society. *Harvard Business Review, 52,* 59-72 (March-April).

McGuire, J.W. (1963). *Business and Society.* New York: McGraw-Hill.

Maitland, I. (1983). House divided: Business lobbying and the 1981 budget. In L.E. Preston, ed., *Research in Corporate Social Performance and Policy,* Volume 5. Greenwich, CT: JAI Press.

Marcus, A. (1985). Business demand for regulation: An exploration of the Stigler hypothesis. In L.E. Preston, ed., *Research in Corporate Social Performance and Policy,* Volume 7. Greenwich, CT: JAI Press.

Molitor, G.T.T. (1980). Environmental forecasting: Public policy forecasting. In L.E. Preston, ed., *Business Environment/Public Policy: 1979 Conference Papers.* St. Louis: AACSB.

Nader, R., Green, M., & Seligman, J. (1976). *Constitutionalizing the Corporation: The Case for the Federal Chartering of Giant Corporations.* Washington, DC: Corporate Accountability Research Group.

Naisbitt, J. (1983). *Megatrends.* New York: Warner.

National Conference of Catholic Bishops. (1987). *Economic Justice for All.* Washington: NCCB.

*National Journal* (1985). *The Influence Industry.* Washington, DC: National Journal (Special Issue, September 14, 1985).

Neal, A.C. (1981). *Business Power & Public Policy.* New York: Praeger.

O'Toole, J. (1985). *Vanguard Management: Redesigning the Corporate Future.* New York: Doubleday.

Pertschuk, M. (1982). *Revolt Against Regulation: The Rise and Pause of the Consumer Movement.* Berkeley: University of California Press.

Posner, B.Z., & Schmidt, W.H. (1984). Values and the American manager: An update. *California Management Review, 26,* 202-216.

Post, J.E. (1983). Business, society and the Reagan revolution. *Sloan Management Review, 24,* 67-73.

Post, J.E., Murray, E.A., Dickie, R.B., & Mahon, J.F. (1983). The public affairs function. *California Management Review, 26,* 135-150.

Preston, L.E. (1975). Corporation and society: The search for a paradigm. *Journal of Economic Literature, 13,* 434-453.

———— (1978-88). *Research in Corporate Social Performance and Policy,* Volumes 1-10. Greenwich, CT: JAI Press.

———— (1983). Teaching materials in business and society. *California Management Review, 25,* 158-173.

———— (1986a). Business and public policy. *Journal of Management, 12* (Yearly Review of Management), 261-275.

———— (1986b). Social issues in management: An evolutionary perspective. In D.A. Wren, ed., *Papers Dedicated to the Development of Modern Management.* New York: Academy of Management.

———— (1986c). *Social Issues and Public Policy in Business and Management: Retrospect and Prospect.* College Park: Center for Business and Public Policy.

———— (1988). *Research in Corporate Social Performance and Policy: International and Comparative Studies.* Greenwich, CT: JAI Press.

Rogers, J. (1983, 1985). *Global Risk Assessments: Issues, Concepts and Applications,* Volumes 1-2. Riverside, CA: GRA.

Sethi, S.P., & Namiki, N. (1983). The public backlash against the PACs. *California Management Review, 25,* 133-144.

Steckmest, F.W. (1982). *Corporate Performance: The Key to Public Trust.* New York: McGraw-Hill.

Steiner, G.A. (1983). *The New CEO.* New York: Macmillan.

———— (1971). *Business and Society.* New York: Random House.

Steiner, G.A., & Steiner, J.F. (1988). *Business, Government, and Society: A Managerial Perspective.* New York: Random House.

Tombari, H.A. (1984). *Business and Society.* New York: Dryden.

Tuleja, T. (1985). *Beyond the Bottom Line: How Business Leaders Are Managing Principles into Profits.* New York: Facts on File.

U.S. Department of Commerce (1979). *Corporate Social Reporting in the United States and Western Europe.* Washington, DC.

———— (1980). *Business and Society: Strategies for the 1980's.* Washington, DC.

Vernon, R., and Wells, L.T. (1986). *Manager in the International Economy.* Englewood Cliffs, NJ: Prentice-Hall.

Vogel, D. (1986). The study of social issues in management: A critical appraisal. *California Management Review, 28,* 142-151.

Votaw, D., & Sethi, S.P. (1969). Do we need a new corporate response to a changing social environment? *California Management Review, 12,* 3-31.

Walton, C. (1977). *The Ethics of Corporate Conduct.* Englewood Cliffs, NJ: Prentice-Hall.

Weidenbaum, M.L. (1980). Public policy: No longer a spectator sport for business. *Journal of Business Strategy, 1,* 1-15.

Williams, O. (1985). Catholic bishops take on economics. *Business and Society Review, 54,* 21-26.

Williams, O., & Houck, J., eds. (1982). *The Judeo-Christian Vision and the Modern Corporation.* Notre Dame, IN: University of Notre Dame Press.

Wilson, G.K. (1985). *Business and Politics.* Chatham, NJ: Chatham House.

Windsor, D., & Greanias, G. (1982). Strategic planning systems for a politicized environment. In L.E. Preston, ed., *Research in Corporate Social Performance and Policy,* Volume 4, pp. 77-104. Greenwich, CT: JAI Press.

Wood, D.J. (1986). *Strategic Uses of Public Policy: Business and Government in the Progressive Era.* Boston: Pittman.

Worthy, J.C. (1984). *Shaping an American Institution: Robert E. Wood and Sears, Roebuck.* Urbana: University of Illinois Press.

# THEORETICAL MODELS AND EMPIRICAL RESULTS:

## A REVIEW AND SYNTHESIS OF
## JAI VOLUMES 1-10

Lyman Reed, Kathleen Getz, Denis Collins,

William Oberman, and Robert Toy

---

In their 1975 publication, *Private Management and Public Policy,* Lee E. Preston and James E. Post proposed a set of formal models, drawn from various sources, of the relationship between business and society. At that time, scholars interested in this subject were scattered among several academic fields—economics, sociology, and political science, as well as management—and were often considered to be on the fringe of their home disciplines, and not associated with any clearly identified academic area. In particular, there was no single research publication specifically focused on their subject matter. In 1978, Preston took on the task of editing a research series focused on corporation-society studies for JAI Press (*Research on Corporate Social Performance and Policy*, volumes 1-10, 1978-1988). This series provided a much needed publication outlet and legitimating focus for academic researchers and students interested in this area.

The subsequent decade brought increasing academic interest in the relationship between business and its social environment. This increased interest was manifest in the growth of the Social Issues in Management Division of the Academy of Management, the appearance of several journals focusing on business and professional ethics, and the publication of an increasing number of articles on corporation-society issues in mainstream management journals. Nowhere was this growth in interest more clearly revealed than in the number and quality of research studies appearing in the annual JAI volumes. The year 1988 marked the end the first decade of publication for the series, as well as the end of Preston's tenure as editor. It therefore seems appropriate at this time to assess the contribution that the series has made to date, and to examine some of the implications of this assessment, both substantive and methodological, for future research. (For an earlier review of the first four volumes in the series, see Useem, 1984.)

In offering this review, we do not intend to suggest that the JAI series contains the main corpus of research on corporation-society relations during this period. On the contrary, as the field has grown in both interest and prestige, representative research has appeared in many leading journals; and significant research monographs are regularly published as well. Our intention here is simply to survey the one source that has consistently and exclusively focused on research in this field during this time period—a source that, indeed, played a pioneering role in the development of the field itself.

The main body of this paper describes and critiques the major research themes found in the series; the principal variables and relationships analyzed are carefully identified, and substantive findings are summarized. The figures included in the paper, and the detailed tabulation of studies in the Appendix, are integral parts of this analysis. (Note that some studies are listed more than once because of the analytical structure of the paper and the Appendix.)

The final section of the paper develops a model for organizing corporation-society research. This model relates both to the studies published in the series and to other work in the area. The model provides the basis for assessing the present state of research as developed in the first ten volumes of this series, and also for suggesting directions for future research.

One additional introductory comment is in order concerning the criteria and terminology used to describe and classify research studies in this review. We are aware of the sometimes emotional debate that can arise concerning the nature and value of "qualitative" vs. "quantitative," or "theoretical" vs.

"empirical," research. Given the stated commitment of the JAI series to "empirical" research, it is apparent that Preston, as editor, accepts qualitative and nonstatistical research as consistent with this criterion. In our own analysis of the published studies, we describe as "empirical" only those studies containing stated hypotheses that are examined statistically using commonly accepted techniques. Similarly, we consider an article "theoretical" only if it sets forth clearly stated propositions that can, at least in principle, be tested empirically. Many excellent articles (including some robust case studies) that are included in the series do not fall into either of these categories; we have classified these as "descriptive," "conceptual," or "methodological," as appropriate.

## MAJOR RESEARCH THEMES

Among the several theoretical models of corporation-society relations presented by Preston and Post in *Private Management and Public Policy,* the broadest and most integrative model is based on the concept of "interpenetrating systems." They explain the rationale for the Interpenetrating Systems (IPS) model as follows: "We assume that the larger society exists as a macro-system, but that individual (and particularly large) micro-organizations also constitute separable systems within themselves, neither completely controlling nor controlled by the social environment" (Preston and Post, 1975, p. 25). (For other general discussions of this model by the same authors, see Preston 1978; Post 1986.)

The idea embodied in the IPS model is that organizations can have important effects on the environment through their actions, and that, conversely, the environment influences and partially determines the nature and scope of these actions by affecting or constraining the structures and responses of the micro systems. It is this ability of the macro- and micro-level systems to change each other's structures, as well as behaviors, that distinguishes the IPS model from other models of the relationship between organizations and their environments.

Figure 1 presents a modified version of the IPS model, which we use as the organizing framework for this survey and review of the contents of JAI volumes 1-10. In the original Preston and Post presentation, the model is described as consisting of two interacting microsystems, subsequently labeled "Institution" and "Society" (Post, 1986). However, from most of their discussion and use of the model, it appears that the two elements might be better described as the "Business System" and the "Political System," since no other components of "Society" are given detailed attention.

We revise the model to identify the political system explicitly, and also to add a third sphere which we refer to as the "Personal-Communal System." This system includes individual, family, and group private interactions, i.e.,

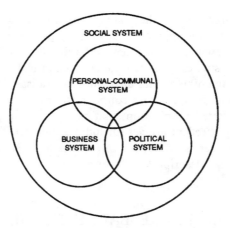

*Figure 1.*   The Interpenetrating Systems Model

human relationships not necessarily involved with business or political institutions. All three spheres—business, politics, and personal-communal life—are, of course, embedded within the larger context of the "Social System," which may contain other dimensions not specified here. Our version of the model emphasizes that there can be binary interactions between business and politics (government regulation), business and personal-communal life (employment issues), and politics and personal-communal life (voting rights), as well as systemic interactions among all three (public policy about drug testing in the work place ). This tripartite version of the IPS model, set within the broad context of the social system as a whole, provides a useful framework for organizing and evaluating the work published in the first ten volumes of the JAI series.

Perhaps the greatest advantage of the IPS concept is that it can accommodate conflict between managerial and societal goals, whether personal or political, as well as processes of goal adjustment and structural change. There is an understanding here that politics, business and personal-communal life are, at the same time, separate from each other and yet interdependent. Each has its own distinct scope, and yet there are many important social processes and problems in which all three domains necessarily interact. These interactions affect all three systems in fundamental ways. Business affects, and is, in turn, affected by the personal-communal and the political systems, and so forth.

Within this framework, the research studies published during the first ten years of the JAI series can be described as falling into two broad categories: (1) studies involving interactions between the business system and the personal-communal system (i.e., "business and society," viewed from a human, and often moral or ethical, perspective) and (2) studies involving interactions between the business system and the political system (i.e., "business and government"). Not surprisingly, very few articles directly address research problems involving interactions among the three systems simultaneously.

Our analysis of the published studies identifies ten major research themes, divided between the two broad categories as follows:

*Business System and the Personal-Communal System*
 (1) Corporate social response patterns.
 (2) Corporate social reporting.
 (3) Corporate social performance.
 (4) Managerial values.
 (5) Corporate misconduct.
 (6) Connection between social and financial performance.

*Business System and the Political System*
 (7) Determinants of government policy toward business.
 (8) Impact of government policy on business.
 (9) Business response to government policy.
 (10) The political character and role of business.

The following sections of this paper summarize and critique the major research findings of the JAI studies in each of these areas, and suggest possible directions for future research. We have refrained from lengthy citations within the body of the text, but the Appendix provides a detailed tabulation of all articles in the first ten series volumes, appropriately classified.

# STUDIES OF BUSINESS SYSTEM— PERSONAL-COMMUNAL SYSTEM INTERACTION

As the phrase "social performance" in the series title might suggest, many of the published studies explore interactions between the business system and aspects of personal or communal (i.e., organization, group) life. According to our analysis, 61 studies involve these aspects of business-society interpenetration. In the inaugural issue of the series, Aldag and Bartol (1978) called attention to the ambiguous nature of the term "corporate social responsibility" and reviewed research in the areas of organizational effectiveness, organization theory and behavior, social attitudes, values, equal employment, and quality of work life. Their coverage suggests the broad range of topics involved.

According to our analysis, twenty-five articles in the series pertain to theoretical and case study analyses of corporate social response patterns; six examine aspects of social reporting; twelve provide empirical analyses of corporate social performance; six examine managerial values; eight deal with the issue of corporate misconduct; and four relate corporate financial performance to social performance.

## Corporate Social Response Patterns

The diverse patterns of corporate response to social issues, a core area of interest for the series from the beginning, are examined in the research studies from three different perspectives: (1) broad corporate policy developments (e.g., "stages" or "degrees" of response), (2) issue-specific responses, and (3) connections with organizational structure.

Many researchers have partitioned the process of corporate social response into various "stages" of development and/or various "degrees" of intensity. Five general patterns of strategic response have been identified: (1) resistance, (2) bargaining, (3) capitulation, (4) termination of relationships, and (5) dissolution of the organization. Case studies reveal that top management plays a pivotal role in both the initiation and the institutionalization of corporate response to social issues. Successful implementation of desirable corporate social policies appears to depend upon: (a) the adoption of a long-term perspective by company managers, (b) the presence and prominence of self-interested external publics, (c) the availability of relevant public funds, and (d) enthusiastic support of both the CEO and public officials.

Specific issues for which detailed corporate response patterns have been examined include plant closings, affirmative action programs, pollution control or abatement, South African withdrawal, the international Nestle boycott, and unemployment. Plant closings were found to be motivated by organizational factors such as organizational tolerance, commitment, strategy, and diversity; concerns about the profitability of local operations, cost of hiring and retraining workers, or conditions within the community were neither necessary nor sufficient reasons for the decision. An organization's response to affirmative action issues was found to be determined by a host of impetus factors, such as social milieu and coalitions, as well as by enabling factors such as financial resources and the availability of minorities and women in the relevant population. Factors facilitating consensus-building among adversarial groups and within stakeholder coalitions were identified in some studies.

Several studies highlight the importance of organizational structure and public issue scanning techniques as determinants of corporate responsiveness to social issues. The structure and functions of corporate environmental and public affairs departments, as well as their role in scanning the environment for relevant public issues, have been extensively described and analyzed.

Much has been learned from these studies of corporate social response patterns, which have included a few studies from other countries as well as the United

States. There are clearly different stages and levels of response to social issues, and the moderating variables (in addition to the passage of time itself) seem to be organizational self-interest, corporate culture, and external pressures, as well as the perceptions and beliefs of top management. Organizational sensitivity to social concerns is heightened by structural features such as the presence of public or environmental affairs offices engaged in public issues scanning.

## Social Reporting

An important aspect of corporate response to social issues is the development of social reports, both for internal and for external distribution. Social reporting has been examined in the JAI studies both as a process—development of social audit techniques and of individual social reports—and in terms of the general status of social reporting in various countries.

There seems to be greater interest in corporate social reporting in Western Europe, where it is sometimes required by law, than in the United States. Companies in the United States release social data primarily in response to regulatory requirements or public pressure, although top executives occasionally determine that the voluntary release of such information is in the company's best interest. Although these studies indicate that social reporting tends to enhance a company's social performance, there is little evidence of its systematic practice in the United States, at least up to the present.

## Corporate Social Performance

The first step in undertaking empirical research on "corporate social performance" is employing the term itself. In the JAI studies "social performance" has been measured or indicated in at least fourteen different ways, including adoption of particular social policies; size of certain budgetary allocations; ratings by panels of stakeholders, employees, or executives; and number of law violations. Use of these numerous and varied measures suggests the multidimensionality of the "social performance" concept itself.

A large number of factors that may influence a company's "social performance" (variously measured) have been explored by the JAI researchers (See Table 1). Variables that were found to have a *significant positive relationship* to social performance include the size of budgetary allocations for customer service and advertising; structural features such as the presence of a public affairs department, a managerial social responsibility committee, a social responsibility officer, or a public policy or social responsibility committee within the board of directors; the practice of social reporting; the importance assigned to integrating social issues with strategic planning; the CEO's personal social concerns; and the public visibility of the firm. Industrial sector was also shown to be a critical variable in these studies.

*Table 1.*    Factors That May Influence Corporate Social Performance

*Factors External to the Corporation*

| | |
|---|---|
| Legal requirements | Salience of issue to relevant publics |
| Pressure by stakeholders | Availability of public funds |
| Public expectations | Action by competitors |
| Community needs | * Industry norms |
| * Community characteristics | State of the economy |

*Factors Internal to the Corporation*

| | |
|---|---|
| * Structure of the board of directors | * Type of employee programs |
| * Routinization of the responsiveness process | * Corporate structure |
| Corporate geographic and business diversity | Corporate strategy |
| Corporate capability to identify issues | * Who controls the corporation |
| Corporate capability to respond to issues | * Corporate size |
| * Attitude of CEO and top executives on the issue(s) | * Corporate visibility |
| Long-term perspective of executives | * Corporate culture |
| Executive commitment to social performance | Corporate power |
| * Personal concerns of individual managers | * Market share |
| Uniqueness of division's social situation | General business philosophy |
| * Managerial values | * Social reporting |
| Perceived impact of social issue of firm performance | * Type of charter |
| Perception of problem as an advertising or marketing opportunity | * Nature of stock ownership |
| | * Hiring strategy |
| Perceived need for corporate legitimacy on the issue(s) | * Profitability |
| Perceived need to improve managerial morale on social issue(s) | * Financial resources |
| | * Customer related expenditures |
| Perceived need to preserve private enterprise system | Previous behavior pattern |
| * Management structure | |

*Note:*    * relationships tested empirically in one or more JAI article.

Variables that yielded confounding results—i.e., a mixture of significant positive and negative, and/or nonsignificant, results—include financial performance; firm size; listings in *100 Best Companies to Work For*; characteristics of employee assistance programs (EAP); and firm size (income), market share, form of organization and pattern of ownership. Community characteristics examined also yielded mixed results.

The major findings of the empirical studies of corporate social performance published in the JAI series are summarized in Figure 2. Statistically significant results between variables are indicated as "pos." or "neg." as appropriate; the notation "mixed" indicates that significant results in both directions were found; the absence of significant results is indicated by "n.s."

Research on the social performance theme presents a set of highly complex measurement problems that need to be analyzed in a more integrative manner.

**VARIABLES RELATED TO COMMUNITY**

| | |
|---|---|
| MINORITY POPULATION IN COMMUNITY (KEDIA & KUNTZ, 1981) | mixed |
| DEGREE OF LOCAL OWNERSHIP (KEDIA & KUNTZ, 1981) | mixed |
| SIZE OF COMMUNITY (KEDIA & KUNTZ, 1981) | mixed |
| COMPANY CONCERN FOR COMMUNITY WELFARE (ROMAN & BLUM, 1987) | pos. |

**VARIABLES DESCRIBING GENERAL CHARACTERISTICS OF FIRM**

| | |
|---|---|
| TYPE OF CORPORATE CONTROL (MITCHELL, 1983) | n.s. |
| FIRM SIZE (LEVY & SHATTO, 1980; COPPERMAN, 1981; KEDIA & KUNTZ, 1981; AUPPERLE, 1984; ROMAN & BLUM, 1987) | mixed |
| FIRM INCOME (KEDIA & KUNTZ, 1981) | mixed |
| INDUSTRIAL SECTOR (COPPERMAN, 1981; AUPPERLE, 1984) | pos. |
| TYPE OF FIRM (KOHLS, 1985) | n.s. |
| DEGREE OF FIRM VISIBILITY (AUPPERLE, 1984) | pos. |

**VARIABLES RELATED TO MARKETING**

| | |
|---|---|
| SIZE OF CUSTOMER SERVICE EXPENDITURE (LEVY & SHATTO, 1980) | pos. |
| SIZE OF ADVERTISING EXPENDITURE (LEVY & SHATTO, 1980) | pos. |

CORPORATE SOCIAL PERFORMANCE

**VARIABLES RELATED TO GOVERNANCE AND OWNERSHIP**

| | |
|---|---|
| FIRM CHARTER (KEDIA & KUNTZ, 1981) | mixed |
| NATURE OF STOCK OWNERSHIP (KEDIA & KUNTZ, 1981) | mixed |
| PROPORTION OF OUTSIDE DIRECTORS (KOHLS, 1985) | n.s. |
| PROPORTION OF INDEPENDENT DIRECTORS (KOHLS, 1985) | n.s. |
| PUBLIC POLICY/SOCIAL RESPONSIBILITY COMMITTEE ON BOARD OF DIRECTORS (KOHLS, 1985) | pos. |
| NUMBER OF SOCIAL RESPONSIBILITY STRUCTURAL FEATURES ON BOARD OF DIRECTORS (KOHLS, 1985) | pos. |

**VARIABLES RELATED TO HUMAN RESOURCES**

| | |
|---|---|
| LISTED IN 100 BEST COMPANIES TO WORK FOR (ROMAN & BLUM, 1987) | mixed |
| LENGTH OF TIME COMPANY HAD EAP (ROMAN & BLUM, 1987) | n.s. |
| HIGH EAP ALCOHOL CASELOAD (ROMAN & BLUM, 1987) | mixed |
| EAP LOCATED EXTERNAL TO COMPANY (ROMAN & BLUM, 1987) | mixed |

**VARIABLES RELATED TO MANAGERIAL CONCERN WITH THE CORPORATE SOCIAL ENVIRONMENT**

| | |
|---|---|
| PUBLIC AFFAIRS DEPARTMENT AS PART OF CORPORATE STRUCTURE (SONNENFELD, 1982) | pos. |
| MANAGERIAL VALUES (KEDIA & KUNTZ, 1981) | mixed |
| SOCIAL RESPONSIBILITY OFFICER AS PART OF MANAGEMENT STRUCTURE (KOHLS, 1985) | pos. |
| SOCIAL RESPONSIBILITY COMMITTEE AS PART OF MANAGEMENT STRUCTURE (KOHLS, 1985) | pos. |
| ANNUAL SOCIAL REPORTING (KOHLS, 1985) | pos. |
| IMPORTANCE ASSIGNED TO INTEGRATING SOCIAL ISSUES WITH STRATEGIC PLANNING (AUPPERLE, 1984) | pos. |

*Figure 2.* Empirical Model: Factors Influencing Corporate Social Performance

The concept of social performance has been utilized in many ways, no doubt depending in part on availability of data and specific interests of individual researchers. No systematic attempt has been made to demonstrate how these various operational definitions are related to one another; nor is it necessarily the case that the measurements used are most appropriate in terms of consistency and general applicability. Some analysts have suggested the importance of "corporate culture" as a factor affecting social performance. Academic researchers need to increase their efforts to develop instruments designed to measure "culture" and other characteristics which may be more useful in improving the social performance of organizations than any of the operational indicators utilized to date.

## Managerial Values

One set of variables that may be associated with the development of desirable social policies and behavior patterns, but which differs significantly from the objective characteristics examined above, involves concepts of personal values and moral reasoning. Two case studies in the series examine the role of values in the managerial interpretation of a company's social responsibility and the managerial decision-making process. In addition, statistical research has revealed that the interpretation of work-related *moral conflicts* does not depend upon gender; however, work-related *values* do vary in relation to gender, age, and job classification. Some terminal value orientations were found to depend upon an individual's status as a manager, union member, or social activist. Researchers also found that different types of organizations exhibit different types of ethical climates.

JAI researchers have attempted to uncover the values that are embedded in organizations and that seem to drive organizational responses and behavior; however, much more work needs to be done in this regard. While there is a substantial general research literature on individual values, research on the nature, source, and influence of organizational values is less well developed. Instruments and constructs necessary to advance research in this important area are greatly needed. There has also been little research in this series on normative issues related to managerial and organizational values. It seems important to discuss what sets of values are most important or best for an organization, and whether or not there are sets of values and priorities that lead to more desirable corporate social performance. For example, is there a set or range of values that generates an appropriate balance between private (e.g., financial) and social performance?

## Corporate Misconduct

The darker side of research on corporate social performance examines factors contributing to corporate misconduct. Factors that have been found to be positively associated with misconduct include firm size, the strength of competition, the level of environmental uncertainty, complexity of the organizational hierarchy, culture, and financial strain. Suggestions offered for reducing the incidence of corporate misconduct include the establishment of social responsibility centers within companies and the development of ethical codes of conduct.

The major findings of the empirical studies of misconduct are represented in Figure 3. The two most often mentioned remedies for corporate misconduct, namely developing codes of ethics and restructuring corporate boards, have not been found to be significantly related to actual evidence of misconduct in these studies. (A negative relationship would, of course, be hypothesized.) It is apparent that analysis of the legal/ethical aspects of corporate policy and behavior presents great research difficulties. Improved instruments for the study of organizational values, mentioned above, could make significant contributions here as well.

## Financial Performance

An important issue in the corporate social performance literature from the very beginning has been whether companies that behave in a socially responsible manner are more or less profitable than others. The findings on this question reported in the JAI series have been mixed (see Figure 4). Companies using formal environmental assessment techniques were found to be better financial performers than those without them, but opposite or nonsignificant results were found for companies making social disclosures. Stockholders were found to be uninfluenced by general social disclosures, but they were shown to react against firms that had not foreseen and responded to new regulations. Stockholders do not necessarily react to good social performance, nor do they necessarily punish poor social performance, unless the latter is expected to result in high future costs.

The theme of financial performance is more prominent in the total corpus of corporation-society research than it is in the JAI volumes, but mixed results are typical throughout this literature. Longitudinal studies might shed some light on the fuzzy results obtained thus far from research on this theme. In addition, measures of financial performance used in these studies may need to be improved; for example, project or division performance might reveal clearer results than those obtained from overall, firm-level financial indicators.

## Business System—Personal-Communal System Research:
## Summary Comments

Future research on interactions between the business system and the personal-communal system should be sensitive to four vital issues that arise

| VARIABLES DESCRIBING GENERAL CHARACTERISTICS OF FIRM | |
|---|---|
| INDUSTRIAL SECTOR (MATHEWS, 1987) | pos. |
| FIRM PROFITABILITY (COCHRAN & NIGH, 1987) | neg. |
| FIRM SIZE (MATHEWS, 1987; COCHRAN & NIGH, 1987) | pos. |
| PRODUCT DIVERSIFICATION (COCHRAN & NIGH, 1987) | pos. |
| FIRM GROWTH (COCHRAN & NIGH, 1987) | pos. |
| INDUSTRY PROFITABILITY (COCHRAN & NIGH, 1987) | n.s. |
| LIQUIDITY (COCHRAN & NIGH, 1987) | n.s. |
| DEGREE OF MULTINATIONALITY (COCHRAN & NIGH, 1987) | n.s. |

CORPORATE MISCONDUCT

| VARIABLES RELATED TO GOVERNANCE AND OWNERSHIP | |
|---|---|
| CODE OF ETHICS (MATHEWS, 1987) | n.s. |
| EXISTENCE OF AUDIT COMMITTEE ON BOARD (JONES, 1986) | n.s. |
| PROPORTION OF OUTSIDE DIRECTORS (JONES, 1986) | pos. |
| NUMBER OF OUTSIDE DIRECTORS ON BOARD AUDIT COMMITTEE (GAUTSCHI & JONES, 1987) | n.s. |
| NUMBER OF INSIDE DIRECTORS ON BOARD EXECUTIVE COMMITTEE (JONES, 1986; GAUTSCHI & JONES, 1987) | mixed |
| SIZE OF BOARD OF DIRECTORS (JONES, 1986; GAUTSCHI & JONES, 1987) | n.s. |
| NUMBER OF ATTORNEYS ON BOARD (JONES, 1986; GAUTSCHI & JONES, 1987) | n.s. |

*Figure 3.* Empirical Tests on Corporate Misconduct

38

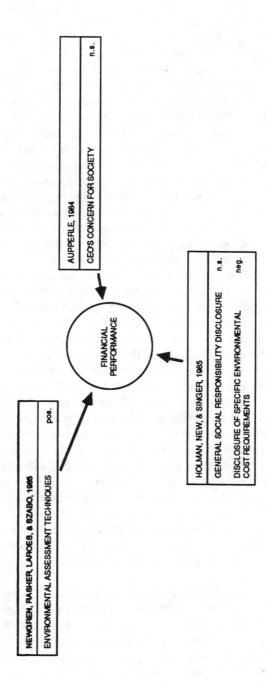

*Figure 4.* Empirical Tests on Social Performance and Financial Performance

from this review: (1) defining and employing key concepts, (2) exploring interdependencies, (3) developing multivariate models (one independent variable impacting several dependent variables, as well as the other way around), and (4) using multiple data bases.

The variety of methods used to model the concept of corporate social performance has hindered the systematic development of knowledge in this area, although the concept itself is intrinsically multidimensional. In addition, the relationship between any given variable and corporate social performance has to be examined from several different approaches, e.g., the perceptions of company executives and stakeholders, the existence and content of particular corporate social policies, and the behavior patterns of individuals within the company and the company as a whole. Real understanding of corporate social performance depends upon many different kinds of information.

After the critical research concepts have been incorporated the second issue is the interdependency among organizational characteristics and social policies and performance. As noted above, evidence on interdependencies is thus far very mixed. We need to develop some theories about such questions as: Why do organizations develop one social policy but not another? Under what circumstances do companies voluntarily initiate some social policies? Closely related to interdependency research is integrative research in the influence on multiple independent and/or dependent variables. Researchers in various studies have found that firm size has a significant *positive* relationship with the size of philanthropic budgets, the presence of mandatory retirement age policies and documentation of performance appraisals, the percentage of minority employees, and the number of law violations; a significant *negative* relationship with the percentage of female officers and with charitable contributions; and *no significant* relationship with many other variables. A comprehensive theory about the relationship between corporate size and personal-communal system variables begs to be developed.

The varied relationships found (and not found) with respect to corporate size illustrate the problems arising from the use of different, unrelated data bases. A more specific example is provided by the conflicting results obtained by Jones (1986) and Gautschi and Jones (1987) in very similar studies of the connection between the structure of boards of directors and the appearance of corporate misconduct. In all cases, conclusions derived from one data base must necessarily be considered tentative until they are confirmed by studies using different data.

Finally, as shown in Table 1, there are many factors relevant to corporate social performance that have not been explored in the JAI series thus far. These factors include the effects of legal requirements, pressure by stakeholders, public expectations, community needs, salience of issues to relevant publics, action by competitors, and the state of the economy, just to name a few. These variables merit careful consideration in future research.

# STUDIES OF BUSINESS SYSTEM-POLITICAL SYSTEM INTERACTION

The second volume of the JAI series included a review of the research on business political activity, which concluded that "there remains a dearth of both significant conceptual and methodological advances in the literature pertaining specifically to business and politics" (Epstein, 1980, p. 1). Subsequent volumes in the series have made a significant contribution to filling this void.

Forty-five articles in the series focus on the interaction between the business system and the political system. These can be divided into four broad categories, as follows: determinants of government policy (7 articles), impact of government policies on business (13 articles), business response to government policy (14 articles), and the political role and character of business (11 articles). The main findings of each of these groups of research studies are the subject of this section of the paper.

## Determinants of Government Policy

The determinants of public policies directed toward the business system, a major research theme in political science, has not been the focus of many studies in the JAI series. Public attention to an issue and agreement within an industry on an issue are shown to be important factors. One JAI study shows that the demographic characteristics of regulatory commissioners can be used to predict the likelihood of their intervention in business affairs.

It is often suggested in the literature that business exerts strong influence over public policy, but the JAI studies do not support this contention. Either the theory of business influence is false or, if the theory is true, then further research is needed in order to substantiate it and to account for these conflicting results. One study in the series indicates that business enjoys a privileged policy position only during economic downturns, and then only when certain broad types of economic policies (supply-side) prevail.

Corporate policy and public policy seem to converge on issues that receive much public attention, and this can be either a source of cooperation between the systems or a source of strain. It seems important to study more closely the variables that contribute to greater business-government cooperation. There is very little discussion in the series about whether or not business involvement in government policy is appropriate, or about how to increase or decrease such involvement. There has also been little study of the interaction between business and other interests in the policy process; the research that has explored this issue seems to indicate that interest groups have little effect on one another except to arouse emotional responses. Finally, very few of the research results related to this theme are generalizable, since most of them are obtained from case studies of very limited scope. More rigorous empirical work is needed in this area.

### Impact of Government Policy on Business

JAI studies of the impact of government policies on business are both conceptual and theoretical, and are often based on supportive case research. From these articles we learn how government policy can affect the development of industries, the risks and operations of firms engaged in international trade, and the ownership of enterprises. Government spending for research, development, and marketing affects both innovation and growth of particular industries.

Particularly germane to this theme are the issues of public ownership and privatization, including public-private partnerships. According to JAI research, privatization has not delivered all the benefits that were hoped for; however, public ownership politicizes decision processes, making this alternative bureaucratic and ineffective. These results suggest that there is a need for more normative discussion regarding government ownership and regulation of business, as well as more empirical research. In particular, there is a need to discover ways to alter some of the difficult tradeoffs indicated in these studies between internal efficiency and external effectiveness. Further, more empirical studies are needed that show the effects of government ownership and regulation on various aspects of the economy—for example, on employment, GNP growth, capital stock, and research and development expenditures.

Finally, findings from case studies need to be made more generalizable. For example, one case study shows that regulation has had a negative impact on development in one industry. Further study might help us better understand the industrial and/or regulatory characteristics that contributed to that result, and how it might be avoided in the future. Further research needs to be done also on issues surrounding the social costs and benefits involved in government intervention. When are the net effects of government regulation on business more harmful than the activities which the regulation is intended to curtail?

### Business Response to Government Policy

Public policies toward business, especially regulatory policies, elicit varied responses. JAI researchers have studied the relationship of various organizational variables to different patterns of business response to government regulation, obtaining the results shown in Figure 5. Firm size, boundary spanning activities, and management ideology are positively related to four regulatory response types: technical, informational, administrative, and environmental management. Proactive and reactive response patterns were found to be determined by specific organizational and contextual variables. In studies of regulatory compliance, profitable and highly leveraged firms are more likely to be in noncompliance, and firm size is not significantly related to compliance behavior.

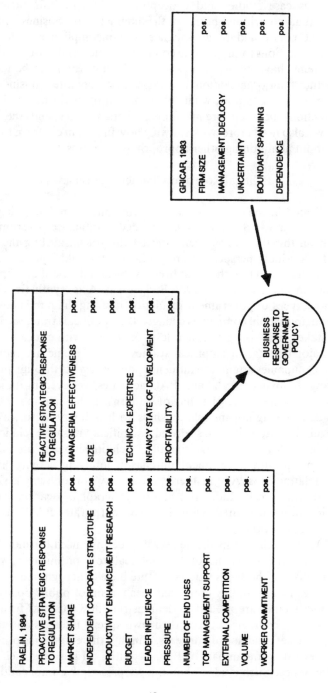

RAELIN, 1984

| PROACTIVE STRATEGIC RESPONSE TO REGULATION | | REACTIVE STRATEGIC RESPONSE TO REGULATION | |
|---|---|---|---|
| MARKET SHARE | pos. | MANAGERIAL EFFECTIVENESS | pos. |
| INDEPENDENT CORPORATE STRUCTURE | pos. | SIZE | pos. |
| PRODUCTIVITY ENHANCEMENT RESEARCH | pos. | ROI | pos. |
| BUDGET | pos. | TECHNICAL EXPERTISE | pos. |
| LEADER INFLUENCE | pos. | INFANCY STATE OF DEVELOPMENT | pos. |
| PRESSURE | pos. | PROFITABILITY | pos. |
| NUMBER OF END USES | pos. | | |
| TOP MANAGEMENT SUPPORT | pos. | | |
| EXTERNAL COMPETITION | pos. | | |
| VOLUME | pos. | | |
| WORKER COMMITMENT | pos. | | |

GRICAR, 1983

| | |
|---|---|
| FIRM SIZE | pos. |
| MANAGEMENT IDEOLOGY | pos. |
| UNCERTAINTY | pos. |
| BOUNDARY SPANNING | pos. |
| DEPENDENCE | pos. |

BUSINESS RESPONSE TO GOVERNMENT POLICY

*Figure 5.* Empirical Tests of Business Response to Government Policy

43

Numerous case studies and conceptual articles on this theme describe variables that contribute both to the character of business response to government policy and to compliance or noncompliance with regulation. Practical suggestions for improving compliance, such as the use of information-based systems, have been put forward. Little discussion can be found about factors other than organizational variables that may affect business response to regulation. For example, what role is played by environmental factors, or by interactions between organizational characteristics and the regulatory system? We also need more work showing how firms can conform to regulatory goals without abandoning other appropriate objectives.

## Political Role and Character of Business

As indicated in the section on the determinants of public policy, business firms engage in a variety of activities intended to influence government policy. Research on this theme has been directed toward unraveling the myth of a monolithic business perspective and influence on public policy issues. Case studies have revealed that there has been a substantial lack of unanimity among companies in reference to the 1981 Budget Tax Acts, synthetic fuel policies, and various types of government regulation. During the public debate on the Superfund, individual companies changed their political strategies due to shifts in their stakes in the issue and their level of conflict with critics.

The major findings of empirical studies on this theme are represented in Figure 6. Companies attempt to influence political events through public policy advertising, lobbying efforts, and PAC activities, yet even in these instances there exists a wide range of behavior patterns. Lobbying and PAC activity have statistically significant relationships with industry sector, a significant positive relationship with firm size, and a significant negative relationship with industry size. PAC activity has a significant relationship with unionization and no relationship with government purchases; lobbying activity has just the opposite relationships. And neither PAC activity nor lobbying is significantly related to firm profit. Industrial sector, geographic location, and market orientation are correlated with level of corporate PAC donations to conservative political candidates.

The JAI research on this theme reveals a definite need for more normative and value-laden discussions of the political role of business, particularly corporate PACs. The series studies to date have either ignored or skirted the ethical issues regarding this important mechanism of public policy influence. In addition, studies are needed to demonstrate how business firms might go about resolving conflicts between their own special interests and the broader industry, market, and social concerns. Finally, there appears to be room for research regarding the impact of PAC activities on business itself, as well as on public policy. Such studies should have prescriptive implications: Should

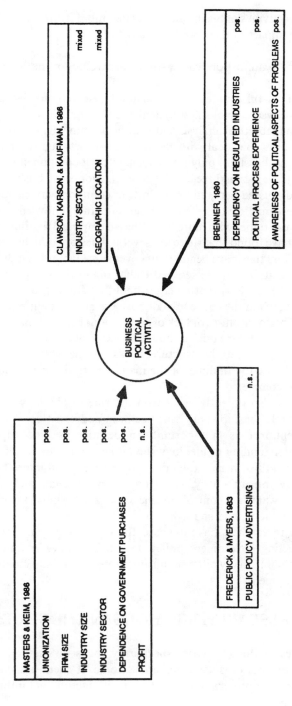

*Figure 6.* Empirical Tests of Business Political Activity

the political activities of business be regulated more stringently? How can firms improve the impact of their political activities?

### Business System-Political System Research: Summary Comments

The most useful and easily understood research articles analyzing the interaction between the business system and the political system are those that provide both theoretical analysis and empirical testing. Of the forty-five articles in the JAI series that deal with the interaction between the business system and the political system, only seven include both components. These articles are distributed among three of the four categories of business-government interaction discussed here, and have little in common with each other.

Future research in this area should integrate knowledge gained from individual case studies with more broad-based empirical findings. For example, researchers have found that there are several types of political activity pursued by business, and they have begun to uncover some factors that determine when some political strategies are selected rather than others. Now the underlying reasons for the patterns that emerge should be studied; a unifying theory is needed. Research in the entire area of business-government relations has been piecemeal. The connection (or lack of connection) between the intent of policies and the effect of those policies should be examined. This work may require more—and more carefully structured—case studies, but it also requires an effort to integrate the findings of the many descriptive case studies that have already been completed.

Research is also urgently needed on the role of ideology in the business-government relationship. This issue has been addressed on a broad level and has been mentioned as an important consideration in some empirical studies. A better understanding of ideology should contribute to all four broad areas of analysis identified here, explaining why business and interest groups try to influence government policy, why government officials and other political stakeholders want to control business behavior, how firms respond to government policies, and so forth.

Although researchers have exposed the myth of one monolithic business interest directing government policy, few articles have examined the many factors—including many different business interests—that actually account for policy developments.

## RESEARCH METHODS IN THE SERIES

Eight articles in the JAI series specifically focus on methodological issues related to corporation-society research. Some of them are concerned with defining relevant domains of research and with factors that influence research

*Table 2.*   Methods Used for Data Collection and Analysis

| Data Collection | Number | Data Analysis | Number |
|---|---|---|---|
| Public Data | 42 | Single Case Studies | 23 |
| Interview | 31 | Comparative Case Studies | 17 |
| Corporate Reports | 24 | Percentages | 12 |
| Survey | 16 | Linear Regression | 10 |
| Observation | 4 | ANOVA | 7 |
| Previous Cases | 4 | Content Analysis | 4 |
| Existing Dasta Bases | 1 | Discriminant Analysis | 4 |
| Historical Documents | 1 | Factor Analysis | 3 |
| Projective Tests | 1 | Ordinary Least Squares | 3 |
| Simulations | 1 | Logit Analysis | 3 |
| | | Canonical Correlation | 2 |
| | | Multiple Regression | 2 |
| | | Chi Square | 1 |

project design; some present and advocate specific research techniques and approaches. All of these articles are appropriately tabulated in the Appendix, and are not further discussed here.

In this section we focus on the research methods that were actually employed in the empirical studies presented in the series. The methods of data collection and analysis used in these studies are listed in Table 2, along with a simple count of the number of studies that employ each method. (Some of the studies employ multiple methods, and are double-counted as a result.)

This tabulation reveals that this collection of research studies lacks the methodological sophistication ordinarily found in organizational research. Public data and corporate reports, along with (and often supplemented by) interviews, are the dominant methods of data collection; there are very few examples of observational studies or the use of specifically developed data-collection instruments. Both public/corporate data and interviews are, of course, subject to serious self-report bias; in addition, public and corporate data may simply omit critical information. With respect to data analysis, although a variety of methods have been used, case studies are by far the most common; statistical analysis is largely limited to simple comparisons of percentages and to linear regression.

This survey makes it apparent that much could be done to improve the rigor of data collection and analysis in this area of research. For example, only one study used Chi-square analysis, although this statistical technique is very useful for determining the significance of differences between percentages and means. Also, since research in this area evidently relies heavily on qualitative methods, a major contribution would be the development and improvement of such methods. The eight methodological articles cited above represent efforts in this direction, but their primary focus is on the improvement of case research.

Moreover, there is little evidence in the series papers to date that the techniques and concepts suggested in these articles have been applied.

From this survey of JAI articles, it would appear that as a given research theme becomes more mature, the methods used to study it become more sophisticated. When a new research theme appears, much basic data accumulation and conceptual work is required to provide a basis for theory development. Theoretical considerations, in turn, then provide the basis for systematic empirical study. Now that a substantial body of conceptual, theoretical, and descriptive work has been accumulated in the JAI series (as well as elsewhere in the literature during the same time period), it would seem likely that future volumes will contain more rigorous empirical studies designed to test existing theories and concepts.

While there is a need for increased rigor in empirical research, there are also dangers in this direction of development. Experience in other areas suggests that empirical research has a tendency to become a dominant paradigm for academic study, and that tests of statistical significance can become ends in themselves. Empirical research that is not based on solid and carefully developed theory contributes little to a field of inquiry. In fact, empirical study that does not evolve from a clear theoretical base may be trivial, misleading, and even erroneous. Therefore, while there is a need for increased empirical rigor in corporation-society research, as befits the increasing maturity of its themes, great care should be taken to try to integrate the various theoretical strains into a unified body from which empirical work can emanate and to which it can contribute.

## CONCLUSION: THE INTERPENETRATING SYSTEMS MODEL REVISITED

According to our analysis, research in the JAI series has focused largely on interactions between the business system and the personal-communal domain, on one hand, or the political domain, on the other. Thus, although ten years of research has developed much substantive knowledge within the broad framework of the IPS model, little work has been done to integrate and synthesize these two broad types of interactions.

A framework for drawing these two different aspects of IPS analysis together is displayed in Figure 7. In this figure the solid lines represent interactions that have been empirically or theoretically examined in the series to date; directions of arrows indicate dependent and independent variables in the various studies. The dotted lines represent interactions that have not yet been studied in the series. The figure serves both as a summary of the research found in the ten JAI volumes, and as a way of identifying relationships and interactions for future research.

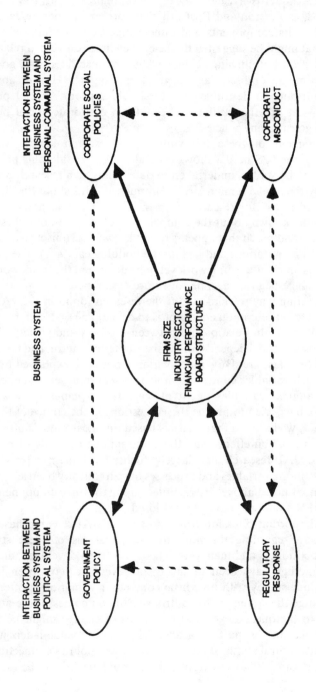

*Figure 7.* The Configuration of Research Found in Volumes 1-10, *Research in Corporate Social Performance and Policy*

If the IPS model is a valid way of conceptualizing business and society relationships, as Preston and Post originally proposed, then research should examine all of its components and dimensions. Some examples of research questions that might be suggested by the broken lines (unstudied relationships) in Figure 7 are the following: Under what circumstances does government regulation stimulate or discourage corporate misconduct? How do government policies contribute to desirable or undesirable corporate social policy and behavior? What are the feedback effects from corporate social policy and conduct on government policies?

Our assessment of these ten volumes of research studies within the framework of the IPS model shows that, although considerable progress has been made by the studies undertaken to date, many rich research possibilities suggested by the model remain largely untouched. This should be both "good news and bad news" for researchers in the field. The bad news is that very little is actually known about the complex relationships among these systems and variables (and much that appears to be "known" is subject to qualification because of data limitations and lack of methodological rigor). The good news is that there is much interesting work yet to be done, and the framework offered in Figure 7 suggests a rich agenda for future research.

One interesting way to think about the research found in the JAI series is to imagine that our common endeavor is to develop a regression model of the factors involved in the relationship between business and society. The value of this regression model depends on the size of the error term, and the questions that should be asked are: How much variance has been explained by research to date? Which variables contribute most to the current level of explanation? What unexamined variables might increase the explanatory power of the analysis? We have tried to pursue these questions in the course of this survey. It is, however, well known that analysis based on linear models often neglects the role of interaction effects, and this criticism can be made of most of the JAI studies. JAI research has largely focused on main effects, and the interactions among variables and processes have frequently been left unstudied. In particular, as noted above, interactions among the three component systems within the IPS model are largely unexplored.

Another important omission from most of the JAI research has been any direct concern regarding the normative implications of these studies for business practitioners and managers. Theory has been developed, and specific empirical findings have been obtained; however, we have been impressed throughout our survey with how little concrete information is offered about ways to change the system or to control specific outcomes. Little attention is given even to the question of what directions of change might be desirable. The reluctance on the part of academics to make value-laden judgments concerning the moral status of the business-society-politics connection is well-known (Frederick, 1986). However, there could be in this literature some development of theoretical bases for making those kinds of judgments, even if the judgments themselves are left to others. At present, even where the description of the status quo clearly implies a moral judgment (as in the case of studies of corporate misconduct), very little is offered regarding processes for bringing about desirable change.

If corporation-society research is going to realize its full potential—namely encouraging the improvement of critical managerial structures and behaviors—then research scholars must find the courage of their convictions and risk expressing them in concrete, prescriptive ways. Many managers are concerned, on both the business and the personal levels, about the moral implications of their behavior. And growing numbers of managers who want to do their own jobs with integrity also desire to be associated with companies that adhere to high social and ethical standards. These managers and their organizations need to find ways to make abstract philosophical concepts understandable and usable within the world of practice. Research directed toward this practical goal would also contribute greatly to academic knowledge and scholarship. The next decade of JAI research should bring about some progress in this direction.

## ACKNOWLEDGMENTS

The authors acknowledge with gratitude the efforts of Professor William C. Frederick for leading the seminar of which this article is a product, as well as for his helpful comments on earlier drafts.

## REFERENCES

[All references not listed here are articles in Lee E. Preston (ed.), *Research in Corporate Social Performance and Policy,* Volumes 1-10. Greenwich, CT: JAI Press, 1978-1988. These articles are individually listed in the Appendix.]

Frederick, William C. (1986). "Toward CSR3: Why ethical analysis is indispensable and unavoidable in corporate affairs," *California Management Review, 28*(2), 126-141.

Post, James E. (1986). "Perfecting capitalism: A systems perspective on institutional responsibility." In Robert B. Dickie & Leroy S. Rouner (eds.), *Corporations and the Common Good.* Notre Dame, IN: University of Notre Dame Press, 45-60.

Preston, Lee E., & Post, James E. (1975). *Private Management and Public Policy: The Principle of Public Responsibility.* Englewood Cliffs, NJ: Prentice-Hall.

Useem, Michael (1984). "Book Review: Corporate Social and Political Action," *California Management Review, 26*(2), 141-154.

# APPENDIX: SUMMARY TABLE OF JAI RESEARCH, 1978-1988

| Author(s) | Volume Year | Topic (Dependent Variable) | Independent Variable | Sample Type and Size | Findings or Propositions |
|---|---|---|---|---|---|
| **Major Theme:** | | **Corporate Social Response Patterns** | | | |
| Aldag & Bartol | 1 1978 | Corporate Social Performance | Not Applicable | Not Applicable | Characteristics of previous research were reviewed; research agenda suggested. |
| Antal | 7 1985 | Responsiveness Process | Not Applicable | Case Study | Responsiveness was affected by the functional areas of the firm and by the issues. |
| Arrow | 1 1978 | Corporate Social Performance | Control Mechanisms | Not Applicable | Characteristics of previous research were reviewed; research agenda suggested. |
| Bauer | 1 1978 | Responsiveness Process | Not Applicable | Comparative Case Studies | Response to social issues can be described in terms of a 3-stage process. |
| Blake | 2 1980 | Multinational Corporations | Not Applicable | Not Applicable | Research on MNCs and their multiple environments is needed. |
| Chaganti & Hamilton | 6 1984 | Plant Closing Decisions | Not Applicable | Comparative Case Studies | Decisions were a function of 4 organizational context factors. |
| Chaganti & Phatak | 5 1983 | Environmental Affairs Officer | Not Applicable | 4 Case Studies | Provided detailed information about the creation and functioning of the position. |
| Fleming | 3 1981 | Public Issues Scanning | Not Applicable | 20 Firms | Characteristics of scanning were reported. |
| Harvey | 6 1984 | Response to Social Problems | Managerial Motivation | Comparative Case Studies | Six factors motivate managers to respond to social problems. |
| Hay & Gray | 7 1985 | Collaboration between Business | Not Applicable | Case Study | Seven contextual factors facilitated collaboration; business and social interest groups' attitudes and behaviors change with collaboration. |
| Heuer | 7 1985 | Development of Corporate Social Responsibility Policies | Acquisition by Another Firm | Case Study | Both internal and external factors contributed to successful project implementation. |

* Empirical Papers

Appendix, continued

| Author(s) | Volume | Year | Topic (Dependent Variable) | Independent Variable | Sample Type and Size | Findings or Propositions |
|---|---|---|---|---|---|---|
| Johnson | 8 | 1986 | Consumer Boycott | Not Applicable | Case Study | Successful boycott went through 7-stage process. |
| MacMillan | 2 | 1980 | Response to Unemployment | Not Applicable | Comparative Case Studies | Community and organizational factors affected response. |
| Mahon | 4 | 1982 | Response Strategies | Not Applicable | Not Applicable | Response strategies were characterized by 5 sequential stages. |
| McGuire | 1 | 1978 | Managerial Motivation; Management Decisions | Managerial Ideology | Not Applicable | Research on the impact of ideology on motivation and decisions is needed. |
| Merenda | 3 | 1981 | Initiation/Institutionalization of Social Programs | Not Applicable | Comparative Case Studies | Top management was instrumental in implementing social programs. |
| Moore & Richardson | 10 | 1988 | Response Patterns | Not Applicable | Comparative Case Studies | Three types of response were identified. |
| Murray | 4 | 1982 | Public Affairs Departments | Not Applicable | 400 Public Affairs Managers | Characteristics of public affairs departments were reported. |
| Paul & Duffy | 10 | 1988 | South Africa Divestment | Not Applicable | Comparative Case Studies | All firms engaged in proactive behavior, but interpreted proactive differently. |
| Post | 1 | 1978 | Response to Social Issues | Not Applicable | Case Study | Response was a function of both external and internal factors. |
| Preston | 3 | 1981 | Corporate Social Performance | Corporate Power | Not Applicable | Research agenda suggested. |
| Sethi | 1 | 1978 | Responsiveness Process | Not Applicable | Comparative Case Studies | Response to social problems can be described in terms of a 4-stage process. |
| Steiner & Steiner | 1 | 1978 | Corporate Social Performance | Not Applicable | Not Applicable | Research agenda suggested. |
| Taylor | 3 | 1981 | Response to Affirmative Action Issues | Not Applicable | Comparative Case Studies | Impetus and enabling factors facilitated positive responses. |
| Zeitlin | 1 | 1978 | Corporate Social Performance | Corporate Control | Not Applicable | Research agenda suggested. |

* Empirical Papers

53

Appendix, continued

| Author(s) | Volume | Year | Topic (Dependent Variable) | Independent Variable | Sample Type and Size | Findings or Propositions |
|---|---|---|---|---|---|---|
| **Major Theme: Social Reporting** | | | | | | |
| Dierkes | 2 | 1980 | Social Reporting in West Germany | Not Applicable | Not Applicable | Status of social reporting in West Germany was reported. |
| Frederick | 1 | 1978 | Social Audit Research | Not Applicable | Case Study | Several factors aided research effort. |
| Guthrie & Mathews | 3 | 1985 | Social Accounting in Australia | Not Applicable | Not Applicable | Evolution of social accounting in Australia was reported. |
| Hogner | 4 | 1982 | Social Reporting | Not Applicable | Case Study | Social reporting was a function of societal demands and firm's need for legitimacy. |
| Malone | 10 | 1988 | Corporate Social Responsibility | Not Applicable | Not Applicable | Development of social responsibility and social performance indicators in Japan were reported. |
| Rey | 2 | 1980 | Social Reporting in France | Not Applicable | Not Applicable | Status of social reporting in France was reported. |
| **Major Theme: Corporate Social Performance and Policies** | | | | | | |
| * Auperle | 6 | 1984 | CEOs' Concern for Society | Organizational Factors | 241 CEOs | Industry sector and firm visibility affected CEOs' concern for society. |
| * Copperman | 3 | 1981 | Mandatory Retirement Policies | Organizational Factors; Industry Factors | 1,636 Firms | Mandatory retirement policies were related to firm size and industry sector. |
| * Keda & Kuntz | 3 | 1981 | 5 Socially Responsible Behaviors | Environmental, Organizational, Managerial Factors | 30 Commercial Banks | Different factors affected different measures of corporate social responsibility; various measures of responsibility were unrelated. |
| * Kohls | 7 | 1985 | Corporate Social Performance | Various Structural Factors | 50 Firms | Some organizational and board structures improved social performance. |
| * Levy & Shatto | 2 | 1980 | Philanthropic Contributions | Firm Size; Customer Service and Advertising Expenditures | 55 Electric Utilities | Contributions were positively related to size and expenditures for customer service and advertising. |

54

* Empirical Papers.

Appendix, continued

| Author(s) | Volume | Year | Topic (Dependent Variable) | Independent Variable | Sample Type and Size | Findings or Propositions |
|---|---|---|---|---|---|---|
| • Mitchell | 5 | 1983 | Social Policies | Corporate Control | 197 Firms | Social policies were not significantly related to type of corporate control. |
| • Ollen & Guthrie | 9 | 1987 | Race of Hired Applicant | Hiring Strategies | Simulation | Merit hiring strategy resulted in the fewest number of blacks hired; minimum competency and quota systems increased the number. |
| • Roman & Blum | 9 | 1987 | Employee Assistance Programs | Various Factors | 440 Firm Sites | Numerous factors influenced Employee Assistance Programs. |
| Siegfried, McElroy & Berniot-Fawles | 5 | 1983 | Philanthropic Contributions | Not Applicable | 240 Firms | Firms' financial factors affected the size of philanthropic contributions. |
| • Sonnenfeld | 4 | 1982 | Corporate Social Performance | Corporate Structure | 6 Forest Products Firms | Firms with public affairs departments had better social performance. |
| Wokutch | 4 | 1982 | Ethical Investment Policies | Not Applicable | 141 Catholic Religious Orders | Characteristics of investment policies were reported. |
| Wokutch, Murrmann & Schaffer | 6 | 1984 | Ethical Investment Policies | Not Applicable | 40 State Public Employee Pension Funds | Characteristics of investment policies were reported. |

**Major Theme: Managerial Values**

| Author(s) | Volume | Year | Topic (Dependent Variable) | Independent Variable | Sample Type and Size | Findings or Propositions |
|---|---|---|---|---|---|---|
| • Derry | 9 | 1987 | Interpretation of Moral Conflicts | Gender | 20 Male and 20 Female Managers | Male and female managers perceived moral conflicts similarly. |
| • Frederick & Weber | 9 | 1987 | Value Preferences | Group Affiliation | 270 Managers, 146 Union Members and 234 Social Activists | There were significant differences in the values preferences of the 3 groups. |
| Isabella | 8 | 1986 | Corporate Social Responsibility | Not Applicable | 40 Electronics Firm Managers | Corporate culture influenced a firm's interpretation of its social responsibilities. |

• Empirical Papers

55

Appendix, continued

| Author(s) | Volume | Year | Topic (Dependent Variable) | Independent Variable | Sample Type and Size | Findings or Propositions |
|---|---|---|---|---|---|---|
| * Ravlin & Meglino | 9 | 1987 | Work Values | Demographic Factors | 1,243 Employees in 40 Firms | Gender, age and job-related differences in work values were found. |
| Stacey | 5 | 1983 | Management Decision | Not Applicable | Case Study | Both economic and social considerations affected a decision to build a nuclear power plant. |
| * Victor & Cullen | 9 | 1987 | Ethical Climate | Organization Type | 146 Members of 4 Organizations | Different ethical climates were found in different organizations. |

**Major Theme: Corporate Misconduct**

| Author(s) | Volume | Year | Topic (Dependent Variable) | Independent Variable | Sample Type and Size | Findings or Propositions |
|---|---|---|---|---|---|---|
| Cacel & Carroll | 6 | 1984 | Executive Compensation | Firm and Market Factors | 287 Firms | Corporate profit and sales, and labor market factors affected compensation. |
| * Cochran & Nigh | 9 | 1987 | Federal Law Violations | Firm and Industry Factors | 683 Firms and Subsidiaries | Firm size, profitability and diversification, and industry sector were related to violations, while liquidity and degree of multinationality were not. |
| Dees | 8 | 1986 | Greenmail | Not Applicable | Not Applicable | Greenmail should not be considered unethical. |
| * Gautschl & Jones | 9 | 1987 | Federal Law Violations | Board Structure | 100 Firms | Most structural characteristics of boards were unrelated to law violations. |
| * Jones | 8 | 1986 | Shareholder Lawsuits | Board Structure | 78 Firms | Most structural characteristics of boards were unrelated to shareholder lawsuits. |
| * Mathews | 9 | 1987 | Regulatory Violations | Codes of Ethics | 212 Firms | The existence of codes of ethics was unrelated to regulatory violations. |
| Sethi | 3 | 1981 | Corporate Crime | Executive Liability | Comparative Case Studies | Establishment of social responsibility centers in corporations was recommended as a way to reduce corporate crime. |
| Yeager | 8 | 1986 | Corporate Crime | Not Applicable | Not Applicable | Characteristics of previous research were reviewed; research agenda suggested. |

* Empirical Papers

56

Appendix, continued

| Author(s) | Volume Year | Topic (Dependent Variable) | Independent Variable | Sample Type and Size | Findings or Propositions |
|---|---|---|---|---|---|
| **Major Theme: Financial Performance** | | | | | |
| * Aupperle | 6  1984 | Return on Assets | CEOs' Concern for Society | 241 CEOs | CEOs' concern for society was unrelated to return on assets. |
| Clarkson | 10  1988 | Corporate Profit | Corporate Social Responsiveness | Comparative Case Studies | Profits and social performance were positively correlated. |
| Holman, New & Singer | 7  1985 | Return on Equity | Social Disclosure | 49 Firms | High expected regulatory costs were negatively related to return on equity. |
| * Newgren, Rasher, LaRoe | 7  1985 | Price/Earnings Ratio | Environmental Assessment Techniques | 50 Firms | Use of environmental assessment techniques was positively related to financial performance. |
| **Major Theme: Determinants of Government Policy** | | | | | |
| * Gautschi | 8  1986 | Regulatory Decisions | Various Individual Attributes | 2,449 FTC Decisions | Four individual attributes affected FTC decisions. |
| Lenway | 5  1983 | International Trade Policy | GATT Rules | 3 Case Studies | GATT rules constrained U.S. trade policy. |
| Marcus | 7  1985 | Deregulation | Business Interests | 3 Case Studies | Deregulation could not be explained by business interests. |
| Post & Baer | 2  1980 | Infant Nutrition Policy | Public Attention | Case Study | Corporate policy and public policy converged when public attention was high. |
| * Quinn | 10  1988 | Tax Policy | Economic Cycles; Prevailing Economic Policies | 15 Years of Corporate Tax Payments in 5 Countries | When supply-side economics prevailed, tax policy favored business during economic downturns. |
| Steiner & Edmunds | 3  1981 | Interest Group Conflict | Various Factors | 2 Case Studies | Conflicts were described in terms of a 5- stage model. |
| Wood | 6  1984 | Food and Drug Act, 1906 | Consumer Interests; Business Interests | Case Study | Regulation benefited both consumers and business. |

* Empirical Papers

57

Appendix, continued

| Author(s) | Volume | Year | Topic (Dependent Variable) | Independent Variable | Sample Type and Size | Findings or Propositions |
|---|---|---|---|---|---|---|
| Major Theme: | | | Impact of Government Policy on Business | | | |
| Eckel | 10 | 1988 | Mixed Enterprise | Various Factors | Not Applicable | Success of mixed enterprise depended upon governmental goals and goal complexity. |
| Foote | 8 | 1986 | Industry Development | Government R&D Support | Case Study | Industry development was closely linked with government spending policies. |
| Gable | 10 | 1988 | Privatization | Various Factors | Case Study | Privatization failed when goals were not clearly articulated. |
| Halal | 10 | 1988 | Business-Government Relationship | Cross-Cultural Communication | Case Studies | Increased communication between societies is leading to convergence of socialism and capitalism in many countries. |
| Jacobs | 7 | 1985 | Neo-Marxist Literature | Not Applicable | Not Applicable | Neo-Marxist literature provides a useful perspective for scholars interested in the business-government relationship. |
| Lenway & Crawford | 8 | 1986 | Environmental Risk | International Politics | Case Study | Disagreement by nations on issues created high risk and uncertainty for MNCs. |
| Monsen & Walters | 4 | 1982 | State-Owned Enterprise | Social and Political Goals | European State-Owned Firms | Nationalization occurred when socialist ideology prevailed; state-owned firms were highly politicized. |
| Sethi & Steidlmeier | 10 | 1988 | Government Involvement in Economy Management | Liberation Theology | Not Applicable | MNCs operating in Latin America must accept role of government in management of the economy, due to the increasing popularity of liberation theology. |
| Vogel | 2 | 1980 | Business Attitude Toward Government | Industrial Development | Not Applicable | State involvement in early industrial development increases cohesiveness between business and government. |
| Waddock | 8 | 1986 | Public-Private Partnership | Environmental Factors | 5 Case Studies | Various environmental factors facilitated successful partnerships. |

* Empirical Papers

Appendix, continued

| Author(s) | Volume | Year | Topic (Dependent Variable) | Independent Variable | Sample Type and Size | Findings or Propositions |
|-----------|--------|------|----------------------------|----------------------|----------------------|--------------------------|
| Windsor & Preston | 10 | 1988 | Socio-economic Environment | State Ownership; Public Authority | Not Applicable | The environment for MNCs is unstable due to intensified competition among firms and nations. |
| Wokutch & McLaughlin | 10 | 1988 | Occupational Injuries | Socio-Political Context | Injuries in 5 Countries | Because the socio-political context differed in different states, comparison of injury data was difficult. |
| Wood | 8 | 1986 | Pharmaceutical Regulation | Various Factors | Case Study | Existing research did not support assertions that regulation had caused marketing delays and reduced innovation in the pharmaceutical industry. |

## Major Theme: Business Response to Government Policy

| Author(s) | Volume | Year | Topic (Dependent Variable) | Independent Variable | Sample Type and Size | Findings or Propositions |
|-----------|--------|------|----------------------------|----------------------|----------------------|--------------------------|
| Buono & Nichols | 6 | 1984 | Response to Regulation | Motive and Orientation | Case Studies | Four responses based on motive and orientation were identified. |
| Chan | 5 | 1983 | Response to Regulation | Not Applicable | Not Applicable | An information-based regulatory system was recommended. |
| Chatov | 1 | 1978 | Study of Regulation | Not Applicable | Not Applicable | Integrating competing theories of regulation would result in better research. |
| Dickie | 3 | 1981 | Response to Policy | Interaction of Business and Government | Case Study | Business and government should appeal to each other's self-interest to induce desired behaviors. |
| Globerman & Schwindt | 7 | 1985 | Response to Regulation | Business-Government Communications | Case Study | Harmonious business-government relations may lead to socially appropriate outcomes. |
| * Gricar | 5 | 1983 | Response to Regulation | Organizational Factors | 34 Foundries | Four types of responses to regulation were related to various organizational variables. |
| Harris | 7 | 1985 | Response to Regulation | Organizational Factors | Case Study | Large firms with experience interacting with government tended to cooperate with regulators. |

* Empirical Papers

59

Appendix, continued

| Author(s) | Volume | Year | Topic (Dependent Variable) | Independent Variable | Sample Type and Size | Findings or Propositions |
|---|---|---|---|---|---|---|
| Logsdon | 7 | 1985 | Response to Regulation | Not Applicable | Case Studies | Responses were characterized as accepting or resisting over 3 stages of issue life cycle. |
| * Marcus & Goodman | 8 | 1986 | Compliance to Regulation; Financial Performance | Organizational Factors | 2 Case Studies | Compliance and financial performance were interrelated, contingent upon organizational factors. |
| Mitnick | 4 | 1982 | Compliance to Regulation | Incentive Systems | Case Study | Compliance required control of both regulators and those regulated. |
| * Raelin | 6 | 1984 | Response to Regulation | Organizational Factors | 114 R&D Projects in 40 Firms | Different organizational factors contributed to proactive and reactive responses. |
| Windsor & Greanias | 4 | 1982 | Corporate Strategy | Stakeholder Interests | Not Applicable | Corporate strategy must adjust to politicized environments. |
| Windsor & Greanias | 6 | 1984 | Corporate-Society Relationship | Not Applicable | Not Applicable | Economic, legal, and political models are useful for understanding the corporate-society relationship. |
| Zashin | 4 | 1982 | Compliance to Regulation | Corporate Strategy | Case Study | Strategic use of judicial process may help. |

**Major Theme: Political Character of Business**

| Author(s) | Volume | Year | Topic (Dependent Variable) | Independent Variable | Sample Type and Size | Findings or Propositions |
|---|---|---|---|---|---|---|
| Brenner | 2 | 1980 | Political Activity | Organizational Factors | 29 Data Communications Firms | Dependency on regulated industries and political process experience increased a firm's use of political activity. |
| * Clawson, Karson & Kaufman | 8 | 1986 | PAC Contributions | Industry Sector; Geographic Location; Ideology | 186 PACs | Industry and location affected PAC contributions; managerial values helped determine contribution patterns. |
| Epstein | 2 | 1980 | Research on Political Activity | Not Applicable | Not Applicable | Conceptual and methodological advances in research on corporate political activity are needed. |

* Empirical Papers

60

Appendix, continued

| Author(s) | Volume | Year | Topic (Dependent Variable) | Independent Variable | Sample Type and Size | Findings or Propositions |
|---|---|---|---|---|---|---|
| Frederick & Myers | 5 | 1983 | Election Outcomes | Public Policy Advertising | Advertisements in 3 Periodicals | Business advertising had little impact on election outcomes; political advertising was not a high priority for business. |
| Kaufman | 6 | 1984 | Lobbying Activity | Intra-Industry Differences | Case Study | Diverse competitive structure within industries led to fragmented political activity by the industry. |
| Mahon | 5 | 1983 | Political Strategy | Stake in Issue; Relationship with Critics | Case Study | Firms selected different strategies based on their stake in an issue and relationship with critics; strategies changed over time. |
| Mahon & Kelley | 10 | 1988 | Political Strategy | Cross-National Differences | Case Study | U.S. firms had adversarial strategies; European firms collaborated with government. |
| Maitland | 5 | 1983 | Lobbying Activity | Business Interest Groups | Case Study | Lobbying reflected both an overall business interest and specialized interests. |
| * Masters & Keim | 8 | 1986 | PAC Contributions; Number of Lobbyists | Organizational Factors; Industry Factors | 1300 Firms | Both organizational and industry variables affected PAC contributions and number of lobbyists. |
| Schlusberg | 2 | 1980 | Political Activities | Not Applicable | Not Applicable | Many business activities were considered political. |
| Swanson | 3 | 1981 | PAC Activity | Not Applicable | Not Applicable | The history of legislation related to corporate involvement in the political process was reviewed. |

Major Theme: Research Methods

| Author(s) | Volume | Year | Topic (Dependent Variable) | Independent Variable | Sample Type and Size | Findings or Propositions |
|---|---|---|---|---|---|---|
| Cavanagh & Fritzsche | 7 | 1985 | Use of Vignettes | Not Applicable | Not Applicable | Use of vignettes for research was recommended. |
| DeFillippi | 4 | 1982 | Research Domains | Not Applicable | Not Applicable | Suggested conceptual dimensions; design is influenced by 6 variables. |
| Fleming | 9 | 1987 | Business Ethics Research | Not Applicable | Not Applicable | Conceptualized and described 8 topics. |

* Empirical Papers

61

Appendix, continued

| Author(s) | Volume | Year | Topic (Dependent Variable) | Independent Variable | Sample Type and Size | Findings or Propositions |
|---|---|---|---|---|---|---|
| Pasquero | 10 | 1988 | Disparity Between Research Literature and Practice | Not Applicable | Not Applicable | Mid-range techniques for research were recommended. |
| Post & Andrews | 4 | 1982 | Case Research | Not Applicable | Not Applicable | Three primary subject categories of research were suggested. |
| Preston | 1 | 1978 | Framework for Analyzing Business and Society Concepts | Not Applicable | Not Applicable | Identified 4 models of interaction. |
| Ravlin & Meglino | 9 | 1987 | Values Research | Not Applicable | Not Applicable | Use of ipsative measures was supported. |
| Szwajkowski | 8 | 1986 | Corporate Misconduct Research | Not Applicable | Not Applicable | Myths about problems in researching misconduct were exposed. |

* Empirical Papers

# CORPORATE SOCIAL PERFORMANCE AND POLICY: A SYNTHETIC FRAMEWORK FOR RESEARCH AND ANALYSIS*

Lee E. Preston

## INTRODUCTION

In his pioneering contribution to the *Handbook of Organizations,* Arthur L. Stinchcombe noted that the study of "the relation of the society outside organizations to the internal life of organizations" was in an undeveloped state; indeed, "the field itself is hardly recognized as a special branch of research . . ." (38, pp. 144–45). Under these circumstances, Stinchcombe suggested that the student or scholar must make a choice as to "what kind of knowledge to seek immediately" among three main alternatives:

(a) to try to establish one proposition well . . . ;

(b) to make distinctions among phenomena in the area or to create (or learn) schemes of analysis which may be of use to others (or to oneself) in analyzing particular problems in the future, which enterprise is called "theory" . . .

(c) to try to increase the credibility of a number of propositions in the area by the use of whatever information comes to hand . . . (38, p. 191).

This paper, along with several others in this volume, is aimed at the second of these three alternatives—making distinctions among phenomena and attempting to create analytical schema for future use. We attempt to develop a framework for research and analysis of the relationship between the business corporation and its social environment, with particular emphasis on describing, explaining, predicting, and evaluating the behavior of firms with respect to *social,* as contrasted with *market* or *financial,* issues and variables.

The need for such an analytical framework seems scarcely open to dispute. Wamsley and Zald note Landau's observation that the "preparadigmatic state" of a discipline is characterized by "a plethora of competing schools, a polyglot of languages, and accordingly, a confusion of logics." They draw upon Kuhn's earlier analysis to point out that an analytical paradigm

sets out a logic or conceptual map by which one proceeds to analyze and from which one draws inferences. It creates and is created by a distinctive coherent research tradition . . . [and] is a sign of maturity in a particular scientific field. . . . [A] paradigm is more global and overarching than a model and, although less precise, it provides the framework for model building and testing. (43, p. 2)

For our purposes, an appropriate analytical framework or paradigm should include at least four critical elements:

(1) A basic conception or model of the *corproate organization,* with specific emphasis on those aspects of the organization that link it to its host environment;

(2) a corresponding conception or model of the *social environment,* or at least of those aspects of the environment most relevant to the analysis of corporation–society relationships;

(3) a conception of the *modes of interaction* between the corporation and its environment, including not only the organization's reception of and response to environmental stimuli, but also its ability to stimulate or alter its environment, both intentionally and inadvertently;

(4) a conceptual basis for *appraising* or evaluating corporate social performance—including both (a) the *process* of corporation–society in-

teraction, and (b) the *results* achieved—from both *internal* and *external* perspectives.

Neither this paper nor this entire volume can provide an analytical framework that fully comprehends all of the complex and multidimensional situations and variables that may arise in the analysis and implementation of corporate social policy. Nevertheless, an outline of the major dimensions of such a framework, and of some possible ways in which they may be more fully articulated, seems worthwhile. At a minimum, this attempt should serve as a basis for additions, corrections, and more detailed development of specific aspects by other contributors to this series and to the general literature. As this process proceeds, the evolving framework should serve as a basis for classifying and codifying research contributions, and for identifying specific hypotheses requiring further investigation and analysis.

## SOCIAL PERFORMANCE AND ORGANIZATIONAL LEGITIMACY

The distinctive characteristic of the business corporation, for purposes of this analysis, is not its specific legal form but rather its social legitimacy as a limited-purpose managerial entity within the larger society. Managerial organizations, whether corporate or not, contrast significantly with voluntary or "expressive" organizations (clubs, churches, etc.) on the one hand, and with units of general government on the other. Managerial organizations are distinguished both by their performance of specialized functions and by their adoption of internal organizational structures and modes of communication and control in order to accomplish these functions. In the basic theoretical model of market capitalism, both the functions themselves and the effectiveness of any specific organization in discharging them are continuously tested in the marketplace. If the functions themselves are not desired by that set of external and impersonal forces roughly referred to as "market demand," or if other competitive organizations are more efficient or effective in performing desired functions, then the specific organization simply ceases to exist. Under opposite conditions, the organization meets "the test of the market" and survives and prospers. Within this simple model, *market* performance is the sole dimension of *social* performance, and successful market performance thus provides both necessary and sufficient conditions for organizational legitimacy. In sum, according to this conception, Friedman's dictum that "The social responsibility of business is to increase its profits" is simply the truth.

The interest in corporate social performance and policy that has developed in recent years involves not so much a rejection of the market model as a realization that it is seriously incomplete as a description of the relationship between large managerial organizations and their host environments. There has, indeed, been some contention that large managerial organizations, and perhaps even coalitions of smaller ones, can manipulate their environments so as to control both market and nonmarket forces and thereby generate their own "success" as their principal organizational output. This thesis—associated with Galbraith, Hacker, Nader, and other social critics—cannot be lightly dismissed, and hence requires a locus for investigation within a comprehensive research framework. It does not, however, provide the sole, or even primary, focus for our analysis. On the contrary, the overriding consideration is the simple fact that managerial organizations of all kinds—and particularly large and complex ones—have multiple impacts on society that are not fully mediated by the market mechanism, even when that mechanism is operating effectively. These impacts reflect the social legitimacy of the organization, and, hence, require managerial attention as well as sytematic external evaluation. Thus, there is a need for a general analytical structure and collection of research techniques that permit the examination of a wide range of organization–environment interactions, impacts, and hypotheses.

The historic and current social legitimacy of the business corporation derived from its economic usefulness—specifically, as a means of amassing capital and directing its use. The historical process by which the corporation was given formal legal sanction is brilliantly analyzed, with particular reference to U.S. experience, in the authoritative study by Hurst (21), who emphasizes that the legal framework developed in response to underlying social and economic relationships, rather than the other way around. The most conspicuous current issues of organizational legitimacy arise not within the law itself, but—as suggested by the title of Christopher Stone's recent book—"where the law ends" (39).[1] Hence, primary interest focuses on the continuing process of organizational legitimation, which involves adaptation to a changing environment, rather than once-and-for-all establishment of a formal legal status for particular organizations or organizational types.

The functional approach to corporate legitimacy, of which Hurst's analysis is the rare and outstanding example in the legal literature, has been typical of traditional economic analysis. Other contemporary analysts, such as Lodge (24) and Cavanagh (13), see the problem of organizational legitimacy primarily in ideological or value terms. And still others, such as Galbraith (19) and Coleman (17), focus on issues of "power", both socio-legal and economic. A major current theme is the search for new bases of legitimacy and legitimation that will respond to "contradictions" and strains within the contemporary system. This theme is addressed in a variety of ways by Bell (9), Harrington (20), and Levy and Zaltman (23). In these latter analyses, the key to continuing (or renewed) organizational legitimacy appears to lie in the resolution of conflicts or discrepancies between *traditional* functions, ideologies, and power relationships on the one hand, and those that are *future-oriented* on the other.

An appropriate conception for analyzing the continuous process of organizational legitimation—whether from a functional or a philosophical perspective—is described by Thompson as the "natural-system approach." He writes:

> [We] assume that a system contains more variables than we can comprehend at one time, and that some of the variables are subject to influences we cannot control or predict . . . Central to the natural-system approach is the concept of homeostasis, or self-stabilization, which spontaneously, or naturally, governs the necessary relationships among parts and activities and thereby keeps the system viable in the face of disturbance stemming from the environment. (41, pp. 6–7)

We would add to Thompson's characterization only the caveat that self-stabilizing activities are not necessarily "spontaneous or natural," but in fact have to be designed and developed within and among organizations. Indeed, the creation of the key structural elements necessary for self-stabilization, and their functional implementation within the management process, is the central problem in designing and executing corporate social policy.

# MODELS OF ORGANIZATION AND ENVIRONMENT

This section develops some elements of a formal model of the managerial organization and, in less detail, a corresponding conception of the social environment in which such organizations "live and move and have their being." The organizational model arises from an initial conception of Parsons (30), as further developed by Thompson (41). The conception of the social environment combines elements from a broad survey of social science literature, and emphasizes some recent contributions and conflicting viewpoints.

## The Parsons–Thompson Model of Organizations

Parsons originally suggested that the structure of a hierarchical organization might be broken down "according to three references of function or responsibility, which become most clearly marked in terms of the external references of the organization to its setting or to the next higher order in the hierarchy." These three elements he termed the *technical, managerial* and *institutional* levels, or sub-systems, within the organization.

The *technical* elements are those that accomplish the specific and distinctive tasks or functions of the organization:

> In an educational organization these are the actual processes of teaching; in a government bureau, the administrative process in direct relation to the public. . . ; in a business firm, the process of physical production of goods, etc. . . . The primary exigencies to which this sub-organization is oriented are those imposed by the nature of the technical task such as the 'materials'—physical, cultural, or human—which must be processed, the kinds of cooperation of different people required to get the job done effectively. (30, p. 60)

Parsons noted, however, that "it does not make sense" to carry out these technical functions without having made some prior decisions about what kinds of technical activities are to be undertaken and how one such activity relates to another. Thus the technical functions within an organization are controlled and serviced by higher level units, which he refers to as the "managerial system." The functions of the managerial system are: (1) to mediate between the technical organization and the users of its "product," and (2) to procure the resources necessary for carrying out the technical function. The managerial system thus looks both *inward,* to control the operations of the technical system, and *outward,* toward both the markets for the products of the technical system and the resources required for its continued operations.

These two levels of functional activity might be sufficient to describe an organization within a social system based solely on market relationships. However, Parsons was thinking in a broader context:

> A formal organization . . . is the mechanism by which goals somehow important to the society, or to various sub-systems of it, are implemented and to some degree defined. But not only does such an organization have to operate in a social environment which imposes the conditions governing the processes of disposal and procurement, it is also part of a wider social system which is the source of the "meaning", legitimation, or higher-level support which makes the implementation of the organization's goals possible. Essentially, this means that just as a technical organization . . . is controlled and "serviced" by a managerial organization, so, in turn, is the managerial organization controlled by the "institutional" structure and agencies of the community. (30, pp. 63–64)

The third, or *institutional,* level of the organization may take many different forms. These "are the mediating structures between the particular managerial organization—and hence the technical organization it controls—and the higher-order community interests which, on some level, it is supposed to serve." Parsons suggested that:

> The foci of this higher level of controls . . . are of three main types, which often appear in combination. One control is universal: The operation of the organization is subjected to generalized norms, valid throughout the wider community. These range from the rules formerly codified in the law to standards of "good practice" informally accepted. So far as control is of this type, the distinctive thing is that no organized agency continually supervises the managerial organization; intervention is likely only when deviant practice is suspected. . . .
>
> The second type of control mechanism is some formal organization which is interstitial between the managerial structure and more diffused basis of "public interest." The fiduciary board which supervises the typical private non-profit organization is the type case, though in many respects *the directors of business corporations also belong in this category.* [Italics added.]
>
> Finally, the third type is that which brings the managerial organization directly into the structure of "public authority" at some level. In our society, this is usually "political" authority, i.e., some organ of government. . . . The relation to superior authority may in turn be "administrative" or "regulative." (30, pp. 64–65)

The basic structure of the Parsons model was extensively elaborated by Thompson, with particular emphasis on the impact of the social environment on all three levels of an organizational system and on the development of criteria and techniques for organizational assessment and control. Wamsley and Zald made extensive use of Thompson's analysis in their discussion of "the internal political economy" of organizations, with a strong emphasis on the role of successive hierarchical levels in "buffering" the technical core activities which constitute the organization's fundamental social purpose. They also stress four specific functions of the managerial and institutional levels:

(1) defining and interpreting goals and missions;
(2) creating and sustaining boundary-spanning roles;
(3) recruiting and socializing elites;
(4) overviewing, controlling and evaluating. (43, Chap. 3)

The Parsons model was also applied explicitly by Post (31) to describe the organizational structure of an insurance company, and to provide a basis for analyzing the varied responses of the insurance industry to social and economic change. (See Exhibit 1).

*Exhibit 1*    Organizational Subsystems of an Insurance Company, An
Illustration of the Parsons–Thompson Model

*Technical Subsystem:*

> *Underwriting,* involving the selection of insurable risks and the calculation of rates.
> *Investment* of insurance premiums in permissible investment options, such as land,
> municipal and industrial bond, and common stocks.

*Managerial Subsystem:*

> *Coordination* of underwriting and investment activities.
> *Sales* activities designed to secure resources (candidates and premiums) for the un-
> derwriting and investment departments.
> *Settlement* of claims that involve distribution of insurance reserve funds to legitimate
> claimants under insurance policies.

*Institutional Subsystem:*

> *Legal* activities directed toward preserving the insurance fund for legitimate claim-
> ants.
> *Public relations* activities directed at providing information and cultivating under-
> standing of insurance activities.
> *Community and public affairs* wherein the insurer's relationship with the local, state,
> and national communities in which it operates is preserved and cultivated (includes
> lobbying).

Source: Post (31), p. 6.

These references suggest the general usefulness and some possible ex-
tensions of Parsons' original conception of the three-level organizational
structure. It is also essential here to emphasize as strongly as possible the
point that changes in the social environment create stimuli and pressures
that cannot be deflected or resolved at the "institutional" level alone, and
that these, in fact, penetrate to the managerial level and even the technical
core. Correspondingly—indeed, perhaps with even greater frequency and
importance—the social impact of organizations originates in the decisions
at the technical or managerial levels, and is recognized at the institutional
level only *after* being received and responded to by the host environment.
An intention to alter this process—so that environmental impacts are
anticipated and, where necessary, modified *before* they actually occur—
is an important stimulus and goal in the development of corporate social
policy.

## The Social Environment

What conception of the social environment will be most helpful in both
the development and the study of corporate social policies and performance impacts? This question is not easy to answer. At one extreme, it is
possible to conceptualize society as a cohesive entity, characterized by a
complex set of common or system-wide attributes—geographic, historic,
institutional, economic, and cultural. However, most analysts are impressed by the extent and significance of internal diversity within society,

the lack of cohesion among its many and varied elements, and, in particular, the relatively weak emphasis on, or even recognition of, goals or purposes for society as a whole, as compared to the clear identity and strength of social subgroups, organizations, and purposive coalitions. Thus, if one wishes to develop a precise analytical conception of the social environment as a basis for either research or managerial policy, an initial and critical choice must be made between an approach based on some conception of *society as a whole,* and hence cast in terms of broadly prevailing trends, themes, and institutions, and one based on a conception that places primary emphasis on *sub-systems,* differentiated groups, and situations of imbalance, conflict, or cooperation. In addition, whichever primary orientation is adopted, there remains a further choice as to the appropriate societal features or group of differentiating characteristics requiring emphasis. Since the number and variety of possible "models" of the social environment appear to be literally unlimited, these analytical choices can best be indicated by example.

## SOCIETY AS A WHOLE

With respect to analytical orientations emphasizing a concept of *society as a whole* and a set of society-wide forces, goals, or trends that form the social environment of any particular organization, many different examples can be identified in the contemporary literature. In a conception that we shall modify slightly below while adapting it to our own purposes, Daniel Bell describes society as a holistic entity composed of three interactive elements—the social structure, the polity, and the culture. (8, p. 12; and 9, p. *xi.*) Bell states that the trifurcation of society into social structure, polity, and culture involves an explicit rejection of philosophical "holism"; and, indeed, as his analysis of "contradictions" progresses, there is some substance to this contention. However, his fundamental orientation—particularly in *The Coming of Post-Industrial Society*—is that the components interact to produce changes in the whole. Indeed, the mere mention of "post-industrial society" implies the existence of a social entity that can be so described, even if its principl characteristics arise from the interaction of component elements.

According to Bell's analysis, a critical change in the social structure—specifically, a shift from an "economizing" society focused on the efficient use of scarce resources to a "post-industrial" society in which "theoretical knowledge" is the key productive factor and its direction and control the central problem for social decision-making—will set off a sequence of changes in the polity and the culture. At the outset, Bell states that these patterns of change are not determinate; however, as the argument progresses he comes to predict a variety of more specific developments, particularly "the subordination of the corporation," as the "economizing mode" is replaced by the "socioligizing mode" as the principal means of directing economic—and, by extension, social and political—activity.

Although Bell's insistence on the primacy of intellectual technology could be interpreted as an "ideological" position, it is not so intended. Indeed, the specific rejection of "old political passions" as guiding forces in modern social life was the main theme of one of his previous works (10), and is explicitly affirmed as the starting point for his more recent analysis (8, p. 34). In direct contrast, Lodge recently reasserted the primacy of ideological considerations; moreover, he argued that the traditional American ideology of pragmatic individualism is rapidly being supplanted by a distinctly different orientation that he terms "communitarianism" (24).[2] However, Lodge's argument is not simply that ideological factors dominate, or at least serve to *define*, legitimacy within the social environment, thus conditioning the process of social change. He further argues that "communitarianism" is in the process of creating a new *Gemeinschaft* in which:

(1) community membership rights replace property rights as the basic organizing social principle;

(2) "community need" replaces individual consumer desire as the dominant economic force;

(3) the central role of the several levels of institutional government as an agency for social planning and direction is greatly expanded; and

(4) a new intellectual synthesis develops that is holistic and significantly "subjective," rather than specialized, rational and deceptively "objective."

A third approach to the analysis of the social environment on a holistic, rather than fragmented, basis stresses the importance of the public policy process, including the institutional framework within which it takes place, as a central integrating element within an otherwise inchoate plethora of social forces. The "institutional-systems" model sketched by Preston and Post (33) represents one attempt to weave together elements from the legal, institutional, and historical literature in order to provide some content to the notion that *society as a whole,* rather than specific sub-units or constituencies, is a significant focus for the analysis of the social environment of any particular organization. One feature of this model is its emphasis on the broad range of social forces that provide *input* into the public policy process, as well as the role of that process in articulating specific goals, constraints, opportunities, and limitations on behalf of *society at large.*

It seems significant that the predictive implications of Bell's functionalist analysis, Lodge's ideological emphasis, and more conventional institutional and historical approaches are essentially similar. All of these analyses suggest an increased emphasis on "sociologizing" and "participative" processes throughout society, and an increased role for "intellectual technology," probably centralized in government, in directing the course of economic and social change, and hence in determining the direction and goals of managerial activity within individual organizations.

## SOCIETY AS A COLLECTION OF SUBSYSTEMS

The alternative analytical conception—that the social environment consists of distinct, although possibly interactive, groups and elements—has, of course, a long intellectual tradition, and has been dominant in the evolution of corporate social policy up to the present time. Indeed, a general predilection to think of society as intrinsically composed of disparate elements and groups is almost unavoidable. And this predilection is reinforced by the fact that the most important example of the long-term evolution of corporate social policy specifically focuses on a single differentiated group within the larger society: the organization's employees and, eventually, their own formal organization, the labor union. Hence, it is not surprising that both the practice and the study of corporate social policy has frequently involved the identification of specific and differentiated constituencies and the discovery (or simply receipt) of their various concerns, needs, and "demands." The common tendency to think along these lines is reflected, for example, in the topical coverage of conferences and collections of essays dealing with corporation–society relationships, such as the pioneering early collection assembled by Mason (27) and the more recent volumes edited by Anshen (3) and McKie (28). (By contrast, a more holistic approach is reflected in the recent Backman anthology(6).)

As an alternative to the actual list of constituencies—employees, stockholders, customers, community citizens, etc.—constituting the social environment, Child offers a more synthetic conception based on four dimensions (omitting the *physical* setting), as follows:

(1) *markets*, both factor and product, where economic considerations dominate and the critical modes of interaction are communication and exchange;[3]

(2) *technical knowledge*, the environmental element that provides the focus for Bell's analysis of "post-industrial" society;

(3) *political environment*, comprised primarily of the institutional structures of government, and their roles with respect to the *other elements;*

(4) *socio-cultural environment,* the attributes of which are, according to Child, "intangible and indiscrete," and include "orientations and values," "life styles," and associations that "can be subsumed by the concept of 'community,' particularly if one does not insist that this must be linked to the notion of a specific territorial base." (15, pp. 14–16)

Commonplace and plausible as a fragmented or "constituency" approach to the analysis of the social environment may be, it is not without major conceptual difficulties. First, there is the simple fact that most individuals, and even most managerial organizations, belong to multiple groups, and that substantial differences in concerns and goals may arise among the several different social coalitions that share some common memberships. This fact, among others, led Olson (29), Schelling (36, 37), and others building upon the earlier theoretical work of Arrow (4) to argue that even clearly identified and significant groups may not be able to act jointly to determine and achieve their own self-interest. Furthermore, even where the goals of specific constituencies *can* be clearly defined Schelling has emphasized the dangers involved in allowing the broad social performance goals of an organization to be determined by "some subset of its customers, . . . employees, . . . whatever ethnic group in the community is most articulate or most threatening, by people who love dogs or by people who are allergic to dog hair" (36, p. 89). He stresses the importance of mutual coercion or uniform practice among all parties involved, the relocation of legal obligations, and public sector leadership— all essentially holistic approaches—in the resolution of such conflicts.

Apart from all of these considerations, when either the formation or the analysis of corporate social policy focuses primarily on specific social groups and constituencies the result is an inevitable emphasis on formal associations and identified interests as they have existed in the *past,* an orientation which, although not necessarily insignificant, may not serve to identify the significant social forces and issues of the *future.* And even in the more synthetic conceptions, as exemplified by that of Child, the process of *interaction* among diverse forces or dimensions of social life is necessarily neglected. However, to the extent that many of the critical problems of modern society arise because of "the simultaneous increase of individualism and interdependence" (40, p. 72), then a conceptualization that permits a balanced emphasis *both* on significant social subgroups *and* on society as a whole is probably essential.

## THE "POLITICAL ECONOMY" MODEL

The "political economy" model of organizations developed by Zald (45), and extended in his work with Wamsley (43) and others, represents an attempt to deal with both the holistic and "specific publics" aspects of organization–environment relationships. This model also develops a parallel framework of internal and environmental structure and process somewhat similar to the more general framework we shall propose below. The analytical scheme classifies the components of the "political economy" of organizations into four categories, as follows:[4]

|  | Environmental | Internal |
|---|---|---|
| Political | 1 | 3 |
| Economic | 2 | 4 |

The elements in the first category (Environmental–Political) correspond roughly to Bell's conception of the "polity"; those in the second (Environmental–Economic), to the physical and economic conditions Bell considers part of the "culture." (It is notable that other broad social and historical conditions included in Bell's concept of "culture" are not specifically mentioned, perhaps because of the narrower focus of Zald's analysis.) Categories three and four contain the essential features of Parson's institutional and technical elements of organizations, respectively; and Parsons' managerial subsystem appears to span the two categories.

An example of the use of the "political economy" model to describe the environment of the Selective Service System (Exhibit 2) illustrates both its strengths and limitations. On the one hand, this conception permits the analyst to identify specific groups, and even named individuals, that may exert critical environmental influence, while at the same time recognizing the presence of the general public and "interested parties with low resources" as elements of the total picture. On the other hand, the specifically "economic" features of the model are not strongly emphasized in this illustration—although, if a "supply and demand" dichotomy were to be adopted instead of the "hostiles and allies" dichotomy used here, then the House Appropriations Subcommittee ("supply") might be separated from the House Armed Services Committee and other "demanders." More important, this illustration suggests that both the basic structure and the specific characteristics of the relevant "environment" vary greatly from organization to organization, and thus that the "political economy" approach, although highly suggestive, is not sufficiently general to serve as the basis of a comprehensive and completely flexible analytical framework.

*Exhibit 2*   "Political Economy" Model of Selective Service System

|               *Hostiles*               |                *Allies*                |
| -------------------------------------- | -------------------------------------- |

*Incontact Influentials*

| Presidential Commission on Draft (1969) | American Legion |
| Supreme Court | V.F.W. |
| Senator Edward Kennedy | National Guard Association |
| | House Armed Services Committee |
| | House Appropriations Subcommittee |
| | Senator John Stennis |
| | Hon. Mendel Rivers |

*Latent Resources with Occasional Contact*

| Assistant Secretary of Defense for | State Governors |
| Manpower & Reserve Affairs | State Adjutant Generals |
| Department of Labor | FBI |

*Interested Parties with Low Resources*

Antidraft Groups
Antiwar Groups
Draft-Age Men

For the basis for the analytical judgment, see Gary L. Wamsley, *Selective Service and a Changing America* (Columbus, Ohio: Charles E. Merrill Co., 1969), *passim*.

Source: Adapted from (43) p. 29.

# A SYNTHESIS

In an attempt to draw together these diverse and important themes and approaches, we suggest here a synthesis of concepts that draws attention to trends and issues arising within society as a whole, while leaving room for the analysis of the special concerns and problems of individual constituencies or institutional entities. This threefold conception parallels to some extent the Parsons–Thompson organizational model presented in the previous section, and utilizes elements of Bell's conception of society as social structure, polity, and culture, along with some of the basic structural features and emphases of Zald's "political economy" model.

The elements of the suggested summary framework are as follows:

(1) A central *core* of basic economic and social conditions, long-term

historical trends, and widely-shared values and behavioral norms. These are the fundamental elements of social life, and determine both the basic characteristics and the effective purposes (whether recognized and stated, or not) of the society. The core includes, of course, Bell's conception of the "culture," along with some underlying aspects of the social structure. Lodge's emphasis on ideology also belongs in the core area.

(2) A higher level structure of formal *organizations,* leadership groups, and institutional arrangements that serve to mobilize and focus the available resources and values-motivations. These are, of course, the "managerial" elements within the larger society, and might be said to constitute the "social structure" *proper,* in Bell's conception.

(3) The formal structure of *law and public policy* explicitly designed to articulate and "institutionalize" the concerns and goals of the larger society; i.e., the "polity."

In Exhibit 3 this threefold conception of the environment is diagrammed alongside the Parsons–Thompson threefold model of an organization, and the two elements are linked by both (1) interaction modes and (2) normative appraisal criteria. The next two sections explain these latter elements of the conceptual scheme.

## INTERACTION MODES

A conventional analysis, and one not inconsistent with Parsons' original conception, might suggest that an organization interacts with the larger society primarily at the "institutional" level. Indeed, the notion that the "institutional" level of the organization deals primarily with the "institutional" (i.e., legal-political) level of the environment underlies the traditional "legalistic" approach to corporation–society relationships, as described in the now-classic article by Votaw and Sethi (42, pp. 192–4). The two other conventional corporate responses they describe also fit easily into our suggested analytical framework. The "industrial relations" response involves the recognition by the corporation of other "managerial" entities (e.g., labor unions) within the social environment, and negotiations with such entities on a bargaining basis. The "public relations" response involves efforts to affect the knowledge, attitudes, or beliefs of members of society, and thus touches—or at least *attempts* to touch—the "core" of the environment, as we have described it.

These examples illustrate efforts on the part of corporate organizations to deal with all levels of the social environment, and not simply with the

*Exhibit 3*   Diagram of Analytical Framework

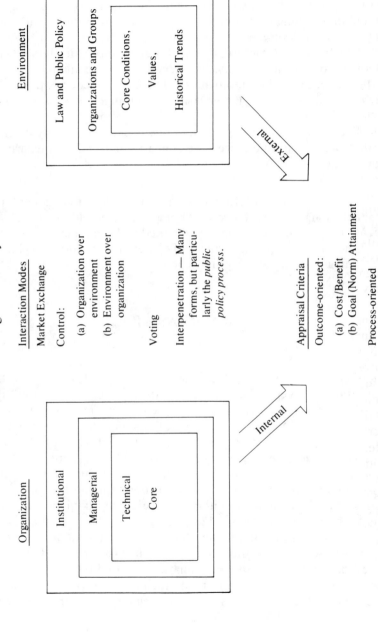

Organization

Institutional

Managerial

Technical

Core

Internal

Environment

Law and Public Policy

Organizations and Groups

Core Conditions,

Values,

Historical Trends

External

Interaction Modes

Market Exchange

Control:

(a) Organization over
    environment
(b) Environment over
    organization

Voting

Interpenetration — Many
forms, but particu-
larly the *public
policy process.*

Appraisal Criteria

Outcome-oriented:

(a) Cost/Benefit
(b) Goal (Norm) Attainment

Process-oriented

formal structure of legal and political institutions. Similarly, forces from all levels of the social environment may penetrate the institutional shell of corporations to affect the managerial level and the technical core. Indeed, one of the striking characteristics of several important new areas of public policy concern—e.g., equal employment opportunity, environmental protection, and occupational health and safety—is that their impact is felt primarily at the technical level of corporate activity. By contrast, other historic areas of public policy evolution have had their principal impact at the managerial level (e.g., collective bargaining, international trade policy) or on the institutional status of the corporation and its relationship to other social entities (e.g., antitrust and regulatory policy, macroeconomic policy).

Most analyses emphasize two sharply contrasting modes of corporation–society interaction: *market exchange* and *control*. The nature of market exchange relationships is familiar. Key characteristics are: (1) the formal independence of the exchanging parties, (2) the voluntary nature of their interaction, and (3) the paradoxical combination of disparity (i.e., differences in resource endowments and tastes) and parity (i.e., the transaction price) that lies at the core of pure market exchange relationships. By contrast, relationships based on *control* involve explicit recognition of both interdependence and inequality among the parties involved. Control, of course, may be exercised by either party over the other. That is, the organization or some coalition of organizations may dominate the environment; or society, operating through its own managerial and institutional superstructure, may control the organization.[5] Conceptions of the domination of society by a corporate "technostructure" or "power elite" imply, of course, the former conception; direct public regulation, as well as the extreme case of government ownership and management, are examples of the latter.

Building upon the earlier analysis by Dahl and Lindblom, among others, Tom Burns identified four modes of interaction "by which we systematize the multifarious traffic of the social world" (12, p. 144). In addition to *market exchange* and *control* (which he termed "bureaucracy"), discussed above, he emphasized two additional modes, the more important of which is *voting*.[6] He noted that, among the identified interaction modes, only *voting* implies some type of formal equality among the voters. However, he further emphasized that "formal equality of voting rights not only does not guarantee equality of influence in the corporate state but systematically underwrites the preservation of inequality of power and influence" (12, p. 160, in ital. in the original). It is notable that, although formal voting has been a characteristic mode of interaction throughout our society and within the corporate structure itself, it has *not* been a significant mode of interaction *among* corporate organizations or *between* them and their environments. A system of corporate federalism, or modern syndicalism, has yet to receive serious consideration, although it may be evolving in *parts* of societies as otherwise disparate as the U.S., France, and the U.S.S.R. A significant aspect of the increased emphasis on *participation* both within organizations and between them and their host environments may be a gradual enlargement of the role of voting, in a variety of forms, as a mode of corporation–society interaction. At a minimum, the emphasis on participative representation and due process—procedural norms ultimately based on an underlying conception of mutuality and equality—seems almost certain to increase (35, 44).

A fourth major mode of organization–society interaction in addition to market exchange and control—and repeating for emphasis that the current importance of voting is limited—may be termed *interpenetration.*[7] Burn's discussion of power-development processes in society, as well as the entire companion essay by Taviss (40) and many other portions of the Marris volume (26), deals with forms of initiative and adaptation that can most conveniently be described under this rubric, although the term itself is nowhere explicitly used. By contrast, Wamsley and Zald refer casually to "the interpenetration of government and business" (43, p. 5) as if the concept were entirely familiar. A very concrete form of interpenetration is mentioned by Arrow, who suggests that one of the principal ways in which "the agenda of organizations" changes in response to the "agenda" of the larger society is through the recruitment of new personnel. As new persons become involved, "new items will appear on the organization's agenda . . . [and] the behavior of the organization will change" (5, p. 59). Arrow's analysis in general emphasizes the cost and informational aspects of the process of interaction and adaptation between individual organizations and society at large.

The concept of "interpenetrating systems," first suggested by Parsons, has become the central focus of our own study of corporation–society relationships. The basic thesis is "that the larger society exists as a macro-system, but that individual (and particularly *large*) micro-organizations also constitute separable systems within themselves, neither completely controlling nor controlled by the social environment" (33, p. 25). The similar characterization by Cohen and Cyert is also worth repeating here:

> The organization and the environment are parts of a complex interactive system. The actions taken by the organization can have important effects on the environment, and, conversely, the outcomes of the actions of the organization are partially determined by events in the environment. These outcomes and events that contribute to them have a major impact on the organization. Even if the organization does not respond to these events, significant changes in the organizational participants' goals and roles can occur. (16, p. 352)

It may be well to emphasize at this point that all four interaction modes here discussed, as well as others that might be suggested, have both a structural and a processual dimension. (The inherent connection of structure and process is also made explicit in Zald's "political economy" model.) Thus, when we speak of *market exchange* as a mode of organization–environment interaction, we include both the *structure* of a social system organized around markets and the *process* by which markets operate to mediate relationships among organizations and individuals and, in general, to provide the traditional market contract basis for organizational legitimacy. Similarly, *control* implies both the existence of a formal control mechanism (ownership, legal authority, etc.) and the actual employment of that mechanism so that one organization or entity directs or limits the activities of another. *Voting* involves the electoral system and voting rights (i.e., structure, however determined) and the electoral process and its outcomes. (The strong analogy between the electoral system and the jury system may serve to reinforce this distinction; in both cases the structure must exist before the process can be used to determine particular outcomes.) Finally, with respect to *interpenetration,* many different structural relationships—like different kinds of markets, different control mechanisms, and different electoral systems—may be utilized within a single interactive decision-making and problem-solving process. Presidential jaw-boning,, activist picketing, Congressional lobbying and advocacy advertising may all be specific structural forms of a broad interpenetration process—as, indeed, they have been with respect to recent public and private attempts to deal with the projected long-term imbalance between national energy requirements and available resources.


## CRITERIA FOR APPRAISAL AND EVALUATION

Most of the discussion of corporate social performance and policy over the past couple of decades—and nearly all of the popular criticism of corporate practices—has assumed the existence of some set of norms, standards, or performance criteria against which corporate behavior might be evaluated, rated, and assigned praise or blame. These appraisal criteria are seldom specifically stated, and almost never examined in detail as to their sources, appropriateness, or mutual consistency. Now that a wide range of social impacts have become recognized as essential concerns of corporate management, the problem of specifying appropriate bases for measurement and criteria for appraisal has become acute. These issues are raised not only by the published judgments of external critics that some forms of corporate behavior are "good" and others "bad," or, indeed, by the rating of entire organizations as "high" or "low" on some unspecified scale of "corporate social responsibility." The significant point is that any organization that takes the problem of social performance seriously must find ways to identify the appropriate sphere or focus of corporate social policy, as well as to discover whether or not any policy adopted or program undertaken has *any* effect whatsoever.

The problem of defining the appropriate *sphere* or focus of corporate social policy has been emphasized by Schelling:

> In discussing "social responsibility" there is a tendency to take for granted that more of it is a good thing. . . . [But] responsibility is often not a quantity (something a person can have more or less of) but a *policy choice,* a choice among alternative values that one can be responsible to. . . . Often the question is not, "Do I want to do the right thing?" It arises in the form, "What is the right thing to want to do?" (36, pp. 88–90)

He also emphasizes that there are "two quite different notions of responsibility. One is like the doctrine of immanence: the responsibility is there. Duty exists. . . . The other is that responsibility is something to be assigned or created or invented" (36, p. 94). Clearly, one's notion of appropriate appraisal criteria will depend considerably on one's underlying concept of organizational legitimacy, and on whether the areas of social impact to be evaluated arise as inevitable consequences of the legitimating activity itself (e.g., provision of desired goods and services in response to market demand) or as extraneous considerations imposed by some external authority or pressure (power) group.

Whatever the specific sphere of corporate activity and/or social impact to be appraised, we may distinguish among appraisal criteria as to whether they are: (1) primarily *internal* or *external* in their frame of reference and application; or (2) primarily *outcome-oriented* or *process-oriented* in character. The conventional mode for evaluating business policy is, of course, *internal* and *outcome-oriented.* This is true not only of the dominant theoretical test—profitability—but also of other conventional corporate goals, both economic and social. Indeed, internal and outcome-oriented criteria are now commonplace in such social performance areas as affirmative action (percentages of minority and female employees within the firm) and environmental pollution. In the latter instance, internal outcome-oriented criteria such as specific pollution emission standards contrast sharply with external criteria such as improvement of ambient air quality levels, restoration of self-cleansing properties to waterways, etc.

In any event, whatever the specific area of social performance involved, and whatever the general character of the goals to be established, the problem of defining and applying appropriate appraisal criteria re-

mains difficult, and, one might add, difficult both intellectually and pro-
cedurally. As Thompson has emphasized:

> Organizations and others assessing them prefer efficiency tests over instrumental
> tests, and instrumental tests over social tests. But efficiency tests are not possible
> when technical knowledge is incomplete or standards of desirability are ambigu-
> ous. . . . Both of these conditions exist at the institutional level of the organiza-
> tion. . . . Organizations are multidimensional, and when they cannot show improve-
> ment on all dimensions, they seek to show improvements on those of interest to
> important elements of the task environment. Organizations especially emphasize scor-
> ing well on criteria which are most visible. . . ; and when it is difficult to score on
> intrinsic criteria, organizations seek extrinsic measures. . . . (41, pp. 97–98)

Internal cost/benefit tests are, of course, the archetype of the rational
organizational decision rule, and numerous attempts to develop such tests
with respect to social performance and impact are illustrated in the survey
of corporate analytical practices by Bauer and Fenn (7). It is no surprise
that these authors found, as Thompson had predicted, that neither the
causal models nor the measurement techniques required for conventional
internal optimization analysis were available, and that the complexity of
the situations confronted probably precluded their development. Hence,
again following Thompson's analysis, there is a tendency for organizations to substitute specific goals or norms—comparison with past
achievement levels, other organizations, external averages, etc.—for the
more usual models of rational optimization when dealing with social issues. When this substitution occurs, the critical issue then becomes the
*source* and *appropriateness* of such goals or norms, and particularly
whether they arise from a perception of immanence within the organization itself (and if so, why and how) or whether they represent the standards or "demands" or external constituencies or authorities.

An alternative to appraising corporate social performance in terms of
*outcomes,* whether justified in relation to cost or to other specific criteria,
is appraising it in terms of *process.* Schelling (28, p. 91) raises the question
of whether corporations are accused of being "irresponsible" (i.e., know-
ingly or unknowingly causing harm) or, by contrast, "unresponsive" (i.e.,
being unaware of, or unwilling to interact with, appropriate constituencies). Since the appropriate constituencies may be both internal (e.g.,
employees) and external (e.g., local communities, public agencies), process analyses and appraisals may, like outcome-oriented analyses, be
both internal and external in focus.

The *process* of corporate responsiveness, rather than the achievement
of specific performance outcomes, has been the major emphasis of two
important research groups during the past several years, the Harvard

Business School group led by Raymond A. Bauer (2) and the University of Pittsburgh group led by William Frederick and David Blake (11). The conviction of these and other investigators that the *process* of organization–environment interaction is the critical focus for study may rest on at least two quite different underlying principles. One principle would be that there is a (demonstrated or assumed) connection between process and outcome, so that the former serves as predictor and/or determinant of the latter. The other, quite different, conception is that the *process* itself is the principal phenomenon, and that both the legitimacy and the appropriateness of any particular *outcome* rests on the *process* by which it is reached. This latter position seems to underlie Ackerman's detailed case studies (1), and is, of course, closely related to more general concepts of voting, representation, and legal due process as central determinants of the legitimacy of actions, decisions, and institutions in many other contexts of our society.

The point, in brief conclusion, is that both final *outcomes* and *processes* can be analyzed and appraised from both *internal* and *external* perspectives, although, again recalling Thompson's observation, the tendency for external criteria to become prominent (even for internal decision making) increases as the gap between the problem under analysis and the requirements of traditional, rationalistic optimization models increases. Equally important, appraisals in terms of *process* will involve entirely different concepts and modes of analysis than appraisals in terms of *outcomes,* and the results of the two may simply be noncomparable. Is the "social performance" of an organization that builds a recreational facility for its employees greater, less, or the same as that of another organization that allows its employees to vote on whether they would prefer a recreation facility or the distribution of its costs in the form of salary bonuses, and then abides by the result?

# CONCLUSION

I have attempted to develop a comprehensive conceptual framework as a guide to the conduct of research concerning corporate social policy and performance. The essential components of the framework are set forth schematically in Exhibit 3, above, and their intended meaning and various intellectual origins are discussed throughout the text.

The usefulness of this framework can be tested in two different ways. One such test is the application of the framework as a means of classifying, relating, and contrasting contributions to the literature. This has, of course, been accomplished in part in the construction of the framework itself; but additional and more extensive surveys could certainly be made, and new contributions can also be placed in perspective as they appear. The second and more important test of the framework is its use as a guide to the development of research questions or hypotheses, and to subsequent execution of research studies. This testing process can occur only over a considerable period of time, and the framework itself will undoubtedly be modified in order to increase its usefulness and correct its deficiencies as such applications proceed. In any event, the suggested framework provides a starting place—and the first conception of its kind presented in the literature, so far as I am aware—for the continuing study of corporate social policy and performance.

# FOOTNOTES

*This paper has evolved out of about a decade of teaching, research and writing about various aspects of the corporation–society relationship. Hence, it cannot avoid repetition of some of the main themes of previous publications, particularly *Private Management and Public Policy* (33), "Corporation and Society: The Search for a Paradigm" (32), and "Strategy/Structure/Performance: A Framework for Organization–Environment Analysis" (34). The first of these publications attempted to develop an overview of the relationship between the business corporation and its social environment, and hence of the inherent connection between *business* policy and *public* policy—and in a form suitable for classroom instruction. The latter two involved rather substantial surveys of the corporation—society (or organization–environment) literature. By contrast, this paper focuses more narrowly on the construction of a research framework, and limits its references to the literature and to related issues both for reasons of space and in order to avoid duplication of material covered by other contributors to this volume.

1. George C. Lodge has pointed out to me that current issues involving property rights—as, for example, with respect to environmental pollution—are formally "legal" in character. However, even here the essential phenomenon seems to be the failure of received legal doctrine to anticipate or to take full account of current concerns. In effect, the law "ends" short of the problem at hand.

2. It is notable that "individualism" is treated by Lodge (and by a long historic tradition) as a society-wide attribute. Thus, it is entirely possible to conceptualize a social *whole* in which "individualism" is a dominant characteristic. A description of society as "individualistic" does not require that all subsequent analysis be conducted in terms of specific individuals and groups, coalitions, organizations, etc.

3. The relation of the firm to its *market* environment is, of course, a principal subject of traditional micro-economics and the special province of the "industrial organization" field. In addition, pioneering studies of the organization-environment relationship such as those Lawrence and Lorsch (22) and Chamberlain (14) focus primarily on *market* environment variables. The complete neglect of environmental variables is a surprising characteristic of some otherwise comprehensive organizational studies, including the classic treatise by March and Simon (25).

4. Of the several different detailed articulations of this category system developed by Zald and his colleagues, the most general is in *45*, p. 231.

5. The two-way nature of these relationships, and also their characteristic instability, is strongly emphasized by Dill, who notes the tendency of both interest group pressures and

regulatory constraints to evolve toward some form of mutual exchange, ". . . a legal and contractual, *quid pro quo* basis" (18, p. 1081, see also pp. 1101–3).

6. Burns's fourth mode of interaction, which he termed "Hobbesian processes," is essentially the process of power-development, which can easily be subsumed within the broader concept of "interpretation" discussed below.

7. In the earlier presentation (33), interpenetration was viewed as a concept broad enough to include market exchange and control, as well as other interaction modes. This general conception is still correct; however, in the present analysis market exchange and control are treated as polar opposites—and therefore separately identified—while interpenetration refers specifically to interaction modes lying between these extremes. (See also the following essay by James Post.)

# REFERENCES

1. Ackerman, R. W., *The Social Challenge to Business.* Cambridge, Massachusetts: Harvard University Press, 1975
2. Ackerman, R. W., and Bauer, R. A., *Corporate Social Responsiveness: The Modern Dilemma.* Reston, Virginia: Reston Publishing Company, Inc., 1976.
3. Ashen, M. ed., *Managing The Socially Responsible Corporation.* New York: Macmillan, 1974.
4. Arrow, K. J., *Social Choice and Individual Values,* 2nd ed. New Haven: Yale University Press, 1963.
5. Arrow, K. J., *The Limits of Organization.* New York: W. W. Norton & Co., Inc., 1974.
6. Backman, J., *Social Responsibility and Accountability.* New York: New York University Press, 1976.
7. Bauer, R. A., and Fenn, D. H., Jr., *The Corporate Social Audit.* New York: Russell Sage Foundation, 1972.
8. Bell, D., *The Coming of Post-Industrial Society.* New York: Basic Books, 1973.
9. Bell, D., *The Cultural Contradictions of Capitalism.* New York: Basic Books, 1976.
10. Bell, D., *The End of Ideology.* Glencoe, Illinois: Free Press, 1960.
11. Blake, D. H., et al., *Social Auditing: Evaluating The Impact of Corporate Programs.* New York: Praeger, 1976.
12. Burns, T., "On the Rationale of the Corporate System," in R. Marris, ed., *The Corporate Society.* London: Macmillan Press, 1974, pp. 121–177.
13. Cavanagh, G. F., *American Business Values in Transition.* Englewood Cliffs, New Jersey: Prentice-Hall, 1976.
14. Chamberlain, N. W., *Enterprise and Environment.* New York: McGraw-Hill, 1968.
15. Child, J., *The Business Enterprise In Modern Industrial Society.* London: Collier-Macmillan, 1969.
16. Cohen, K. J., and Cyert, R. M., "Strategy: Formulation, Implementation, and Monitoring," *J. Business,* 46(3), July 1973, pp. 349–67.
17. Coleman, J. S., *Power and the Structure of Society.* New York: W. W. Norton & Co., Inc., 1974.
18. Dill, W. R., "Business Organizations," in J. G. March, ed., *Handbook of Organizations.* Chicago: Rand McNally & Company, 1965, pp. 1071–1114.
19. Galbraith, J. K., *Economics and The Public Purpose.* Boston: Houghton Mifflin, 1973.
20. Harrington, M., *The Twilight of Capitalism.* New York: Simon and Schuster, 1976.
21. Hurst, J. W., *The Legitimacy of the Business Corporation in the Law of the United States 1780–1970.* Charlottesville: The University Press of Virginia, 1970.

22. Lawrence, P. R., and Lorsch, J. W., *Organization and Environment: Managing Differentiation and Integration*. Boston: Division of Research, Graduate School of Business Administration, Harvard University, 1967.

23. Levy, S., and Zaltman, G., *Marketing, Society, and Conflict*. Englewood Cliffs, New Jersey: Prentice-Hall, 1975.

24. Lodge, G. C., *The New American Ideology*. New York: Alfred A. Knopf, 1976.

25. March, J. G., and Simon, H. A., *Organizations*. New York: John Wiley & Sons, Inc., 1967.

26. Marris, R., ed., *The Corporate Society*. London: Macmillan Press, 1974.

27. Mason, E. S., *The Corporation In Modern Society*. Cambridge, Massachusetts: Harvard University Press, 1959.

28. McKie, J. W., ed., *Social Responsibility and the Business Predicament*. Washington: Brookings Institution, 1974.

29. Olson, M., Jr., *The Logic of Collective Action*. New York: Schocken Books, 1968.

30. Parsons, T., *Structure and Process in Modern Societies*. New York: The Free Press, 1960, Chap. II, pp. 59–98.

31. Post, J. E., *Risk and Response*. Lexington, Massachusetts: D. C. Heath, 1976.

32. Preston, L. E., "Corporation and Society: The Search for a Paradigm," *Journal of Economic Literature*, Vol. XIII, June 1975, pp. 434–453.

33. Preston, L. E., and Post, J. E., *Private Management and Public Policy*. Englewood Cliffs, New Jersey: Prentice-Hall, 1975.

34. Preston, L. E., "Strategy/Structure/Performance: A Framework for Organization-Environment Analysis, " in H. B. Thorelli, ed., *Strategy+Structure=Performance*. Bloomington: University of Indiana Press, 1977.

35. Preston, L. E., and Post, J. E., "The Third Managerial Revolution," *Academy of Management Journal*, Vol. 17, No. 3, September 1974, pp. 476–486.

36. Schelling, T. C., "Command and Control," in J. W. McKie, ed., *Social Responsibility and the Business Predicament*. Washington, D.C.: Brookings Institution, 1974, pp. 79–108.

37. Schelling, T. C., "On The Ecology of Micromotives," in R. Marris, ed., *The Corporate Society*. London: Macmillan Press, 1974, pp. 19–64.

38. Stinchcombe, A. L., "Social Structure and Organizations," in J. G. March, ed., *Handbook of Organizations*. Chicago: Rand McNally & Company, 1965, pp. 142–193.

39. Stone, C. D., *Where the Law Ends: The Social Control of Corporate Behavior*. New York: Harper & Row, 1975.

40. Taviss, I., "On Contemporary Social Change," in R. Marris, ed., *The Corporate Society*. London: Macmillan, 1974, pp. 65–86.

41. Thompson, J. D., *Organizations in Action*. New York: McGraw-Hill, 1967.

42. Votaw, D., and Sethi, S. P., *The Corporate Dilemma*. Englewood Cliffs, New Jersey: Prentice-Hall, 1973.

43. Wamsley, G. L., and Zald, M. N., *The Political Economy of Public Organizations*. Lexington, Massachusetts: D. C. Heath and Company, 1973.

44. Wilson, I. H., *Corporate Environments of The Future*. New York: The President's Association, Special Study No. 61, 1976.

45. Zald, M. N., "Political Economy: A Framework for Comparative Analysis," in M. N. Zald, *Power in Organizations*. Nashville: Vanderbilt University Press, 1970, pp. 221–261. (See also following "Comment," by F. L. Bates, pp. 262–269.)

# RESEARCH ON PATTERNS
# OF CORPORATE RESPONSE
# TO SOCIAL CHANGE

James E. Post

## I. INTRODUCTION

*Field in Search of a Focus*

Twenty years ago, William Foote Whyte described the study of human relations as a "field without a focus." His point was that while many people understood the importance of the field there had failed to emerge a coherent framework for its study. More recently, Preston (21) has argued that the study of corporation and society relationships is still in search of a paradigm, or in Whyte's phrase, a "field without a focus."

Frustrating the search for a paradigm is the intrinsic difficulty of designing research that will specifically illuminate critical corporation–society issues, since theory and research design are reciprocally linked. Traditional disciplines may be limited in their perspective, but they provide both theory and methodology by which inquiries can be pursued. The absence of a central conception in the corporation–society area corresponds to the absence of a methodological base from which basic research into the subject can evolve. We are faced with a chicken and egg dilemma; must the integrative theory precede the research design, or vice versa? In this paper, that question is discussed in the context of a line of continuing research into the manner in which corporations respond to social change.

## The Design of Inquiry

Relatively few specific corporation–society studies have been conceived, designed, researched, and published. Among them are those by Ackerman (1), Murray (14), Post (17) and Sethi (24,25). Because research design has been a particularly thorny issue in this field, and because research design is intrinsically tied to the search for an integrative theory, it is useful to raise the question of how one goes about creating an inquiry into the study of the corporation and society. Two distinct approaches have been popular to date. One approach, illustrated by the Ackerman (1), Murray (14), and Council on Economic Priorities (8) studies, selects a current corporation–society issue (pollution, minority affairs, employee safety), examines its life history, and analyzes the manner in which it has affected particular firms and/or industries. This approach often leads to intra-industry comparisons of particular firms' responses to the same issue and to comparative histories of the life cycle of, and responsiveness of industries and firms to, different social issues. An alternative approach, illustrated by Orren (15) and Sethi (24), is to select a proposition (e.g., the purpose of all management activity is to maximize control over the use of assets) and test it across a sample of firms and/or industries. As Mintzberg (13) has pointed out, the inductive and deductive approaches these examples suggest are extremes which, in other fields, have become integrated parts of the scientific approach to the development of knowledge. However, this integration of inductive and deductive research has not yet emerged in the study of the corporation and society.

Churchman (7) has argued that there is no single "scientific" approach to the development of knowledge in a field. Rather, there are a variety of historically recognized approaches to research that differ most significantly in terms of what "guarantor" endorses the validity of their findings. At their best, methodologies (sampling, experimenting, etc.) reflect different kinds of known statistical or mathematical "guarantors." In a field such as corporation–society relationships, however, where the central issues are broad in nature and defy the narrow sophisticated research methods that have known guarantors, we must look to the underlying design of research to determine what ensures the validity of findings. In part, this becomes a matter of clearly framing the central questions and asking what is appropriate to their analysis.

Several years ago, at an annual meeting of the Academy of Management, a session was held on research developments in the corporation–society field. During the meeting, questions were raised as to where the central research questions lay, and how more sophisticated methodologies might be brought to their analysis. Robert Ackerman, well known for his studies in the area, responded that while endorsing the call for the application of more sophisticated methods to research, it should not be overlooked that the corporation–society area is inhabited by a great many "elephants." It is a field replete with very large issues and problems that defy methodologies of intensive, but narrow, perspective.

The need for a holistic framework in designing research becomes clear when one looks at a specific case. A brief personal example illustrates the point. Until several years ago, the bulk of studies in the corporation–society area focused on a specific social issue and its impact on a particular industry and member firms. Inter-firm comparisons had been made, but no one had studied how the management of a single firm simultaneously responded to many different issues, each at a different stage in its own life history. The beginnings of a corporate responsiveness model, as articulated by Ackerman and Bauer (2), Preston and Post (22), and Votaw and Sethi (26), had suggested a process involving managerial awareness of an issue, commitment toward response, and actual implementation. However, this model had not been tested in the context of a single firm facing many issues.

To analyze this question, it was necessary to find a candidate firm that would allow itself to serve as the research case. Once such a firm was found and the study initiated, it became clear that the responses of the firm to different issues could not be comprehended without knowing something about the factors motivating its management, the role of the firm in the industry, the historical development of the company, and the history of the industry itself. To understand these, in turn, one had to look at other historical analyses of the evolution of the industry and the many competitive trends that had shaped it during that time. The result was not a narrow study of a specific question, but the pursuit of an elephant! To understand how the management of Aetna Life and Casualty responded to an agenda of public issues in the early 1970s, it was necessary to go back to the very beginning of the American insurance industry and trace two hundred years of market trends, public policy trends, organizational trends, and regulatory trends. It was only against the backdrop of this continuous industry and social history that one could analyze the nature and character of the Aetna's responses to change in the 1970s (17). In this research, the guarantor of validity was not a proven methodology, but the conceptual framework that facilitated the study's design.

*Where Ignorance Lies*

Kenneth Berrien has argued that it "is only by erecting conceptual frameworks that we discover where ignorance lies, and take appropriate steps to fill the gaps" (4, p. 60). The necessity of conceptual models to illuminate areas where gaps in knowledge exist can be illustrated by a brief recounting of the way in which the "interpenetrating systems" model evolved. In 1972, Lee Preston and I began to address ourselves to the literature of the corporation–society area. But the idea of doing a literature search of the area proved both difficult and frustrating. Try as we might to organize it, the literature seemed to go off in so many directions, embracing so many issues and topics, that it seemed to defy synthesis and order.

In time, we identified the views of several major authors—Adam Smith, Karl Marx, Milton Friedman, and John K. Galbraith—around which the literature (data point) clustered; but it was still necessary to search for a means by which each view could be criticized and evaluated against the others. We eventually chose to "translate" each of the key conceptions into the common language of systems theory (22, Ch. 2). Our central assumption was that the firm and society were social systems, related to one another in some not yet fully understood way. In this framework, the similarities and differences between the market model and the exploitation model became sharp and clear—each saw an "exchange process" between the firm and society, but differed on the relative benefits accruing to the various subsystems through the process of exchange (consumer surplus versus surplus value). Galbraith's concept of a technostructure dominating social values could be viewed as a suprasystem dominating many individual social systems (firms and other organizations). And the legal model could be seen as a process by which the suprasystem (society) established the rules of the game for each of the social units within it. Some evidence suggested that each of these views did indeed have a grain of truth in it. Our problem lay not in choosing among them (for no one choice could explain the "deviant" situations explained by the other models), but in finding an integrating conception.

The systems literature provided what was to become both an alternative way of viewing the corporation–society relationship (model), and a set of concepts that could embrace all of the inductive evidence that seemed to support one or another of the extant models. The new concept was that of *interpenetrating social systems*. According to Talcott Parsons (16), social systems are interpenetrating when they not only influence one another but also *mutually* influence the processes by which they continue to interact over time. As applied to the study of the corporation and society, this concept permitted an emphasis on the process of corporation–society interaction without predetermining what form that interaction must take. It facilitated an analysis of behavior that reflected both social conflict and harmony; and, unlike other models, the presence of either harmony or conflict between the corporation and society was not the primary theoretical concern. Rather, this model focused attention on the *processes* of interaction (market and public policy), the kinds of behavior exhibited by corporations and other social actors, and the patterns of response whereby harmony or conflict evolved. A framework for understanding the processes of interaction was the gap in knowledge that the interpenetrating systems model sought to fill.

## II.  THE INTERPENETRATING SYSTEMS PERSPECTIVE

As a conceptual approach to the analysis of the corporation and society, the interpenetrating social systems perspective operates at two distinct levels. Originally conceived as an integrator of the prevailing legal, economic, and technostructure models, it is a macro level model of the *nature* of the corporation–society relationship. In this context, it provides a distinctive way of thinking about the corporation and society in general—i.e., as social systems which influence one another and the processes by which they continue to interact over time—which contrasts with the conventional economic and legal/political approaches.

The second level at which the interpenetrating systems perspective operates is the micro level of the specific firm and the ''society of relevant publics'' (17, pp. 7 & 8) interested in its economic and social performance. At this level of analysis, the research questions are focused on those variables influencing the performance and behavior of the firm, the identification of its relevant publics, and the factors influencing the responsiveness of the firm and relevant publics to one another.

At the macro level, the interpenetrating systems concept functions as a deductive model, providing logical propositions for research and inquiry. At the micro level, it provides a framework within which empirical evidence can be organized and structured. Potentially, at least, the analysis of specific cases of corporation–society relations in this framework will facilitate a collection of applied knowledge about the processes of interaction between the firm and its external environment.

### As a Model of the Corporation-Society Relationship

The conventional legal, economic, and technostructure models concentrate on individuals or social classes as the relevant social units of analysis. The interpenetrating systems model, however, specifically assumes that the appropriate social units for analysis are the institutions of society—i.e., corporations as whole entities and relevant publics in society that have an institutional context (government agencies, public interest groups, etc.).[1] This is not to say that individuals or classes are inappropriate foci; rather, they are inappropriate if one wishes to analyze the corporation and society as social systems.

At the macro level of analysis, two principal questions are, "What is the *nature* of the corporation-society relationship?" and "What determines the *scope* of corporate responsibility?" These are the questions to which *Private Management and Public Policy* (22) was specifically addressed. These questions appeared to be the central questions underlying much popular debate about the economic and social performance of the modern corporation in society. While certain kinds of economic and social performance raise public issues and create specific social conflicts, performance in general is not a macro-level research question. Rather, at the macro level, attention focuses on identification of significant performance areas and the source and character of public expectations about the performance that corporations should render, and, thus, on the underlying issue of the *nature* of the corporation–society relationship. Similarly, the public debate surrounding the "social responsibility" of business seemed to indicate that there was an underlying question about the *scope* of responsibility that corporations had in society. The public arguments that corporations did have responsibilities, and that those responsibilities transcended the marketplace but were not unlimited in nature, seemed to reinforce the proposition that the scope of corporate responsibility differed with the circumstances of a particular firm's relationship with society. Our formulation of a theory of primary and secondary involvement, in turn, was an attempt to deal with the underlying determinants of *scope* at the macro level (22, Ch. 1).

The social systems terminology proved well-suited to the type a level of analysis just described. It facilitated a critique of the conventional legal, economic, and technostructure models in terms of the significant differences in the conception of the nature of the corporation–society relationship and a comparison of views about the scope of micro unit responsibility (22, Ch. 2). Out of this critique, it eventually became clear that each of the corporation–society models (including the interpenetrating systems model) articulated a thesis about the nature of the corporation in society. While each of the conventional models has descriptive weaknesses, insofar as they are unable to describe all of the observed reality of corporation–society interactions, each model does address the question of how the corporation, as a social unit, "fits" with the larger society as a social unit.

## Status/Behavior/Performance

Every organization develops a set of structural relations with elements in the external environment over time. Through the organization's life history, these relations may evolve into such "roles" as industry leader, community leader, and so forth. As Epstein (11) has argued, as the organization grows in size, these relations multiply and various kinds of power begin to accrue. In my study of the American insurance industry (17), this structure of relations with elements in the environment was seen as defining the organization's social *status*—i.e., its place in the scheme of things.

A corporation's status, or the power which derives from it, can, itself, produce social conflict. More often, status operates as a set of conditions leading to outcomes that might be considered unsatisfactory *performance* by the corporation. This concern with corporate impact and corporate performance is the wellspring from which arguments both defending and criticizing the corporation have drawn abundant evidence. Most importantly, the connection between the actual performance of corporations and the status of those entities (using such indicators as size, assets, or market share) has been widely argued, but not convincingly proven. One reason this connection is not yet clear is that a crucial research link is missing between the concepts of status and performance.

The "missing link" that is necessary to bridge the gap between the macro-level concepts of status and performance is a comparable macro-level conception of corporate *behavior* in response to social change. In the field of industrial organization, it has becom part of the conventional wisdom to note that the structure of a market (competitive, monopolistic) influences the conduct of actors in that market. Conduct, in turn, determines the actual performance that society receives in the form of prices, product quality, and consumer surplus. The writings of Bain (3) and Caves (6) represent classic efforts in the definition of this relationship. We now suggest an analogous relationship in the corporation–society field: *The status of an organization will influence its behavior; its behavior will determine the kind, and quality, of its economic and social performances.*

The macro-level conception of behavior has not been explicitly addressed as a research problem in the past. Indeed, a review of the literature dealing with organization/environment interaction (17, Ch. 1), led to the identification of two basic models of behavior; the empirical research study which built on that base identified a third, conceptually new, behavior model. The two familiar behavior models are the adaptive and proactive models. The *adaptive model* assumes that there are various states of organization–environment relations in which the entity can operate. Some are more preferred than others by management. When external disturbance occurs in the environment, it prompts management to respond in a way that moves the organization toward a more preferred available state. This is accomplished by management's assessment and evaluation of the change, its consideration of internal decision variables, and the application of known and previously used decision rules (e.g., "never bargain with protestors on the first day"). The external shocks and their influence on the internal decision variables of the organization serve to change the actual state of the firm's relations with the environment. As Cyert and March (9) have written, whether the new state is more preferred or less preferred determines the likelihood that the decision rule will be used again in the future.

Whereas the adaptive model assumes that environmental change occurs first, and is then followed by an organizational reaction, the *proactive* (or manipulative) *model* assumes that an organization's management continuously analyzes its internal interests (decision variables) and applies previously successful decision rules in an effort to change the environment and achieve a state of external conditions that are most favorable for the organization's operations. This manipulative or proactive approach means that, in principle, management can authorize any action that will increase or improve the opportunities for achievement of organizational goals. As with the adaptive model, decision rules and actions that successfully lead to a preferred state are likely to be used again in the future; those that fail will not. Management undergoes a learning process whether its behavior is adaptive or proactive or both (17, Ch. 1).

The conceptual fit between these models of organizational action and the basic models of corporation–society relationship is illustrated in Figure 1. The central difference between the adaptive and proactive models is the assumption about where change initially occurs—i.e., in the adaptive model, the environment is the source of change; in the proactive model, the organization is the initiator. The validity of either of these stimulus-response conceptions of organization/environment relations is itself a subject for empirical inquiry.

In the analysis of the insurance industry and social change, this stimulus-response conception of corporation–society relations was tested and found insufficient to explain all of the cases analyzed. Out of this research, which is discussed in greater detail below, a third and new conceptual model of organizational behavior was articulated. The *interactive model* proceeds from the assumption that the organization and the environment are both changing simultaneously, though not at the same rate. Hence, rather than focusing on a single temporal change and a specific response, the appropriate research focus for assessing organizational behavior in response to a performance issue is a longitudinal one.[2] In this context, an organizational action may be viewed as neither the defensive reaction prescribed by the adaptive model, nor the offensive

*Figure 1.* Corporation and Society: Status and Behavior Models*

| Models of the Corporation–Society Relationship | Models of Organizational Behavior | Characterized by . . . . . |
|---|---|---|
| LEGAL MODEL | Adaptive | adherence to rules of the game |
| | Proactive | cooptation of regulatory agencies |
| MARKET MODEL | Adaptive | competition |
| | Proactive | attempts at monopolization |
| EXPLOITATION MODEL | Adaptive | search for new exploitation opportunities |
| | Proactive | extraction of surplus value |
| TECHNOSTRUCTURE MODEL | Adaptive | countervailing power |
| | Proactive | technocratic dominance of social goals and values |
| INTERPENETRATING SYSTEMS MODEL | Adaptive | reactions to perceived threats |
| | Proactive | attempted manipulation of other actors |
| | Interactive | continuous action and reaction to evolving social trends and issues. |

*Adapted from Post (17, p. 14)

manipulation prescribed by the proactive model. It may be seen as a response calculated to stimulate or continue interaction between the entity and the environment. If so, it can be assessed by examining a longitudinal relationship, the process of interaction, and the resulting *pattern* of behavior.

## As a Model of the Firm and Its Environment

At the micro level of analysis, the appropriate social unit for analysis is a specific firm and those segments of society that constitute its "relevant publics" (17, Ch. 1). The interpenetrating systems model provides a general framework within which the analysis of a specific corporation–society relationship can be undertaken. In addition, and perhaps more importantly, the interpenetrating systems perspective provides some sense of where the important issues lie in the relationship of a specific firm to its social environment.

Every individual firm renders a great number of social and economic *performances*. That is, its activities usually have a large number of different impacts on society. The number of employees, their average wage level, the contribution to local or regional output, the magnitude of goods and services purchased from local vendors, and the amount of contributions to local charities are but a few of the many performance impacts a firm has on its social environment. At the micro unit level, these performance impacts can be identified and evaluated. (Indeed, much of the "social audit" literature is concerned with the development of performance indicators.) On the society side of the corporation–society equation, it can be said that various relevant publics have expectations about the kind and quality of the firm's economic and social performances. Indeed, this concept has been extended to the point of saying that a firm faces a social issue whenever there is a gap between some actual performance which it is rendering and that performance which *any* relevant public expects from the organization (19). In the modern social environment, any relevant public which is dissatisfied with the performance of an organization can apply pressure to the firm to meet expectations or can attempt to use the legal system to require improved performance.[3] Hence, at the level of an individual firm, the focus is not on the abstract concept of social and economic performance, but on the expectations which particular elements of the public have of *that* firm's performance compared to the actual performances being rendered.

The firm's *social status* or position in society is another interpenetrating systems concept which can be applied to corporation–society research at the micro level. A firm's status reflects its relations with the rest of the world and is a function of such varibles as its position in an industry, the importance of the industry to society (e.g., energy vs. candy), the size of its employment, and its importance to the local or regional economies in which it operates. Recognition and articulation of such variables make possible comparisons within categories, within geographical areas, and within asset or sales categories. More importantly, status emphasizes that the relationship between a firm and its environment is multidimensional in nature, as well as in manifestation (performance). This, in turn, raises the possibility of finding associations between combinations of status variables and performance outcomes.[4] In my study of management and social change in the American insurance industry, for example, it was found that one company's (Aetna Life & Casualty) rather unique performance in the urban affairs area (e.g., first insurer to create a department of social responsibility) and its trendsetting activities in the equal employment opportunity area were related to its prominence in the local headquarters community and a longstanding involvement in urban redevelopment.

A firm's social status is altered as it responds to changing performance expectations. That is, when changing public expectations are viewed as the immediate manifestations of underlying social change, then an organization's underlying responsiveness to change is manifested by its *behavior* in coping with new performance issues. Inductive observation indicates that a firm's behavior is attributable to various types of stimuli, including legal requirements, public pressures, and management initiative (12). In analyzing a particular organization's response to performance issues, then, the researcher can search for those factors that manifest changing legal rules, new or increased pressures from relevant publics, and the values that lead management to direct the firm as they do. In the study of the insurance industry, for example, it was found that different combinations of legal change, public pressure, and management objectives existed in the "life cycle" of each of the public issues examined. Other research studies have pointed to the relation between certain kinds of behavioral stimuli and the resultant corporate behavior (18, 20). Indeed, it is this concept of stimuli producing predictable patterns of corporate behavior that underlies the organizational decision rules of the adaptive and proactive behavior models discussed above. It was also the application of this set of concepts to the analysis of the Aetna's behavior in response to a variety of performance issues that eventually gave rise to the conclusion that the adaptive and proactive models did not describe all types of organizational response to change, and that there also existed an "interactive pattern" of response (17, Ch. 9). Examples of these patterns are further discussed below.

*Figure 2.* The Corporation and Society: An Interpenetrating
Systems Perspective

At the Macro Level

| STATUS ⟶ | BEHAVIOR ⟶ | PERFORMANCE |
|---|---|---|
| Legal Model | Adaptive Model | Social Performance |
| Market Model | Proactive Model | |
| Exploitation Model | Interactive Model | Economic Performance |
| Technostructure Model | | |
| Interpenetrating Systems Model | | |

At the Micro Level

| STATUS ⟶ | BEHAVIOR ⟶ | PERFORMANCE |
|---|---|---|
| *Variables:* | *Affected by:* | *Variables:* |
| *Scope* of involvements; | Legal requirements; | *Salience* of issue to "society" of |
| *Continuity* of relationship; | Pressure from relevant publics; | relevant publics (external); |
| *Salience* of issue to firm (internal). | Management goals and purposes. | Public *expectations* of performance; *Actual* performance impacts of firm's behavior. |

## III.   PATTERNS OF RESPONSE: FINDINGS FROM THE INSURANCE INDUSTRY

The study of management and social change in the American insurance industry was conceived as a means of testing the hypothesis that a corporation's behavior in response to various public issues, at different stages in their own life history, would vary with the extent of the interpenetration between the firm and society. To conceptualize this interpenetration, the *scope* of the firm's involvements with its relevant publics as well as the *continuity* of those relationships was examined. Hence, scope and continuity were identified as the key indicators of the corporation's status. The performance issues selected for examination were "mostly economic performance" issues in three instances and "mostly social performance" issues in two other instances. The life history of each issue was examined, and Aetna Life & Casualty's response to each issue was studied over that life history, The gap between the company's actual performance and the public's expectations was expressed in terms of the *salience* of the issue to both the firm (internal salience) and the relevant publics (external salience). Over time, of course, the salience of the issue to both the firm and society changed.

Because the research was very much exploratory in nature, precise relationships between the scope of involvements, continuity of relationships, salience of issues, and actual corporate behavior in response to the issues could not be hypothesized. Rather, the research question was posed in this manner: what factors account for the responses of a single organization to different public issues during a given period of time when each issue is at a different stage of its life history? The research was undertaken by interviewing managers, regulatory officials, executives of competitors, and members of external groups and associations, as well as extensive examination of records and published and unpublished documents bearing on the controversies and the company's responses. Beginning with about fifteen issues that were important in the insurance industry between 1960 and 1972, five were selected for the most detailed analysis. The three "mostly economic performance" issues included inflation and the life insurance business, the inner city fire insurance market, and no-fault automobile insurance proposals. The two "mostly social performance" issues included equal employment opportunity and community affairs. As the research proceeded, it became obvious that in order to comprehend the actions of the focal organization, it was necessary to understand the company's historical development, its role in the life and nonlife components of the industry, and the competitive, organizational, and public policy trends that had shaped the environment for insurers in the 1960s and 1970s.

When assessed in this context, a set of relationships and explanations for behavior became not only more logical but more reasonable in the sense of the industry's whole history. It was found that the responses of the Aetna Life & Casualty Company to the five selected issues (and eventually the remainder of the original sample of fifteen) fell into three distinct patterns. Two were quite conventional and could be traced throughout the company's history: one involved *reaction* to change in the environment (adaptive behavior model); the second involved efforts by the company to *promote* change in the environment (proactive behavior model). It was found that both approaches began to fail the firm during the late 1960s. Two notable failures (inflation in the life insurance business and the inner city fire insurance market) are discussed below. Out of these failures came an eventual recognition of the need for a new approach to the changing environment (interactive behavior model). The Aetna's response to the issue of no-fault auto insurance represented such a response, one which recognized the simultaneously changing corporate goals and social goals. This approach emphasized the need for actions to keep corporate and public goals continuously harmonized. These three cases are summarized below as individual examples of the basic adaptive, proactive, and interactive patterns of response.

*Example 1. The Reactive Pattern*

A major public issue in the United States during the 1960s was the growing impact of inflation on personal savings and investment. The life insurance industry had been directly affected by inflation earlier than many other industries. Although usually sold as a form of protection, life insurance actually competes against other forms of investment for investor dollars. When corporate earnings increase, as they did during the 1960s, and inflation eats away at the real value of insurance policies, dollars tend to flow away from life insurance toward more attractive investment alternatives. The actual investment performance of life insurance deviated greatly from that which an investing public had come to expect from "good" investments during the 1960s.

The gap between investor expectations and the actual performance achievable through investing in life insurance was serious, and the industry was moved to respond. Since there was no effective way of convincing investors that their expectations should be lowered, thus making life insurance appear attractive again, the industry's leaders began to search for other responses. An early effort was a public relations campaign to convince the public of the need for an anti-inflationary campaign to curb government spending. Although the campaign featured a film called "Trouble in Paradise," detailing the woes that befell nations that favored deficit spending and inflationary wage increases, neither the federal government nor the American public was inclined to alter its spending habits.

Public relations having failed, a number of insurers began to embark on a course of product development designed to join the safety of the traditional life insurance policy with the higher returns of common stock investment. This effort to improve actual performance and meet investor expectations led Aetna Life & Casualty to innovate in the "variable products" area by developing and selling variable annuities. This approach eventually led Aetna to acquire a subsidiary that specialized in variable products and to portray their sales staff as financial consultants. By the early 1970s the company had developed a variable life insurance policy (VLI) that combined the safety of life insurance and the variable investment return of a stock portfolio.

Overlapping regulation was the most formidable obstacle to the marketing of this product innovation. The states had regulatory jurisdiction over any new life insurance policies and had to approve the underlying concepts as well as the policy forms. Since the variable life insurance policies had a variable return component that was tied to the performance of a common stock fund, the Securities and Exchange Commission also sought to exert regulatory jurisdiction, ruling that salesmen had to be registered securities dealers and that VLI contracts could only be sold under restricted conditions. In 1972, Aetna Life and Casualty sold the first variable life insurance policy in the United States.

The opposition of the securities industry was understandable, and it sought to convince the SEC of the need to severely limit VLI sales. A ruling in January 1973 exempting VLI policies from SEC regulation was reconsidered by the SEC and VLI sales were halted. Only sales in conjunction with qualified pension and profit-sharing plans were permitted. Yet, because of their insurance characteristics, even these limited sales of VLI had to be approved by the state insurance commissions. In 1974, only 23 states had given such approval and these did not include the crucial insurance markets of New York, New Jersey, Pennsylvania, Illinois, or California. Variable life was effectively excluded from the market.

Finally, in October 1976, the SEC adopted regulations that permitted life insurance companies to sell individual VLI policies. Of the eighteen insurers that once indicated a desire to sell the product, however, only Equitable Life Assurance Society of the U.S. indicated an intention to market the product. With investor confidence in the stock market having declined precipitously during the mid-1970s, the late approval of VLI was not perceived as an action that would substantially enhance insurers' competitive positions. As one executive commented, "It's a fine step— and only five years late!"

The SEC's late approval was but the final act in a play that took sixteen years to reach its denouement, but whose ending could have been foretold well beforehand. The effort to create variable life insurance was, at its core, a reaction to change in the environment. The scope of Aetna's involvement in the life insurance business made investor choices an extremely salient matter; for investors, the issue was less salient because other investment options were available. The company's status as a major seller of life insurance made a product response reasonable; the fact that development did not begin until *after* investor shifts had begun, (i.e., reaction to change) doomed the response to failure. The complexity of the regulatory environment undermined the prospects of a timely adaptation by the company. The adaptive behavior pattern was conventional but destined to fail in an environment where buyers had choices outside the industry.

*Example 2: The Proactive Pattern*

Unlike life insurance, which has had to compete for its buyers, fire insurance (and its casualty insurance offspring) has long been considered a necessity. This character as an essential service has produced a number of fundamental problems for the industry. Since businessmen cannot secure loans without insured inventories, the availability of fire and casualty insurance protection is a basic commercial need. Because there is also a consumer need for "reasonable" prices, insurers are not permitted by state insurance departments to price their product as they would like. The result of this availability/pricing squeeze was that by the mid-1960s, fire and casualty (e.g., crime) insurance was nearly unavailable in the inner-city areas of many American metropolitan areas. Withdrawal from the inner-city insurance markets was an increasingly popular response to the high loss-ratios that insurers had encountered in the cities. The urban riots of 1967 injected one further element into a largely bleak insurance picture—the catastrophic loss. Following the riots, over $75 million of claims were filed with insurers. The shock of that experience provided insurers with a serious problem, but also a unique opportunity to change the insurance environment of the inner city.

The scope of involvement in the inner city for a major stock fire insurer like Aetna was very extensive. Stock insurance companies supplied nearly eighty percent of coverage in force. Hence, large losses, followed by riots, made the question of performance highly salient for the industry as well as for inner-city residents.

When President Lyndon B. Johnson appointed a special commission to look into the causes of the urban riots, a special advisory panel was created to analyze the insurance aspects of the riots. Taking testimony from many sources, this panel analyzed the insurance environment of urban areas. A parade of witnesses representing the major stock insurers presented a concerted position. They advocated a government reinsurance program to safeguard the private carriers from excessive and catastrophic losses. In return, there was the promise of cooperation in developing property-by-property inspection plans (rather than redlining whole areas) and a pooling plan to insure the less-preferred (but not all) risks. In short, the stock companies would commit themselves to remain in the inner-city fire insurance market if they could retain discretion in normal underwriting cases and get federal reinsurance protection for catastrophes such as riots.

Opposition to the industry plan was intense. The insurance commissioner of California testified that the industry was practicing political brinksmanship, refusing to insure inner-city properties unless they received the backup commitment. Timing favored the insurers: 1968 would be an election year, and if the summer of '68 was the powderkeg that 1967 had been, the states could be forced into incredibly expensive pooling plans. The insurance commissioner from Michigan noted that a federally subsidized reinsurance plan, in the absence of increased exposure in the urban areas, could actually produce a better financial and underwriting result. Reinsurance would not induce insurers to go into the inner-city market—at best, it might persuade those companies already selling in that market to stay.

Convincing federal and state governmental authorites of the need for a government-supported backup arrangement was an intensely political act, and the stock insurance companies pursued a common political strategy: argue the need for such a system and threaten to abandon the inner city en masse if it were not enacted. The strategy succeeded. In January 1968, the President's National Advisory Panel on Insurance In Riot-Affected Areas submitted its report calling for a voluntary system that would include individual inspection of properties, notification of steps required to make properties insurable, and creation of a pool to guarantee insurance for reasonably maintained properties. These were the so-called "Fair Access to Insurance Requirements" (FAIR) plans. State reinsurance pools would be created as industry backups and a federal reinsurance mechanism would also be established for catastrophic losses. Within the year, Congress enacted legislation to implement the Panel's recommendations.

By mid-1969, twenty-seven states, representing 75 percent of the property insurance premiums collected in the United States, enacted legislation creating the state insurance pools. Yet, riot-occasioned losses had declined to $15 million, a development which reduced the value of the federal reinsurance commitment to the insurers. Not surprisingly, since that time the FAIR Plans have continued to face the twin problems of insurer dumping (placing most inner-city risks in the state pools) and the threatened withdrawal of the companies from the underwriting pools.

The proactive approach of the stock companies can be understood as a result of a concern with an unsatisfactory performance in the inner city (i.e., high loss ratios). The high salience of the problem led to a search for a means to close the gap between actual performance and management expectations. The riots presented an occasion for the companies to attempt a manipulation of the regulatory environment toward creation of a reinsurance plan. The dependency of inner-city publics on the stock insurers made the availability of fire insurance a highly salient matter to this group as well. A federal Congress, confronted with an industry with significant involvements and serious economic problems as well as a public that faced immense social and economic problems if the insurers withdrew, endorsed the reinsurance plan. The behavior of the insurers was directly influenced by their status as sellers and the performance problems they suffered. The behavior of Congress was influenced by the salience of the issue to the public and the industry, and the implications that flowed from the companies' threatened withdrawal.

*Example 3: The Interactive Pattern*
The central role of the automobile in American society obscures the fact that its history dates back less than 100 years. The scope of insurer involvement with the driving public has changed greatly. In the course of the last fifty years, automobile insurance has been transformed from a tentative new kind of insurance coverage to a regulated product and, most recently, to a major social problem. The problem, of course, is the externalities of injury and death associated with automobile use and misuse. The protection of innocent victims has long been a public policy matter, beginning with financial responsibility laws in the 1920s and extending to compulsory liability systems. As the need for automobiles increased, and the need for liability insurance increased as well, the notion of refusing insurance to a poor driver became unacceptable. Moreover, great pressure was exerted on insurers to keep the cost of insurance at "reasonable" levels. Hence, in auto insurance, a classic availability/pricing dilemma developed.

As the problems worsened during the 1960s, new proposals emerged. The most notable was the comprehensive no-fault reform scheme offered by Professors Keeton and O'Connell in 1965. Despite the industry's underwriting and loss ratio problem (high internal salience), the basic industry response to the no-fault proposal was opposition. A listing ship, it seemed, was more attractive than an unknown ship. Hence, for most insurers, the conventional reactive response to change was opposition. An exception to this pattern was Aetna Life & Casualty, one of the nation's largest auto insurers, where the head of the underwriting department authorized a study of the impact of the Keeton–O'Connell plan on a sample of recent automobile claims. The results of that study led the underwriting staff to endorse the concept. Considerable skepticism from sales executives and others within the company had to be overcome, but by late 1967 a management policy position in support of the concept had crystallized. This position became public during the Department of Transportation study in 1968, and the Aetna's position was a matter of public record well before the DOT findings were issued in 1970.

The ground on which the Aetna had positioned itself exposed it to criticism of various types. Nevertheless, the company became an open advocate of no-fault reform and the first automobile insurer to publicly urge the states to adopt such plans. Its lobbying efforts were directed toward this end, and in 1974, when several "counterfeit" no-fault plans had been adopted in various states, Aetna Life & Casualty became the first auto insurer to advocate the establishment of federal standards for no-fault plans.

What did the company gain from such a posture? Regulatory authorities would certainly require rate reductions if the savings were as great as anticipated. Hence, no windfall profits were likely to accrue. Also, the fears that such a system might alter normal marketing arrangements in favor of mass marketing was dismissed when the company strengthened its commitment to the prevailing agency sales system. Hence, there was probably neither financial nor competitive advantage for the company.

A study of the circumstances surrounding the case of no-fault insurance suggests that Aetna's management endorsed the no-fault concept because it was responsive to an issue that was highly salient to both the driving public and major insurers like the Aetna. The extensiveness of the company's auto insurance business and its interest in remaining in that business gave it both a distinct status as a supplier of insurance coverage and a role as a key actor in any potential reform of the automobile reparations system. In supporting no-fault insurance, the company publicly endorsed a set of reforms that would serve the driving public's need for available coverage and reasonable prices and the insurers' needs for adequate rates. On its own, this case seems to signal an approach that recognized the continuous interaction and changing goals of the public and the firm. In this, it departed from both the adaptive and proactive approaches to coping with change.

There was more than a trace of organizational learning associated with Aetna's endorsement of no-fault insurance. By the late 1960s the company's responses to other public issues showed a distinct shift away from the conventional adaptive and proactive patterns of response toward a more interactive pattern. The key change seems to have been a top management recognition of the need to continuously narrow the gap between changing public goals and the company's performance. To do this, it has responded to the new demands of social involvement with a functional structure for dealing with community and corporate responsibility matters headed by a Vice President for Corporate Social Responsibility. On "mostly social performance" issues like urban investment and equal employment opportunities it has consistently attempted to sense changing public goals and act in advance of new legislative requirements. On "mostly economic performance" issues, such as the automobile, mal-practice, and product liability insurance dilemmas, it has attempted to interact with regulatory agencies and relevant consumer publics to define mutually accommodating solutions. While not always successful, there has been a clear preference for interactive, rather than reactive or ma-nipulative behavior since the early 1970s.

# IV. CONCLUSIONS

*Theory Building*

The study of the corporation and society relationship has attracted scholars who are interested in both the applied aspects of the relationship (e.g., conflict management) and the more theoretical.[5] Any theory that would deal with this field, however, must ultimately confront the reality of extensive and continuing corporation–society interaction. According to Robert Dubin, an applied theory necessarily has to have the real world as its point of origin. "It is exceedingly difficult to say something about the real world without starting in the real world. Observation and descrip-tion of the real world are the essential points of origin for theories in applied areas . . ." (10, p. 18). Documentation of the interaction between corporations and society is extensive, and the many volumes of observa-tions, anecdotes, and case studies are regularly supplemented by the con-tinuing tale of interaction told in the pages of the *Wall Street Journal,* the *New York Times* and local newspapers throughout the world.

The extensiveness and the richness of this inductive base does not guarantee theoretical formulations, however. What is required for the "central theoretical conception" of which Preston (21) wrote is a creative leap from the data base to a conclusion from which other deductive prop-ositions might emerge. Dubin's essay, "Theory Building in Applied Areas," makes the point in the following manner:

Theories . . . represent levels of generalization beyond a statistical summary of data points. Any generalization which starts from the data points generated by observation and description is arrived at through an inductive process. . . . What further conclu-sions the researcher wishes to draw from the correlation depends upon his skill and cleverness in reaching an inductive generalization at a level higher than the correlational conclusion. . . . [In this way] we have reached an inductive conclusion that is already removed from the data base from which it originates. . . . [Having] started from sound observation and description, we could well be on the road to developing new theory. (10. p. 18)

The search for a creative generalization, in Dubin's context, has rarely been successful in the study of the corporation and society. It is ironic that, while there seems to be relatively little argument in academic circles about the importance of the field, only parsimonious encouragement is given to theoretical scholarship in the area. Yet the need for such an investment of scholarly effort is apparent. Our vast data base does not, by itself, make clear where the information is lacking. If anything, we probably have too much raw material and unstructured data and insufficient ways of organizing it.

One purpose of the patterns of response research has been to establish a set of behavioral categories, conceptually and theoretically distinct, into which the body of observations of corporate behavior may be placed. The interpenetrating systems theory raised behavior to the foreground as an important matter for research. In *Risk and Response,* two familiar behavior models were articulated and a third model derived from the study of how the management of one firm simultaneously responded to multiple environmental issues. Articulation of the interactive behavior model represented the kind of creative leap from the data base to which Dubin referred. Further testing of these models is the next research step.

## Broadening the Data Base

The existence of three distinct patterns of response to change at Aetna Life & Casualty was confirmed by the actions of other firms in the insurance industry. Nevertheless, it was not clear whether the patterns were unique to the insurance industry, or applicable to other industries and corporation–society relationships. There is a clear need to test the patterns of response concepts against a larger body of empirical data. If the patterns are to be a set of useful analytical concepts, their existence has to be demonstrated in a broad variety of environmental change cases.

Because environmental change touches the core of management activity and policy decision making, there is reason to believe that patterns of response similar to those identified in *Risk and Response* will be found in other industries, and with regard to other types of environmental change. Having found some similarities in the manner in which an organization coped with change, irrespective of its economic or social character, the question of whether these patterns will apply under various kinds of environmental change remains. To push this line of research forward, a subsequent study has been constructed to test the patterns of response hypotheses. A series of "high salience" issues in a variety of industries has been drawn from conflicts reported in the popular press. This pool of cases has been supplemented with a number of historical cases of organization/environment conflict. The sample has been segmented by the type of underlying environmental change, utilizing four categories of change: economic, technological, sociocultural, and political.

The three basic patterns of response (reactive, proactive, interactive) are now being applied to the analysis of these cases. A working sample of cases has been selected for detailed study. Although the results are still preliminary, there is strong reason to believe that the behavior patterns discussed above hold over this sample.

Henry Mintzberg (13) has made the simple, yet insightful, observation that all fields of research have an interplay between deductive models and inductive observations. Especially as it applies to the study of the corporation and society, there is a back-and-forth movement between the development of models based on past experience and evidence and the testing of those models against new empirical cases and evidence. The truth of Mintzberg's observation is probably best seen by reference to the manner in which my own research into patterns of corporate response to change has evolved.

The research described in the aforementioned evolution is not applied research in the study of the corporation and society. Unlike those studies that have chosen to focus on managerial tools for coping with environmental change, this line of study has concentrated on the manner in which organizations *do* respond to change. And since it concentrates on how firms *do* respond, rather than how they *should* respond to change, it is not normative in its nature.

The analysis of the corporation-society relationship as interpenetrating systems raised the issue of behavior to the foreground. In the context of analyzing the question of how one firm simultaneously responds to multi-

*Figure 3.* Evolution of Patterns of Response Research

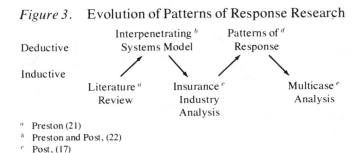

<sup></sup> " Preston (21)
<sup></sup> Preston and Post, (22)
<sup></sup> ' Post, (17)
<sup></sup> Post, (17)
<sup></sup> ' Post, (19)

ple issues at various stages in their life history, several behavioral patterns were identified. The question that remains to be answered is whether these patterns apply in all cases, or whether additional patterns emerge when the interpenetration variables differ. The definition of those variables and the manner in which they correlate with behavior patterns is a matter that seems certain to demand additional research in the years ahead. The research into the relationship between status, behavior, and performance reflects the continuing search for a paradigm in the study of the corporation and society.

# FOOTNOTES

1. This emphasis on institutions as the focal units for analysis recognizes that institutions are the *central* actors in modern political economies. To be sure, there are important management/society issues regarding *managerial* conduct and social conduct in the personal ethical context. In discussing the corporation–society relationships, however, it is clear that the institutions of society have an existence quite distinct from those individuals who manage or inhabit them for a limited period of time.

2. This perspective serves to focus attention on the "life history" of the issue and the evolving patterns of response exhibited by individual firms. The concept of a public issue's life history is discussed by Wilson (27) and an application is made in Post (18).

3. The mechanisms whereby a relevant public can actualize its interest and accomplish its objectives differ, but the framework in which this occurs is the public policy process (22, Chs. 5,6).

4. It is also important to recognize that this concept offers a framework into which all of the industrial organization literature on structure → conduct → performance relationships can be incorporated.

5. Curriculum trends in the business and society field indicate some movement away from the more critical "social role/impact of business" approach typified by Sethi (23) toward a more "managerially oriented" approach as typified by Ackerman and Bauer (2) and Carroll (5). This may signal a shift in teaching away from more conceptual treatments of the subject in favor of more applied approaches.

# REFERENCES

1. Ackerman, R., *The Social Challenge to Business*. Cambridge, Mass.: Harvard University Press, 1975.
2. Ackerman, R., and Bauer,. R. A., *Corporate Social Responsiveness: The Modern Dilemma*. Reston, Va.: Reston Publishing Co., 1975.
3. Bain, J. S., *Industrial Organization*, rev. ed. New York: John Wiley and Sons, 1968.
4. Berrien, K., "A General Systems Approach to Organizations," in *Handbook of Industrial and Organizational Psychology*, Marvin Dunnette, ed., Chicago: Rand McNally & Co., 1976, pp. 41–62.
5. Carroll, A., ed., *Managing Corporate Social Responsibility*. Boston, Mass.: Little, Brown and Company, 1977.

6. Caves, R. E., *American Industry: Structure, Conduct, Performance*. 2nd edition. Englewood Cliffs, N.J.: Prentice-Hall, Inc., 1967.
7. Churchman, C. W., *The Design of Inquiring Systems*. New York: Basic Books, Inc., 1971.
8. Council on Economic Priorities, *Paper Profits*. Cambridge, Mass.: (MIT Press, 1972).
9. Cyert, R. M., and March, J. G., *A Behavioral Theory of the Firm*. Englewood Cliffs, N.J.: Prentice-Hall, Inc., 1963.
10. Dubin, R., "Theory Building in Applied Areas," in *Handbook of Industrial and Organizational Psychology*, Marvin Dunnette, ed. Chicago: Rand McNally & Co., 1976, pp. 17–39.
11. Epstein, E. M., "Dimensions of Corporate Power," Parts 1 and 2, *California Management Review*, Vol. XVI, Nos. 2 and 4, 1973–74.
12. Hinckley, C. P., and Post, J. E., "The Performance Context of Corporate Responsibility" in *The Unstable Ground*, S. P. Sethi, ed. Los Angeles: Melville Publishing Co., 1974.
13. Mintzberg, H., "Policy As a Field of Management Theory," *Academy of Management Review*, Vol. 2, No. 1 (January 1977) pp. 88–103.
14. Murray, E. A., Jr., "The Social Response Process in Commercial Banks: An Empirical Investigation," *Academy of Management Review*, Vol. 1, No. 3 (July 1976) pp. 5–15.
15. Orren, K., *Corporate Power and Social Change: The Politics of The Life Insurance Industry*, Baltimore, Md.: Johns Hopkins University Press, 1974.
16. Parsons, T., "An Approach to Psychological Theory in Terms of the Theory of Action," in *Psychology: A Study of Science*, Sigmund Koch, ed., New York: McGraw-Hill Book Co., 1959, Vol. 3, pp. 612–711.
17. Post, J. E., *Risk and Response: Management and Social Change in the American Insurance Industry*, Lexington, Mass.: D. C. Heath, Inc., 1976.
18. Post, J. E., "Strategy and Orientation as Determinants of Patterns of Corporate Response to Social Conflict," Working Paper, Research Program in Management and Public Policy, Boston University, 1977.
19. Post, J. E., *Corporate Behavior and Social Change*, Reston, Va.: Reston Publishing Company, 1978.
20. Post, J. E., and Mellis, M., "Corporate Responsiveness and Organizational Learning," *California Management Review*, Spring, 1978.
21. Preston, L. E., "Corporation and Society: The Search for a Paradigm," *Journal of Economic Literature*, Vol. 13, No. 2 (June 1975) pp. 434–453.
22. Preston, L. E., and Post, J. E., *Private Management and Public Policy*, Englewood Cliffs, N.J.: Prentice-Hall, Inc., 1975.
23. Sethi, S. P., *Up Against The Corporate Wall*, Englewood Cliffs, N.J.: Prentice-Hall, Inc., 1971, Rev., 1974, 1977.
24. Sethi, S. P., *Japanese Business and Social Conflict: An Analysis of Response Patterns with American Business*, Cambridge, Mass.: Ballinger, 1975.
25. Sethi, S. P., *Advocacy Advertising and Large Corporations*, Lexington, Mass.: D. C. Heath, 1977.
26. Votaw, D., and Sethi, S. P., *The Corporate Dilemma*, Englewood Cliffs, N.J.: Prentice-Hall, 1973.
27. Wilson, I. H., "Socio-Political Forecasting: A New Dimension to Strategic Planning," *Michigan Business Review* (July 1974).

# CONCEPTUAL FRAMEWORKS AND STRATEGIES FOR CORPORATE SOCIAL INVOLVEMENT RESEARCH

Robert J. DeFillippi

---

A major challenge in any new area of scientific interest is laying out the domain for research, such as specifying the boundaries and structures of the entire domain of relevance within which one may wish to conduct research (Runkel and McGrath, 1972). The study of corporate social involvement—i.e., of the relationship between corporate activity and social issues—has received an increasing amount of research attention, reflected in a significant increase in the amount of theoretical and empirical work, over the past decade. With the amount of research interest expanding, and with the amount of research resources (time, manpower, funding, and goodwill of research participants) limited, it is vital that we assess the directions taken by current research and identify priorities for future research efforts.

A review of major corporate social performance and policy issues reveals a wide range of substantive topics addressed, ranging from corporate governance, employee health and safety, to the involvement of business firms in public policy controversies surrounding environmental pollution, urban development, affirmative action, and consumer product safety (Steiner and Steiner, 1977). The topical choices of business and society researchers identify important areas of corporate social involvement but provide little guidance to new scholars in their conceptualization of research problems or in their development of appropriate research designs.

The present paper is an effort to analyze the strategic choices reflected in current research on corporate social involvement. Two sets of choices are explored: (1) those involving *conceptualization* of the corporation-society relationship; and (2) those involving *design* of the research study. The analysis does not assume that researchers make their conceptual or methodological choices on any particular grounds (scientific, opportunistic, stylistic or aesthetic), but it does assume that any completed research study has a discernable set of characteristics that can be located within the choice dimensions of the classification scheme. The discussion proceeds in four parts: the first describes four dimensions of research conceptualization and illustrates them with examples from current research. Part two discusses three dominant conceptual frameworks (Business Policy, Pressure/Response, and Public Policy) within the corporate social involvement organizational literature that represent different patterns of conceptual choice. Part three characterizes some alternatives in research design and illustrates them by reference to the research designs used by exponents of the three conceptual frameworks. The final section identifies three constraints on conceptual and methodological choices and suggests some ways of overcoming them.

# BASIC CONCEPTUAL DIMENSIONS

Four main dimensions are readily observable within current attempts to conceptualize research on corporate social involvement: Focus of Research, Locus of Control, Standards for Evaluation and Levels of Analysis. Each involves several options; however the options are not mutually exclusive and a given research study may contain elements of several options within any conceptual dimension (See Table 1.)

## Focus of Research

"Focus of Research" addresses the choice of what aspect of corporate social involvement to study. Bourgeois (1980) has conceptualized the business policy literature in terms of "process" vs. "content" ap-

## Table 1.  Conceptual Dimensions and Alternatives

FOCUS OF RESEARCH

| *Process* | *Content* | *Impact* |
|---|---|---|
| Sequence of events: "How does corporate social involvement occur?" | Substantive responses: "What form does corporate social involvement take?" | Primary (direct); Secondary (indirect): "What effect does corporate social involvement produce?" |

LOCUS OF CONTROL

| *Internal* | *External* | *Interactive* |
|---|---|---|
| Organizations: Top management values, social issues specialists, organizational structures, systems of planning, control and reward. | General environmental trends<br><br>Specific (task environment) | Environment<br><br>Organization (reciprocal casualty) |

CRITERIA FOR APPRAISAL

| *Internal* | *External* |
|---|---|
| Process | Process |
| Outcome | Outcome |

LEVEL OF ANALYSIS

| *Micro* | *Macro* |
|---|---|
| Organizational; Intra-organizational: Division Department Group Individual | Inter-organizational: Institution Industry Network Organization set |

proaches, and a similar conceptual distinction is apparent in the corporate social involvement literature as well. A "process" approach focuses upon the sequence of events by which a form of social involvement is proposed, decided upon, and implemented. Murray (1976) suggests that social involvement begins with top management recognition of a social issue and its relevance for the organization, commitment to a course of action and communication of top management commitment through policy development. This stage is followed by a process of technical learning during which staff specialists are selected to gather information about the social issue and the organization's current involvement and develop ideas about methods to initiate, plan and control social response action. The stage of administration learning includes the modification of existing planning and control mechanisms, organizational structures, and incentive systems to accomodate corporate social involvement. The institutionalization phase concerns the involvement of operating units in implementing corporate social policies and programs.

The "content" approach to corporate social involvement focuses upon the form, content and occurrences of substantive responses to social issues. Examples of specific substantive responses typically assessed by the "content" approach include advocacy advertising and public relations (Sethi, 1977), lobbying and electoral political involvement (Epstein, 1969, 1976), litigation and other legal-judicial actions (Stone, 1975), research and development on social issue related technologies (McGraw-Hill, 1977), technical-engineering modifications of work place operations (Gricar, 1979), the creation of new positions, committees, departments and other organization structures for social issue involvement (Holmes, 1976), the pronouncements of new corporate policies within annual reports and official policy documents that reflect social involvement (Ernst and Ernst, 1978), establishment of programs with personnel, budget and authority to carry out social involvement activities (Moskowitz, 1974, 1975), and reported corporate compliance with private agency or governmental standards for social performance (Council on Economic Priorities, 1972, Clinard and Yeager, 1979).

A major conceptual effort by students of both the content and process approaches has consisted in the development of typologies for classifying and summarizing different patterns of corporate social involvement. These schemes differ in detail but attempt to classify different firms according to commonalities in the content of their social involvement (Gricar, 1978, Sethi, 1975), the processes of involvement (Ackerman, 1975) or both (Buono and Nichols, 1980).

A third potential focus of research on corporate social involvement assesses the impact of corporate social activity on social issues. Most social impacts induced by corporate activities are the secondary consequences or side-effects of actions taken primarily for economic purposes. Indeed, deliberate corporate social programs may have far fewer and less important social consequences than the unintentional, indirect social impacts of a firm's economic involvement (U.S. Department of Commerce, 1979). Research addressing primary and secondary social impacts has been undertaken by a wide variety of social accountants or auditors: academic social scientists, social issue activists and public interest organizations, the legislative and executive branches of federal, state and local governments and their commissions and regulatory agencies, private consulting firms, and corporate management and corporate staff specialists. Impact assessors may differ in their assessment objectives and informational needs and the resulting assessments of corporate social involvement will reflect these differences (American Institute of Certified Public Accountants, 1977).

## Locus of Control

"Locus of Control" involves the researcher's assessment of the extent to which corporate social involvement responses are influenced by internal (organizational) factors or external (environmental) factors. Post (1978) describes three conceptual models that hold different assumptions about locus of control: Business Policy, Pressure/Response, and Public Policy.

Business Policy models of corporate social involvement conceptualize the firm as possessing considerable discretion and autonomy from external pressures in selecting and implementing social policies and programs. The major constraints on management action exist within the firm and include such factors as the values and philosophy of top management, the conflict of authority between staff and line managers, the inadequacy of financial control systems in explaining and evaluating social involvement costs and benefits, and the inability of performance appraisal and compensation systems to either recognize effective social performance or to reward it (Ackerman, 1973). Management process audits attempt to identify and assess internal organizational arrangements for identifying social issues, formulating policy, implementing programs and evaluating, rewarding, and controlling social performance (Bauer, Cauthorn and Warner, 1978; Kelly and McTaggart, 1978).

Pressure/Response models of corporate social involvement view management action as highly constrained by external factors such as legal requirements, stockholder expectations, customer demands, technology trends, economic conditions, political programs, union and supplier contractual obligations, national media (T.V., newspaper) coverage of social issues and pressures for internal reform or external governmental intervention and control by public interest organizations (Vogel, 1978). The model suggests that corporate social involvement consists in an ad hoc series of tactical responses—public relations, legal or bargaining—to immediate social pressures (Sethi and Votaw, 1969). The social response is incremental and social policies and social goals only emerge as a consequence of a precedent setting pattern of tactical commitments to a course of action (Lindblom, 1959).

The Public Policy model differs from the others in its assumption that the organization participates in and helps shape its own external environments, social expectations, and legal requirements. This model emphasizes anticipatory management through early warning assessment and intervention. Environmental assessments utilize a variety of forecasting techniques such as Delphi (Linestone and Turoff, 1975), cross impact analysis (Pfeffer and Salanick, 1978), computer simulation modeling (Forrester, 1969, Meadows, 1972) and scenario creation (O'Toole, 1979) to identify environmental trends and possibilities that warrant corporate social attention and involvement. Firms that fail to forecast adequately their social environment are expected to have fewer social policy options available than firms that engage in long range environmental assessment (Wilson, 1976).

The Public Policy model thus assumes that early awareness of emerging social issues maximizes the firm's opportunity to influence the demands placed upon it and the range of performance options available. A considerable amount of corporate external relations activity is thus devoted to anticipating and influencing legislative and regulatory agency developments potentially affecting a firm or industry's mandated social involvement (Weidenbaum, 1977).

Post (1978) refers to the interpenetration of environmental and organizational boundaries as a defining characteristic of the Public Policy model. To make an analogy from statistics, the three models represent three effects upon corporate social involvement observed in an analysis of variance: the main effect of organizational characteristics (Business Policy model), the main effect of environmental characteristics (Pressure/ Response model) and the interaction effect of organization and environment (Public Policy model).

## Criteria for Appraisal

"Criteria for Appraisal" refers to the determination by a researcher of the set of performance criteria against which corporate social involvement responses are to be compared and evaluated (Preston, 1978). This dimension is recommended on the grounds that whether one conducts normative research on how corporations should be socially involved or descriptive research on how corporations are socially involved, both research efforts rely upon some "yardstick" for measurement of observed corporate social involvement.

Preston distinguishes among appraisal criteria by whether they are primarily internal or external in their frame of reference and application and primarily outcome or process oriented in the activities they measure. Preston's framework thus suggests four sets of appraisal criteria: Internal process, external process, internal outcome and external outcome. Each set of criteria reflects a different conception of corporate social involvement and suggests a different focus of research and level of analysis.

Internal process criteria attempt to measure the extent to which socially desirable organizational arrangments are present in the observed firm. For example, to what extent is there evidence of top level management concern for a social issue? Does corporate policy exist on the issue? Are staff specialists responsible for managing the issue? (Bauer, Cauthorn and Warner, 1978)? Internal process assessments measure the presence or absence of such arrangements on the presumption that particular organizational arrangements facilitate corporate social involvement (Holmes, 1978).

Internal outcome criteria measure the impact of corporate social involvement activities upon business operations. For example, what is the impact of affirmative action hiring policies and procedures upon the cost of employee recruitment-selection and on the percentage of minority and women employees constituting the firm's work force? Such an assessment may present a comparison of internal costs with internal benefits, or a comparison of the costs and hiring records of firms having affirmative action policies and procedures with firms not having them.

External process criteria assess the types of inter-organizational arrangements existing between a firm and those external groups, organizations and forces which generate demands or pressures for corporate social involvement, for example, the state of relations between a firm and its local community in terms of its sponsorship of community development programs and use of local supplies. Such assessments may reveal whether inter-organizational relations are friendly or antagonistic, stable or unstable, and thus provide clues on future demands and the means by which demands will be articulated.

External outcome criteria evaluate the actual impact of corporate economic and social involvement upon society. For example, what is the impact of an industrial firm's manufacturing activity on levels of environmental pollution? To what extent have the firm's pollution control activities contributed to the reduction in overall pollution in its area? Impact assessments are very difficult to conduct for a single firm or organization because social issues such as pollution reflect the cumulative effects of the actions of a great variety of participants. A firm may be highly "efficient" in removing 98 percent of all particulate matter from its smoke stacks, yet "ineffective" in reducing the overall level of particulate matter in the atmosphere surrounding it. For this reason, appraisals of impact often require aggregation of the behavior of a variety of actors affecting an issue and thus the level of analysis shifts from a single firm (micro) perspective to a more macro analysis of larger aggregates of firms.

## Levels of Analysis

"Levels of Analysis" identifies the type of entity whose social involvement activities are assessed. Candidates for corporate involvement research can be hierarchically arranged from small or micro to increasingly large or macro units of analysis: individual, group, department, division, organization, inter-organization (interaction between two organizations), organization set (organizations with whom a firm is in direct contact), network (relation between organizations not necessarily in direct contact), industry, institution (Perrow, 1978).

The selection of boundaries for designating research as either micro or macro is somewhat arbitrary and often reflects disciplinary traditions. In organizational psychology, a macro level study focuses on the department or division; the same research unit is a micro study for organizational sociologists whose definition of macro level research begins with the study of inter-organizations or organization sets. These units are still micro from the vantage point of industrial economists whose own research focuses on industries as their unit for study. Political scientists and historians may view industries as a relatively micro unit in their own research on political systems and economic and social institutions.

Commentators on corporate social involvement generally place the outer limit on micro level research at studies of the firm and its relevant publics (Post, 1978; Preston, 1980). Research at the micro level includes studies focusing on individual attitudes, values, perceptions, beliefs and behavior with respect to social issues (Aldag and Bartol, 1978); studies of group composition, cohesion and normative expectations as determinants of quality of work life (Hackman, 1976); and studies of single firm involvement in social issues (Ackerman, 1975 Murray, 1976). These studies focus on intra-organizational and organizational units for analysis.

Macro studies of corporate social involvement focus on inter-organizational units of analysis and include research on the activities of political action committees in influencing the regulation of business (Epstein, 1979), the collective response by the Tobacco industry to social and regulatory pressures to restrict tobacco use (Miles and Cameron, 1977); the study of regulatory enforcement actions against industries of varying market structure and profitability (Clinard and Yeager, 1979) and research comparing the institutional relations between government and business in the political economies of different countries (Lindblom, 1977).

## ALTERNATIVE CONCEPTUAL FRAMEWORKS

The preceeding discussion has examined four conceptual dimensions and alternative choices in each available to researchers. When certain alternatives are very widely used, they become the basis for the development of different conceptual frameworks (Runkel and McGrath, 1972).

Table 2 profiles three alternative conceptual models for the study of corporate social involvement and the conceptual choices involved in each. These three models were initially introduced under the "locus of

## Table 2. Profiles of Conceptual Frameworks

| Conceptual Dimensions | Business Policy | Pressure/ Response | Public Policy |
| --- | --- | --- | --- |
| Mode of Strategy-Making | Entrepeneur | Adaptive | Planning |
| Focus of Research | Process | Content | Impact |
| Locus of Control | Internal | External | Interactive |
| Criteria for Appraisal | Internal Process Internal Outcome | External Process Internal Outcome | External Outcome Internal Outcome |
| Level of Analysis | Micro: organization division department | Macro: organization set inter-organization | Macro: institutions industries |

control" dimension, to characterize three different views of the relative influence of internal versus external factors on corporate social involvement. The three models bear a striking resemblance to Mintzberg's (1973) description of three modes of strategy-making—Entrepeneurial, Adaptive and Planning—and thus suggest some points of theoretical convergence between the corporate planning and corporate social involvement fields of study.

The Business Policy model reflects an Entrepeneurial strategy mode, with the emphasis placed on managerial commitment and initiative as the starting point for corporate social involvement (Ackerman, 1975; Murray, 1976). The model also focuses on the processes of issue identification, response selection and implementation, and utilizes internal process and outcome criteria in evaluating the influence of organizational arrangements upon social involvement activities and performance. Moreover, the individual firm and its subunits (e.g. divisions, departments) typically constitute the units of analysis for research (Ackerman and Bauer, 1976).

The Pressure/Response model reflects an Adaptive model of strategy making in its emphasis upon incremental, disjointed responses to immediate external pressures (Sethi and Votaw, 1969). The model also focuses on the content of political bargaining, legal maneuvering and public relations posturing with specific external pressure groups. It utilizes external process and internal outcome criteria to evaluate the success of a firm in managing its external relations. Typical units for analysis include the organization and its set of external pressure groups (Sethi, 1979).

The Public Policy model reflects a Planning mode of strategy formation in its emphasis upon an integrated pattern of planned organizational response (Post, 1976). The model focuses upon corporate efforts to achieve substantial impact upon the definition and resolution of social issues and utilizes both internal and external outcome criteria to assess organizational efficiency in satisfying internal demands and organizational effectiveness in shaping and satisfying external societal demands. Typical units for study include industries (Hirsch, 1975) and major institutions of the political-economy (Lindblom, 1977).

## Choices in Research Design

The six design features listed in Table 3 provide a basis for describing, classifying and comparing some of the research design strategies employed in empirical studies of corporate social involvement.

## Research Purpose

"Research Purpose" assesses whether a research effort is primarily attempting to *build,* or to *test,* theory about the phenomena under investigation. For phenomena about which little is known, much research effort is directed toward identifying and describing phenomena. This *descriptive* phase of research should lead to a *concept development* phase where research attention focuses on the identification of key variables, both those internal to the phenomena and external variables that may affect the phenomena. The next phase is *hypothesis-generation,* where research efforts focus on specifying the relations between and among the variables identified. In the third phase, *internal validation,* hypotheses are tested to see whether they accurately represent the phenomena in question. Those hypotheses surviving the test of internal validation are then subject to *external validation,* in order to determine the degree to which relations originally observed in a limited sample of the phenomena also apply to other samples from the same or different populations (Schendel and Hofer, 1979).

Much research on corporate social involvement has focused on theory building. The preceeding discussion of alternative conceptual frameworks suggests that research efforts have moved beyond description into concept development. The Business Policy approach is perhaps the most theoretically advanced framework and lends itself to the generation of hypotheses for subsequent testing. Thus far, however, research based on this approach has largely consisted of studies which elaborate the original conceptual framework but do not provide an empirical test of specific propositions. The Pressure/Response model is less precise in its specification of relations between variables. Use of this model has gen-

*Table 3.* Choices in Research Design

| | | |
|---|---|---|
| *RESEARCH PURPOSE* (Inductive/Deductive) | *Theory Building* Exploration Description Hypothesis generation Validation | *Theory Testing* Verification Hypothesis testing |
| EXPERIMENTAL CONTROL (Internal Validity) | *Non-Experimental* Natural setting Learning setting (e.g., classrooms) | *Experimental/ Quasi-experimental* Lab experiments Experimental simulation Field experiments |
| SAMPLE SCOPE (External Validity) | *Case Study* Single case Multiple (corporation) case | *Comparative* Single population sample Multiple population sample |
| TIME INTERVAL (Dynamic-Static Relations) | *Longitudinal* Retrospective Prospective | *Cross-sectional* |
| LEVEL OF DATA (Numeric Measurement and Manipulations) | *Qualitative* Unstructured data collection Non-statistical analysis | *Quantitative* Structured data collection Statistical analysis |
| RESEARCH PRODUCT | *Verbal Models* Concepts and heuristics | *Mathematical Models* Prediction |

erated an increasing variety of concepts and variables to describe the range of corporate response options available; but the work to date fails to specify the conditions under which a particular response pattern is likely.[1]

The Public Policy model, as represented in the research of James Post, has moved beyond description of corporate response patterns to the identification of various environmental conditions (technological, economic, political, cultural) likely to affect the public policy response of a firm or industry. His latest survey of case studies of corporate social policy concludes with a series of general propositions illustrated by the following:

The stimulus or motivation for change in organizational behavior can derive from the pressure of changed legal rules of the game, pressure from the firm's relevant publics, or from the initiative of management. (Post, 1978, p. 284)

Propositions such as this reflect an early phase of theoretical development. A major theoretical gap is the identification—in testable form—of the specific environmental or internal conditions likely to be associated with various patterns of corporate social involvement. Until such specific hypotheses are developed, one must expect future research in the area to continue to be of an inductive, hypothesis-generating nature.

*Experimental Control*

"Experimental Control" describes the degree to which a research design allows the investigator to control the variables of interest. Research designs differ in the "experimental control" dimension from almost complete control (the lab experiment) to total absence of control (a natural event). Control is largely determined by the conditions under which data collection occurs. Intermediate controls are obtainable by the use of quasi-experimental and experimental designs in natural settings (Campbell and Stanley, 1963).

Most research on corporate social involvement occurs in natural settings where little or no experimental control exists. The three conceptual frameworks described earlier are based on field research and to date have largely generated additional field research. Some observers suggest that the phenomena subsumed under corporate social involvement research are too complex to be replicated within experimentally controlled settings (Post, 1978; Preston, 1978). Moreover, our review of the three conceptual frameworks suggest that current theory is too imprecise to permit the formulation of hypotheses amenable to experimental assessment.[2]

*Sample Scope*

"Sample Scope" refers to the degree to which the data used in a study are representative of a larger class of entities (population). This can range from a case study, whose findings permit limited empirical generalization, to large sample studies whose findings are generalizable across a wide range of similar settings.

Research using any of the three conceptual models has consisted largely of case studies. The Business Policy perspective is particularly characterized by single case research. The Conference Board has sponsored several surveys to assess and compare corporate response organizational arrangement across a variety of firms and industries, but such studies have been essentially descriptive and unrelated to any systematic theory of corporate involvement (McGrath, 1976). A growing number of surveys of managerial attitudes and values also exist, but these generally have a limited focus that precludes generalization to the responses of their employing organizations (Aldag and Jackson, 1977; Cavanaugh, 1976). However, some surveys have attempted to link managerial values and attributes to the perceived social performance of their employing firms (Sturdivant and Ginter, 1977). Continued research on links between top management values and corporate response may make it possible to assess key theoretical assumptions (e.g., Entrepeneurial social initiatives) of the Business Policy perspective.

Comparative research based on the Pressure/Response model is beginning to appear. A comparative analysis of the responses by pharmaceutical and food processing firms to criticism of their marketing of infant milk formula in less developed countries suggests hypotheses regarding industry and firm level differences in patterns of both business strategies and social responses (Sethi and Post, 1979). Comparative research using the Public Policy model is limited to cross-cultural comparisons of differences in institutional arrangements between business and government (Lindblom, 1977). Post (1978) has compared case histories compiled from a variety of sources but the absence of systematic data collection and measurement procedures across cases reduces the external validity of his findings.

In summary, research on corporate social involvement is only beginning to move beyond single case studies to comparative studies of a variety of firms in different industries and cultural settings. The current state of research suggests a trend toward comparative case studies in which an attempt is made to retain the conceptual and substantive richness of the case study with the empirical generalizability of the comparative study. Research involving larger sample surveys is frequently limited to non-theoretical, descriptive studies.

## Time Interval

"Time Interval" describes whether a research study is based on data covering a single time point (cross sectional) or over some longer period (longitudinal). The time interval dimension refers to the data itself, not to the data collection process. A single data collection effort involving a retrospective assessment of events over a time period constitutes a longitudinal study, as does a prospective design for collecting data at several time points in the future. Prospective studies provide more internal validity for identifying and assessing antecedent conditions and their consequences (Darran, Miles and Snow, 1976).

Most research studies by proponents of the three conceptual models have relied on retrospective studies assessing events occurring over an extended time period; and this emphasis on a longitudinal perspective is not unwarranted. A common theoretical assumption of all three major perspectives is that corporate social involvement activity results from processes which occur over time. Ackerman (1975) and Murray (1976) suggest that the "institutionalization" of corporate social response to a social issue typically takes about eight years. Such long time periods make prospective studies prohibitively time consuming and expensive. However, Preston (1980) has warned that exclusive reliance on longitudinal studies (which are also usually case studies) may retard efforts to collect precise data for detecting specific patterns of corporate social involvement behavior across a wide variety of firms, industries and general social environmental conditions. A recent example of cross-sectional research is Reeder's (1978) doctoral dissertation comparing relations between corporate level policies and plant level programs of social involvement across large, geographically dispersed and small, geographically concentrated firms. A second example is a questionnaire survey of Canadian firms comparing corporate-wide social policies with a firm's stage of involvement in specific social issues (Preston, Dierkes and Rey, 1978). More cross-sectional research focusing on specific external and internal factors associated with corporate social involvement is likely.

*Level of Data*

"Level of Data" refers to the extent to which methods of data collection and analysis permit quantitative versus qualitative descriptions, comparisons and evaluations. These differences reflect in part the degree to which methods of data collection are structured and methods of data analysis transform raw data into a form suitable for statistical manipulation.

Most research on corporate social involvement relies upon qualitative methods of data collection (unstructured observation, interviews and document reviews) and analysis (clinical insight and inductive categorization). Some of the comparative research has yielded quantitative data on corporate-divisional relations (Reeder, 1978), on the relation between firm size and social involvement (Preston, Diekes and Rey, 1978), and firm profitability and social involvement (Bowman and Haire, 1975; Bragdon and Marlin, 1972; Sturdivant and Ginter, 1977).

To the extent that research on corporate social involvement relies upon qualitative methods of data collection and analysis, the resulting research findings will usually take the form of verbal models of corporate social involvement. Verbal models are most valuable as heuristic devices for demonstrating the richness and complexity of a phenomenon and for inspiring new insights and understanding. However, the informational needs of both business and government require more precise description and estimation of the antecedents and consequences of corporate social involvement which only mathematical models can provide. The formulation and validation of such models requires a substantial increase in both the amount and the quality of quantitative research in this area.

# CONSTRAINTS ON CONCEPTUAL-METHODOLOGICAL CHOICES

The preceeding discussion of research conceptualization and design choices suggests that there is a gap between the verbal models and qualitative research methods employed in many studies of corporate social involvement and the mathematical models and quantitative methods that characterize other domains of social science research, and that efforts should be made to increase analytic rigor in both conceptualizing and empirically examining corporate social involvement phenomena. Such a development would appear consistent with the "normal science" paradigm (Kuhn, 1962).

The existence of a conceptual/methodological gap raises two related questions: Why does the gap exist? How can it be reduced?

The first question deserves extended intellectual attention and the present discussion can only offer some hypotheses for further consideration. Three hypotheses are offered here to account for the conceptual and methodological shortcomings cited earlier. These hypotheses suggest that phenomenological, disciplinary, and data access factors have constrained conceptual and methodological choices. Each factor is presented with a discussion of possible correction actions. The discussion concludes with a description of the author's current research which incorporates many of the recommendations discussed earlier.

*Phenomenological Complexity*

The phenomenological hypothesis holds that phenomena associated with corporate social involvement are so recent, relatively unknown and intrinsically complex that verbal models and qualitative analyses represent appropriate conceptual and methodological strategies. Without challenging the phenomenological premise, which has been argued in a variety of social research domains (Hatten, 1979), one may still question the conclusion that verbal models and qualitative analyses are the only appropriate responses to complex social phenomena. An additional response is to partition a complex phenomenon into more limited domains of inquiry for theoretical and empirical focus. (Merton, 1968). The three conceptual frameworks (Business Policy, Pressure/Response, Public Policy) described earlier represent three broad partitions of scholarly effort within which further subdivisions of theoretical and empirical focus can develop. For example, the Public Policy model offers a rich domain for intensive research focus on corporate involvement and influence upon such substantive policy areas as electorate politics (Epstein, 1979), health (Sethi and Post, 1979) and government regulation (Chatov, 1978). Implementing a limited domain strategy will require a considerable expansion in the amount and variety of scholarly study of corporate social involvement.

### Disciplinary Background

A second explanation for the limitations of corporate social involvement research emphasizes the business policy backgrounds of many researchers in this field. Hatten (1979) has characterized business policy scholarship as emphasizing broad verbal models and qualitative case research methods. An emphasis upon case research is reinforced by professional and institutional demands upon business policy faculty to develop teaching cases for classroom use and for distribution by the Intercollegiate Case Clearing House. One remedy would be to encourage research contributions from representatives of a variety of disciplines. No single discipline can encompass the complexities inherent in corporate social involvement phenomena but different disciplines offer unique perspectives on selected aspects of the research domain. Economics, political science, and sociology offer a rich array of conceptual and methodological tools for constructive application to the study of corporate social involvement. Increased understanding of corporate social involvement phenomena will most rapidly develop if contributors with different disciplinary backgrounds employ their specialized skills to enrich the conceptual and research base already established.

### Data Access

A third explanation for the preponderance of case study and descriptive research activity lies in the perceived barriers to developing data bases amenable to explanatory model building and quantitative assessment. Corporations are alleged to be highly secretive about their efforts to influence social issues and public policy (Stephenson, 1973). Moreover, the expense of obtaining data from corporate sources has limited the scope of most research efforts. One remedy to these difficulties may be to look to publicly available information on corporate behavior. Numerous departments of the federal government compile data on business activity and access to much of this data is available under the Freedom of Information Act. Moreover, federal data on corporate activity provides a convenient access point for comparative assessments of a large number of business organizations across a wide range of issues and forms of social involvement. Implementation of a government data access strategy will require that business and society scholars develop greater familiarity with government data archives and procedures for their access. Data archives are also available at state and local government agencies.

## IMPLEMENTING ANALYTIC RESEARCH STRATEGIES

To illustrate how more analytically-oriented conceptual and methodological strategies may be employed in corporate social involvement research I will describe briefly my own ongoing study of constituency (interest group) influence on regulatory agency decision making. (De-Fillippi, 1981) The conceptual framework selected for assessing business and non-business interest group impacts on regulatory decisions was the Public Policy model, where a research focus on business impacts on the social (in this case regulatory) environment is directly applicable.

Employing the public policy conceptual framework directed me to a consideration of the interpentration of constituency and regulatory agency boundaries and thus the interaction between business policy and public policy. Moreover, the public policy framework suggested that research attention be directed toward an appraisal of the impact of business and other constituency efforts on the definition of social issues (in my study, the regulatory agency's agenda) and their resolution (agency decision making on agenda items). Finally, the public policy framework suggested a macro-level analysis including trade associations and co-alitions of organizations representing industry and non-industry constituencies.

A review of the research literature on business-government relations revealed a variety of case studies of business efforts to influence specific issues in specific government agencies, but very little empirical research that systematically compared the success of different constituencies and their influence tactics across a range of issues. Available literature also suggested a variety of influences on agency decision behavior, including characteristics of the constituency, the nature of constituency demands, the variety and intensity of influence behavior, and the issue context in which constituency influence behavior occurs. These variables and the working hypotheses concerning their impact upon agency decision making represent vital conceptual and hypothesis generation contributions of qualitative case research.

In developing a research strategy for modelling and assessing the impact of these factors on agency decision making, I elected to employ data available from the Consumer Product Safety Commission on two hundred business and consumer organizations and individuals petitioning the agency for rule making action between 1973 and 1980. The selection of a federal agency was more than a data access tactic. The choice also limited the scope of my research to a specific policy arena (consumer product safety) and a specific public policy mechanism for constituency influence (the petitions process). Thus my data access choices also limited my domain of inquiry to an area sufficiently narrow to permit analytic model development and quantitative assessment.

Before implementing an analytic research strategy one should be aware of potential risks arising from its misuse. One risk is that data availability may replace theoretical or policy relevance as the criterion for selection of research projects. The issues requiring scholarly attention are too important to be subordinated to data access opportunities; data access choices must be subordinated to problem identification.

A second risk is the overinterpretation of research findings. For example, my data base on constituency influence behavior is limited to "public behavior" documented in agency records. A review of literature on constituency-regulatory agency relations suggests that a considerable amount of constituency influence occurs informally and in private settings (Nader and Serber, 1976). Results from a study based solely on *public* behavior by constituencies and agency officials must qualify and delineate its findings to that domain.

A final risk is that of assuming that any single research strategy is sufficient to analyze the complexities of corporate social policy and performance. The complex and multifaceted phenomena to be addressed in this area provide abundant opportunities for both independent and coordinated research efforts employing a variety of conceptual and methodological approaches. Each approach has its strengths and limitations, but the employment of multiple approaches increases the cumulative knowledge gained and provides an empirical basis for validating our concepts and increasing our confidence in the results generated by each research strategy.

## SUMMARY

This paper has examined the conceptual and methodological choices reflected in current research on corporate social involvement. Most research in the field reflects a descriptive level of conceptual development in contrast to the explanatory models common in the basic social science disciplines. Qualitative case studies and descriptive surveys are the dominant research methods in contrast to the social science trend toward quantitative assessment and modelling of complex phenomena.

Explanations for the gap between corporate social involvement research and social science disciplinary research include the inherent complexity of corporate social involvement phenomena, the limited number of researchers active in the field, the institutional and professional role demands upon faculty to devote research time to the development of teaching cases and the difficulties and expense in accessing data from business sources.

Recommendations for overcoming constraints on corporate social involvement research include the employment of limited domain strategies for theoretical and research focus, an increase of research involvement by scholars from a variety of disciplinary backgrounds, and greater reliance on governmental sources for data access. An example of an analytic study that attempts to overcome some of these conceptual and methodological limitations is presented.

## ACKNOWLEDGMENTS

The author thanks Barbara Grey Gricar of Pennsylvania State University for comments on an early version of this paper presented on May 5, 1980 at the Joint National Meeting of the Institute of Management and the Operations Research Society of America.

## NOTES

1. Sethi (1975) has compared corporate response patterns of Japanese and American firms and has thus begun to develop and examine broad hypotheses on the relation between cultural differences as a moderator of the impact of social pressures on corporate response patterns.

2. Hegarty and Sims (1976) have employed experimental methods to assess the impact of heightened competition on unethical decisions by individuals.

## REFERENCES

Ackerman, R., *The Social Challenge to Business*. Cambridge: Harvard University Press, 1975.

Ackerman, R., and R. Bauer, *Corporate Social Responsiveness: The Modern Dilemma*. Reston: Reston Publishing Co., 1976.

Aldag, R., and K. Bartol, "Empirical Studies of Corporate Social Performance and Policy: A Survey of Problems and Results." In L. Preston (ed.), *Research in Corporate Social Performance and Policy*, vol. 1. Greenwich: JAI Press, 1978, pp. 165–200.

Aldag, R., and D. Jackson, "Assessment of Attitudes Toward Social Responsibilities." *Journal of Business Administration* 8 2(1977):65–80.

American Institute of Certified Public Accountants, *The Measurement of Corporate Social Performance*. New York: AICPA, 1977.

Bauer, R., L. Cauthorn, and R. P. Warner, "The Management Process Audit Manual." In L. Preston (ed.), *Research in Corporate Social Performance and Policy*, vol. 1. Greenwich: JAI Press, 1978, pp. 265–278.

Bourgeois, L. J., "Strategy and Environment: A Conceptual Integration." *Academy of Management Review* 5 1(1980):25–39.

Bowman, E. M., and M. Haire, "A Strategic Posture Toward Corporate Social Reporting." *California Management Review* 18 2(1975):49–58.

Bragdon, J. H., and J. T. Marlin, "Is Pollution Profitable?" *Risk Management* 19 4(1972):8.
Buono, L., and L. Nichols, "Researching Corporate Responsiveness: From Conceptualization to Data Collection." Paper presented at TIMS/ORSA Joint National Meeting, Washington, D.C. (May 5):1980.
Campbell, D. T., and J. C. Stanley, *Experimental and Quasi-Experimental Designs for Research.* Chicago: Rand McNally, 1963.
Cavanaugh, G. F., *American Business Values in Transition.* Englewood Cliffs, N.J.: Prentice-Hall, 1976.
Chatov, Robert, "Government Regulation: Process and Substantive Impacts." In L. Preston (ed.), *Corporate Social Performance and Policy,* vol. 1., 1978, pp. 223–54.
Clinard, M., and P. Yeager, et al., *Illegal Corporate Behavior.* Washington, D.C.: U.S. Department of Justice, Law Enforcement Assistance Administration, 1979.
Council on Economic Priorities, *Paper Profits.* Cambridge, Mass.: MIT Press, 1972.
Darran, D., R. Miles, and C. Snow, "Organizational Adjustment to the Environment: A Review." Paper presented at the Annual Meeting of the American Institute for Decision Sciences, Washington, D.C., 1975.
DeFillippi, R., "Constituency Influences On Regulatory Decisions: A Multivariate Model". Dissertation Proposal. Yale University, 1981.
Epstein, E., "The Emergence of Political Action Committees." In H. E. Alexander (ed.), *Political Finance.* Beverly Hills, CA: Sage Publications, 1979.
———, "Corporations and Labor Unions in Electoral Politics." *Annals of the American Academy of Political and Social Science,* 1976.
———, *The Corporation in Americal Politics.* Englewood Cliffs, N.J.: Prentice Hall, 1969.
Ernst and Ernst, *Social Responsibility Disclosure Survey of Fortune 500 Annual Reports.* Cleveland, Ohio: Ernst and Ernst, 1978.
Forrester, J. W., *Urban Dynamics.* Cambridge, Mass.: M.I.T., 1969.
Gricar, B. G., *The Environmental Imperative Created by Government Regulation: Predicting Organizational Response.* Ph.D. Dissertation, Case Western Reserve University (August):1979.
Hackman, R. J., "Group Influence on Individuals." In M. D. Dunnette (ed.), *Handbook of Industrial and Organizational Psychology,* Chicago: Rand McNally, 1976.
Hatten, K. J., "Quantitative Research Methods in Strategic Management." In D. E. Schendel, and C. W. Hofer (Eds.), *Strategic Management,* Boston: Little, Brown and Company, 1979.
Hegarty, W. H., and H. P. Sims, Jr., "The reinforcement of unethical decision behavior: An experiment." Proceedings of the Eighth Annual Conference of the American Institute for Decision Sciences, pp. 250–252, 1976.
Hirsch, P. M., "Organizational Effectiveness and the Institutional Environment." *Administrative Science Quarterly* 20(1975):327–344.
Holmes, S., "Adopting Corporate Structures for Social Responsiveness." *California Management Review* 21 1(1978):47–54.
———, "Executive Perceptions of Corporate Social Responsibility." Business Horizons 19(1976):34–40.
Kelly, D. W., and R. T. McTaggart, "Guidelines for Social Performance Case Studies." In L. E. Preston (ed.), *Research in Corporate Social Performance and Policy,* vol. 1. Greenwich, Conn.: JAI Press, 1978, pp. 287–291.
Kuhn, T., *The Structure of Scientific Revolutions.* Chicago: University of Chicago Press, 1962.
Lindblom, C. E., *Politics and Markets.* New York: Basic Books, 1977.
———, "The Science of Muddling Through." *Public Administration Review (Spring):1959.*
Linstone, H. A., and M. Turoff, *The Delphi Method: Techniques and Application.* Reading, Mass.: Addison-Wesley, 1975.

McGrath, J. E., "A Multi-facet approach to classification of individual, group, and organizational concepts." In B. Indik, and K. Berrien (eds.), *People, Groups, and Organizations: An Effective Integration,* New York: Teachers College Press, 1967, pp. 191–215.

McGrath, Phyllis, *Managing Corporate External Relations.* Report #679. New York: The Conference Board, 1976.

McGraw-Hill, *Economics Department Survey of Preliminary Plans for Capital Spending.* New York: McGraw-Hill Publications Co., 1977.

Meadows, D. et al., *The Limits to Growth.* New York: Universe Books, 1972.

Merton, R. K., *Social Theory and Social Structure.* New York: The Free Press, 1968.

Miles, R. H., and K. Cameron, "Coffin Nails and Corporate Strategies: A Quarter Century View of Organizational Adaptation to Environment in the U.S. Tobacco Industry." Working Paper No. 3. Research Program on Government-Business Relations. New Haven: Yale School of Organization and Management, 1977.

Mintzberg, H., "Policy as a Field of Management Theory." *Academy of Management Review* 2 1(1977):88–103.

――――, "Strategy-Making in Three Modes." *California Management Review* 16 2(1973):44–53.

Moskowitz, M., "Profiles in Corporate Responsibility." *Business and Society Review.* 13(1975):28–42.

――――, "46 Socially Responsible Corporations." *Business and Society* 7 8(1974).

Murray, E. A., "The Social Response Process in Commercial Banks: An Empirical Investigation." *Academy of Management Review* 1 3(1976):5–15.

O'Toole, J., "What's ahead for the Business-Government Relationship." *Harvard Business Review* (March-April):1979.

Perrow, C., *Complex Organizations: A Critical Essay.* Glenview, Illinois: Scott, Foresman & Co., 1978.

Pfeffer, J., and G. Salancik, *External Control of Organizations.* New York: Harper and Row, 1978.

Post, J., *Corporate Behavior and Social Change.* Reston, Va.: Reston Publishing Co., 1978.

――――, *Risk and Response.* Lexington, Mass.: D. C. Heath, 1976.

Preston, L. E., "Business, Society and Public Policy: Current Research and Research Approaches." In L. E. Preston (ed.), *Business Environment/Public Policy: 1979 Conference Papers,* St. Louis: AACSB, 1980.

――――, "Corporate Social Performance and Policy: A Synthetic Framework for Research and Analysis." In L. E. Preston (ed.), *Corporate Social Performance and Policy,* vol. 1. Greenwich, Conn.: JAI Press, Inc., 1978.

Preston, L. E., M. Dierkes, and F. Rey, "Comparing Corporate Social Performance: An Analysis of Recent Studies in Germany, France, and Canada, and Comparison with U.S. Experience." *California Management Review,* 1978.

Reeder, J., "Corporate Social Involvement at the Local Level." *Proceedings of the 38th Annual Meeting of the Academy of Management,* pp. 356–59, 1978.

Runkel, P. J., and J. E. McGrath, *Research on Human Behavior.* New York: Holt, Rinehart and Winston, Inc., 1972.

Schendel, D. C., and W. C. Hofer (eds.), *Strategic Management: A New View of Business Policy and Planning.* Boston: Little, Brown and Company, 1979.

Sethi, S. P., "A Conceptual Framework for Environmental Analysis of Social Issues and Evaluation of Business Response Patterns." *Academy of Management Review* 4(1979):63–74.

――――, *Advocacy Advertising and Large Corporations.* Lexington, Mass.: D. C. Heath, 1977.

————, *Japanese Business and Social Conflict: An Analysis of Response Patterns with American Business*. Cambridge, Mass.: Ballinger Press, 1975.

————, "Dimensions of Corporate Social Performance: An Analytic Framework." *California Management Review* 7 3(1975):58–65.

Sethi, S. P., and J. Post, "Public Consequences of Private Action: Marketing of Infant Formula in Less Developed Countries." *California Management Review* 21 4(1979):36–48.

Sethi, S. P., and D. Votaw, "Do We Need a New Corporate Response to a Changing Social Environment?" Part II, *California Management Review* 12 1(1969):17–31.

Steiner, G. A., and J. Steiner, *Issues in Business and Society*. New York: Random House, 1977.

Stephenson, L., "Prying Open Corporations: Tighter than Clams." *Business and Society Review* 8(Winter 1973):42.

Stone, C. D., *Where the Law Ends*. New York: Harper & Row, 1975.

Sturdivant, F. D., and J. L. Ginter, "Corporate Social Responsiveness: Management Attitudes and Economic Performance." *California Managment Review* 19 3(1977):30–39.

U. S. Department of Commerce, *Corporate Social Reporting in the United States and Western Europe: Report of the Task Force on Corporate Social Performance*. Washington, D.C., 1979.

Vogel, D., *Lobbying the Corporation: Citizen Challenges to Business Authority*. New York: Basic Books, 1978.

Weidenbaum, M., *Business, Government and the Public*. Englewood Cliffs, N.Y.: Prentice-Hall, 1977.

Wilson, I., *Corporate Environments of the Future*. New York: The President's Association, Special Study #61, 1976.

# THE THOMPSON-PAGE CONTRIBUTION TO SOCIAL ISSUES RESEARCH

John F. Mahon

---

James D. Thompson, who died in 1973, was a recognized leader in management thought. Robert Avery in his eulogy for Thompson noted that:

> Students of organization and administration will be reaping dividends for a long time from Jim Thompson's investment in ideas. (1974:4)

Thompson's ideas are often cited in the leading texts of both organizational behavior and management policy (Pfeffer and Salancik, 1978; Galbraith and Nathanson, 1978). It is a tribute to his brilliance and foresight that *Organizations in Action*, a thin volume, 177 pages, has served as such a rich and varied source of new concepts and research ideas. Researchers in the social issues arena, however, have apparently felt that Thompson provides little stimulus for theoretical or empirical research relevant to corporate social responsiveness. The "empirical" criticism has often been made of Thompson's work. It is argued that the level of abstraction is such as to make empirically-based investigations difficult, if not impossible, to perform.

It now appears that Thompson was well aware of this problem with his work and that he undertook some action to resolve it. The resolution involved Thompson's sponsoring doctoral dissertation work along empirical lines to extend and/or modify his theoretical contributions. One such thesis, undertaken by Robert R. Page, with Thompson as chairman, was completed in 1971. Page died shortly thereafter, and the thesis was never published, Page's thesis is clearly an extension of Thompson's work, and it serves as a linking pin between Thompson's contributions and the more recent research literature in corporate response to non-market aspects of the environment.

The purpose of this paper is to illuminate the intellectual roots of social issues research in the Thompson-Page collaboration and the substantive work of Page. It is clear that when Thompson finished *Organizations in Action* he began to refocus his energies and talents on broader organization-environment relationships. His writings and research took him away from economic considerations of the firm to an analysis of the role of business in a larger social framework. The titles of some of his last works are indicative of this shift: "The Regeneration of Social Organizations" (1971); "Society's Frontiers for Organizing Activities" (1973); "Social Interdependence, The Polity, and Public Administration" (1974)' and "Technology, Polity, and Societal Development" (1974).

## THE THOMPSON-PAGE LEGACY

*Organizations in Action* was Thompson's attempt to address what he saw as the critical organizational problem: coping with uncertainty. His analysis of this issue laid the early framework and conceptual foundation for the pattern of response literature and the research in corporate involvement in public policy that was to follow. Although Thompson confined himself primarily to economic and technical issues, his emphasis on response patterns was extended by Page to include corporate response to social issues and changing public policy agendas.

Thompson notes that organizations act in certain ways because they must. Organizations are expected to produce results, and that requires them to act in a rational manner. Yet, any uncertainty threatens their capability to do so. For Thompson, the central problem for complex organizations is dealing with uncertainty which arises from technology and the environment. This thesis allows Thompson to make a creative leap in theory building. If the afore-mentioned concepts and relationships hold true, then ". . . organizations with similar technological and environmental problems should exhibit similar behavior; *patterns should appear.*" (1967: 1, 2, emphasis added)

In order to investigate these relationships, Thompson frames the argument in an open/closed system perspective drawing heavily on the works of Weber (1947), March and Simon (1958), and Parsons (1960). He analyzes the tension that exists in an organization seeking certainty but constantly faced with uncertainty, and parallels that argument with the dynamics of open and closed systems operations. The pressure of the dynamic interactions between certainty and uncertainty requires the organization to act and to organize (or structure) itself in order to survive and operate.

The action response of the organization is characterized by "homeostasis," a process of self-stabilization where the organization spontaneously balances and alters the relationships among the parts and activities (both internal and external) to insure organizational survival when faced with uncertainties generated in the environment. This process alone is not sufficient to ensure corporate survival when the environment becomes more complex.

The structural response is oriented to controlling uncertainties in the environment while simultaneously providing some measure of control over technological uncertainties. The foundation of this analysis is Parsons' (1960) distinction among technical, managerial, and institutional sub-systems within the organization. The technical sub-system is concerned with the technical tasks of the enterprise (e.g. underwriting in insurances, assembly line production in automobile manufacturing). The other two sub-systems, according to Thompson, protect and insulate this technical sub-system (Thompson uses the term "technical core") from uncertainties. The managerial sub-system serves as the link between the technical and institutional sub-systems, and it provides direction and control for the organization. The institutional sub-system is the linking pin between the overall organization and its environment. This system is concerned with the maintenance of organizational legitimacy and the enterprise's interaction with other institutions and agencies of the community.

Although recognizing the importance of the institutional sub-system in the management or organization-environment relationships, Thompson did not explore its full potential. Corporations, because of their intimate familiarity with economic planning and technical management, have often ignored the challenges posed by changing public policy agendas and the increased interest in the social responsibility of the firm. This area of interaction involves the greatest uncertainty for the firm and receives the least treatment in *Organizations in Action*.

Page's thesis, *Organizational Response to Social Challenge: Theory and Evidence for Two Industries,* was an attempt to take Thompson's theory into the social arena. He observed that organizations seem to move only when pushed. Even when it is quite obvious that an issue is building and must be confronted, the firm cannot be expected to adapt or change automatically unless forced to do so. In a clear link with the notion of interpenetrating systems (Preston and Post, 1975), Page observes that:

> Organizations are slow to adapt to environmental pressures, and if they are powerful
> enough, they don't adapt. The society in which they are situated has to. (1971:241)

## Six Areas of Conceptual Development

Thompson and Page's work was instrumental in the genesis and development of six distinct lines of inquiry. These research paths are being pursued by researchers in social issues in management, organizational behavior, and strategic planning. They are:

- Thompson's recognition of the interdependency between the organization and the environment was a clear signal to researchers. He was one of the first supporters of the necessity for research that would simultaneously analyze the corporate and societal response mechanisms and their interdependencies with one another. Preston and Post (1975) picked up on this notion, and applying systems theory as a conceptual filter, developed the interpenetrating systems model. This approach recognizes the interdependent relationship between actors, but notes that they can influence one another *both* directly and indirectly.
- Thompson provides further support for this interpenetration between the organization and society when he addresses *domain and domain consensus.* Domain, in its essence, is the expectation that actors in the corporate-environment relationship hold concerning corporate behavior. This expectation involves both traditional economic issues (e.g., provide jobs, good products at reasonable prices, etc.) and social issues (e.g., product safety, concern for the environment and the local community, etc.). It is his analysis of this relationship that serves as the basis for several strands of current research in business and society and in strategic planning.
- The expectations concerning economic and social issues, when linked with the concept of *domain* consensus, forms a basis for the current *effectiveness/effficiency distinction* in the strategic planning literature. Pfeffer and Salancik (1978) and Hofer and Schendel (1978) explore this relationship in great detail.

- Thompson also makes it quite clear that there is a difference between subjectively determined organizational goals and operative policies which can be objectively verified. The former category is the articulation of goals made by the organization. The latter category, operative policies, requires us to analyze the interaction between the organization and the environment. Post's (1976) articulation of the reactive, proactive, and interactive modes of corporate response is a clear example of what Thompson meant by operative policies. In analyzing corporate societal relationships, a reliance on the statement of organizational goals by the firm is clearly insufficient. We must look at these operative goals as well.
- Thompson appears to place great faith in organizational boundary spanning activities as providing a solution to the uncertainty problem that the organization faces. Thompson's faith in this area has been supported by the growing research into boundary spanning activities (Adams, 1976; Aldrich and Herker, 1977; Miles, 1975, 1980).
- Page's work, largely unrecognized, moved Thompson's theoretical approach clearly into the social issues arena with an empirical focus. Page's thesis in 1971 addressed the trade association as a political actor in the public policy process, and offered some early ideas on stakeholder analysis. In addition, Page may have been one of the first researchers to investigate corporate response patterns to social issues.

## THOMPSON-PAGE AND SOCIAL ISSUES RESEARCH

In order to demonstrate the relevance of the Thompson-Page contribution to social issues research, I have selected three issues of current research activity for more detailed discussion: (1) corporate involvement in the public policy process and business-government interaction in the political arena; (2) corporate responses to social issues; and (3) stakeholder analysis.

*Corporate Involvement in the Public Policy Process and the Political Arena*

This area of study has been investigated by a number of researchers (Bauer, Pool, and Dexter, 1964; Epstein, 1969, 1973, 1974, 1980, 1980a; Lindblom, 1968, 1977; Post, 1976, 1978, 1978a; and Preston and Post, 1975). Page's study was an extension of the previously existing works on this subject.

The central concept in Page's thesis was:

> . . . that when an organization is challenged by a serious threat to its operations,
> it responds by resisting the demanded change, and the resistance takes the form
> of a *patterned sequence of actions* to restore compatability with the environment.
> (1971: *x, emphasis added*)

Page was concerned with the broad issue of the relationship of the organization to its environment. He wanted to examine ". . . how certain business firms maintain viability over a period of time when confronted by a challenge from the environment that creates uncertainties about relationships vital to their functioning." (1971:2)

Page accepts from Thompson that the motive for corporate action is the alleviation of uncertainty. In its simplist form, Page's theory is that challenge threatens the ability of the firm to function, which in turn creates considerable uncertainty. Uncertainty often arises out of social and political (non-market) forces, but a significant challenge has to come from a vital element in the firm's environment. A vital element is an external actor or force whose role relationships with the organization are essential to the organization's present method of operating. For example, for many large organizations, the federal government is a vital element of the environment.

Page's analysis, although controversial and exploratory in nature, was firmly grounded in theory and empirically verifiable. He pursued this work through an in-depth analysis of two unrelated environmental/corporate situations: (1) The issue of automobile safety, particularly during the period 1956-1966; and (2) the controversy surrounding the drug industry and the promotion of ethical drugs during 1956-1962. The situations were similar in that each involved the federal government as the challenger; and both were concerned with social issues important enough to involve vital elements in the organization's environment, thereby ensuring a good test of Page's postulated corporate response patterns. A secondary reason for this choice was the availability of information on the situations; since both issues involved the federal government, and they both received a great deal of publicity.

Page used publicly available documents and the practitioner's literature (*Fortune, Wall Street Journal, Business Week,* and so forth) to construct a chronological record of organizational and governmental actions. The main interest of the study was in the *response patterns* of the organizations involved. This longitudinal research allowed Page to determine if there were sequential changes in organizational responses to the challenges as time progressed, and thereby confirm or deny the existence of the hypothesized patterns.

It is important to note that the level of analysis in this study was the *industry,* not the individual firm. The automotive analysis was focused on the actions of the Automobile Manufacturers Association, and in the drug investigations he used the Pharmaceutical Manufacturers Association. Page's study is therefore, first of all, a record of the participation of these industry groups in the public policy process.

## Corporate Ressponse to Social Issues

Page described his study as ". . . a report of *how* organizations respond. . . . The test is whether complex business organizations exhibit the postulated pattern in their responses to challenges." (1971:51)

Research in this area has proceeded along two distinct, yet related paths. Bauer (1978), Ackerman and Bauer (1976), and Murray (1974) working at Harvard, and Sethi (1971, 1973, 1975, 1978) as well as others have attempted to analyze corporate response from an *internal* perspective, focusing on the process of internal adaptation to social issues and demands. The other path has analyzed the relationship of the corporation with the environment from an *external* perspective (e.g., Galbraith, 1967; Lindblom, 1968, 1977), where the research begins from the societal or public policy viewpoint. Post (1976, 1978, 1978a, 1980) has also viewed corporate response to social issues from an external viewpoint but at a more micro level, including an analysis of the response patterns of individual firms within the same industry to a common problem (the infant formula controversy, Post & Baer, 1980). Page took an external perspective, with the trade association as the focal organization. This use of the trade association as the "organization" was unique and advanced for the time.

Page notes that there are a limited number of options available to the organization to resolve environmental uncertainty. These options fall into five broad response patterns (or strategies):

1. Total Resistance—The organization refuses to change, repulses the challenge, and/or forces the environment to adapt to the organization.
2. Bargaining—The organization bargains or compromises so that adjustment on both sides is required.
3. Capitulation—The organization adapts or gives in to the environment's demands.
4. Termination—The organization may end the relationship with the challenger, seek a replacement or change its environment.
5. Cessation of activity—The organization may be unwilling or unable to adapt or make the demanded changes, and therefore disbands. (Page, 1971:36-53)

The response patterns involve different levels of costs to the organizations, and also demand different amounts of coordination of organizational elements and sub-systems.

These responses are undertaken because any disruptions or disturbance in the "role-set agreement" between the organization and its environment threatens corporate goals, stability and viability. The concept of "role-set agreement" refers to the set of reciprocal expectancies or exchanges that govern the relationship between the organization and any element of the external environment. A particular role relationship includes bundles of rights and responsibilities. Rights are things of value or privilege gained by one actor in the process, while responsibilities are the duties or obligations offered in exchange for these rights. As a consequence, both the product and process of these role agreements are essential to organizational continuity and success. This approach clearly reflects the key aspects of Preston and Post's (1975) notion of interpenetrating systems, whereby actors influence one another directly and indirectly through an interaction process.

The response strategies noted above are very broad, but a variety of specific tactics may be associated with each (See Figure 1). If the firm elects to resist the change (the first strategy), it can either ignore the challenge (give no outward response) or engage in persuasion or propaganda. The organization can try to discredit the issue, or deny its existence or legitimacy, by acclaiming the legitimacy of present organizational behavior. The firm could also attempt to discredit those promoting the issue, acclaim the organization's social responsibility by emphasizing what the firm is doing in this area or in other areas, or has done in the past. The enterprise can also issue countercharges of irresponsible behavior directed toward the challengers. If all these tactics fail, the organization can engage in diversionary tactics; that is, the existence of the issue is admitted, but responsibility or legitimacy for dealing with the problem is disclaimed.[1] If the challenge can be resolved by these tactics, no changes in exchange agreements are necessary; and the organization can continue on with little or no changes in actual operations. Page notes that the organization would logically act only when the cost of inaction is higher than the cost of action (assuming both are known or estimated).

If resistance proves futile, the firm will seek out compromises (the second strategy). This is more threatening to the firm than resistance as it involves the renegotiation of role relationships and exchange agreements. Again, there is a patterned sequence of responses. The first tactic the enterprise can pursue is to offer positive inducements, in essence an attempt is made to buy off the challenger. If this is ineffective, negative inducements can be applied (for example, threats, warnings, sanctions,

*Figure 1.* Page's Response Patterns/Strategies

| | RESISTANCE | BARGAINING | CAPITULATION | TERMINATION | CESSATION |
|---|---|---|---|---|---|
| | Ignore | Positive inducements | Concede | Cease relationship with the challenger | Dissolve the organization |
| | Persuasion/ Propaganda<br>• discredit<br>• deny<br>• question legitimacy<br>• acclaim organization's social re-sponsibility<br>• counter charges | Negative inducements<br><br>Expand the conflict (build coaltions) | Seek best solution for firm<br><br>Seek exoneration<br>• promote social responsibility<br>• enchance prestige | | |
| | Diversionary Tactics | | | | |

TACTICS

143

and so forth). There is a danger here in that this tactic could result in adverse reactions from the challenger and other environmental elements.[2] The firm could also expose the conflict to other members of the role set, thereby gaining sympathetic allies as well as preparing them to accept changes in their role agreements with the organization with less resistance if the firm loses the challenge. This a dangerous tactic because it brings into question the ability of the firm to cope with challenges. The strength and stability of the enterprise is questioned and other members of the role set may themselves seek new exchange arrangements.

If these two general strategies fail, the organization can capitulate on the issue. Basically the organization concedes to the challenger on the major point of controversy. As a consequence the exchange agreements with the challenger change, and some or all other exchange agreements of the organization will have to be renegotiated. Although the organization gives-in, it will seek the best arrangements for its interests in the new exchange agreements. In addition it will seek exoneration by promoting an image of social responsibility in an attempt to enhance its prestige and perhaps receive some payoff from the concession. It is entirely possible that capitulation may be one of the first tactics used by the firm, if the costs of giving in are not too great, or the gain in prestige or image offsets them.

Two other general strategies are available to the firm. One would be for the enterprise to terminate the relationship with the challenging elements. This may be the first choice of the organization in responding to the challenge if the challenger's role is unimportant. The final strategy would be for the firm to dissolve itself, to cease to exist. If all other strategies and tactics are unsuccessful, this is the final and most drastic option available. All roles and relationships end with this response.

Pfeffer and Salancik offer response strategies and tactics consistent with those developed by Page. In addition, Pfeffer and Salancik note the importance of trade association activity as a method of limiting the demands of the environment on an organization; and observe that "In spite of the pervasiveness of trade and industry associations, there is remarkably little literature about them" (1978:179). Richards, writing on organizational goal structures, addresses the issue of organization responses to external demands within a strategic management framework. He notes that the initial response to external change by the corporation is resistance or divestment where possible. In addition the firm can use rhetorical support, tactical diversions, environmental co-optation, compliance, proaction, and advocacy (1978:78–82). All of these responses appear consonant with Page's typology.

In addition, Page's response patterns, and interactions between the organization and the government, parallel Preston and Post's notion of interpenetrating systems, where the interpenetrating systems model emphasizes that the various systems are related and that they interact in a variety of ways and processes that the systems themselves shape (1975, Chapter 2). In essence the elements in the system shape their relationships and the process that those relationships will follow.

Finally, the research of Kenneth Thomas (1976) and Gladwin and Walter (1980) on responses and modes of conflict resolution reflect the earlier developments of Thompson and Page. These authors note that management can attempt to overcome the opposition, try to avoid conflict, or accommodate the opposition. The firm can also attempt to collaborate with its opponents or attempt to reach a compromise. Thomas was one of the first researchers to lay out these various options in a managerially useful framework, and many of the tactics and strategies he offers are consistent with Page's developments. Post (1978a) utilized Thomas' model in a comparative analysis of five firms and their approaches to coping with social conflict (the infant formula controversy).

Page's first proposition is of relevance to this area of research, and is well supported in his analysis.

> The resistance of an organization to challenge will take the form of a *patterned behavior sequence* until some sort of compatibility with the environment is restored. The pattern is based on actions that create the least uncertainty for the organization. (1971: 37).

## Stakeholder Analysis

Research in the area of stakeholder analysis and management has grown in recent years. Ansoff (1965), Dill (1976), MacMillan (1978), Rothschild (1976), and Freeman (1980) have all attempted to address the importance of various publics ("stakeholders") on managerial action and discretion. Thompson and Page also worked on this issue. Thompson addressed the stakeholder problem through his analysis of the use of boundary spanning structures, organizational domains, and the assessment criteria used by environmental elements in evaluating organization action (1967:Chapters 3, 6, 7).

Page observed, following Thompson et al. (1959), that business firms are administered organizations and that they exist within and related to an environment. Page builds on the open systems framework of Thompson, noting that the firm has to convert inputs from the environment into outputs. A key factor in this process for Page is the notion of exchange—including exchange with both internal and external elements—to provide support for the organization. In order for these exchanges to take place, there has to be an exchange agreement between the elements. According to Page, this agreement involves what is to be given and received by each participant, both in substantive terms and in behavioral expectations.[3] Page defines these agreements as "roles." Although Thompson does not use the term "role," the essence of this exchange agreement notion is contained in his discussion of domain, dependence, and environment (1967:25–29). Page argues that the organization's behavior in one of its roles can be challenged by a dissatisfied element (or stakeholder) in the environment. This vital element may demand that the organization take on new responsibilities or obligations toward that element, or that the organization give up previous rights. Such a challenge may present a serious threat by being potentially disruptive not only of one role (or exchange agreement) but of other roles as well. To capture this relationship, Page offers a proposition for further study:

> When the demand concerns a social issue, resistance comes about, not particularly because social responsibility as such is resisted or the aims of business are evil by design, but because some, and perhaps all, of the interrelated roles in the role set will have to be readjusted and defined.[5] (1971:27)

This leads to a consideration of how roles become redefined as a result of these challenges. There are four methods by which a redefinition of roles could come about:

1.  Relationships may change gradually by changes in the accepted norms and values of individuals comprising the related groups (e.g., change in mandatory retirement age to 70);
2.  A particular exchange agreement could be redefined over a significant time period by small issues slowly eroding away a set position and effecting change in perceived privileges and obligations (e.g., women in business);
3.  The organization could grow more powerful in relation to an environmental element and force a more advantageous bargain for itself (e.g., growth of General Motors and its relationship to suppliers);
4.  From some element or combination of elements in the environment an issue could arise that threatens the continued functioning of the organization (e.g., Chrysler's situation). (Page, 1971:20–21)

Conceptually, this relationship is shown in Figure 2. Page is developing a composite picture of the business organization. Individuals occupying positions interrelated to other positions by means of roles form sub-units. The interconnection of all these subunits forms the total system (organization). This relationship is dynamic, and is depicted in three "frames" representing the organization's position at sequential points in time in

*Figure 2.* Dynamic Relationship between the Organization and its External Role Set

| *FRAME ONE* | *FRAME TWO* | *FRAME THREE* |
|---|---|---|
| Visible roles set in place. | The role set is disturbed. | Adjustments are made in the role set. |
| Relationship understood and clear and satisfied. | Exchange agreements no longer satisfactory | New exchange agreements entered into with other roles. |
| Support from internal and external elements obtained and secure. | A challenge is posed for the organization to respond to. | The challenge is dealt with in a satisfactory manner. |
| | Requires the organization to act in order to restore equilibrium (i.e., get back to frame one situation). | Equilibrium is restored and support assured. |

TIME ⟶

147

Figure 2. Page is concerned with the processes involved in making the adjustments between frames two and three. How does the firm adapt to challenges that upset exchange agreements already in force? This problem is particularly acute when we consider the multiplicity of exchange agreements an organization has with internal and external elements.

Simply put, Page makes the point that resistance to social issues arises out of corporate concern that its relationship with one or more key stakeholders in its domain will have to be renegotiated in a lengthy, time consuming process. As noted, once the firm engages in this process with one stakeholder, other agreements with other stakeholders may have to be renegotiated as well, and so on in a continuous bargaining process since all the stakeholders are interrelated.

## RECENT CORPORATE RESPONSES TO SOCIAL ISSUES

Gatewood and Carroll (1981) have investigated the response of three corporations to three very difficult issues with large social impact. The three firms and issues are Procter and Gamble, and Rely Tampons; Firestone and the 500 series of steel-belted tires; and Ford and the Pinto. My own investigation of the chemical industry's response to recent superfund legislation (Mahon, 1981) provides an additional example of recent corporate action for study in the light of the analytical scheme set forth here.

The superfund legislation that became public law in 1980 was subjected to intense debate starting in January 1979. The legislation was designed to provide a fund ($2.6 billion) to pay for the clean up of hazardous waste sites. The monies for the fund were to be raised from taxes on the chemical and petroleum industries, with the bulk of the funds coming from the chemical industry. The chemical industry's initial response to proposed superfund legislation was that the hazardous waste problem was not severe and that the scope of the problem was not well known. In addition, they argued that the problem was really the result of behavior of unconscionable midnight haulers and other unscrupulous people and efforts should be made to punish the guilty parties. As Robert Roland (1979), president of the Chemical Manufacturers Association, noted:

> One of the things that we must all realize in discussing the solid-waste disposal problem, including toxic or hazardous wastes, is that it is not just the problem of the chemical industry. It is a result of society's advanced technology and pursuit of an increasingly complex lifestyle.

Later, Roland was even more specific.

> The administration's bill unfairly singles out the chemical and related industries to bear a disproportionate burden of clean-up costs. In doing so, it fails to adequately reflect the society's responsibility for resolving a problem which everyone has helped create and for whose solution everyone should help pay. (*Chemical and Engineering News,* June 25, 1979)

The chemical industry attempted to deflect criticism and to deny the necessity of this type of legislation arguing that current laws were sufficient and that any large superfund would cause severe economic damage to the industry and to individual firms. The industry group also advocated different (and less expensive) legislation focused on the problems of *abandoned* waste sites.

> Robert A. Roland, CMA President, said the association considers the superfund approach to be a "one-shot panacea which unwisely imposes economic burdens on companies that did not create the problems which superfund attempts to address". And he stressed that the industry is "on record" in favor of a new law specifically dealing with abandoned dumpsites. (*Chemical Week,* September 5, 1979:19)

In addition to these public statements, the chemical industry launched a $6 million public relations campaign to point out the positive side of the chemical industry. All this was in vain, as Congress eventually passed superfund into law. After the passage of the bill, the CMA noted that they would do their best to make it work and that it reflected the intense work that the CMA put into this legislation.

The Gatewood and Carroll (1981) piece provides similar patterns involving three different firms in three different industries. Their analysis of the Proctor and Gamble handling of Rely shows that the firm first argued that there was no correlation between toxic shock and their tampon, and that their in-house tests supported this conclusion. When the Center for Disease Control announced publicly that Rely was a major element in toxic shock, the firm argued that the information and data was too limited and fragmentary for any conclusions to be drawn. In addition, Procter and Gamble protested that exhaustive coverage in the news media biased the results, that the data were inaccurate and the interviewing techniques suspect.

However, Procter and Gamble halted production of Rely and eventually withdrew the product from the market. But this did not occur until after Harness, the chairman and executive noted that he was:

> . . . determined to fight for a brand, to keep an important brand from being hurt by insufficient data in the hands of a bureaucracy. (Rotbart and Prestbo, 1980:21)

When Procter and Gamble did withdraw the product, Harness observed that:

This is being done despite the fact that we know of no defect in Rely tampons and despite evidence that the withdraw of Rely won't eliminate the occurrence of toxic shock syndrome. (Procter and Gamble News Release, September 22, 1980)

Firestone's handling of the 500 series tire is very similar. Firestone's initial arguments were that there was nothing wrong with the tire and that any problems were caused by customer abuse. The firm constantly tried to block investigations of its tire and publicly questioned the motives of the investigators. The organization deflected requests for more detailed information on the grounds that it would cost a great deal of money and require a large amount of time and effort. Eventually, Firestone was compelled to initiate what was to become one of the largest recalls in history.*

Ford's response to the investigation surrounding the Pinto was also similar, but far more sophisticated. Ford lobbied against federal standards which would have forced the redesign of the Pinto gas tank for over eight years. Their tactics involved offering arguments successively that could only be worked on one at a time, arguing that the problem was the people not cars and ". . . accompanying each argument, no matter how ridiculous, with thousands of pages of highly technical assertions that would take the government months or, preferably, years to treat." (Gatewood and Carroll, 1981:14)

Even after the Federal Government proved that auto fires were a real and growing problem, Ford countered with a new position: There were auto fires, but rear end collisions rarely happen. Later Ford would argue that regardless of fire, people would have died anyway from the force of the impact. In the later stages of the disagreement, Henry Ford warned, "If we can't meet the standards when they are published, we will have to close down," for example, adopt Page's ultimate strategy. (Dowei, 1977:54)

## CONCLUSIONS

The four incidents reviewed here amply demonstrate that Page's strategies and tactics are relevant to an analysis of the business-government relationships that exist today. The chemical industry at first resisted, using tactics shown in Figure 1, then began to bargain and finally capitulated. This pattern is repeated in the Procter and Gamble, Firestone, and Ford situations. It does seem true that firms will move only when pushed. This "pushing" may, as these short cases demonstrate, involve time and constant pressure on the firm to obtain some movement.

*See additional analysis of the Firestone 500 experience in the essay by Elliot Zashin in this volume. Ed.

From a managerial perspective, all of these firms, with the exception of Procter and Gamble, incurred some additional negative costs. Although these costs in some instances are difficult to measure, they are nonetheless real. The chemical industry's actions severely damaged their political image in Congress and publicly embarrassed their supporters. We can only speculate, but it seems logical to assume that their credibility will be lowered as Congress begins debates this year on Clean Air and Clean Water Act amendments.

Firestone is still suffering from the court cases, congressional hearings and bad press over the 500 tire issue. Their share of the market has fallen by one-half of one percent, a loss that amounts to millions of dollars (Louis, 1978:45). Ford has discontinued the Pinto line and announced last year a major loss in North American sales which they attributed to the publicity surrounding the Pinto case.

The only firm to realize any positive gain from a publicly embarrassing situation was Procter and Gamble. They realized an increase in favorable public attitude following the removal of Rely from the market (Rotbart and Prestbo, 1980:21). These gains came as they proceeded through Page's response patterns. After Procter and Gamble admitted that there might be a problem, they followed up with positive action. They pledged research expertise to investigate toxic shock, financed and directed an education program about the disease and issued a warning to women not to use Rely. Thus, instead of merely claiming that they were good citizens, they backed up their position with concrete action. They capitulated, it is true, but they also sought exoneration through enhancing their prestige and promoting their own social responsibility.

The Thompson-Page research into social issues has gone largely unnoticed. Their analysis is important to several current areas of inquiry and it demonstrates that Thompson's theoretical contributions could be useful in empirical studies. The Thompson-Page research should thus be in the mainstream of current investigations in the social issues in management areas.

# ACKNOWLEDGMENT

The author wishes to thank Professor Paul J. Gordon of Indiana University for bringing Page's work to his attention.

# NOTES

1. J.P. Stevens' battle with unionization attempts may be a classic example of a firm following a long pattern of resistance to challenges from the environment. This particular example may also demonstrate the futility of a strategy of resistance in the face of committed opponents prepared to wage a lengthy battle.

2.  See Post and Mahon (1980) for an analysis of a situation where an industry made threats that resulted in extremely adverse reactions by other elements in the environment.

3.  This link between behavioral expectations and organizational performance aligns closely with Post's (1978b) model of Status—Behavior—Performance.

4.  Post and Mellis's (1978) investigation of Polaroid's response to the women's movement is another excellent example of the dynamics of Page's proposition.

# REFERENCES

Ackerman, R. W., *The Social Challenge To Business.* Cambridge, MA: Harvard University Press, 1975.

Ackerman, R. W., and R. Bauer, *Corporate Social Responsiveness: The Modern Dilemma.* Reston, VA: Reston Publishing, 1976.

Adams, J. S., "The Structures and Dynamics of Behavior in Organizational Boundary Roles." In M. Dunnette (ed.), *Handbook of Organizational and Industrial Psychology,* Chicago: Rand McNally, 1976.

Aldrich, L., and D. Herker, "Boundary Spanning Roles and Organizational Structure." *Academy of Management Review* 2(1977):217–230.

Ansoff, H. I., *Corporate Strategy.* New York: McGraw-Hill, 1965.

Avery, R. W., "James D. Thompson: A Memorial." *Administrative Science Quarterly* 19(1974):3–4.

Bauer, R., "The Corporate Response Process." In L. Preston (ed.), *Research in Corporate Social Performance and Policy,* vol. 1. Greenwich, CT: JAI Press, 1978; pp. 99–122.

Bauer, R., I. Pool, and L. Dexter, *American Business and Public Policy: The Politics of Foreign Trade.* New York: Atherton Press, 1964.

*Chemical, and Engineering News,* "Bill Proposes Hazardous Waste Cleanup Fund." (June 25, 1979):27.

*Chemical Week,* "CMA Blasts Superfund Plan on Dump Cleanups." (September 5, 1979):19.

Dill, W., "Strategic Management in Kibitzer's World." In H. Ansoff, R. Declerck, and R. Hayes (eds.), *From Strategic Planning to Strategic Management,* New York: Wiley, 1976.

Dowei, M., "How Ford Put two Million Firetraps on Wheels," *Business and Society Review* 23(Fall 1977):26–55.

Emshoff, J., and R. Freeman, "Who's Butting Into Your Business." *The Wharton Magazine* 4(1979):44–48ff.

Epstein, E., *The Corporation in American Politics.* Englewood Cliffs: Prentice-Hall, 1969.

———, "The Dimensions of Corporate Power." Part 1, *California* Management Review 16(1973):9–23.

———, "The Dimensions of Corporate Power." Part 2, *California Management Review* 16(1974):32–47.

———, "Firm Size and Structure, Market Power and Business Political Influence: A Review of the Literature." Paper presented at the Bureau of Economics of the Federal Trade Commission Conference on the Economics of Firm Size, Market Structure and Social Performance. Rosslyn, VA:(January 17–18, 1980).

———, "Business Political Activity: Research Approaches and Analytical Issues." In L. Preston (ed.), *Research in Corporate Social Performance and Policy,* vol. 2, Greenwich, CT: JAI Press, 1980; 1–56.

Freeman, E., "Stakeholder Theory and Strategic Management." Paper presented at the Academy of Management Meeting. Detroit: (August, 1980).

Galbraith, J. K., *The New Industrial State.* Boston: Houghton Mifflin, 1967.

Galbraith, J. K., and D. Nathanson, *Strategy Implementation: The Role of Structure and Process.* New York: West, 1978.

Gatewood E., and A. Carroll, "The Anatomy of Corporate Social Response: The Rely, Firestone 500, and Pinto Cases." *Business Horizons 24(1981):9–16.*

Gladwin, T., and I. Walter, "How Multinationals Can Manage Social and Political Forces." *The Journal of Business Strategy* 1(1980):54–68.

Hofer, C., and D. Schendel, *Strategy Formulation: Analytical Concepts.* New York: West, 1978.

Lindblom, C., *The Policy Making Process.* Englewood Cliffs, NJ: Prentice-Hall, 1968.

———, *Politics and Markets: The World's Political-Economic System.* New York: Basic Books, 1977.

Louis, A., "Lessons From the Firestone Fracas." *Fortune* (August 28, 1978):45.

MacMillan, I., *Strategy Formulation: Political Concepts.* New York: West, 1978.

Mahon, J. F., *The Corporate Public Affairs Office: Structure, Process and Impact.* Doctoral Dissertation. Boston University, 1981.

McNeil, K., and J. Thompson, "The Regeneration of Social Organizations." *American Sociological Review* 36(1971):624–637.

Miles, R., "Role Conflict in Boundary and Internal Organizational Roles." Unpublished manuscript, Yale University, 1975.

———, "Organizational Boundary Roles." In G. Cooper, and R. Payne (eds.), *Current Concerns in Occupational Stress,* London: Wiley, 1980.

Murray, E., *The Implementation of Social Policies in Commercial Banks.* Doctoral Dissertation. Harvard University, 1974.

Page, R., *Organizational Response to Social Challenge: Theory and Evidence for Two Industries.* Doctoral dissertation. Indiana University, 1971.

Pfeffer, J., and G. Salancik, *The External Control of Organizations.* New York: Harper and Row, 1978.

Post, J., *Risk and Response: Management and Social Change in the American Insurance Industry.* Lexington, MA: D.C. Heath, 1976.

———, *Corporate Behavior and Social Change.* Reston, VA: Reston, 1978.

———, "Research on Patterns of Corporate Response to Social Change." In L. Preston (ed.), *Research in Corporate Social Performance and Policy,* vol. 1. Greenwich, CT: JAI Press, 1978; pp. 55–78.

Post, J., and M. Mellis, "Corporate Responsiveness and Organizational Learning." *California Management Review* 20(1978):57–63.

Post, J., and E. Baer, "Analyzing Complex Policy Problems: The Social Performance of the International Infant Formula Industry." In L. Preston (ed.), *Research in Corporate Social Performance and Policy,* vol. 2. Greenwich, CT: JAI Press, 1980; 157–196.

Post, J., and J. Mahon, "Articulated Turbulence: The Effect of Regulatory Agencies on Corporate Response to Social Change." *Academy of Management Review* 5(1980):399–407.

Preston, L., "Corporation and Society: The Search for a Paradigm." *Journal of Economic Literature* 13(1975):434–453.

———, "Corporate Social Performance and Policy: A Synthetic Framework for Research and Analysis." In L. Preston (ed.), *Research in Corporate Social Performance and Policy,* vol. 1. Greenwich, CT: JAI Press, 1978; pp. 1–26.

Preston, L., and J. Post, *Private Management and Public Policy.* Englewood Cliffs, NJ: Prentice-Hall, 1975.

Richards, M., *Organizational Goal Structures.* New York: West, 1978.

Roland, R., "Toxic Scapegoats." *Washington Post* (April 2, 1979):15.

Rotbart, D., and J. Prestbo, "Killing a Product." *Wall Street Journal* (November 3, 1980):21.

Rothschild, W., *Putting It All Together*. New York: AMACOM, 1976.

Sethi, S., *Up Against the Corporate Wall: Modern Corporations and Social Issues of the Seventies*. Englewood Cliffs, NJ: Prentice-Hall, 1971.

————, "Corporate Social Audit: An Emerging Trend in Measuring Corporate Social Performance." In D. Votaw, and S. Sethi (eds.), *The Corporate Dilemma: Traditional Values Versus Contemporary Problems*, Englewood Cliffs, NJ: Prentice-Hall, 1973.

————, "Dimensions of Corporate Social Performance: An Analytical Framework for Measurement and Evolution." *California Management Review* 17(1975):58–64.

————, "An Analytical Framework for Making Cross-Cultural Comparisons of Business Responses to Social Pressures: The Case of Japan and the United States." In L. Preston (ed.), *Research in Corporate Social Performance and Policy*, vol. 1. Greenwich, CT: JAI Press, 1978:pp. 27–54.

Taylor, B., "Managing the Process of Corporate Development." In B. Taylor, and J. Sparkes (eds.), *Corporate Strategy and Planning*, New York: Wiley, 1977.

Thomas, K., "Conflict and Conflict Management." In M. Dunnette (ed.), *Handbook of Industrial and Organizational Psychology*, Chicago: Rand McNally, 1976.

Thompson, J., *Organizations In Action*. New York: McGraw-Hill, 1967.

————, "Society's Frontiers for Organizing Activities." *Public Administration Review* 33(1973):327–335.

————, "Social Interdependence, The Polity and Public Administration." *Administration and Society* 6(1974):3–20.

————, "Technology, Polity, and Societal Development." *Administrative Science Quarterly* 19(1974):6–21.

Thompson, J., P. Hammond, R. Hawkes, B. Junker, and A. Tuden, *Comparative Studies in Administration*. Pittsburgh: University of Pittsburgh Press, 1959.

# RADICAL MODELS OF THE BUSINESS-GOVERNMENT RELATIONSHIP

David Jacobs

The business literature on the relationship between government and corporations has often been concerned with the ways that private enterprise is controlled by the state and the strategies that can be developed to avoid these controls. Research in other social science disciplines has generally dealt with the opposite link between business and government. Marxists and social scientists with a less radical bent in disciplines such as sociology and political science have spent more time on the question of how modern corporations affect political institutions. An emphasis on this aspect of the interdependent relationship between business and the state rests on the assumption that the huge resources of the modern corporation can be readily translated into political influence. If that assumption is correct, it is natural to pay attention to the political impact of the modern corporation because the resources of these organizations are so vast in comparison with the resources of all of the other potential participants in the political arena.

Because the relationship between corporate resources and political influence is an important question, these matters have inspired much debate. But, attempts to deal with these issues have been handicapped by the lack of comprehensive theories (Preston, 1975). One result is that most of these discussions have an ad hoc quality. According to Kuhn, in his seminal work on the philosophy of science, a good theory focuses attention on the exact questions that must be answered if understanding is to increase. Without shared assumptions imposed by theory, the parties in scientific disputes generally talk past one another, In this situation, the hidden agenda of most debates is definitional while the evidence that is used to support one position frequently can be used to validate others. It follows that even flawed attempts to develop theoretical perspectives on the relationships between corporations and the state should be of great interest to students of business and government because verifiable theories are the basis of scientific progress.

Recently new interest in this area has been stimulated by Neo-Marxist attempts to develop comprehensive models of business-government relationships. Because these new perspectives can be used to broaden our understanding and because they offer the promise of further development, Charles Lindblom (1982) in his presidential address to the American Political Science Association called for a new awareness of Neo-Marxist work on the relationship between business enterprise and the state in capitalist democracies.

Therefore, an accessible survey of this work should be a worthwhile endeavor. In this essay I will review these new perspectives with particular emphasis on the ways that they can be used to enhance our knowledge of the political role of the modern corporation. Two criteria will be used to evaluate these incipient theories. First, what is their intuitive appeal? Second, to what extent can they be tested? This article will conclude with a final section on the inherent tradeoffs involved in the various methodological tests that can be applied to neo-Marxist and other perspectives on government and business.

# NEO-MARXIST THEORIES OF THE STATE

*Historical Origins: The Failings of Elitism*

If we are to understand the current debate, it will be necessary to look briefly at the starting point. Although there were differences in emphasis, before 1970 there was only one major radical view of the state in American social science, and it is here that we should begin our survey.

Elitists started with the premise that there was a consciously organized upper class that dominated American politics. This view was not Marxist since ownership or control over the means of production was not emphasized. Rather than focus on control of productive resources, in what was probably the most important work on elitism, C. Wright Mills argued that corporate leadership was only one of the many ways to enter what he called the "power elite." Thus, lawyers from prestigious firms, generals, and the presidents of established universities were seen as equal participants in the activities of this tightly organized class. What counted for Mills and the other elitists (Hunter, 1963; Domhoff, 1967) was (1) the proper social background which allowed men to reach eminent positions in various hierarchies, and (2) the close interpersonal links between members which allowed this established elite to control all political decisions that mattered.

Some elitists put greater emphasis on economic resources (Hunter, 1963; Lynd and Lynd, 1929; 1937) but the connection between economic and political domination was never carefully delineated. Much greater emphasis was placed on personal interactions between members. Thus, shared experiences and the contacts established at the "right" schools allowed people with the correct family backgrounds to join an organized political *and* social elite which used their combined influence to control all important political outcomes.

It was not difficult to generate plausible criticisms of this view. To political moderates, elitism seemed to be a sophisticated exercise in conspiracy theory. This criticism was not refuted by the evidence that elitists used to support their case. At the national level, elitists appeared to be guilty of eclecticism. Disparate facts were gathered but one often had the sense that only part of the evidence was being presented, and that those facts which were presented sometimes could be interpreted in other ways.

In addition to sampling bias imposed by ideological preconceptions, the individual interests of members of the elite presented fundamental problems. Why should the CEO of a corporation engaged in automobile manufacturing or the president of an Ivy League college care about price supports on milk or the taxes paid by the drug industry? In both instances, attention to the parochial interests of one's own organization would seem to be immensely more profitable. Yet a central tenet of elitism held that the power elite controlled all decisions that mattered. Thus, even before Olson's (1966) seminal work on the distinction between individual and collective interests had appeared, it seemed difficult to believe that members of a power elite would neglect important personal interests in order to spend valuable time on matters that often would be only distantly related to their private goals.

Other criticisms were generated by the left. To Marxists, the picture painted by elitists seemed to be too individualistic and ahistoric. Rather than think in terms of idiosyncratic relationships between individuals which were based on shifting resources, Marxists sought less eclectic and more historical explanations for the economic basis of the power of the dominant class. The neo-Marxist view of politics also began to be colored by a core dilemma in Marxist thought.

According to sacred texts, the socialist revolution was an inevitable consequence of the inconsistencies that were fundamental to capitalism. However, it became increasingly difficult to defend this view. By the middle of this century, it was apparent that autonomous socialist revolutions did not seem to occur in nations where capitalism was most advanced.

One intuitively appealing way to account for the persistence of capitalism involved the political sophistication of the dominant class. If this class were clever enough to allow mild reforms, capitalism could be temporarily sustained. This view required that the ruling class be willing to give ground when it was expedient. But the notion that a power elite controls all political outcomes so that they are consistent with its own short run interests, as many elitists seemed to believe, conflicts directly with a strategy of short-run accommodation for long-run survival.

The emphasis on politics as a way to sustain capitalism also demanded that the existing political order be perceived as legitimate by important majorities even though these majorities were being exploited according to Marxist thought. Given the contradictory relationship between their actual circumstances and the positive attitudes of workers about the legitimacy of existing arragements, the exploitive nature of these arangements could not be transparent. But if a power elite was able to control all political outcomes and guarantee that these outcomes were in accord with its interests, this domination should be obvious to vital majorities; and capitalism would no longer be tenable. In any society in which some get more than others, effective mechanisms for retaining the allegiance of the have-nots must be present. Because Marxists held that capitalism was an unnatural system that should have collapsed already, these mechanisms were particularly vital to a Marxist view of politics in advanced capitalism. Elitism offered no solution for the dilemma.

Now that the historical origins have been described we can turn to the first of recent neo-Marxist attempts to develop theories about the relationships between the capitalist state and the corporations.

## Instrumentalism Versus Structuralism

By the beginning of the 1970s several new developments became apparent. Some of the more extreme European Marxists had been arguing that the persistence of capitalism was due to a fusion between the monopolistic corporations and the state which used force to preserve the conditions for capitalistic accumulation (for a detailed summary in English see Jessop, 1982. For a critical review see Poulantzas 1969; 1973). In contrast to American elitism, this view at least provided hypotheses about the economic foundations of political domination, but it was not easily believed when economic reforms and the relative absence of coercion in advanced capitalism were considered. The fact that this perspective could be used to generate falsifiable hypotheses also made some

Marxists uneasy (Bierne, 1979). In response to the inadequacies of both American elitism and European notions of the state as the property of "monopoly capital," a new perspective began to emerge.

The first task for the proponents of this new perspective was to find a convenient label for the opposition. This was accomplished by going back to the original texts. At one point in his writings Marx had clearly stated a central tenet of the opposition's case when he argued that the state is but an *instrument* of the ruling class. Because both elitists and the radical European Marxists who emphasized the fusion between the state and "monopoly capital," appeared to believe that the state was completely controlled by the ascendant class, *instrumentalism* seemed to be a reasonable label for both points of view.

The political imagery adopted to handle the anomalous persistence of capitalism perspective involved the implicit use of what is commonly known as system theory. If capitalism was still around when it should not be, perhaps the reason was that the state acted to regulate this unstable system and thereby reduce or ameliorate the harmful effects of the inherent contradictions in capitalism. According to this new perspective, which came to be known as *structuralism*, the state acted as an autonomous entity that was not controlled by any group of capitalists. Instead, politicians in office and state bureaucrats were seen as having long run interests in the survival of existing political and economic arrangements. Therefore, when it was necessary, office holders could act against the parochial, short run interests of some corporations to introduce reforms that would help to insure that capitalism would survive (for initial statements see the early works of Poulantzas, 1977; 1978; Althusser, 1977. For a sympathetic review without jargon see Gold et al., 1975).

At first glance this new formulation appeared to represent a giant step forward. It helped to explain why the predicted demise of capitalism was so late in coming. It also seemed intuitively plausible that office-holders and public administrators had their own independent interests and the necessary autonomy to express these interests in public policies. With this view in mind, the reforms introduced by the American New Deal or the various socialist parties in Europe could be explained without violating Marxist dogma about the nature of politics in advanced capitalism. Thus, while segments of business might have various short run interests that were inimical to the survival of the capitalist system, office holders occupying a position above the day-to-day contest for profits could introduce selective reforms that would allow capitalism and the generation of profits to continue.

The structuralist perspective was enthusiastically received, but there is a fundamental flaw in the underlying logic that is instructive to anyone who is tempted to use what social scientists call system theory. It is absolutely vital to the scientific method that theories be stated in a way that allows them to be disproved. No theory can ever be proven; all that can be done is to deduce narrow predictions from a theory and see if these predictions are true. But even if predictions from the same theory are confirmed an infinite number of times, the theory in question still cannot be regarded as proven because its predictions could always be right for the wrong reasons. An infinite number of other theories may exist which could generate the same predictions and it never will be possible to eliminate all of these potential alternative theories. As Popper (1965) pointed out, all that can be done in science is to refute a theory by showing that predictions based on it are false. Therefore, the scientific method requires that conceptual formulations be stated so they can be disconfirmed.

But as long as structuralists hold that the state acts independently with *any set of policies* to preserve capitalism, then *any* political outcome can be used as evidence for this systemic orientation. If, for example, a political outcome hurts workers and the poor while helping the largest corporations, then a structuralist can argue that the state is acting to sustain existing arrangements because such outcomes preserve the unequal relationships that are fundamental to capitalism. If, on the other hand, the state acts to help the subordinate classes while hurting the largest corporations, a structuralist still can argue that capitalism is being sustained because these political outcomes legitimize current economic and political arrangements while undercutting dissident justifications for actions against the existing order. No matter what happens, structuralism remains intact. This tautological quality means that structuralism is not very useful and it also may help to explain why so many Marxists found it so beguiling. It simply could not be refuted.

It is important to note that this objection does not apply to some variants of instrumentalism. The term ''monopoly'' refers to diminished competition. Therefore, if European instrumentalists are correct and the state is controlled by private monopolies, firms operating in less competitive markets ought to obtain favorable political outcomes. There are several plausible reasons for believing this hypothesis. First, participation in an uncompetitive industry allows a firm to charge higher prices (Scherer, 1980) and, as long as controls on costs are maintained, this condition should result in heightened profits (for summaries of the statistical evidence for this relationship see Vernon, 1972; Weiss, 1971). Because those who seek elected office are constantly in need of money, it is not difficult to believe that exchanges of mutual benefit between corporations and candidates take place. Thus, Pittman (1976; 1977) found that campaign contributions were more likely to come from executives employed by firms in uncompetitive industries, while Mann and McCormick found that lobbying expenditures were greater when firms faced uncompetitive markets. It should also be less difficult for firms to act together to achieve political ends when sales in an industry are controlled by a few firms, because it will not be as easy to free ride and benefit from rewards won by others (Olson, 1966).

Investigations that examined political *outcomes* such as taxation and tariffs have not supported either the profitability or the organizational hypotheses. Salamon and Siegfried (1977) for example, found that federal taxes paid by firms in an industry were *lower* when an industry was uncompetitive, while Jacobs (1983) found no connection between four different measures of competition and property tax rates on manufacturing. Research on tariffs designed to protect industries from foreign competition also has not supported the hypothesis that political outcomes will be more favorable to firms in less competitive industries. Neither Caves (1976) nor McPherson (1972) could find a relationship between concentration and heightened import barriers. Thus, even though there is evidence that firms in less competitive industries spend more to influence political outcomes, there is not much quantitative evidence that they are successful.

However, instrumental Marxists may be referring to the size of corporations, not to concentration, when they use the term "monopoly." Marxists are often less than precise when they employ economic terms, so this interpretation cannot be ruled out. A close relationship between size and political influence also seems plausible for several reasons. First, successful attempts to influence political outcomes probably involve significant fixed costs. It is unlikely, for example, that the relationship between expenditures on lobbying or political advertising is linear. Limited expenditures probably have no effect, but once a significant threshold is reached, both activities may become quite useful. Therefore, it is reasonable to believe that the large enterprise will be more able to afford the minimum outlays that will be required for effectiveness. A second justification for a hypotheses that size matters concerns resources that already are present. The large firm with attorneys, public relations experts and executives with extensive political contacts can participate effectively in politics at a reasonable cost, because these useful tools have already been acquired (Useem, 1982).

Some empirical evidence supports the hypothesis that large firms will be most likely to attain their political goals. Siegfried, for example, found that the *size* of the median firm in an industry was inversely related to effective national tax rates on the entire industry, while Salamon and Siegfried (1977) reported that excise tax rates on motor fuels were reduced in states where the petroleum industry was dominated by large firms. Jacobs (1983) found that regions with the largest manufacturing enterprises had lower property taxes on manufacturing. Thus, the corporate size version of instrumentalism has not been refuted. Although the instrumentalists probably overstate their case when they argue that the state always is controlled by the largest firms, we need more quantitative results that will let us identify the exact circumstances when this condition does and does not hold.

Regardless of the other inadequacies of instrumentalism those variants which are relatively specific about the economic resources that lead to political power can be used to generate falsifiable hypotheses. By contrast, the structuralist alternative to instrumentalism relies on systemic or functional logic, and its hypotheses are not falsifiable. That omission means that the structuralist perspective is of questionable worth. Plastic conceptualizations that can be stretched to fit any outcome often generate great initial enthusiasm, but their appeal tends to be short-lived. Perhaps that explains why new formulations of greater interest to non-Marxists who are not puzzled by the continued existence of capitalism have appeared even after the structural alternative became popular.

## Class Theories of the State

It is worth remembering that one of the main Marxist criticisms of elitism was that this perspective did not take history into account. But neither structuralists nor instrumentalists are in a position to find fault on this matter. Instrumental Marxists appear to believe that, regardless of the historical circumstances, the capitalist state inevitably will be controlled by the powerful corporations; structuralists hold that the state invariably acts as an autonomous thermostat which continually readjusts the capitalist system. There is no room in either perspective for the unique interplay of historically contingent events. This is unfortunate because, as Marx pointed out, men do not make history under conditions of their own choosing. Instead, contemporary political actors are constrained by the organizational residues of past struggles which have left the institutions and rules that control present and future events.

This omission of history in the prior theories led to the development of class conflict perspecitves of the state (for statements see Esping-Anderson et al., 1976; Block, 1977; Offe, 1976). In this view, political outcomes and the organization of the state are the result of an ever changing contest between the subordinate classes and the corporations. The economically ascendant will have an automatic edge in this contest, of course, but their supremacy will never be complete. Because capitalism is assumed to be inherently unstable, all attempts to resolve the contradictory forces at work in the system can only result in temporary solutions. It follows that workers and other subordinate groups will never be completely neutralized or totally co-opted. In periods of crises such as depressions when confidence in capitalism is diminished or in wars where dependence on the support of workers is enhanced, explicit or implicit bargains must be struck with workers and their allies; but when labor is weakened, the necessity to reach such accords will be greatly reduced. Thus, the actions of the state can be represented as a vector diagram where the strength of the unequal contestants is weighted by historically unique events which act in concert to determine how political disputes will be resolved.

There is much that is commendable in this interactional model. Even if Marxist economics is flawed and capitalism is dynamic rather than unstable (Schumpeter, 1936), a treatment of history as the result of ongoing conflicts between the haves and the have-nots captures a fundamental element of political reality (Lasswell, 1936; Key, 1949). All that is required to use this view is an acceptance of the plausible notion that an unequal access to economic resources has important effects on politics in advanced capitalist democracies. This perspecitve is not limited to an assumption that reality can only be described as a fixed sum game where one party's benefits must result in equivalent losses by the other contestant. Often, both parties can realize gains by agreeing to pass on the costs of their accommodation to unrepresented third parties. To acquire a contented and malleable labor force, for example, management can agree to wage increases in concentrated industries because the costs can be conveniently passed on to unorganized consumers (statistical evidence for this is provided by Dalton and Ford, 1977; Jenny, 1978). The history of business tax legislation and labor law is filled with equivalent compromises (Lowi, 1964).

But there are additional criteria that a theory should meet. Because the class perspective operates at such a high level of abstraction with elements borrowed from other perspectives, it is difficult to use it as a unique source of falsifiable hypotheses. For example, both the class conflict and instrumental positions hold that political contests between the corporations and their adversaries will not be equal, so a finding that the corporations often win can be used to support either view. Although it is not easy to develop a crucial test of the class perspective, this perspective does offer some implicit instructions as to how quantitative research should be conducted. First, an emphasis on history calls for longitudinal analyses of the political process. Second, an emphasis on the interactional nature of politics suggests that statistical investigations into the determinants of outcomes should employ measures of the strength of both the corporations and their opponents. Third, an emphasis on the effects of idiosyncratic historical events which combine to produce unique outcomes implies that quantitative analyses should be designed to look for statistical interaction (for examples of time series analyses of the political process that begin to meet some of these criteria see Snyder, 1975; Synder and Kelly, 1976; Griffin et al., 1982; 1983; Frey and Schneider, 1978; and Devine, 1983).

However, there are some unanswered questions associated with the class struggle imagery. One central issue that has not been discussed in sufficient detail concerns the precise ways that class interests are aggregated to form an internally consistent set of demands. There has been much recent work on this subject by neo-Marxists. One major research stream has attempted to demonstrate that corporate executives and board members act as a consciously organized class to realize their political aims.

The most rigorous approach to this issue has not proven to be very fruitful. Elegant mathematical models have been constructed to map the intercorporate networks that are generated when executives and board members from one firm sit on the boards of others (Mariolis, 1975; Mintz and Schwartz, 1981; Mizruchi, 1982). Unfortunately, the findings have not allowed us to examine the political impact of the resulting networks because investigators generally have used dissimilar mathematical techniques applied to data collected at different times. Until indentical measures are constructed from data collected at a sufficient number of equal intervals, or until measures of the network characteristics of enough comparable industries or regions are available, it will not be possible to gauge the relationship between these linkages and political outcomes. Thus, while there is much plausible speculation about the political effects of interlocks between corporations, no empirical documentation of their consequences has yet appeared (Aldrich, 1979).

Other investigators have used less rigorous methods to examine the political organization of corporate elites. In an article on transportation policy that was informed by the class perspective, Whitt used intensive interviews with executives to examine the organization of corporate interests. He found that business leaders generally reached a consensus about public issues before the corporate case was presented to the politicians. Thus, even though the resulting compromise may have hurt some firms, Whitt claims that unanimity frequently was imposed before lobbying and other political activities were begun.

In another article that used similar techniques, Useem (1982) developed an argument that may account for the apparent inconsistency between the personal and class interests of executives. Recall that if the previously discussed class or elite theories are correct, corporate actors must be willing to spend scarce time on wider systemic matters that frequently will not appear to be relevant to the parochial interests of their firms. Useem begins his effort to account for this anomaly with the well-established axiom that business organizations must constantly strive to reduce uncertainties in their external environment (March and Simon, 1958; Thompson, 1967). One way to accomplish this is to develop methods to "scan" important aspects of the organization's environment. Thus, the senior executives in Useem's sample saw participation on the boards of firms in different industries and service in the government as a vital way to gain useful knowledge about business conditions. Useem's respondents also believed that attempts to use these contacts to pursue the private interests of one's firm are not acceptable. Therefore, he argued that intra-class conflicts tend to be suppressed because selfish behavior results in exclusion from these important networks. Useem goes on to claim that these interactions between executives lead to a common framework that is applied to most problems. The result, according to Useem, is substantial consensus about political matters among senior executives employed by the largest corporations.

Some statistical work that is relevant to the class perspective on the state also has appeared. In an original analysis that ultimately was not convincing, Hicks et al. (1978) attempted to demonstrate that the political resources of the largest corporations are used to interfere with redistributive public policies in the American states. Unfortunately, the factor scores that were used to gauge the political strength of workers and management were highly correlated (.85) so the resulting regression coefficients cannot be trusted. In any case, a supposition that the largest corporations use their considerable resources at the state level to interfere with the political interests of the least affluent is difficult to justify on substantitive grounds. Since these enterprises will be better able to shift increased costs forward to consumers, the comparatively small taxes that are levied by the states should not be terribly important to them. Research on decisions about the location of new plants, for example, shows that state tax differentials have little impact (Bloom, 1955; Thompson and Mittila, 1959). Other work shows that workers and the poor often do worse politically in states with *smaller* enterprises. Jacobs (1978) found that labor legislation was less favorable to workers in states with more small businesses while Jacobs and Waldman (1983) showed that the total incidence of taxation was more regressive in states where small firms predominate.

Additional statistical investigations have attempted to develop generalities about the political cohesion of workers. In contrast to the neoclassical treatment of strikes as a breakdown in bargaining found in the economics literature, Synder (1975) and Synder and Kelly (1976) present time series regressions which show that strikes often occur in response to purely political conditions. After looking at the prewar and postwar determinants of work stoppages in France, Italy and the United States, they conclude that when labor relations are not institutionalized and union recognition is problematic, strikes frequently are used by workers to influence the political system. Other work has attempted to gauge the political impact of racial cleavages among workers. In a test of historical analyses developed by Bonacich (1976) and Key (1949) and Jacobs (1978) found that when there are more blacks in a state, and workers are divided on racial grounds, labor legislation, as measured by right-to-work laws and unemployment compensation, is least likely to be favorable to workers. This finding remained when the southern states were removed from the analyses. Thus, some empirical research has begun to describe how the interests of workers are translated into political outcomes, but much more needs to be done on this subject.

However, the version of class theory that has been presented assumes that political influence can be won only through organization. What has been implicit in the preceeding discussion is an assumption that without cohesion and the resulting ability to engage in coordinated political activities, the political interests of corporate elites or their opponents cannot be expressed in legislation. But there is an important version of the class perspective on the capitalist state which holds that political organization is unnecessary. This version also deals with a major difficulty in the prior formulations, and it is well worth some discussion.

## Class Politics without Class Organization: Unbalanced Exchange Theories of the State

In a seminal article that was partly based on Offe's (1976) work, Block (1977) developed a perspective on the state which identifies business investment as a major determinant of political outcomes (for a similar argument by a non-Marxist, see Lindblom, 1977). Block starts with the premise that elected office holders in capitalistic democracies will be highly dependent on reasonable levels of economic activity, but that activity will be subject to the independent investment decisions of private investors. In the absence of sustained private investment, unemployment will increase dramatically and support for elected regimes will decline sharply. As a result, political authorities will be replaced in the next election. This relationship is well documented. Tufte (1979), for example, finds substantial evidence that reduced confidence and the resulting effects of a downturn in the business cycle have significant negative effects on the political fortunes of incumbents.

One consequence of this argument is that political authorities should be quite responsive to the preferences of major private investors. Regardless of their party or ideology, elected officials who wish to stay in office must seek outcomes that will be in the general interest of investors, or capital will be diverted to sources outside of the country. Because a major share of private investment is generated by firms rather than individuals (Thurrow, 1979), this dependence on investment also means that public decisions ought to follow the interests of corporations even if their agents do not attempt to act as a unified class. According to this formulation, business domination over political outcomes can be maintained in the complete absence of any political coordination among corporate elites. The threat of diminished business confidence should be more than enough to guarantee this result.

Lindblom (1977, p. 185) summarizes this argument concisely when he notes that:

> Businessmen only rarely threaten any collective action such as a concerted restriction of function. Ordinarily, they need only point to the costs of doing business, the state of the economy, the dependence of the economy's stability and growth on their profits or sales— and simply predict, not threaten that adverse consequences will follow on refusal of their demands. . . . But prophecies of some kinds tend to be self-fulfilling. If spokesmen for business predict that new investment will lag without tax relief, it is only one short step to corporate decisions that put off investment until tax relief is granted.

According to this logic, politics in capitalistic democracies will generally be controlled by business interests even if their agents make no attempt to coordinate their political activities and act as a unified class.

This perspective is impressive for several reasons. First, Block provides refinements which explain how reforms can be introduced even if they are not consistent with the short run interests of the corporation. He argues that in periods of crises business attitudes become less important. During a severe depression, for example, when further reductions in business confidence are unlikely and popular demands for reform are at a peak, legislation which is not consistent with short run business interests can be expected. When a nation is engaged in total war and labor is scarce, political outcomes also may be more likely to favor workers rather than management.

Second, an emphasis on the effects of independent decisions about investment also provides a solution for a major problem with all of the perspectives which imply that some form of class organization is necessary. Block's formulation removes the necessity to believe that businessmen get involved in political disputes that are not relevant to their private interests. As long as office holders are dependent on the effects of independent decisions about investment, system-wide matters that are irrelevant to individual businessmen can be completely ignored and business interests still will be politically dominant. Thus, a belief that corporations are influential does not require a supposition that businessmen conspire together to achieve their political aims.

This formulation also has the added advantage of being more consistent with Marx. The following quote shows this convergence and also provides a concise summary of the argument:

> By returning to Marx's suggestion that the historical process unfolds 'behind the backs' of actors (including ruling class actors), it is possible to locate mechanisms that shape the workings of the capitalist state. These mechanisms operate independently of any political consciousness on the part of the ruling class. . . . The structural position of state managers forces them to achieve some consciousness of what is necessary to maintain the viability of the social order. . . . However, the fact of consciousness does not imply control over the historical process. State managers are able to act only on the terrain that is marked out by the intersection of two factors—the intensity of the class struggle and the level of economic activity (Block, 1977, p, 27).

Moreover, despite statements to the contrary by Lindblom (1977), it should be possible to test this argument. Good indicators of the phases of the business cycle are readily available, and these are highly responsive to the degree of business investment and confidence. When these indicators are falling, politicians should be under great pressure to enact programs that favor business, so that confidence will be restored. Therefore, if the Block-Lindblom idea is correct, time series regressions should reveal a significant independent relationship between increases in business investment and public policies that are consistent with business interests. In a preliminary and as yet unpublished study, Jacobs (1984) finds no relationship between lagged indicators such as percent change in real GNP, percent of industrial capacity utilized, or manufacturing profits in a given year and effective tax rates on manufacturing corporations. But the indicators that were employed in this study may not be responsive enough to the investment activities of the largest firms. In any case, tests like this point to a fruitful area for further inquiry.

## Recapitulation

This concludes the inventory of Neo-Marxist images of the political role of the corporation. While judgements about the plausibility of these four models can be left to the reader, it might be fruitful to compare them on their ability to generate testable hypotheses.

*Instrumentalism.* Even though the instrumental imagery may be a bit naive, variants that identify sources of business power can be tested by seeing if measures of these resources predict political outcomes that favor business interests. A series of quantitative investigations designed to test these ideas may at least help us to identify the circumstances when the instrumental model is or is not correct. Moreover, if predictions from the instrumental model are generally found to be true, subsequent studies that focus on the details of a few decisions may be able to shed light on the exact connections between the most important business resources and favorable political outcomes.

*Business Confidence.* As I have just noted, the Block-Lindblom idea that political outcomes that bear on business interests are controlled by the need to maintain business confidence also can be tested, although only time series techniques will be appropriate. If this image is correct, we can expect that legislation will be enacted that favors business interests whenever investment starts to fall.

*Class Struggle.* The class struggle imagery developed by Esping-Anderson et al. (1976) and others, on the other hand, is more of a framework that can be used to guide research. As long as proponents suggest that under some historical conditions business may lose political contests, but the precise conditions are left unspecified, no exact predictions can be tied to this view. But it still should be possible to develop longitudinal measures of the comparative political strength of corporations and their opponents, and to test the predictive utility of these measures with historical contingencies explicitly taken into account. It follows that while this perspective is not directly refutable, it should be useful as a way to generate important longitudinal studies of business–government relationships.

*Structuralism.* The structuralist alternative is probably the least useful of the four models because of its tautological construction. Explanations that can be stretched to fit any outcome are of limited value in a scientific enterprise.

One aspect of this discussion which needs more attention is the precise way that these images of the relationship between corporations and the state can be tested. In the following section, I will conclude this essay with a comparatively detailed treatment of the strengths and weaknesses of some of the more common research designs that have been used to examine business-government relationships.

## METHODS OF STUDYING BUSINESS-GOVERNMENT RELATIONSHIPS

It is possible to classify research designs that are commonly used to study political outcomes by (a) their breadth, and (b) their objectivity of method.

Studies which focus on a small number of political decisions can be contrasted with those where the researcher attempts to generalize about many outcomes. Studies which use subjective methods such as observation or nonquantitative summaries of the historical record also can be compared to studies that use statistical or purely mathematical techniques to gauge the effects of various explanations of the political process. Figure 1 shows a two-by-two table which cross-classifies research designs on these two diminsions. These comparisons are presented to highlight the strengths and weaknesses of methods that fit each quadrant.

## Quadrant I

The procedures in quadrant one have been the most commonly used methods to investigate business-government relationships. Case studies which are based on a researcher's subjective impressions of a few political outcomes have provided the basis for most of the work on how political decisions are made (Dahl, 1961; Bauer et al. 1963, are good examples). Because of its close focus on actual behavior, this technique is best suited for the development of new insights about the interactions of the immediate participants. The rich detail provided by case

*Figure 1.*   Cross Tabulation of Methodological Approaches to the Study of Models of Political Outcomes

|  | Subjective Methods | Objective Methods |
|---|---|---|
| **Micro (Limited Sample)** | I<br>Studies that look at a limited number of decisions using observational techniques (typical case study e.g., Bauer, Pool and Dexter) | II<br>Studies of a limited number of decisions that use quantitative techniques to gauge the independent effects of various determinants (e.g., surveys or roll call analysis) |
| **Macro (Large Sample)** | III<br>Studies of decision processes in many governmental units with multiple observers (e.g., James Q. Wilson's study of 9 police departments) | IV<br>Quantitative studies of the relationship between corporate resources and public outcomes using aggregate data (e.g., Salamon and Siegfried) |

studies certainly has been useful, but it will always be difficult to know if the results from such studies can be applied to other settings or times. A major problem with work in quadrant one, therefore, is the generalizability of the results.

Another problem concerns the reliability of subjective observations. To what extent do researchers see what they thought they were going to see? Undoubtedly, there are some observers of the political process who can put aside their preconceptions and view the data with an open mind, but this attribute may be rare. Even if it is not, how is a reader to identify the particular observers whose work can be trusted? There is no doubt that statistical analyses also are as vulnerable to the individual researcher's preconceptions, but the effects of these biases often can be corrected by a reanalysis of the original data. Individual researchers may be biased, but the ongoing competition for scholarly recognition insures that important quantitative results will be reanalyzed by investigators who do not share the preconceptions of the original researcher. This correction, unfortunately, is difficult to apply to findings generated from observational data, so questions about the reliability of findings typically remain unanswered.

Thus, while rich insights about the political process have been provided by the case study method, this work has led to the discovery of few general rules. With conclusions from the previous observational studies in mind, the most that can be said is that a circulation of diverse interests based on a variety of resources has shaped the outcome of some political contests. What has been missing is a sense of cumulation.

*Quadrant II*

Even though generality still may be problematic, research that fits the constraints found in the second quadrant of figure one has several comparative advantages. This work uses quantitative methods to gauge the determinants of a limited number of political decisions. Examples include regression analyses of votes in a legislative body (Burstein and Freudenburg, 1978; Welch, 1980) or the statistical analysis of surveys which are designed to explain how a small number of political decisions are reached. One advantage of such techniques is that they penetrate the black box of the governmental process with techniques that produce comparatively reliable estimates of the immediate causes of a few political actions. These research designs can be used to generate a relatively detailed account of why some interests prevailed and they have the added advantage of being subject to reanalysis.

When each study is viewed in isolation, the major difficulty with research that fits in this quadrant is that we cannot be sure whether the findings will hold in other places or in other periods. But when the results of such studies correspond, or if validated hypotheses can be advanced to account for systematic discrepancies, then this objection will not matter. Thus, while generality may be a problem, the offsetting advantages of a detailed and reliable explanation of how a limited number of political decisions are made makes approaches in the second quadrant quite useful.

## Quadrant III

Work in the top two quadrants runs the risk of concentrating on the trees while losing sight of the forest, but research in the lower quadrants often suffers from the opposite fault. In an attempt to generalize about the determinanats of a large number of political outcomes, the researcher may ignore useful detail. This fault may even pose a methodological threat. When many diverse political decisions are included in a single analysis, the investigator may be attempting to generalize about processes which are in fact not comparable. A time series analysis of political decisions which occur during some fundamental changes in the political process, for example, may be misleading even if the researcher attempts to introduce proxy variables to control for the idiosyncratic aspects.

Research in quadrant three provides an example of some of these potential shortcomings. The most common research design that fits these constraints involves an examination of a large piece of the historical record in an attempt to develop generalizations about the causes of political change. The insightful study by Chambliss (1964) into the orgins of vagrancy statutes in England from the thirteenth to the eighteenth century provides a good example of the strengths and potential weaknesses of this use of historical methods. Chambliss found that vagrancy laws were established and administered to control the supply of labor for the ultimate benefit of powerful employers. When labor was scarce, these laws were vigorously enforced to restrict the mobility of workers and weaken competition for this vital commodity. But there is a vexing problem with the historical techniques that Chambliss uses. The historical record from 1250 to 1750 is vast. To what extent did Chambliss' Marxist sympathies cause him to ignore anomalous facts in that vast record? Other historically oriented social scientists also have access to the same sources, of course, so studies which use these methods can be replicated by skeptics. Nevertheless, a perennial question about historical research is the extent that scholars with different political orientations will reach similar conclusions when the same records are scrutinized.

Another more costly way to apply subjective techniques to a large number of political outcomes involves the use of multiple observers who simultaneously report on the political process in many governmental units (for example see Gamson, 1966; or Wilson, 1971). With this design, aspects of the political process that are difficult to quantify can be studied without losing much detail and the conclusions will be more general than those which are based on a single case. Particularly when graduate students from the same department are used as observers, their similar perspectives may lead to problems with systematic bias but, if there are enough cases, at least the effects of idiosyncratic or random differences in observer perceptions may be averaged out. Equivalent techniques also have been used to study historical records. Gamson (1975), for example, used student coders to develop quantitative measures of the organizational characteristics and the success of a sample of movement organizations which sought to resist or bring about political change. Because so few of the previous studies of these organizations used quantitative techniques, this investigation was quite informative. It follows that the multiple observer method can be most productive, but the high cost of this design means that it will not be used as often as it should be.

## Quadrant IV

Research in quadrant four has many advantages. The use of statistical techniques to study the causes of numerous political outcomes is generally undertaken because conclusions from such designs are both general and reliable. Cross-sectional studies which compare the determinants of public policies across state, local or national governments, or investigations which use time series regressions to gauge the determinants of historical changes, generally have the added advantage of using secondary sources which are available to other investigators (for examples of cross-sectional work see Hewitt or Jacobs, 1978; for examples of time series research with a Marxist orientation see Griffin et al., 1982; 1983; and Devine, 1983). For these reasons and because of the emphasis on history in Marxism, many quantitative sociologists with Marxist sympathies are beginning to use time series techniques to assess the relationships between sources of business power and the actions of the state.

This new research style offers many advantages when it is compared to the previous case studies and historical investigations, but some problems remain. First, because the researcher is interested in generalizing about many political decisions, the behavior of the immediate participants frequently is ignored. The result, of course, is a sacrifice of much useful information. This sacrifice often is justified by the unspoken but questionable assumption that the state can be safely treated as a black box because the behavior of this institution is entirely subject to external inducements and constraints. Second, the causal relationships that come between the independent and dependent variables frequently are left out of the regression equations. Thus, when the regression coefficients for business resource variables are significant, the intervening influence processes that connect these economic resources to political outcomes must be inferred. It is reasonable to argue, however, that the actions which elites use to convert economic resources into political gains will rarely be open to public scrutiny, so these intervening processes will not be easy to measure. In any case, the first question that should be investigated is whether there are any statistical relationships between business resources and public policies which benefit corporations. If the answer to this question is yes, the next step should be an empirical delineation of the intervening processes.

The new emphasis on history in the social science literature on business-government relationships means that the use of time series regression techniques offers considerable promise, but there still are some significant difficulties that have not been completely solved. Recall from the previous discussion that Neo-Marxist theories of the state stress historically contigent events. Arguments that take the form, X will cause Y when Z and W are present in sufficient strength, are both common and plausible. The problem, however, is that multiple regression in general, and time series regression in particular, is ill suited to testing for the kinds of statistical interactions that are implied in such a model.

The introduction of multiplicative terms, where one variable is multiplied or divided by another, to test for statistical interaction often introduces severe problems of multicolinearity (Hannon, 1971). This difficulty frequently is compounded in time series regressions because longitudinal data tends to be highly aggregated in the first place. Typical time series regressions are computed on yearly averages for an entire nation. The averaging process which creates these variables removes outliers by converting variation around a mean to a mean. Therefore, time series variables tend to be closely related to one another even before multiplicative interaction terms are introduced. These problems can be partially overcome by the use of dummy variables, but this technique requires an assumption that many important historical processes can be correctly represented with dichotomous measures which make no allowance for continuous effects. All of these estimation problems often are heightened by the limited number of observations that are availiable. It follows that researchers should be cautious when they make conclusions about business-government relationships from time series results. It also is apparent that the connections between theory and empirical manipulations will require sophistication when Neo-Marxist conceptualizations of the state are tested.

Nevertheless, because most of the previous work in this area has relied on methods that led to noncomparable results, the use of time series designs to examine these questions offers much promise. One way that any area of knowledge should be judged is by the number of validated generalities that have been accumulated. If this criterion is applied to social science research on business-government relationships, it is apparent that much still needs to be done. The extensive reliance on case studies and historical techniques in this literature has meant that we have almost no cumulative knowledge. It is quite possible that if researchers with different points of view were to study the same political decisions about business interests with conventional techniques, the results would be similar to those found when pluralists and elitists examined the distribution of power in the same city. When this happened, pluralists found that the power structure was pluralistic while elitists found that politics in the same city was dominated by a power elite. The use of techniques that fit in quadrant four should help us to avoid such unfortunate results.

## CONCLUSIONS

In this paper, I have tried to do two things: summarize the recent neo-Marxist work on business-government relations, and provide a short discussion of some of the advantages and disadvantages of different methods of testing models of these interactions.

It can be seen from the first section that neo-Marxist treatments have not reached the status of definitive theory. Perspectives overlap and important elements remain metaphoric and untestable. Nevertheless, as Lindblom has noted, a close examination of this work should be useful to non-Marxist students of business and government. Perhaps the best way to develop new insights in any discipline is to look at how scholars with quite different assumptions approach the same issues. Because of an unfortunate tendency to overuse jargon, the Neo-Marxist theoretical work on this subject has not been very accessible to non-Marxist scholars. Therefore, I have tried to present the useful aspects of these approaches with special attention to those elements which will be most appealing to scholars who do not believe that capitalism is an inherently unstable system which can only be maintained by force and fraud.

As I noted at the beginning of this essay, most of the work in sociology and a large part of the research on these questions in political science has concentrated on how the state is controlled by business interests. The question of how business is controlled by the state has not been investigated as much, at least in sociology. But even if one's interests focus more on how business can avoid being controlled by the government, Neo-Marxist treatments of the state still should be useful because they shed light on some of the ways that businesses can resist these controls.

On a more general note the relationship between business and government is bound to be reciprocal. Government, with its unique access to coercion and its dependence on majorities which must be based on at least some of the votes of the less affluent, can hardly be expected to ignore the marketplace. Business, on the other hand, with its almost complete monopoly of the production of new wealth, can hardly be expected to ignore politics. As long as exchange cannot take place without property rights and these rights are conferred by government, we can expect that business will attempt to control political outcomes. But what has been missing so far are useful models of these processes which are subject to empirical refutation.

## ACKNOWLEDGMENT

I wish to thank David C. Colby for his thoughtful comments.

# REFERENCES

Aldrich, Howard E. *Organizations and Environments*. Englewood Cliffs: Prentice Hall, 1979.

Althusser, Charles H. *For Marx*. London: New Left Books, 1977.

Bauer, Raymond A., Ithiel De Sola Pool, and Lewis A. Dexter. *American Business and Public Policy*. Cambridge, Mass: MIT Press, 1963.

Bierne, Piers. "Empiricism and the Critique of Marxism on Law and Crime." *Social Problems* 26 (1979):373–85.

Block, Fred. "The Ruling Class Does Not Rule: Notes on the Marxist Theory of the State." *Socialist Revolution* 33 (1977):6–28.

Bloom, C. C. *State and Local Tax Differentials*. Iowa City: Bureau of Business Research, 1955.

Bonnacich, Edna. "Advanced Capitalism and Black/White Relations." *American Sociological Review* 41 (1976):34–51.

Burstein, Paul and William Freudenburg. "Changing Public Policy: The Impact of Public Opinion, Antiwar Demonstrations and War Costs on Senate Voting on Vietnam War Motions." *American Journal of Sociology* 84 (1978):99–122.

Caves, R. E. "Economic Models of Political Choice: Canada's Tarrif Structure." *Canadian Journal of Economics* 9 (1976):278–300.

Chambliss, William. "A Sociological Analysis of the Law of Vagrancy." *Social Problems* 12 (1964):46–67.

Dahl, Robert A. *Who Governs?* New Haven: Yale University Press, 1961.

Dalton, James P. and E. J. Ford. "Concentration and Labor Earnings in Manufacturing." *Industrial and Labor Relations Review* 31 (1977):47–61.

Devine, Joel A. "Fiscal Policy and Class Income Inequality." *American Sociological Review* 48 (1983):606–622.

Domhoff, G. William. *Who Rules America?* Englewood Cliffs, N.J.: Prentice Hall, 1967.

Esping-Anderson, Gosta, R. Friedland, and E. O. Wright. "Modes of Class Struggle and the Capitalist State." *Kapitalistate* 4/5 (1976):186–220.

Frey, Bruno S. and Friedrich Schneider. "An Empirical Study of Politico-Economic Interaction in the United States." *Review of Economics and Statistics* 60 (1978):174–183.

Gamson, William A. "Rancorous Conflict in Community Politics." *American sociological Review* 31 (1966):71–81.

———. *The Strategy of Social Protest*. Homewood, Ill: Dorsey, 1975.

Griffin, Larry, Joel Devine, and Michael Wallace. Monopoly Capital, Organized Labor and Military Expenditures," in Michael Buroway and Theda Skocpol (eds.), Marxist Inquires: Studies of Labor, Capital and the State. *American Journal of Sociology* 88 (1982):S113–S154.

———. "On the Economic and Political Determinants of Welfare Spending in the Post-World War Two Era." *Politics and Society* 12 (1983):331–72.

Gold, P. A., C. L. Lo, and E. O. Wright. "Recent Developments in Marxist Theories of the State." *Monthly Review* 27 (1975):29–43.

Hannon, Michael T. "Problems of Aggregation," in Hubert Blalock (ed.), *Causal Models in the Social Sciences*. Chicago: Aldine-Atlerton, 1971.

Hewitt, Christopher. "Deomcracy and Equality in Industrial Societies." *American Sociological Review* 42 (1977):450–63.

Hicks, Alexander, Roger Friedland, and Edwin Johnson. "Class Power and State Policy." *American Sociological Review* 43 (1978):302–315.

Hunter, Floyd. *Community Power Structure*. Garden City, N.Y.: Anchor Books, 1963.

Jacobs, David. "On The Determinants of Class Legislation: An Ecological Study of Political Struggles between Workers and Management." *Sociological Quarterly* 19 (1978):469–480.

———. "Concentration, Scale and Political Influence: A Cross-Sectional Examination of Business and Public Policy." Presented at the *Academy of Management Meetings* (August) 1983.

Jacobs, David and Don Waldman. "Towards A Fiscal Sociology: Determinants of Tax Regressivity in the American States." *Social Science Quarterly* 64 (1983):559–565.

Jenny, Fredrick. "Wage Rates, Concentration and Unionization in French Manufacturing Industries." *Journal of Industrial Economics* 26 (1978):315–27.

Jessop, Bob. *The Capitalist State*. New York: New York University Press, 1982.

Key, V. O. *Southern Politics*. New York Vintage Books, 1949.

Kuhn, Thomas S. *The Structure of Scientific Revolutions*. Chicago: University of Chicago Press, 1962.

Lasswell, Harold D. *Politics: Who Gets What, When and How*. New York: McGraw-Hill, 1936.

Lindblom, Charles F. *Politics and Markets: The World's Political-Economic Systems*. New York: Basic Books, 1977.

———. "Another State of Mind: Presidential Address, American Political Science Association." *American Political Science Review* 76 (1982):9–21.

Lowi, Theodore. "American Business, Public Policy, Case Studies and Political Theory." *World Politics* 16 (1964):679–714.

Lynd, Robert S. and Helen M. Lynd. *Middletown*. New York: Harcourt, Brace and World, 1929.

———. *Middletown in Transition*. New York: Harcourt, Brace and World, 1937.

Mann, H. M. and K. McCormick. "Firm Attributes and the Propensity to Influence the Political System." In John Siegfried (ed.), *The Economics of Firm Size, Market Structure and Social Performance*. Washington: Federal Trade Commision, 1980.

March, James G. and Herbert Simon. *Organizations*. New York: John Wiley, 1958.

Mariolis, Peter. "Interlocking Directorates and the Control of Corporations." *Social Science Quartely* 56 (1975):425–529.

McPherson, C. B. *Tariff Structures and Political Exchange*. Unpublished Ph.D. Dissertation. Chicago: University of Chicago, 1972.

Mills, C. Wright. *The Power Elite*. New York: Oxford University Press, 1959.

Mintz, Beth and Michael Schwartz. "The Structure of Intercorporate Unity in American Business." *Social Problems* 29 (1981):87–103.

Mizruchi, Mark S. *The American Corporate Network*. Beverly Hills, CA: Sage, 1982.

Offe, Clause. "Structural Problems of the Capitalist State." In Klaus Von Beyme (ed.), *German Political Studies*. Beverly Hills, CA: Sage, 1976.

Olson, Mancur. *The Logic of Collective Action*. New York: Shocken, 1966.

Pittman, R. "The Effects of Industry Concentration and Regulation on Contributions in Three 1972 U.S. Senate Campaigns." *Public Choice* 27 (1976):71–84.

———. "Market Structure and Campaign Contributions." *Public Choice* 28 (1977):37–52.

Poper, Karl R. *The Logic of Scientific Discovery*. New York: Harper Torchbooks, 1965.

Poulantzas, Nicos. "The Problem of the Capitalist State." *New Left Review* 58 (1969):58–75.

———. *Political Power and Social Classes*. London: New Left Books, 1973.

———. *State Power, Socialism*. London: New Left Books, 1978.

Preston, Lee. "Corporation and Society: The Search for A Paradigm." *Journal of Economic Literature* 13 (1975):434–453.

Salamon, Lester and John Seigfried. "Economic Power and Political Influence." *American Political Science Review* 71 (1977):1026–43.

Scherer, F. M. *Industrial Market Structure and Economic Performance*. Chicago: Rand McNally, 1980.

Schumpeter, Joseph. *The Theory of Economic Development*. Cambridge: Harvard University Press, 1936.

Siegfried, John. *The Relationship between Economic Structure and the Effect of Political Influence*. Unpublished Ph.D. Dissertation, Madison: Univeristy of Wisconsin, 1972.

Synder, David. "Institutional Setting and Industrial Conflict: Comparative Analyses of France, Italy and the United States." *American Sociological Review* 40 (1975):259–278.

Synder, David and William Kelly. "Industrial Violence in Italy 1878–1903." *American Journal of Sociology* 82 (1976):131–161.

Thompson, James D. *Organizations In Action*. New York: McGraw-Hill, 1967.

Thompson, W. R. and John Mittila. *An Econometric Model of Postwar Industrial Development*. Detroit: Wayne State University Press, 1959.

Thurrow, Lester. *The Zero Sum Society*. New York: Penguin, 1979.

Tufte, Edward R. *Political Control of The Economy*. Princeton, 1978.

Useem, Michael. "Classwide Rationality in the Politics of Managers and Directors of Large Corporations in the United States and Great Britain." *Administrative Science Quarterly* 27 (1982):199–226.

Vernon, John M. *Market Structure and Industrial Performance: A Review of Statistical Findings*. Boston: Allyn and Bacon, 1972.

Welch, W. P. "The Allocation of Public Monies: Economic Interest Groups." *Public Choice* 35 (1980):97–120.

Weiss, Leonard. "Quantitative Studies of Industrial Organization," in M. D. Intrilligator (ed.), *Frontiers in Quantitative Economics*. Amsterdam: North-Holland, 1971.

Whitt, J. Allen. "Toward a Class-Dialectial View of Power: An Empirical Assessment of Three Competing Models of Political Power." *American Sociological Review* 44 (1979):81–99.

Wilson, James Q. *Varieties of Police Behavior*. New York: Atheneum, 1971.

# THE CORPORATE RESPONSE PROCESS*

Raymond A. Bauer

## INTRODUCTION

This document is an attempt to develop a structured agenda for empirical research, analytical writing, and development of the topic which has generally been known as "corporate social responsibility." The substitution of the term "corporate responsiveness" for the more generally popular label is in itself a reflection of our improved understanding of the phenomenon under consideration.

As one looks at firms in the process of becoming "responsive," the distinction between "social" and "business" issues breaks down in a variety of ways. One reason is the indeterminate status of the issues. In some instances community relations activities may be virtually devoid of business advantage, and in others the business aspect will be dominant. In most instances they can be viewed through a business lens or a social lens, or both—and it makes a difference. The same can be said of equal employment, employee health and safety, consumerism, pollution abatement, even corporate giving. Another reason is that the individual issues interact with each other, a current example being the energy crisis and pollution abatement programs. And a final, and less well understood, consideration is the extent to which issues which are substantively dissimilar can pose similar or identical problems. The problem of scanning the environment for changing consumer values is not much different from scanning it for emergent social demands. On the level of implementation, the institutionalization of *any* new policy has certain features in common with any other new policy, whether the issue be social or exclusively business. The establishment of a corporate-wide uniform purchasing policy faces many of the same organizational problems as does a policy of equal employment opportunity. From either, one can learn lessons applicable to the other.

We are witnessing the development of a ''responsive'' corporation, one that is learning to institutionalize novelty. And if the corporation is in fact learning, it should be increasingly capable of handling new issues whether they be ''business'' or ''social.'' It is reasonable to expect the development of a new breed of managers. They will probably have different values, as has been rather widely suggested. But, probably more importantly, they will be accustomed to and skilled at organizational change.

## THREE STAGES OF RESPONSIVENESS

At times the words available to us are more precise in their connotation than are the phenomena to which we refer. Roughly speaking we may say that the response process consists in realizing that some issue exists, deciding whether to do something about it, and—if the answer is affirmative—deciding what to do about it, and finally doing something. But there are flaws even in this low-keyed statement. ''Realizing that some issue exists'' implies that the issue has some defined meaning independent of the observer, whereas a crucial part of the process is the giving of a definition. ''Deciding'' implies some intellectual process which, if not rational, is at least deliberate, and this is far from necessarily so. Furthermore, the sequence of steps which seems so natural indicates a degree of orderliness that is illusory. For example, the issue continues to be redefined in the process of implementation, and the process of implementation is often the means for identifying and defining new issues.[1]

With all these caveats on the limitations of language, I will proceed to treat the response process under the three headings of *identification, commitment,* and *implementation.* The literature on corporate responsiveness and the private expressions of concern by businessmen place a heavy emphasis on the first two stages, stressing the desirability of early "detection" (seldom does anyone acknowledge the active process of "defining" what is out there) of issues, and a wise selection of what issues to respond to at what time.

Let us imagine the response process as something that begins when an issue has reached the point where it should be considered seriously and ends when implementation is in some sense "complete." My own sense of the meaning of "complete" may be illustrated with the issue of equal employment opportunity. "Completeness" does not mean that the job is entirely done in that minorities and women have achieved employment parity. "Completeness" means that organizational changes have been made—and stabilized—so that, if they continue to function as intended, "parity" (whatever that means) will be achieved within some agreed-upon time period. Thus, the completion of the response process is not the accomplishment of a particular goal but the changing of behavior so that the goal will be accomplished and will continue to be accomplished. Whether this nice distinction will hold up in the real world is in itself a very interesting empirical question. An historical study of the relationship of the U.S. Steel Company to the C.I.O. in the thirties indicates the distinction is meaningful [ 10]. U.S. Steel institutionalized revised control and reward systems and a system of supervisory training to introduce a new era of labor relations. After some years this system atrophied as the new mode of labor relations became routine. I would regard the response process as completed at the point at which the new management procedures were in effect and required no more than routine attention.

If we take this view of the response process from beginning to end, research to date indicates that speed in identifying issues or in committing the organization to action may be overemphasized for most of the social issues that are of present concern. At least they have been overemphasized relative to implementation if one is intent on shortening the response process as a whole. Even when responses have been mandated by law, the process of implementation may take a decade or more in well-run companies with well-motivated managers, particularly when the required behavioral changes are complicated.

It is not my intention here to argue or document the actual or potential complexity of the implementation phase of the response process at this point. For some issues the implementation phase may in fact be quite short and simple. A change in contributions policy *can* be accomplished rather rapidly. The point to be made is that the relative importance, complexity, and duration of the three processes of identification, commitment, and implementation will vary from issue to issue and probably from organization to organization. One of the causes of variation in all phases of the response process may be the perceived legitimacy of the actions to be taken, and this, in turn, is likely to be closely, but possibly imperfectly, related to the extent to which the issue is seen to be akin to the organization's regular business activities. Other sources of variation will be the initial clarity of the issue, the urgency of the issue, the viability of proposed actions, the structure of the organization, the number of organizational levels involved in implementation, the extent to which an issue cuts across the ways in which business organizations are structured to handle issues, the extent to which an issue is seen as appropriate for the private sector, and so on.

The above sources of variation probably are most associated with variations among issues (rather than among industries, and individual firms) though industries and individual firms may have characteristics that affect their position on some of these dimensions. In any event, what is important is to recognize the possibility or probability of intrinsic reasons for variation in the relative importance and difficulty of the several phases of the response process, particularly on an issue-to-issue basis. This will not only identify key stages of the process which are most in need of facilitation, but probably illuminate the response process in general[6].

## IDENTIFICATION OF ISSUES

*Detection of Issues*

A variety of formal and semiformal procedures exists for identifying existing, and anticipating future, developments of potential importance to business organizations. These procedures go under such names as environmental scanning, early warning systems, technological and social forecasting, future analysis, and the like.[2] The sources and content of inputs are too numerous to permit enumeration, but they vary from informal scanning of the media and conversations with persons of varying expertise, to formal econometric and demographic analysis and forecasting, to the writing of future scenarios and forecasting via the Delphi technique, using panels of experts under controlled conditions, to the sensitive monitoring of the legislative process. Some of the work is done within the firm, and some is syndicated by various commercial organizations. The collection, evaluation, and analysis of such inputs is usually relatively centralized in some function as long range planning to the extent that it concerns the future. As it concerns the present, it is more likely to relate to some function such as finance, marketing, purchasing, and so on.

Information about the existing state of the world relating to regular business concerns is gathered and processed relatively routinely by regularly established functional units of the organization. The uses and usefulness of such information is fairly well established on the basis of long experience. To the extent that information pertains to the future and/or to issues progressively remote from regular business issues, both the gathering and use of the information is less well organized and understood. This may, perhaps, be tautological, but it directs our attention to the need to understand better the use of such information, and to the instability of arrangements for gathering and using it.

As of now we have not been able to develop a satisfactory conceptual approach to handle the full scope of the problems associated with the anticipation and detection of issues relevant to corporate responsiveness. For a beginning, several approaches suggest themselves which may yield convergent information and understanding, and thus will eventually permit us better to grasp the overall phenomenon.

The first is the study of *formal arrangements* for environmental scanning. Probably this will yield most if it is done on a comparative basis where the comparison is made between traditional and "new" issues. The comparison would include the formal arrangements for gathering such information, the ways in which the two types of information are processed in the organization, the ways in which traditional types of information are used for "new" purposes and vice-versa (e.g., demographic projections used both for market analysis and anticipating social problems).

Studies may concentrate on *particular areas of concern.* For example, how is a given firm organized to handle external information relevant to equal employment opportunity with regard to such things as: impending legislation and regulation, interpretations of existing legislation, public attitudes toward the issue, developments in civil rights and the feminism movement, the existence and tactics of interest groups, the experiences of other firms in dealing with the issue, technical developments such as information on possible biases in tests of ability, impending developments such as opportunities for ethnic minorities?

There is also merit in detailed studies of *individual incidents* or in the origins of *specific programs* in which the firm is engaged. Such case studies are especially useful for illuminating the sorts and sources of informational inputs which would not be identified by a more frontal approach to environmental scanning. The ideal approach would be to take a random sample of important actions—both regular business and "other"—taken within the firm and trace their origins backward to identify what external inputs, if any, precipitated the action in question. Such an approach paralleled by tracing the course of a random sample of inputs (recognizing that such inputs may be blocked, distorted, or lost) would probably be the conceptually ideal method of understanding the detection process. The magnitude of such an effort and its demands on individual organizations almost certainly make it impractical. Yet, it does underscore the merits of individual case studies which trace the input origins of specific incidents and actions.

The preceding discussion has focused on anticipation and detection of issues—the establishment of the fact that "something" relevant is out there. Even the judgment of relevance involves some element of definition of the issue, a matter to which we now turn.

### Definition of Issues

The process of issue definition begins with the decision as to what type of information is relevant, and therefore determines what channels of information will be monitored, the way in which one organizes to monitor information, and the type of personnel who are selected to do the monitoring. The next stage is the determination of the relevance of specific information. This will be affected by the previous decision as to what *types* of information an organization has concluded are relevant, but modified by such additional factors as the organizational position of a particular individual—both where he is located, and how he relates his own career to the organization—and his personal characteristics. The final stage is the giving of substantive meaning to what has been perceived, answering the question, "What is it?" In all probability the second and third stages are separable only analytically, since a decision of relevance clearly implies at least some provisional attribution of meaning.

An organizational "decision" as to what types of information are relevant will be reflected in the formal scanning mechanisms that are established. Surveys have been made to study the existence of such mechanisms from time to time. Such studies should be extended, and the existence of formal scanning systems should be analyzed by the nature of their coverage and by relevant characteristics of firms. Survey data, however, are unlikely to give much understanding of the functioning of such systems. Therefore, surveys should be considered as complementary to the case studies of such systems suggested above. Such information should be valuable in understanding the responsiveness of individual firms and of firms in various industries. Individuals will also vary in the content of the personal "scanning systems," e.g., what they read, whom they associate with, and so on. Such behavior will be integral to understanding the responsiveness of individual firms.

The attribution of substantive meaning to "something out there" can, of course, be a matter of infinite complexity. However, two pairs of categories seem to be of value in studying the attribution of meaning. These are whether an issue is seen as "social" or "business" and whether it constitutes a "threat" or an "opportunity." As a matter of fact, a given issue may change status on these dimensions in the course of its consideration.

A good example of an issue which went through several stages of redefinition was identified by Edwin Murray in his study of a bank's policy of offering free checking to the elderly [11]. When the bank was first approached by the elderly the issue was seen as one that posed both a social and a business threat. As the public relations possibilities were explored it was seen as offering a social benefit and a possible minor business payoff that did not offset the main business threat. Further analysis revealed a business advantage. In the end, the package prepared for the elderly was seen as an opportunity which was quickly exploited in another market.

It would appear that the response process functions best when an issue has been perceived from both a "business" and a "social" perspective and when both threats and opportunities have been explored. But it is not clear when and how this occurs nor how rapidly and thoroughly it can be expected to happen. This might be studied as a distinct aspect of the response process across a number of firms and a number of issues. It is likely, however, that the process of giving meaning to an issue is so integral to the response process as it proceeds through time that it may be easier and more fruitful to study it in the context of longitudinal studies of responses to specific issues.

*Summary*

The process of identification, of detecting and defining issues, is one aspect of the corporate response process which can be treated as analytically distinct. When it can, or should, be studied empirically as separate from other aspects of the response process is a matter of research strategy, opportunity, and probably of the particular problem to which it is addressed. Categories of research which have been identified are:

1. Studies of formal or semiformal arrangements for scanning the environment. This would include surveys of the existence of such arrangements and more intense studies of their functioning, including the uses to which such information is put. A useful strategy might be to compare the collection and use of regular "business" and "social" information.

2. Studies of detection and definition of issues associated with specific issue areas. Relative to the preceding category of research, these studies should permit a better exploration of the uses of information, and of the role of both formal and informal informational inputs.

3. Studies of specific incidents and actions to trace the informational

inputs that precipitated them. This permits a further exploration of informal sources of informational input, and the relative effectiveness of various sorts and sources of information as it actually affects action.

4. Studies of the process of giving substantive meaning to issues, with specific reference to facilitating the process whereby both "business" and "social" aspects, and both "threats" and "opportunities" are considered as appropriately as possible.

## COMMITMENT TO ISSUES

A key phase in the response process is the selection of issues to which to respond, and eventual commitment to an effective organizational response, by corporate officers with sufficient clout. This phase is not well understood, has been little researched, and is likely to be difficult to research. The conventional way of referring to this phase of the response process is "deciding which issues to respond to." This phrasing has three misleading connotations. It implies deliberateness, discretion, and a one-shot process with a relatively short duration.

The process whereby a business firm becomes committed to some course of action is almost invariably less elegant, more complex, and less marked by conscious deliberation than is implied by the word "decision." This is true for regular business matters as well as for matters outside of regular business concerns.[3] Furthermore, as should be quite obvious, many of the issues on which business is being asked to respond are matters of law, and the operative question is not that of whether to respond or not, but rather when and how to respond, and with what degree of commitment. Finally, the process is one of long duration. Where the undertaking of a program is in fact discretionary, making the initial commitment may take months or years.

With respect to mandated issues, conformance to the law is quite variable, and this variability is founded in the same sorts of perceptions and decisions as are implied as the basis for deciding on whether to respond to "voluntary" issues. Decisions as to when and how to respond on mandated issues deserve as much, if not more, attention than decisions to respond to voluntary issues. The latter are not as important to society—if we may take passage of a law as evidence of priority—and they may have less consequence for the firm. Furthermore, decisions to respond to non-mandated issues are more complicated, both as to how they *ought* to be made and how they actually *are* made.

Whatever the limited rationality and limited coherence of regular business decisions, decisions on "social" policies are far less orderly, as might be expected. Ideally, the selection of social issues on which to respond would reflect some coherent strategy; and decisions would be implemented in a manner consistent with that strategy. Guidelines for selection of social issues to which to respond ought to include such criteria as the intrinsic importance of the issue, the appropriateness of the private sector as the locus of response, the capability of business and of the individual firm in particular to deal with the issue, and its fit with *some* coherent strategy.

Studies should continue of both prevailing and best practice in exploration of the extent to which the process of issue selection and commitment can or ought in fact to be rationalized. Attention should be concentrated on the roles of chief executive officers, of corporate social responsibility committees, and of boards of directors, of corporate staff, and of line officers in a position to take independent initiative. These studies should be executed with only a tenuous assumption of a straightforward notion of rationality. Experience with the study of regular business decisions suggests the possibility that prevailing practice may reflect more wisdom than is quickly apparent.

In addition to studies of current decisions to respond to nonmandated social issues, studies should be made of recent past actions of business firms. A fair amount of literature on this topic exists. It should be reviewed with an eye to answering questions of the appropriateness of various activities for private sector response both from the point of view of where social priorities should be set, and whether or not given types of activity fit the skills and resources of businessmen and business firms. Where such activities seem appropriate for business to undertake, reasons for success and failure should be reviewed.

## The Timing of Commitments

The foregoing pertains to *how* organizational commitments to social responses are made. There is also the question of *when*—the timing of such commitments. To a large extent, perhaps entirely, *when* is tied to *how*. It is notorious that the automobile industry was aware of the safety issue but did not act. The industry responded to signals from the marketplace, but not to nonmarket signals. What must be remembered, however, is that the process of decisionmaking affects both the content and the timing of the firm's commitment. Moreover, the initial commitment is only the beginning of a much longer process in which top management, with varying degrees of conscious deliberateness, reassesses its objectives and its allocation of attention, energy, and other resources to meet the objectives to which it is ostensibly committed.

When we consider that this process continues over a long time—and that much of it occurs inside the heads of top executives and/or in meetings of top executives—the difficulty of researching it becomes obvious.[4]

Such research is intrinsically difficult. Mental processes cannot be observed directly by researchers, and—to the extent that they are largely unconscious—not even by the actor himself. Furthermore, these are the sorts of actors who, by virtue of their business and the importance of what they are doing, present the most difficult problems for sustained research access. For these reasons, research on the commitment process may require compromises which one would like to avoid—such as reconstructing events which are much more reliably studied while they are occurring. In addition, when commitment occurs at a level below the top, a number of questions become interesting. Why does a group, division, or department decide to adopt certain policies or programs that are not sponsored throughout the corporation? Why are some operating units generally more progressive than others in the same corporation? Is this related to the content or circumstances of the business?

For a variety of reasons, the ideal research design for studying the commitment process would be to establish continuing research sites in a number of firms which would vary on a variety of dimensions. There is good reason to believe that all of the following dimensions affect both the extent and the content of corporate commitment to social issues: consumer vs. industrial market; divisionalized vs. integrated structure; progressive vs. conservative management; expanding vs. stable vs. contracting market; expanding vs. stable vs. contracting firm; prosperous vs. nonprosperous; regulated vs. unregulated; local regulation (utilities) vs. national regulation (airlines). Even with a certain amount of ingenuity of research design (such as use of a Latin square) it would be manifestly impossible to maintain continuing research sites to cover all these dimensions. Under ideal *practical* circumstances, one would aim at a few intensive research sites coupled with more extensive exploration along these various dimensions.

The reasons for studying the commitment process in an ongoing research site are to pick up individual issues as soon as possible, and to understand the context in which the issue arises and is handled. The latter point may need some explication. Any executive treats any new issue in the context of his ongoing responsibilities. These ongoing activities determine whether or not he notices the issue, the amount of attention he gives it, how he defines it, and whether and how he will pursue it. Such matters are best understood if observed as they occur.

Again, if we were to specify ideal conditions, the commitment process would be studied in the context of the overall process of implementation, since the maintenance of commitment is as important as its initial establishment. When we have known what was happening throughout an organization which was dealing with a "social" issue it became a matter of obvious interest to relate top management perception of what was occurring to our own perception of what was occurring. In some instances top management's perception was manifestly incorrect. The problem was not so much one of incorrect factual information, but more of inadequate understanding of the process being managed. However, our developing general understanding of the implementation process may make possible substantial compromises on the extent to which all dimensions of the implementation of specific policies need be observed in order to understand the commitment process.

Recognizing that practical constraints will force relaxation of conditions for ideal research on the commitment process, there are a variety of types of studies which should prove worthwhile, and which generally speaking have not been done: chief executives dealing with one or more "social" issues, preferably over some period of time; boards of directors doing the same; the operation of "social responsibility committees" of boards of directors; the operation of other social policy committees within business firms. Among the questions to be explored are: Is there coherence, whether conscious or not, to the pattern of things to which a firm is committed? Do "social policies" fit into an overall corporate strategy? Who effectively makes commitments? What is the process whereby a perceived issue results or does not result in commitment? How is continued commitment managed during the process of implementation?

Ingenious researchers may well find ways of designing such studies so as to amplify their powers of illumination. For example, line managers must regularly deal with matters that are beyond their primary competence. For these matters a system of staff roles has evolved to provide advice to line management on such matters as public and governmental relations, technical topics, marketing and advertising, and so on. Current issues of social responsiveness have expanded the number of such staff roles. Thus, the commitment process involves line managers in learning to use a new set of advisors. The development of this advisory relationship may be studied in comparison with the use of established advisors.

The resolution to commit an organization to any new policy is an intensely personal one. The conventional approach, which, as might by now be expected, I find to be inadequate, is to discuss this in terms of the values of executives. No doublt values are important, but there are cognitive dimensions which may be of equal importance. The way a person sees the world is not necessarily the way he wishes it were; and the way he sees it working is not necessarily the way he wishes it would work. The corporate counsel for Executive A may tell him something is legal, but the counsel for Executive B may tell him the opposite. People vary in their tolerance of ambiguity and in their capacity to rationalize. While such dispositions are probably related to certain patterns of values, the relationship is undoubtedly complex and imperfect. Studies of the commitment process invite consideration of the fullest range of personal and background variables, and, whether studied or not, they will be relevant.

Finally, it is necessary once more to assert that what can be separated analytically cannot necessarily be separated empirically. The commitment process must be understood in the context of the entire response process. I have pointed out that the implementation phase places continuous demands on the commitment process. The identification phase has similar relevance. The detection subphase will determine whether an issue will be raised, and the definition subphase will determine what is reacted to. The interface between the identification and commitment phase will be an interesting point of observation for purposes of understanding how well each serves the other.

*Summary*

Analytic writing and empirical research on the commitment phase of the response process are needed. The commitment phase should be viewed as a complex social-psychological process of extended duration which is separable only analytically from the identification and implementation phases. A number of dimensions were identified which may be presumed to affect the extent and content of the response process. In addition, because of the intensely personal nature of the commitment process, as full a range as possible of personal and background characteristics should be taken into consideration. Several types of research may be suggested.

1. Studies of *commitment-making entities*, managers, and committees which commit business organizations to the pursuit of major objectives. Insofar as possible, such studies should be done in the context of regular business activities, and should compare the handling of regular business and social issues as well as the interaction of the two. The focus here is on the go/no-go decisions, and the relation or lack thereof of social policy to corporate business strategy.

2. The *management of commitment* through the course of the implementation process, the review and maintenance of commitment, and its communication to the organization.

3. Micro-studies of the *commitment process*, including detailed studies of the actual circumstances precipitating specific commitments, the social-psychological process of learning to use new types of staff advisers, the role of values, cognitive models of social and organizational processes on commitment, and so on.

4. Studies which focus on the *locus of initiative* for commitment within a firm. The ability to create commitment may be relatively widely distributed in the firm, and the matters on which commitments are made may vary with the locus of the initiative taken. Furthermore, the commitment

process itself may vary in dependence on the locus of initiative. Thus, a middle-level manager will face a different situation if he initiates a commitment that can be fulfilled with resources already under his control than if he must obtain those resources from higher levels of management.

# IMPLEMENTATION OF POLICIES AND PROGRAMS

Problems of implementation vary on a number of dimensions. The distinction between policies and programs is intended to signal one of those dimensions. A *policy* may be a broad statement of principle designed to guide behavior across a wide range of situations, e.g., being a good corporate citizen. Or it may pertain to some particular domain of activities such as support for higher education, equal employment, and so on. As the abstract and general become more concrete we begin to talk about *programs,* which are specific bundles of activities designed to convert policies into action. Such programs may range from a regular review of hiring practices to the establishment of a system for delivery of food to needy families in the community. The dimension, as indicated, is from the general and abstract to the specific and concrete.

Policies and programs themselves vary as to the locus of initiative and the locus of execution. Generally speaking we may identify three types of policies and programs: (1) those initiated and executed at the corporate level; (2) those initiated at the corporate level and executed at the operating level; and (3) those initiated and executed at the operating level. The discussion will be organized along these three categories. Since the implementation problems of policies and programs initiated at the corporate level and executed at the operating level are apparently by far the most complex, we will discuss them last.

Problems of implementation also vary according to the structure of the organization, particularly between product/market divisionalized firms and single business firms. Because the product/market divisionalized firm is dominant among large firms, our discussion will be directed toward that particular form with qualifications entered when relevant.

## Initiation and Execution at the Corporate Level

Social policies and programs initiated and executed at the corporate level tend to be limited to corporate giving and the involvement of top management and staff in outside activities. Generally speaking, the implementation of such policies and programs causes the least organizational difficulty, since they do not require the participation of other units of the organization. The major limitation on such policies and programs seems to be the lack of enthusiasm of managers on the operating level for the drain which these activities put on corporate funds[5] and top executive time and energies. This source of strain between headquarters and operating divisions is in itself probably worth studying in a period in which the chief executive's activities are being directed increasingly outside the firm, and in which corporate headquarters is pressuring operating units to execute policies which have been initiated at the corporate level.

From my present perspective, policies and programs initiated and executed at the corporate level do not seem to provide a very rich area of research, although some aspects are not totally without interest. The implementation of corporate giving is worth studying from several perspectives. If there is an explicit policy, what provision is made for keeping the program consistent with that policy? To what extent is the actual execution consistent with stated policies? If there are inconsistencies, what forces affect this distortion? Where top executives are involved in outside activities, what controllable factors affect their effectiveness? For example, a large national company moved into a medium-sized midwestern city. The chief executive began showing up at meetings of community organizations accompanied by staff members who did support work for the organizations. This set an example for other firms and substantially enhanced the contribution of the business community to the larger community. Are there any strictly managerial problems associated with programs both initiated and executed at the corporate level?

*Initiation and Execution at the Operating Level*

Here I shall define "initiation" as either undertaking a policy or program that falls outside of corporate policy or implementing an activity covered by corporate policy with a degree of commitment that clearly exceeds corporate commitment. Thus, some divisions of firms which have been studied show a degree of commitment to pollution control or equal employment opportunity that cannot be explained by corporate commitment. Some divisions have aided minority businesses in the absence of a corporate policy to this effect. In some corporations, corporate officers have deliberately refrained to this point from establishing a corporate policy on occupational health and safety, "leaving it to the divisions." Community relations programs are often initiated at the level of the local plant.

The term "operating level" also requires some specification. To the extent that operating units such as groups or divisions are composed of smaller operating units (divisions in groups, and departments in divisions) which are relatively autonomous businesses, the problems of implementation at the group or divisional level should be a minor version of those for implementing a corporate-wide policy which has to be executed on the operating level. The problem, in a nutshell, is one of how to get a relatively autonomous unit whose executives are rewarded on the basis of financial performance to undertake activities to which they are not accustomed and for which they are not rewarded.

*Within* any business unit, the problems of implementation seem to be little different than those of implementing a corporate policy on the same issue. To be specific, if a department head becomes committed to a community relations program, the job before him is —except in a few ways I will specify—similar whether he came to it out of personal conviction or because of pressure from headquarters. Aside from some probable difference in his own level of enthusiasm for the task, it also seems likely that the organization is likely to respond with more alacrity to a locally initiated policy or program for the simple reason that it is more likely to be clearly relevant to that segment of the business and/or one or more of its constituencies. This, however, is a difference in motivation rather than a difference in the management task of execution. However, this possible difference in motivation may offer an interesting research control. For example, it would be interesting to compare two manufacturers of electronic components (or any other type of business), one of which had adopted a policy under its own initiative, and the other of which had adopted a parallel policy under pressure from corporate headquarters. While the sample would be small and the control over motivation crude, it is conceivable that such a comparison might give us some clue as to which aspects of implementation are intrinsically difficult, and which are simply neglected due to the relatively low priority given social issues of primary interest to someone else.

The fact that an operating business may be a subdivision of a larger corporation may be a matter of particular interest. There is some evidence that independently owned business firms devote more resources to human services than do organizations which are owned by larger firms. It may well be that corporate pressure on operating units to deliver profits reduces the social initiative which those operating units can take. Since it is likely that the policies and programs which operating units would initiate on their own will tend to be related to the long-run welfare of their particular businesses (however imprecisely), it may be that the divisionalized corporate structure bears adversely on the long-term welfare of its components—at least in this particular way. On the other hand, there may be offsetting factors, such as the availability of corporate resources of money and expertise. Both the processes at work, and their relative impacts on responsiveness, are worthy objects of study. Because of the fact that there may be offsetting factors, some form of quantitative approach such as a survey may be an appropriate means for determining which dominates the other.

A policy or program initiated within an operating unit may produce a different learning process than one initiated corporate-wide. Because the head of an operating unit has direct control over operating personnel he can initiate and terminate actions quite freely, and, since the lines of communication are short, he has a better chance to "learn by doing" than higher level officers do. He can also alter policy as a result of this experience. The significance of this difference will become clearer when I discuss the effect of organizational structure on implementation of policies initiated on the corporate level and implemented on the operating level. Other research questions relevant to the implementation of policies and programs initiated and executed at the operating level will be covered in the section which follows.

*Initiation at the Corporate Level and Execution at the Operating Level*

Policies and programs initiated at the corporate level and executed at the operating level are both most characteristic and most complex to implement. The major categories of issues that confront the business firm today—pollution, urban and minority affairs, occupational health and safety, product quality and safety, consumer relations, and good community relations—are generally corporate-wide in their significance, or at a minimum are of importance to more than one division in large corporations. They are also matters for which top corporate officers feel responsibility. However, they must all be executed by the functional personnel of the operating units, by engineering, production, marketing, personnel, and purchasing, under the direct control of lower-echelon general managers.

*Structural Difficulties:* The difficulty of implementing policies such as these has been pointed out a number of times.[6] It lies in the circumstance that the overwhelming majority of large American firms are organized according to a product/market divisionalized structure. The reason for this structure is the multiplicity of businesses in which such corporations are involved. Because of the diversity of markets and technologies involved, it is impossible for corporate officers to exercise the judgments required to run such a variety of businesses. Accordingly, the heads of the various "businesses" ( a business may be a "department" of a "division", which is in turn a member of a "group" below the corporate level) are expected to exercise considerable autonomy, and generally are held responsible only for demonstrating an adequate financial performance.

Corporate efforts to enforce new policies or programs in such a situation run up against three obstacles: (1) they require operating managers to do something to which they are not accustomed; (2) they violate the autonomy which such managers have come to regard as their right; (3) they appear to prejudice the financial performance of the businesses, and therefore threaten the manager's immediate bonus as well as his track record for promotion. In addition to these obstacles, corporate headquarters is handicapped by the lack of an information system by which to assess and monitor the performance of operating units on matters relating to new policies.

Under these circumstances, the institutionalization of a new policy is a long and complex process. Ackerman has identified three stages through which this process goes. Stage I is that at which the chief executive officer becomes committed and communicates this commitment to the organization. This produces little or no organizational change. At Stage II a staff specialist is appointed. The specialist defines the problem (studies relevant laws, assesses expectations, and so on), identifies what needs to be done, formulates an explicit statement of policy (this *may* have been done earlier), and develops a rudimentary information system. Despite the activity of the staff specialist, there is likely to be little effective change of behavior at the operating level during this phase.

Stage III is one of institutionalization. Operating managers build the implementation of the policy into their business plans. A budget is allocated, objectives are set, personnel are trained when necessary, an ongoing information system is established and perhaps supplemented by a system of internal auditors, proper administrative procedures are designed and implemented, and performance on the objectives of the polic, is built into the evaluation of executives.

In effect, the successful implementation of a corporate social policy (and it may be true for any corporate-wide policy) in a divisionalized firm requires the revision of the firm's system of reward and control. And it seems plausible to us that as policies become thoroughly institutionalized the control and reward systems required to establish them would be likely to atrophy when the changed behavior becomes "standard practice." (The historical look at the United States Steel Company previously mentioned supported this.)

## IMPLEMENTATION RESEARCH

Research already done at Harvard and elsewhere gives us at least a partial glimpse at virtually every phase of the implementation of corporate-wide policies in divisionalized firms. But there remains much research to be done. I have tried various schematics for presenting the research that seems worth doing, but even a very elaborate one does not display all of these opportunities. A major difficulty lies in the fact that there are several equally attractive bases on which they might be organized.

*Implementation of Specific Policies*

To begin with, as of now there appears to be no adequate road map of the full range of administrative problems and tasks associated with the implementation of policy on any one of the existing active social issues to which corporations are attempting to respond. Nor is there a sound knowledge basis for the execution of the various activities within each stage level. It would appear, for example, that it is highly desirable to have operating line personnel involved in the formulation of detailed policies and in the setting of goals. Yet, some firms are not following this route. The execution of a first cut "social audit," which may cover only a few policy issues, seems a necessary step in moving toward institutionalization, yet it regularly encounters delays due to organizational resistance. The types of information systems required for monitoring various policy areas present different technical and organizational problems. We know little about this. Efforts to change systems of executive evaluation seem confined to a few issues; such efforts are also few in number, and no one knows how they will work out.

It is necessary to expand our knowledge of the implementation of policy in each of the current areas, to study the problems of specific subphases, and to do it on a comparative basis. Comparisons involve both the handling of one social issue with that of another, and the handling of social issues with that of regular business issues on which corporations are institutionalizing policies throughout the firm. Intermediate issues, such as consumer programs and community relations, which may have an immediate tangible business payoff in many instances, should be of particular interest since in some instances they will be seen as "social," in some "business," and in some a mixture. Furthermore, in all instances attention should be paid to the extent and ways in which a given issue may alternately be seen as a "social" and a "business" one. There is no issue on the present social agenda that cannot and has not been seen in both contexts.

*The Implementation Role*

The implementation of corporate-wide policies demands certain activities which at present do not seem to fit within any appropriate role, either from their performance or, to the extent the specific activities are the job of others, for their coordination. In the past several years, corporate staff functions with such labels as public affairs, community affairs, urban affairs, or even public relations are turning their attention inward for the purpose of bringing about organizational change. On the whole they lack either the legitimacy or the competence for this task. They meet resistance from other staff and from line operators and they must learn new skills. One must assume that a new staff role may be evolving; however, the evolution of this role requires continued study.

## The Importance of Structure

The business context deserves a good deal of attention. At a first glance it would appear that the structure of divisionalized firms reveals all of the qualitative manifestations that I have spelled out. Yet, the institutionalization of new policies in firms which are organized along functional rather than divisional lines does not seem to proceed more rapidly [11]. However, the process itself is in certain respects qualitatively different. In brief, the learning process in the functionally organized firm seems to be like that which was suggested for policies initiated and implemented at the operating level of a product/market divisionalized firm.

## Responsiveness and Profitability

The relationship of profitability to responsiveness needs more attention. A few years ago this issue was seen as simply one of the availability of monetary resources—"If you are rich you can afford to be responsible." There is, of course, a great deal of plausibility to the notion that a marginal firm in a marginal industry will have little interest in "frills," There are numerous press accounts of a capital starved steel industry trying to fend off pressures to comply with pollution abatement laws. However, this issue has not been pursued in any rigorous fashion. Furthermore, the resource scarcity of unprosperous firms is not likely to be limited to money. Executive time and attention are also scarce resources, and on some issues and in some situations may be more critical than monetary resources. Certainly research to date indicates strongly that the implementation of social policies is strongly affected by the amount of top executive attention these issues get.

Ackerman [2] adds an interesting variation to this theme. He suggests that the crucial variable may not be profitability *per se,* but the rate at which the firm is expanding. Invoking the concept of the economy of incentives within the firm, he suggests that opportunities for promotion are a function of the rate of expansion of the firm, and that a chief executive who has many promotional opportunities to dangle in front of his subordinates is likely to get their attention when he favors a change in their behavior.

One more variation is also plausible. This one stresses executive time and attention as well as managerial skill as possible crucial variables. The argument is that an executive group that can afford to devote considerable energy to managing organizational innovations is likely to be one that has its regular business affairs well under control. This argument can be extended by saying that if the executive group is skillful at handling the implementation of new policies it is also likely to be adept at handling routine business, which presumably would be less demanding. According to this argument, a responsive firm should be prosperous, but it does not follow that a prosperous firm would be responsive.

Since all of the above hypotheses about the relationship of business profitability to business responsiveness are plausible, chances are that under some circumstances each is likely to manifest itself in varying degrees under some circumstances. While no one piece of research is likely to establish the entire set of contingent relationships which may manifest themselves, attention to these various possibilities across a wide variety of studies can bring the proper illumination to the relative roles of various types of resources in corporate responsiveness.

### The Generality and Specificity of Responsiveness

I have casually referred to ''responsiveness'' and to some organizations as being more ''responsive'' than others as though responsiveness were a unitary phenomenon. There is a certain amount of legend to the effect that a business firm that is ''responsible'' on one issue will be so on all. This is, at best, imperfectly true. A firm that is excellent on consumer issues may be fair on employment and atrocious on pollution. To some extent such variations may be a function of the nature of the business, or such circumstances as the relative importance of a particular firm in a given community. It may also be a matter of historical accident, of a given executive's preoccupations, and so on.

Both generality and specificity of responsiveness are matters of importance; and there are certain obvious reasons for expecting variations in patterns of responsiveness. One would not expect an industrial goods manufacturer to foster a program of consumer education in a school system, though retailers such as Sears Roebuck have done so. One would expect a local utility to show more concern for its local community than for the nation at large. To the extent that it has a large fixed plant investment it will ''logically'' be interested in the economic and social vitality of the local community, and the general good will of whatever community it is beholden to for rate increases. A toy manufacturer will be interested in product safety, a steel manufacturer in water and air pollution, and so on. Any firm that feels it is both highly visible and dependent on public good will is likely to be concerned with vulnerability to ''third sector'' action. Other such ''rational'' relationships can be imagined.

A first item of research interest would be to establish the extent to which patterns of corporate responsiveness reflect such ''rational'' differentiations of response. The interesting findings would be those that did not fit the pattern. For example, a company's structure might inhibit a response that would otherwise seem "rational." Thus, a nationwide utility or retailer might have a great deal more trouble mounting an effective community relations program than would a local utility or retailer. Or, one might look for a differential rate of implementation of policies which had more and less direct relevance to the business, not necessarily because top management was more enthusiastic about policies of more direct relevance—though this might well be so—but because operating managers were more convinced of their legitimacy. One ought also to look to the extent that a pattern of selective responsiveness is a matter of conscious overall business strategy. A best guess is that at this time such an overall deliberate strategy would be rare.

*Learning Responsiveness*

The notions of "selective" responsiveness and "general" responsiveness are not incompatible as such, if the selectivity is in fact strategically based. If the corporation is undergoing a transformation to a more adaptive organizational entity, then it should be acquiring general skills for selecting and implementing responses. From what we have seen, if this is taking place it is happening only occasionally and imperfectly. One would expect some skills for implementing new policies to be rather general ones which would cut across regular business and "social" issues. Yet, one finds a corporation which has within the last few years established corporate-wide policies on computer usage and on purchasing, and it is only by chance that it finds out that the same organizational procedures would appear to be applicable in the area of equal employment opportunity. This may be true in other policy areas also, but the connection had not yet been made.

While many firms view responsiveness as a general phenomenon at the commitment phase ("How do we decide what we should be doing?"), few, if any, see it as such at the implementation phase. Yet, since the implementation phase of the response process is generally the most complicated and prolonged, the acquisition of skill in implementation is a crucial aspect of the development of more responsive business firms. This learning may occur in one of two ways. It may happen within individual organizations, or it may happen via research which converts existing experience into the sort of "social knowledge" referred to previously. And, in turn, the social knowledge can be of two sorts. One would be substantive in the sense of codifying generalized aspects of the response process. The other would be process oriented and focus on how organizations can learn responsiveness from their own experience.

Research on organizational learning of responsiveness should in the first instance focus on a full variety of corporate efforts to implement broad policies whether they be related to regular business concerns or social concerns. Methods may range from the establishment of staff positions, the appointment of committees, the manning of committees, the socialization of management, the formulation and communication of policies—and by what means and with what personnel—devising of information systems, changing evaluation systems and so on. Distinctions should be made among procedures which are highly general, (e.g., involved in the formulation of policy those who will have to implement it), those which are peculiarly suited to specific organizations, and those which are issue limited.

Special attention should be paid to instances in which learning does and does not occur, both across issues and across organizational units. For example, it is usual for some operating units to be more advanced in responsiveness, yet other units fail to learn or even resist learning from the advanced divisions. The nature and role of such advanced divisions should be studied. Various patterns may emerge. Such divisions may be sufficiently distinctive that their problems of responsiveness are qualitatively different from those of other divisions. A highly profitable division, using high technology and thus requiring highly educated personnel, may find responsiveness compatible and relatively easy in comparison with a division in different circumstances. Such a division may influence other divisions in a delayed and general fashion by supplying a disproportionate number of personnel who are promoted to corporate ranks.

Our experiences suggest, however, that failure to learn across operating units is less easily explicable than these comments suggest. We have seen instances which cannot be explained by differences in business circumstances. It is a phenomenon that requires understanding.

*Summary*

The implementation phase of corporate responsiveness has until recently been virtually ignored as a research topic. While it has received a fair amount of attention recently, it deserves considerable additional ongoing attention. Types of research which are required are:

1. Detailed road maps of the problems of implementing specific types of policies, such as pollution control, equal employment opportunity, occupational safety and health, community relations and such industry-specific programs as minority lending by banks. Such research should be oriented to the time dimension of implementation, focusing on the phases which the implementation process goes through, identifying the administrative problems characteristic of each phase, and the administrative options that are likely to succeed or fail. The thrust of this research is not at

the technical aspects of implementation, e.g., how to measure emissions or locate minority or female employees, but at the administrative task of ensuring that what should be done is in fact done.

2. Various roles are key to the implementation process. In particular, I have noted that an overall implementation role may be evolving that merits continued attention. Additionally, the role of the chief executive officer and any other personnel who may be especially relevant would merit research.

3. The various activities involved in the implementation process such as design of information systems, changes in executive evaluation, and the like, are themselves administratively sufficiently complicated to warrant separate research attention.

4. A basic premise of this agenda is that beyond reacting to specific issues the business corporation may be becoming more generally responsive. If this is true, then it ought to be developing a general capability for implementing new policies as they come along. If this learning process is taking place spontaneously, that process should be a focus of attention. Additionally, research should be directed at those aspects of successful implementation that can be codified and transmitted so as to facilitate the learning of responsiveness in the corporate world.

# FOOTNOTES

*This is a portion of a larger manuscript entitled "An Agenda for Research and Development on Corporate Responsiveness," completed in 1974. Professor Bauer was at work on a review of subsequent research results and modifications of his initial research design in the light of experience and more recent developments at the time of his death.

1. For a fuller exposition of my view of such processes see [8, Ch.1].

2. This general topic has been the subject of considerable research. A researcher starting to work in this area should consult [4].

3. For well-conceptualized studies of regular business "decisions" see [5] & [9].

4. My continued reference to "top management" requires clarification. In complex business organizations, more than one level of management is often in a position to make commitments on matters of social concern. A division head or even a department manager may take initiative on his or her own. To the extent that he commands the relevant resources and has jurisdiction over a meaningful organizationl segment, he or she is, for our purposes and in this context, "top management."

5. The uninitiated reader may be surprised at the notion that "underlings" can constrain the boss's spending. In fact the funds available at the corporate level may be quite limited. A public broadcasting executive complained to me that it was very difficult to get support from divisionalized firms: "The money is all down in the divisions and when headquarters asks them to support a public T.V. program they couldn't care less."

6. For an especially pertinent exposition see [1] & [2].

# REFERENCES

1. Ackerman, R.W., "How Companies Respond to Social Demands," *Harvard Business Review,* July-August, 1973, pp. 88–98.
2. Ackerman, R.W., *The Social Challenge to Business,* Cambridge, Massachusetts: Harvard University Press, 1975.
3. Ackerman, R.W., and Bauer, R.A., *Corporate Social Responsiveness: The Modern Dilemma,* Reston, Virginia: Reston Publishing Company, Inc., 1976.
4. Aguilar, F.J., *Scanning the Business Environment.* New York: The Macmillan Company, 1967, p.66.
5. Aharoni, Y., *The Foreign Investment Decision Process,* Harvard Business School, Division of Research, 1966.
6. Bauer, R. A., Cauthorn, L. T., and Warner, R. P., "The Management Process Audit Manual," see Appendix A.
7. Bauer, R. A., and Fenn, D.H., Jr., *The Corporate Social Audit.* New York, The Russell Sage Foundation, 1972.
8. Bauer, R. A., and Gergen, K. J., *The Study of Policy Formation:* New York, The Free Press, 1971, p.2.
9. Bower, J. L., *Managing the Resource Allocation Process,* Harvard Business School, Division of Research, 1970.
10. Houget, G. R., *United States Steel and the Acceptance of Unionism: Some Implications for Contemporary Management,* Unpublished paper, April 21, 1973.
11. Murray, E. A., Jr., *The Implementation of Social Policies in Commercial Banks,* Doctoral Thesis, Harvard Business School, 1974; See also Cases 12–15 in [3].

# CASE RESEARCH IN CORPORATION AND SOCIETY STUDIES

James E. Post and Patti N. Andrews

## INTRODUCTION

Today, some fifteen years since its beginning as a recognizable area of management scholarship, the business and society field can cite much progress, even while acknowledging that a number of problems continue to pose a challenge. The academic successes include curriculum development, teaching materials, and an expanding cadre of teachers and scholars identifying with the field. The number and variety of courses and approaches to curricula continue to expand. Faculty have increasing number of texts, case collections, and visual tools on which to draw in designing their courses. Additionally, the membership of the Social Issues in Management Division of the Academy of Management has grown from a handful of members in 1970 to nearly 500 today.

The most serious continuing challenge involves the research base of the field. Few things have proven as consistently frustrating to interested scholars, students, and observers as the substance and methodology of business and society research. The diversity of research questions, the variety of theoretical perspectives from which those questions have been approached, the number of different research tools employed, and the unevenness with which they are applied have all provoked serious and substantial criticism.

While some of this criticism seems unjustified for a field still in search of a central focus (Preston, 1975), a considerable amount is warranted. To the extent that anecdote, opinion, and ideology have characterized much of the published material, subjectivity and bias are real problems. "Informed speculations" dominate the methodology landscape. An occasional survey, statistical analysis of time series data, or other quantitative analysis can be found in the early literature of the field. Today, while more of the latter can be found, case research remains a vital form of inquiry. By "case research," we mean a whole range of research methodologies in which the case study is central, whether singly, in sequence, comparative, or as part of a larger research effort.

The criticisms of case research—poor generalizability, subjectivity bias, no degrees of freedom—are familiar but have not significantly diminished the volume of research that employs this approach. Of thirty reports published from original research in Volumes 1-3 of *Research in Corporate Social Performance and Policy,* for example, eighteen employed case research as a major methodological part of the study. Case research remains a popular approach to inquiry in the field because it is well-suited to the study of many important questions about the corporation and society where sheer complexity of issues renders other methodologies inappropriate.

Case analysis as a research effort can yield much more than mere description of facts. What this field can learn from neighboring disciplines is to use a case for its full theoretical potential. Its potential for theoretical payoff comes in part from the variety of techniques which fall under the umbrella of the general term "case research": the single case study, a sequence of case studies, comparative case analysis, or phased research in which cases play a major role.

- The *single case study* has a familiar but tainted image in the corporation and society field. In the broader world of research single cases—such as the contribution to anthropology of the "Lucy" discovery (the "missing link")—have lead to powerful theories. So have *sequential cases*—such as successive single case studies of dying patients—contributed to theories of death in sociology. Corporation-society research that proceeds in phases may use single or sequential cases as well (see Taylor, 1979 and 1981).

- *Comparative cases* are familiar in the corporation-society field. A number of comparative case analyses may be examined in the first three volumes of this series as well as in Randall (1972), Murray (1974), Jesaitis (1969), and Unterman (1968).
- *Phased research,* in which cases play a limited role—e.g., pilot study—use cases in conjunction with other research techniques. A recent example of the potential contribution of cases to a larger study may be found in Mahon (1982) where cases were used early in the research effort to generate research questions. This was followed by an extensive quantitative analysis of the public affairs data[1] and used to build some theory about public affairs structures and activities. The theory was then examined in the context of another case study.

# A PERSPECTIVE ON CORPORATION-SOCIETY RESERACH

The literature of the corporation-society field can be organized along two principal dimensions. The first relates to whether the researcher's focus is primarily on the corporation, either individually or as an institution, or society, as manifested in its institutions, for example, government— or in specific social problems or issues—e.g., environment protection. Only a few studies have emphasized the interaction process between business and its environment, thereby bridging the boundary between the two (Epstein, 1969; Post and Mahon, 1980).

A second dimension of the literature of the field ranges from theoretical to applied. It is possible to distinguish between those studies which are relatively more theoretical in their approach to the corporation-society relationship (Galbraith, 1967; Lindblom, 1977; Friedman, 1962; Rawls, 1971) and those which are relatively more applied or practical in nature (Ackerman, 1975; Ackerman and Bauer, 1976; Murray, 1974; Stone, 1975; Sethi, 1977). These studies have in common a concern with either corporate management of a changing social and political environment or societal management—e.g., regulation, direct action, or public policy— of important problems of corporate social and economic performance.

The central themes of the corporation-society field as reflected in the literature can be illustrated in terms of the dimensions mentioned above. The typology is illustrated by topics in Figure 1A and by reference to specific studies in Figure 1B.

## The Applied Perspective

The topics and studies in Quadrant I of each of the figures are those which tend to have a managerial focus and which are primarily concerned

*Figure 1A.*  Literature of the Corporation-Society Field

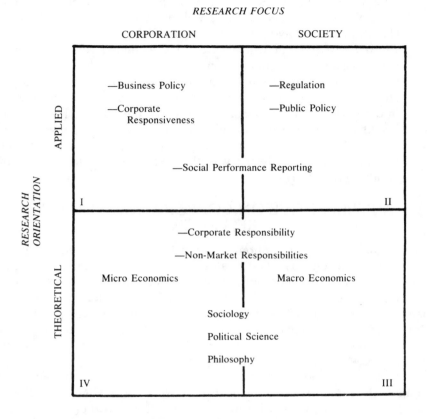

*RESEARCH FOCUS*

with questions of how companies manage their responses to a changing social and political environment. Many "corporate responsiveness" studies fall squarely into this area, as do studies from business policy which deal with the strategic impact of regulation, social trends, and public issues. The literature of this entire area emphasizes a concern with the running of private sector organizations, and the way in which those organizations do or should respond to environmental change. The writings of Ackerman (1973, 1975), Ackerman and Bauer (1976), Hanson (1979), Murray (1976), and Post (1978) all manifest a concern with organizational repsonsiveness to external change.

Quadrant II also reflects an applied perspective, but from a societal or public sector orientation rather than the private one that characterizes Quadrant I. Unlike Quadrant I studies, in which the research generally adopts a perspective from within the firm, the researcher's perspective in Quadrant II studies is "in society"; and the dominant concern is a

*Figure 1B.* Literature of the Corporation-Society Field

RESEARCH FOCUS

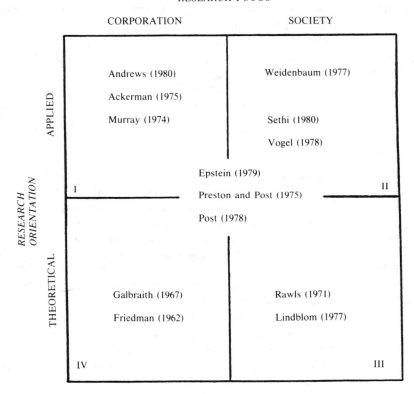

CORPORATION                          SOCIETY

APPLIED

Andrews (1980)                    Weidenbaum (1977)

Ackerman (1975)

Murray (1974)                     Sethi (1980)

Vogel (1978)

Epstein (1979)

I                    Preston and Post (1975)                    II

Post (1978)

RESEARCH ORIENTATION

THEORETICAL

Galbraith (1967)                  Rawls (1971)

Friedman (1962)                   Lindblom (1977)

IV                                                            III

social problem or the external effects of corporate performance. The literature of antitrust, industrial organization, and regulatory policy generally speaks to the way in which society, through public policy, can alter, influence, and shape corporate performance.

Spanning the boundary between Quadrants I and II are various studies of corporate social performance measurement. Ranging from Bauer and Fenn's (1972) discussion of the corporate social audit to more sophisticated attempts to match internal and public performance on a common set of measurement dimensions (Preston, 1978; Kelly, 1978; Rey, 1980; Dierkes, 1980), the literature of corporate performance measurement represents applied studies that span the private sector/public sector boundary. In addition, a number of studies have examined the responses of both private and public sector organizations to the same phenomenon. For example, the Investor Responsibility Research Center (IRRC) annually publishes analyses of issues that are the subject of stockholder resolutions. It includes descriptions of the positions of the businesses involved, those of regulatory agencies, public action groups, and other institutional actors. Moreover, there are a number of especially interesting studies from an applied perspective that deliberately examine what actions both corporations and society can (should) take with regard to specific events or issues. Epstein's (1979) analysis of political action committees (PACs), for example, stresses both the considerations that should govern a corporate management's commitment to a PAC and the considerations society, through the Federal Election Commission and the Congress, must give to the PAC phenomenon.

## The Theoretical Perspective

Although the applied literature of the field is extensive, a far greater number of analyses take theoretical perspectives (Quadrants III and IV). Quadrant III includes an emphasis on the societal consequences and aspects of business and modern economics, while Quadrant IV identified studies that tend to focus more sharply on business as an institutional force in society. Scholars from such disciplines as economics (Marris, 1974; Friedman, 1962; Galbraith, 1967), sociology (Zeitlin, 1978), political science (Orren, 1974), and philosophy (Rawls, 1971; Nozick, 1975) have analyzed the relationship between the corporation and society or the issues spawned by that relationship. The abundance of this literature and the continuing efforts of political scientists, sociologists, economists, and historians to undertake research that deals with questions of corporation and society underscores both the importance of the subject and the opportunities for discipline-based research.

## Summary

The research dimensions and perspectives discussed in this section have two important implications for research design. First, they can help a researcher clearly specify whether it is the corporation, society, or the interactive processes that are the principal focus of analysis. Whatever the reason for undertaking a case research project, the researcher is well advised to be explicit about what is to be accomplished and why he or she has selected to use a case approach rather than some other alternative. The more explicit the researcher can be in answering these questions, the better the job she/he will have done in framing the research question itself.

Second, the researcher will be forced to clarify the relationship between theory and data. The design of a research study will differ greatly according to its primary concern—whether to simply explore the "what is" of a particular social problem or to examine that problem in light of *a priori* theoretical statements. It is against this background of substantive focus (corporation, society, or both) and research perspectives (theoretical, applied) that the discussion of case research must proceed.

## TYPES OF CASE RESEARCH

Case research can be used in many areas in need of systematic inquiry for a range of theoretical purposes. One aim of this paper is to entice the researcher who has made a choice about focus to make a similarly explicit choice about whether the primary effort should be to describe, explore, explain, or predict. With so much description and exploration already in the literature, many areas of research may be ready for the latter two aims.

There are four broad categories of case analysis, each of which describes a distinct genre of research. While in reality these categories overlap, sharp distinctions are drawn here to emphasize differences in primary purpose. *Descriptive* case research attempts to present a coherent picture of the facts that constitute a particular problem, organization, or object of study. Descriptive case research is characterized by an accurate representation of events, and while they may include some interpretation of data or drawing of inference, there is little evidence of conscious analytical purpose to the case report.

*Exploratory* case research is a deliberate form of "mucking around," done for the purpose of identifying issues, problems, or unique facets of a complex situation or organization. Exploratory case research has a more deliberate analytical purpose than the descriptive focus in that the researcher is undertaking the accumulation of facts for the purpose of identifying or clarifying research questions, or developing hypotheses for further study. Certain implicit ideas inevitably guide the researcher's exploration.

The descriptive and exploratory types of case research are characterized by a primarily inductive approach that requires assembling all available facts that together render a description without major gaps. The principal methodological problem with descriptive and exploratory case research involves the need for a guarantee [embodied in Churchman's (1971) "guarantor"] that the factual landscape has been swept sufficiently clean. If there are important facts that have escaped the researcher's net and these leave holes in the picture, the representations made about the case will be inherently flawed, and the conclusions drawn suspect. Nothing undermines the credibility of descriptive or exploratory case research as seriously as disclosure that important factual evidence was excluded

or never sought. Hence, the critical need in such descriptive or exploratory case research is comprehensiveness of data collection and truth-
fulness in representation to the reader.

*Explanatory* case research is somewhat less grounded in factual presentation than the descriptive and exploratory types. The distinctive feature of the explanatory case research is its starting point: an explanatory
work begins with a proposition, hypothesis, or conflicting statements of
theory that the case study is used to test or prove. In this context
explanatory case research is a device for advancing theory by empirical
testing of theoretical propositions.

An extension of the explanatory studies, *predictive* analysis is the
ultimate form of case research. Such a research study will have gathered
together all relevant factual data, identified and analyzed key issues, and
concluded with one or more hypotheses or predictions about future developments. Usually, such predictions take the form of scenarios. These
scenarios may focus on external events or they may focus on clusters
of internal characteristics—such as, Bruce Scott's (1971) analysis of the
stages of growth through which companies evolve and of the characteristics which distinguish each stage of development.

Not surprisingly, case research is most frequently found in inquiry of
an applied nature. The concern with "practical"questions of organizational and social functioning has led scholars to study questions that
have a substantial impact on the operations or organizations or the
smooth functioning of society. Thus, in terms of Figure 1, case research
is most prominently found in applied/corporation and applied/society
quadrants. The business policy, corporate responsiveness, and applied
public policy literature frequently highlight descriptive and explanatory
case analyses that focus on important research topics and/or key events—
for example, Chrysler bailout, Love Canal, or Bay of Pigs invasion.

It is important to note that case research has also been used to build
or to test theory in the study of the corporation and society. Max Weber's
(1947) study of bureaucracy, and formulation of ideal types, can well be
viewed as a theoretical construct built upon extensive case research.
The Miles and Snow (1978) study of organization/environment relationships repeatedly draws on case studies to develop key conceptual propositions. Unlike Thompson (1967), whose discussion of organization/en-
vironment relations was almost wholly theoretical in its original
presentation, and subsequently tested through the empirical case research
of others (Page, 1972), the distinctive feature of the Miles and Snow
work is their systematic building of theory through a series of explanatory
and predictive case analyses.

The usefulness of case research to both the building and verification
of theory underscores Henry Mintzberg's (1977) assertion that research

is really a continuous process of inductive and deductive analysis. Case research may be undertaken either for the purpose of building an empirical base upon which hypotheses and research propositions can be predicted or used as a device to test and examine previously articulated hypotheses or propositions. It is important for the researcher to know what is to be accomplished with the research and to refrain from misusing the findings developed from one type of case research as "proof" at other levels. A well-done descriptive case research effort ought not to be used for predictive purposes, and an explanatory case research effort, which has not attempted to sweep in all relevant available facts to adequately describe, ought not to be cited as factual example for propositions other than those tested. Much of the methodological criticism of case research stems from the careless citation of case research for purposes other than that for which the case was researched and written.[2] Table 1 presents the four categories of case research to help the individual(s) planning research to be clear on the primary purpose of the effort.

## DEFINING THE SUBJECT OF CASE RESEARCH

What is the appropriate subject (object) of case research? The question is important, for the researcher must provide some boundaries that define the subject being researched. This becomes difficult in practice, however,

*Table 1.* Types of Case Research

| Types of Case Research | Focus | Characteristic Uses |
|---|---|---|
| Descriptive | *What* occurred? | Develop an empirical baseline for studying the subject. Occasionally used to illustrate a theoretical point. |
| Exploratory | *How* did the event develop, or the organization act? | Pilot study; provide insight for structuring a larger analysis. Used to clarify variables, so as to permit more focused analysis in subsequent stages of research. |
| Explanatory | *Why* did the event or organizational action occur? | Build a theory. Test two conflicting theoretical propositions. Add new variables to the analysis of previously studied questions. |
| Predictive | *What* will happen when such conditions arise again? | Test and verify theoretical propositions. Articulate a new theory? |

for researchers often find themselves with the proverbial ball of twine that continues to unravel in ways that reveal new connections and directions. So, while it is true that bounding is an essential step in case research, there is a reality that everything is related to everything else and that the effort to delimit the scope of case research is somewhat arbitrary.

Case research can be focused in a number of ways. It is always best to search for a "natural" or recurrent context in which a case can be defined. The bounding will always be factual in nature but will inevitably require some conceptual abstraction to make the definition precise. "Natural" configurations are easiest to work with because they require the least amount of conceptual abstraction and definition. Thus, cases that are limited to an entity, such as a particular organization, are easier to define than those dealing with an issue, trend, or social phenomenon. Preston (1978) has argued that good research in the study of corporate social policy and performance requires that the researcher have a firm grasp of the organization, the environment, and the processes by which they interact. It is possible to select any of these components as the basis for bounding the case, though the degree of abstraction necessary to clarify the boundaries may differ considerably depending on the choice.

Listed below are some of the common boundaries given cases in the corporation and society field. The first four concentrate on the corporation as the focal unit of analysis, the next four concentrate on society, and the last two focus on processes of interaction among institutions. The ten types of case research subjects are summarized in Table 2.

*Table 2.*   The Subjects of Case Research

*Focus on the Corporation*

1. *A Single Organization.*     Case studies of business firms, regulatory agencies, or public groups. Little abstraction necessary to define boundaries—i.e., a highly natural configuration. Evaluation criteria are comprehensiveness of factual material.

2. *An Organizational Subunit.*     Focus is on a particular department or structural subunit of the organization. Bounding is more difficult than in #1, because organizations do not include the same scope of activities in departments of the same name. Evaluation criteria are comprehensiveness for descriptive studies, subtlety for explanatory and predictive studies.

3. *An Organizational Practice.*     Case studies of programs, activities, or policies. Bounding is made difficult by definitional difference among organizations. Evaluation criteria rest on factual completeness and comparison with other organizations.

*Table 2.* (Continued)

4. *An Industry.*    Some definitional difficulty, but generally includes competitors, potential competitors, and producers of substitute goods/services. Bounding is generally based on product line definitions. Criteria for evaluation rest on factual completeness and comparison with other industry analyses.

*Focus on Society*

5. *Segment of Society.*    Focus on specific stakeholders in society. Bounding problems are definitional in nature—i.e., need to specify who is within the definition and who is outside. Criteria for evaluation rest on precision of definition as measured against alternative definitions (e.g., does "community" mean only groups and institutions, or general citizenry?).

6. *A Social Phenomenon.*    Focus on a significant event or happening in society (e.g., the drive to put a man on the moon, "corporate Watergate" disclosures, or new conservatism). Bounding problem is one of definition—i.e., distinguishing the phenomenon from the general history of the period. Evaluation criteria include precision of definition, and comparative insight into phenomenon.

7. *A Social Issue.*    The most popular subject for case studies in business and society field. Definitional problem is significant—i.e., what is a social issue? Bounding will be an increasingly relevant criteria in evaluating such studies.

8. *Society as a Whole.*    Occasionally the subject of case studies, an entire country or culture (e.g., Japan) is most difficult to bound properly. Evaluation criteria must include comprehensiveness or factual presentation, and comparative insights into multidimensional cultural aspects.

*Focus on Processes of Interaction*

9. *Public Policy Process.*    How actors of different, often conflicting interests find bases to accommodate one another and resolve problems. Difficult to separate the process from the organizations or institutions that are directly involved. Evaluation should focus on the author's skill in distinguishing the process aspects from the substantive aspects of the subject.

10. *Direct Action.*    Campaigns, boycotts, and so forth to influence other institutions. Bounding is often done by focusing on events (e.g., Campaign GM, Nestlé Boycott). Evaluation criteria include comprehensiveness of factual presentation, and comparison with alternative explanations.

## 1. A Single Organization

Case studies of business firms, regulatory agencies, or other organizational units in their entirety are among the most common forms of case research. The organizational case study requires very little abstraction to define the boundaries of the case, the organization being a very natural unit for analysis. More difficult to meet is the criterion of comprehensiveness of factual information because of the sensitivity and confidentiality of internal documents, interviews, and so forth. An alternative is to organize a case around only objectively verifiable data—such as publicly available. This approach allows the researcher to comment on "operative policies" of the organization, even while unable to comment on its "stated policies" and intentions (Post, 1978). Such an approach may be satisfactory for explanatory or predictive case research although insufficiently comprehensive for descriptive case research. For examples of explanatory case research see Chatov, 1978; Post, 1978; and Sethi, 1977.

## 2. An Organizational Subunit

This type of case research concentrates on a particular department or structural subunit—such as division—of an organization. The researcher's concern may be with the manner in which a particular staff unit relates to operating divisions on social issues matters—e.g., equal employment opportunity—the way in which a subunit functions within the framework of the whole organization—e.g., Competition Bureau within the Federal Trade Commission—or the degree to which the internal functioning of a subunit within the organization depends upon its relations to external entities—for example, community relations office. Research at the subunit level can create more pitfalls than organizational units in their entirety. A subunit's boundaries are more fluid and less easily fixed for research than those of an entire organization; in addition, subunits across different organizations may have more differences than similarities. Under such circumstances, the researcher must take care to be as explicit as possible in defining the subunit within the context it operates.

## 3. An Organizational Practice

Specific organizational practices are frequent targets for social issues researchers. Single case and comparative case analyses of such practices as affirmative action programs (Taylor, 1979), corporate philanthropy (Callaghan, 1975), and political activities (Brenner, 1980; Epstein, 1980) are representative of the approach. Problems often occur because of the difficulty of precisely defining the practice, or class of practices, to be researched. For example, philanthropy is often a part of a business firm's community relations or public affairs activities, providing a rationale for the actual disbursement of charitable gifts. Case research on philanthropic practices would have to relate philanthropic practices to the community affairs or public affairs efforts of the organization. The limitations of the research must be clearly specified. The field research itself may be the first indication that the practice as originally defined encompasses several seemingly discrete areas. The practice may be only understood in the context of some other area of corporate behavior, and the researcher must be prepared to revise the original conception of the topic—e.g., philanthropic practices—in favor of a more precise definition of the subject—for example, philanthropy in the service of community relations goals.

### 4. An Industry

While product line definitions may be quite appropriate in some case research, there are situations in which the definition of the topic may call for a broader definition of the industry. Case research on the political impact of the oil industry, for example, requires inclusion of not only the integrated major producers but also the independent producers, marketers, and refiners, the wildcat operators, oil service companies, and so forth. What drives the determination of the industry definition is the theoretical requirement that the definition meet the needs of the research question and the theory being pursued.

Definitions that meet such needs are important to search for in case research, for they frequently have a bearing on the behavior of firms in response to social issues. For example, the infant formula industry consists of firms which do not exclusively manufacture and sell infant formula products. Rather, some are food companies which sell formula as part of a line of milk-based products, while others are pharmaceutical manufacturers which sell formula as a health care product through a medical sales system (Post and Baer, 1979). As suggested, the behavior of these firms varies in ways related to their differing orientations to conducting business.

In addition to case research which concentrates on the firm or industry, it may concentrate primarily on society or some portion thereof as the focal unit for analysis. Listed below are several categories of "society-oriented" types of case research.

### 5. Segment of Society

The study of specific social groups, "stakeholders," or "relevant publics" can also be made using case research. Institutional investors (Purcell, 1979), church organizations (Vogel, 1978), and public interest networks (Gerlach, 1978) have all been the focus of case research efforts. Familiar definitional problems exist. For example, are churches institutional investors or proponents of shareholder resolutions? In terms of the topical definition, such choice will make a difference. If the focus is on institutional investors, churches may be a subset of such investors in the research. If, however, the researcher's real interest is the behavior of churches, their investment behavior regarding resolutions must be viewed as one of a number of social activities in which they engage. This specification of the context in which the focal segment is to be analyzed is a crucial research step that too often is seen as secondary in importance to gathering information. In truth, it is quite important that the researcher may be reasonably specific in placing the facets of the project into a logically appropriate arrangement. Thus, one more precise way of defining the example study mentioned above so that behavior is the focal question would be as a study of "the institutional investor behavior of denominational churches in the United States." The initiation of shareholder resolutions may be left to be considered as one type of behavior.

## 6. A Social Phenomenon

Case research often focusses on major events or social phenomena. The creation of NASA and the drive to put man on the moon, the aborted campaign to build the SuperSonic Transport (SST) (Horwitch, 1982), grass roots politics as reflected in the TVA (Selznick, 1965), the economic regulation of the New Deal (Chatov, 1978), or the present development of a synthetic fuels industry are but a few examples of social phenomena that have been examined in ways that emphasize the business/government/society relationship. A critical problem in such research is to define the phenomenon at the outset in sufficient detail so as to distinguish the case analysis from a general history. A conceptual proposition or hypothesis can facilitate case research. Sethi's study of advocacy advertising (1973), identifies a phenomenon, describes it in detail, and then uses organizational studies to further elucidate the significance of the advocacy advertising phenomenon. See also Sethi's study of executive liability trends (1981) and Horwitch's (1980) research on large scale social projects such as synfuels. In each, the key is a clear description of the phenomenon followed by research that illuminates the complexity of that phenomenon and enriches understanding of factors and forces affecting it.

## 7. A Social Issue

The most prevalent of all types of case research in the business and society field is the study of specific social issues, which have long dominated the published literature of the field. Methodological problems exist with respect to these studies. The thoroughness and subtlety of analysis has often been in question. Too often, these studies have been little more than scrapbook collections of material gleaned from secondary sources with little or no primary investigation. At the same time, with appropriate controls and theoretical guidance, quality research with useful theoretical payoff may and should be designed using materials already published in an astute manner. Social issue case studies and research can make a greater contribution if they rise beyond the purely descriptive level.

Today, research on social issues should focus on the identification of explanatory variables and prediction of future developments, beginning with a conceptual definition of what constitutes an issue. For example, the senior author has argued that a social issue exists whenever a gap exists between the public's expectations of an organization or industry's proper performance and the actual performance of that organization or industry (Post, 1978). Thus, redlining practices, doing business in South Africa, worker exposure to toxic substances, marketing infant formula in developing nations, and dumping taconite in lakes and streams all have in common a definitional similarity. Whereas the analysis of one more incident of industrial effluent discharge is not very helpful research for the business and society field, and analysis of a pollution control problem in terms of a given definition or concept—e.g., public issue life cycle may serve to illuminate a new facet of business/government/society relations or suggest a variation on the basic way public issues evolve which adds new knowledge to the field.

In the 1980s the scholarly significance of social issue analysis must come from the researcher's needs to be skilled at either doing an analysis of the larger problem in a context—for example, the substantive analysis of bank lending practices—or from systematic analysis in terms of an *a priori* definition or concept of the issue.

### 8. Society as a Whole

Occasionally, an entire society will form the basis of case research of corporation-society interaction; at the society level each society is one case. Most notable in this type of research are the efforts of Sethi (1978) and Lodge (1975) to compare the business/government/society relationship in Japan with that of the United States. As critical reviews of both efforts indicate, such analysis is fraught with conceptual, methodological, and factual problems. The most telling criticism may well be that institutional interrelationships are so culturally specific, and so entwined with the entire fabric of the society, that nothing less than expert treatment of each nation can produce a truly insightful analysis.

More promising than the inevitably broad national comparisons, however, is more narrowly focused study of an institution which arises out of a societal setting. Dickie's (1981) recent study of the interaction between government, multinational firms, and social interests in the development of the Indonesian securities market and Monsen and Walters' (1980) analysis of public enterprises in Western European nations suggest a direction such cross-cultural research might take.

Finally, there are case studies that focus primarily on processes of interaction among social institutions or between institutions and individuals. In particular, there are opportunities for case research on the public policy process and direct corporation/society interaction.

### 9. Public Policy Process

The political processes through which public and private interests are reconciled provide rich opportunities for case research. The bounding of the research can be accomplished by focusing on a particular piece of legislation (Redman, 1973), an administrative agency decision—e.g., FTC, NLRB—or a court opinion—(for example, First National Bank of Boston vs. Bellotti). Much legal research has concentrated on the judicial process as a way of defining and resolving social conflicts, and useful predictive analyses might be developed in this context. In evaluating such research, the researcher must distinguish the type of case research being undertaken—descriptive, exploratory, explanatory, predictive— and whether the author is attempting to analyze the process or the substantive issue on which the political process is acting.

### 10. Direct Action

Public action campaigns, boycotts, and so forth, represent distinct forms of direct social action taken against an organization or idea. Bounding may require that a stream of events be defined as a direct action campaign—e.g., Nestlé boycott, even if a formal campaign has not been announced (e.g., Moral Majority's review of television advertising). The researcher's explanation when compared with alternative explanations offered by participants or other observers needs to be balanced and to offer greater insight than any single viewpoint.

## METHODOLOGICAL ISSUES

The process of case research must address a number of important methodological issues—for example, to what extent must the information be collected "systematically"? Must there be a uniform presentation? How does one identify and distinguish fact from interpretation or inference? These questions of methodology, in turn, are related to the purposes for which a case study is used. Issues of methodology are addressed in the process of inquiry.

Systematic inquiry can and has been done in many different, legitimate ways. C. West Churchman in the *Design of Inquiring Systems* (1971) argues that the key for the inquirer is to recognize that certain fundamental questions—what guarantees the value and validity of the work ("who is the guarantor"), and what is the relation between observed fact and *a priori* assumptions—must be answered in advance to insure the integrity of the inquiry. The models of inquiry in the field are relatively few in number, and researchers inevitably gravitate toward original research rather than the replication of other studies. Substantively, in the sense of covering the territory in numerous contexts, this is healthy for the field; but methodologically, there are perils for researchers.

There are a number of useful papers on methodology in a previous volume in this series and more in the present volume. In particular, Aldag and Bartol's (1978) article on empirical studies, Frederick's (1978) paper on social auditing methodology, and Bauer's (1978) paper on analyzing the corporate response process each present important insights into the problems encountered in designing research studies. Papers by Epstein (1980), Post and Baer (1980), Dierkes (1980), and Rey (1980) in Volume 2 also highlight methodological issues.

Three propositions about methodology can be set forth. First, most research in this field is "qualitative," rather than "quantitative," because the questions are more amenable to qualitative research. Second, many of the research questions require the use of multiple techniques rather than any single technique because the probability of a single technique providing a comprehensive answer is very low. Research is more appropriately viewed as a *process of inquiry* requiring many tools, rather than the application of a single technique in a series of replications. Third, case research has proven to be an especially useful approach because it is well suited to analysis of the complexity of business/government/society relations. The weaknesses of case research are not unique; they are the fundamental problems of all inquiry. With appropriate attention to those weaknesses, the case study is a legitimate form of research in this field.

"Quantitative research" in the sense of large sample-based research has been infrequently done in the business and society field, although it does achieve prominence in industrial organization and applied public policy areas, and in the study of such topics as corporate ownership and control and executive attitudes on social policy matters. The prerequisite for quantitative analysis is, of course, an adequate data base. Where time series data exist, as in the Economic Censuses or IRS collections, statistical analysis can be fruitfully pursued. But there have been relatively few such data bases in the business and society field. Recent collections of data on corporate boards of directors (Sethi, 1979), public affairs offices (Boston University, 1981), and political action committees (Epstein, 1979) improve the prospects for more quantitative research in the future.

"Qualitative research," particularly in the form of case studies, participant observation, and interviews, has been the foundation of most empirical work in the field. This is not unusual, since it has been necessary to create factual and descriptive documentation of what is actually occurring as a starting point. Today, a baseline of information has been created in many areas of the field, and the need for explanatory research is increasing. While qualitative research can continue to make significant contributiuons, it must become increasingly concerned with the testing of hypotheses.

An especially important example of the continuing importance of qualitative research can be found in Philip Burch's (1972) study of corporate ownership and control. For several decades following the Berle and Means (1932) study of corporate ownership patterns, more sophisticated quantitative studies of time series data concluded that there was a nearly total separation of stock ownership by family interests and effective control of management policy in those large corporations. Burch's study painstakingly drew on insider insights to reassess the influence of familiar ownership interests and produced a fundamental reexamination of the ownership/control relationship. More recently, Edward Herman (1981) has reexamined a portion of the data base and addressed anew the relationship of ownership and control and the social implications thereof.

The point, simply stated, is that the research technique to be used must fit the question being asked. Qualitative analysis does not sacrifice scholarly rigor by its mere use. Indeed, good qualitative studies are the key to the creation of useful and valuable bases for quantitative analysis.

## THE PROCESS OF CASE RESEARCH

Case research is often a euphemism for qualitative research. While some authors view the case study as but one type of qualitative research (Duncan, 1979) on a par with interviewing and participant observation, such a conception is too narrow for this discussion of case research. Properly conceived and executed case research must incorporate the data acquired through interviews and observation but will also draw on available quantitative data. Although it is not a quantitative technique itself, case research that sweeps in all relevant data makes the inclusion—and analysis—of quantitative material inevitable. Thus, a research case study is more than just qualitative research, and something other than a simple qualitative technique. It is, rather, a basic way of thinking about complex issues.

The process of inquiry that distinguishes case research is different from but not entirely dissimilar to the process that guides experimental or more narrowly focussed research studies. Experimental and quasi-experimental research is characterized by a straight-line process which requires beginning with theory in the form of testable hypotheses. Such a process tends to place primary emphasis on the verification of existing theory. Generation of new theory from such a process is possible but is not the primary goal. This process is like that of Kuhn's (1962, 1970) "normal science." Figure 2 illustrates the major steps in the straight-line process and is derived from Isaac and Michael (1971) and Campbell and Stanley (1963).

Case research is one of a family of processes called by Glaser and Strauss (1967) the "constant comparative method." These processes differ most widely from the straight-line process in their *iterative* character. With the theory choice decisions made (see Figure 3) and the preconceptions and assumptions made explicit, the process begins with selection of data. Iteratively, each data "slice" is collected, coded, and analyzed. This process-within-a-process insures that the most theoretical value is extracted for the effort. The data is collected because the theory needs it. It is coded relative to the explicit theoretical goals and preconceptions, and previous data slices. It is analyzed for its potential contribution to concepts (categories and their properties).

Conceptually, there are several process-within-process cycles. Each cycle widens and moves the research in steps from 1) the collecting-coding-analyzing of the data; to 2) examining new data slices for their similarities to other data and categories; to 3) examining new data slices for their differences from other data and categories; and so on with repeated comparisons of new data and concepts to what has already been developed through the latter stages of hypothesis development and theory integration. Figure 4 illustrates the movement conceptually from the theory choice to the theory level and accompanying data.

### Theory Choices

*First choice.* A central methodological question for the researcher is whether the case research is being undertaken to develop or to test theory. This decision on the primary purpose of the research will have dramatic impact on both what is to be done, and the sequence in which those activities are to be conducted. The choice is between "theory generation" and "theory verification." Either purpose can employ case research, but this choice of purpose will influence type (descriptive, exploratory, explanatory, or predictive) and the manner in which the subject (see Table 2, supra) is definitionally bound.

*Figure 2.*   Straight-Line Research Process[a]

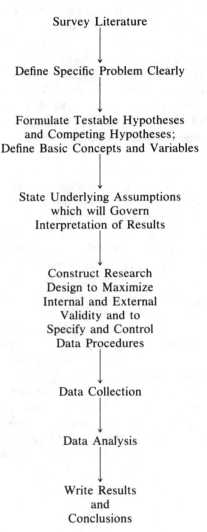

Survey Literature

Define Specific Problem Clearly

Formulate Testable Hypotheses
and Competing Hypotheses;
Define Basic Concepts and Variables

State Underlying Assumptions
which will Govern
Interpretation of Results

Construct Research
Design to Maximize
Internal and External
Validity and to
Specify and Control
Data Procedures

Data Collection

Data Analysis

Write Results
and
Conclusions

*Note:* [a]This schematic is a simplified picture of the process Isaac and Michael (1971) propose as
necessary for carrying out valid, reliable, scientific research.

*Figure 3.* Two Primary Theory Choices

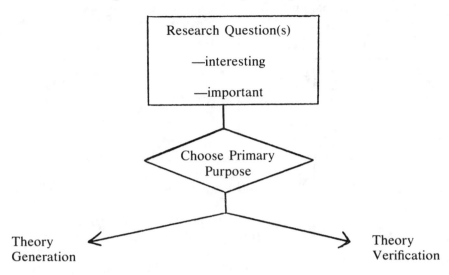

If theory verification is desired, the researcher may use either the familiar straight-line process (Figure 2) of literature review and hypothesis testing or explanatory or predictive case research as appropriate ways to test theory (Post, 1978; Merenda, 1981). If theory generation is the primary purpose, a different and less familiar process must be used which keeps the building of theory prominently first. Descriptive, exploratory, and explanatory case research may be employed to generate theory; but the research process begins with the question of what kind of theory the researcher is pursuing.

*Second choice.* Theory may range from substantive to formal in nature. That is, it may apply only to a specifically defined context(s), called substantive, or it may conceptually embrace a number of substantive areas, more formal. For example, a researcher might study the patterns of pricing behavior in one industry, and then proceed to develop a theory of pricing that was derived from known information about pricing behavior in many industries. This general theory of pricing would be a formal theory, embracing many substantive areas. The theory could then be verified by testing it in other industries, preferably not those used in its development.

Substantive and formal theory can be either developed through an inductive process or deduced from other theory areas. The researcher must recognize the importance of determining whether the questions are at a substantive or formal level; for example, is the purpose to develop

*Figure 4.* Theory Level Choices and Beginning of Constant
Comparative Method for Theory Generation

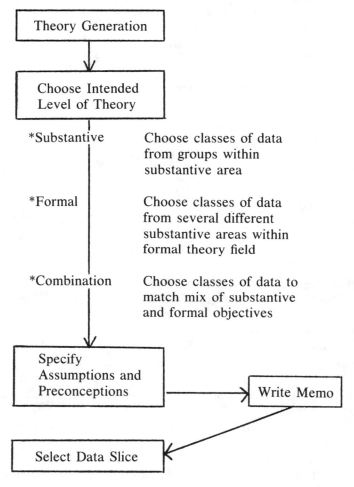

theory dealing with a narrower substantive area (e.g., social policy implementation), or more general theory (e.g., implementation of *all* corporate policies)? Similarly, one sometimes asks a question at a conceptual
level ("What is the model of corporate policy implementation?") and
then considers a specific context or substantive setting (e.g., affirmative
action programs) in which questions about policy implementation may
be examined.

In the study of the corporation and society, theory development has
usually been grounded in factual examples; and case studies of companies

and social issues have been the foundation of most conceptual propositions. Quite often, however, authors have proposed to leap from data analysis in one or two substantive areas to a general theoretical formulation. Sethi's (1975) comparison of social responsiveness in the United States and Japan, for example, suffers from an overly ambitious attempt to generalize to a model of social responsiveness from data on only two countries. Such "great leaps" would be more likely to succeed through a more systematic blending of formal and substantive theory development.

Between the extremes of purely substantive theory and purely formal theory lies a third possibility that is most appropriate in the social policy and performance area. This possibility is one of multiple layers of substantive theory between the descriptive data of an area and the formal theory. The analysis of patterns of corporate response (Post, 1976) provides an illustration. A detailed analysis of how one firm responded to many issues in the same time period provided a first collection of data and some initial concepts (reactive, manipulative, and interactive patterns). Using these definitions, a larger sample of cases organized by type of firm (manufacturing, service, trade) and by type of external change (economic, political, values, technological) was studied (Post, 1978). The analysis of this data helped sharpen the conceptual definitions and allowed the data analysis to be framed into a formal theory of how corporations behave in the face of external change. Mahon (1982), Sonnenfeld (1981), and Logsdon (1981) have since tested various facets of this theory in their own research.

The appropriateness of each of the theory-choice possibilities outlined above depends on the researcher's own goals and purposes. Glaser and Strauss (1967) reported that formal theory was infrequently developed directly from data, although there were a number of noteworthy instances in which such had occurred. The more familiar pattern was for theory to be developed first at a substantive level; then, the theory of several substantive areas was joined into a formal theory. The researcher needs to articulate this theoretical objective at the outset of a study, for it guides both the way the problem will be defined and the process of data collection. For these reasons it is desirable that the purpose be explicitly written out before data collection begins.

## Case Research and the Comparative Method

As discussed previously, the single case study has its greatest value when used as a means to describe a complex phenomenon or as an exploratory device to discern possible dimensions of the issues that may lend themselves to more precise analysis. The single case study probably cannot serve as a basis for a broad generalization nor as the ground for disproving an established generalization (Lijphart, 1971:619). Comparative case analysis, however, has greater explanatory and predictive value. Indeed, comparative case analysis can be employed to either build theory from data or to verify an extant theory against additional facets of reality. Used in either way, legitimate comparative case analysis has a number of stringent methodological requirements similar to those already discussed.

First, the researcher's purpose—such as, to build theory or to verify theory—must be decided and made explicit. Second, the kind of theory being pursued—substantive, formal, or some combination—must also be made clear. A crucial aspect of these steps is the articulation of *a priori* assumptions and preconceptions that will inevitably guide the collection of data (see Figure 4). For example, a researcher who is studying the issue of plant closings must articulate both the analytical perspective (theoretical or applied) and the substantive perspective (corporation or society) being brought to the study. It is a matter of setting forth "where you're coming from" in the design of the research.

The third step is the identification of types and classes of data to be compared according to "theoretical relevance." Theoretical relevance is the criterion which continually guides data selection throughout the research process. The question being asked is "What do the concepts thus far developed tell us about (a) the next appropriate slice of data, and (b) where to look for it?" Usually, the researcher will have to decide which of several slices of data to examine next, a decision which should be made on the basis of greatest incremental contribution to the emerging theory.

The underlying method (see Figure 5) is an iterative process that moves the researcher through four stages, beginning with: Ⓐ *data;* whose Ⓑ *categories* and their properties are developed; until Ⓒ suggested *hypotheses* are formed, based on a reduction of the original categories and properties; and finally, all these Ⓓ for a dense, well-integrated *theory* with no more major modifications needed. Depending on the scope of the particular research project, this process can take months or years.

First in the process is a procedure of sampling in which the researcher collects, codes, and analyzes each data "slice" and decides what data slice to collect next and where to look (Figure 5, Ⓐ).

In a way that Churchman (1971) describes as Leibnitzian, the first step in the data search is to look for similarities in the data that suggest a category (Figure 5, Ⓑ), although differences which appear must also be noted. The next slice of data is then selected which has a similarity to the last in terms of the category or property under examination. This effort serves to verify the usefulness of the category, establishes its basic properties, and delimits where and when and to what extent the category

*Figure 5*.  Interactive Constant Comparison Research Process[a]

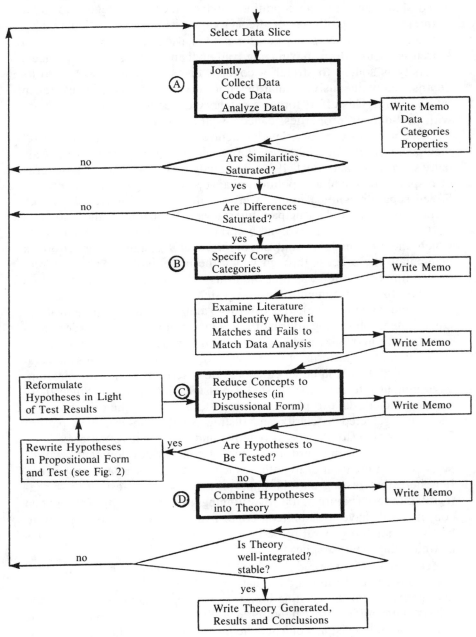

*Note:* [a]This schematic is a substantially simplified picture of the process Glaser and Strauss (1967) take their readers through. Glaser and Strauss do not present their process in flow chart form.

exists (thus, enabling prediction). Because differences are also being noted along the way, the conditions under which the category (or later in the process, hypotheses or theory) varies will also be articulated.

A second part to category development is also required where the data search is focussed on maximizing, rather than minimizing, differences. Diversity is sought to stretch a concept to its limits and push it to its depths. Simultaneously, similarities not previously noted are also taken into account. This effort forces a category conceptually tight and dense with well-defined properties, called "well-integrated."

These ideas of category development can be illustrated through a review of research undertaken by the senior author at Aetna Life & Casualty some years ago (Post, 1976). The study was concerned with patterns of response to social and political change. The company's responses to fifteen separate political issues were detailed and documented through archival research and participant interviews. Of the fifteen, the responses to twelve of the issues involved a corporate coping with problems over which the firm had no control, or in several instances, an effort to manipulate the process through which the issue evolved. The apparent or "contingent truth" was that the firms either reacted to, or attempted to shape the environment. This suggested two possible categories (reactive and manipulative); the careful examination of the organization-environment interchange during the evolution of each issue made it possible to both maximize and minimize the differences between responses. In so doing, two patterns of response were "defined". For those several issues which did not fit either category, close scrutiny of the organization-environment interaction suggested a possible third pattern. Since there was insufficient data to prove such a pattern, as with the others, a new issue was selected to clarify and distinguish the "interactive" pattern from the previously discussed reactive and manipulative patterns.

In Figure 5, ©, the third major part of concept development requires parsimonious creation of hypotheses from the categories and properties. It is here that testing may be appropriate as well as testing of the integrated theory (Figure 5, Ⓓ). A well-integrated theory with well-defined concepts will have a delimited scope, making it neither too narrow to be useful nor too general to be helpful. Delimiting bounds the contexts in which the theory applies.

According to Glaser and Strauss (1967), it is *after* core categories have been constructed from the data that similarities, convergences with, and divergences from the existing literature may be established. The reason this is done after core categories are constructed, is to minimize the amount of tunnel vision along one theoretical track brought to the analysis of the case. In their view the best theory is "grounded" theory, and the purer the grounding—that is, the less adulterated it is by pre-existing theoretical concepts—the greater its ultimate value.

## The Guarantor

Case research most dramatically departs from large sample studies supported by sophisticated statistical analyses on the question of what guarantees the validity of the research. In addition to adherence to the straight-line process, statistical analysis gains its power from sufficient degrees of freedom, tests of significance, and confidence levels. Case research does not have any comparable features, and its validity is heavily dependent on the researcher's skill and depth of understanding of the subject studied. Indeed, it is the research process itself that is a key guarantor of the validity of case research. Here we must distinguish, once again, among the various types of case research.

*Descriptive* case research only intends to describe reality. It is valid, therefore, if all relevant facts are woven into the description, and other persons who are familiar with the subject acknowledge the comprehensiveness of each case. This is precisely where many case books used for teaching in the business and society field fall woefully short of acceptable research standards. (For example, having been a participant in the controversy over infant formula marketing in developing nations, the senior author has yet to see one published case study on the controversy that is adequate in terms of factual presentation. Thus, on a substantive level these are not good descriptive case *research* works because they do not meet the standard of comprehensiveness. This may, of course, be satisfactory for teaching and discussion purposes.)

The validity of *exploratory* case research rests more on the concepts than on specific facts. In a recent article Campbell (1975) describes how degrees of freedom in a single case study come from each piece of data which saturates (in our terms) a concept. When the research purpose is the illumnnination of critical issues, the test of validity must be whether other scholars find the results illuminating. Occasionally, a researcher will undertake a single case study from a particular perspective in order to determine whether or not an issue exists *from that point of view.* Although this is a legitimate activity, it limits the validity test to one of whether others, with that same point of view, believe that critical issues have been raised. At some point the researcher can so narrow the peer group as to leave no outside guarantor available!

When the purpose of the research is to *explain* and/or *predict* behavior, it is essential that the researcher have in mind an appropriate process in advance and adhere to that plan throughout the project. Adherence insures valid control for which the process is designed. The constant comparative method is an especially powerful method to use in explanatory or predictive case research. The guarantor of validity is the density (to the saturation point) and delimited scope (for applicability and generalizability) of the resultant theory.

As the process of collecting, coding and analyzing successive "slices" of data and as category–, hypothesis–, and theory-building continue, a certain blurring of decisions or thoughts can occur. If during each iteration of each step in the process, however, the researcher takes care to write in memo form the categories and properties suggested by the data, a more consistent and logical analysis is likely to emerge. A similar practice of recording events and ideas as the process proceeds is used by the lab scientist who keeps carbon-copied notes in a spiral-bound book. The process of memo writing forces conceptualization early on and throughout the process. It is most valuable in dealing with conflicting evidence, so that the questions, puzzles, and apparent dilemmas suggested by the evidence are not lost. If preserved, these thoughts can become the clues to future conceptualization.

As Glaser and Strauss (1967) suggest and as others have subsequently demonstrated, case research, properly constructed and executed, can be both rigorous and credible in its quality and theoretical contribution. Moreover, the use of comparative case analysis—such as, several cases matched on theoretically relevant criteria—offers substantially more potential for generalizability than the single case study. None of this can be done very well from an "armchair," however. A process such as the one detailed in this paper is as demanding as many other forms of research. Most important, it provides a means of "building up" the base of substantive theory in the field.

## LARGE PROJECTS, LITTLE STEPS

Perhaps the most intriguing aspect of case research is the way in which it can complement and enhance other research techniques. There are times when the holistic perspective of a case analysis is precisely what is needed to move the frontier of understanding forward. There are other times when surveys or other large scale methods are more appropriate. Most important, there are many important research questions that require, indeed demand, that a combination or sequence of techniques be employed to produce progress in knowledge about the subject. Examples of the different roles case research has played in recent research follow.

In 1976, the senior author began a study of the international infant formula industry and the conflict surrounding competitive marketing of formula products in less developed countries. Comparative descriptive cases of the competitive strategies and behavior of five companies provided an important factual and exploratory base. The research on these firms progressed to an explanatory level when the purpose was to understand how these industry leaders would respond to national legislation and the World Health Organization's code of marketing conduct (Post, 1980). Subsequent research steps were facilitated (and made possible by the filling of a "factual void") by this intensive work and have involved large surveys in a number of developing nations.

A second example involves the Boston University research project on "The Public Affairs Function in the American Corporation." As discussed by our colleague, E. A. Murray, Jr., elsewhere in this volume, exploratory case studies of how four individual companies managed their public affairs functions clarified important practices and internal relationships—for example, public affairs and corporate planning—and suggested a possible continuum of structures, shaping factors, and evolutionary development. The clarifications were important in the construction of a survey instrument, and the suggestions about the evaluation of public affairs units studied. In this manner case analysis has been used in concert with, and as a complement to, other types of inquiry. In so doing, it provides an excellent example of how the systematic pursuit of significant questions can yield a considerable improvement in our understanding of the corporation in society.

## CONCLUSION

As the study of corporation and society relationships and interactions proceeds, it is to be expected that our research will become both more refined and more extensive. If our substantive theory continues to grow in systematic ways, the possibilities for formal theory development will improve as well. In both the generation of substantive theory, and the testing of formal theory, case analysis has much to offer. The systematic development, and extension, of research in the study of the corporation and society can become the hallmark of the second decade of this field. By focusing our research this way, we are likely to give to it the central focus and definition that it has needed. As we have argued in this paper, the key to systematic development lies not in the application of any single technique but in the creative and imaginative pursuit of an elusive truth.

## NOTES

1. The data from which this analysis was drawn is reported in *Public Affairs Offices and Their Functions: A Summary of Survey Results* (Boston University School of Management, Public Affairs Research Group, 1981).

2.  Cases made available through the Intercollegiate Case Clearing House (ICCH) are almost universally prepared as "teaching cases." This purpose often results in a slanting or withholding of information for pedagogical reasons. Such gaps render these cases flawed for most research purposes.

# REFERENCES

Ackerman, Robert W., "How Companies Respond to Social Demands." *Harvard Review* (July-August), 1973.

Ackerman, Robert W., *The Social Challenge to Business*. Cambridge, MA: Harvard University Press, 1975.

Ackerman, Robert, and Raymond Bauer, *Corporate Social Responsiveness–The Modern Dilemma*. Reston, VA: Reston Publishing Co., Inc., 1976.

Aldag, Ramon J., and Kathryn B. Bartol, "Empirical Studies of Corporate Social Performance and Policy: A Survey of Problems and Results." In Lee E. Preston (ed.), *Research in Corporate Social Performance and Policy*, vol. 1. Greenwich, CT: JAI Press Inc., 1978, pp. 165–200.

Bauer, Raymond A. "The Corporate Response Process." In Lee E. Preston (ed.), *Research in Corporate Social Performance and Policy*, vol. 1. Greenwich, CT: JAI Press, Inc., 1978, pp. 99–122.

Bauer, R. A., and D. H. Fenn, Jr., *The Corporate Social Audit*. New York: The Russell Sage Foundation, 1972.

Berle, A. A., and Gardner Means., *The Modern Corporation and Private Property*. NY: The Macmillan Co., 1933.

Boston University School of Management Public Affairs Research Group. *Public Affairs Offices and Their Functions: Summary of Survey Responses*. 1981.

Brenner, Steven N., "Influences on the Decision to Use Business-Government Relations: A Study of Computer Time-Sharing Firms." Unpublished doctoral dissertation. Harvard University, 1972.

Brenner, Steven N., "Corporate Political Activity: An Exploratory Study in a Developing Industry." In Lee E. Preston (ed.), *Research in Corporate Social Performance and Policy*, vol. 2. Greenwich, CT: JAI Press, Inc., 1980, pp. 197–236.

Burch, Philip H., *The Managerial Revolution Reassessed*. Lexington, MA: D. C. Heath, Inc., 1972.

Callaghan, D. W., "Management of the Corporate Gift-Giving Function: An Empirical Study of the Life Insurance Industry." Unpublished doctoral disseration. University of Massachusetts/Amherst, 1975.

Campbell, Donald T. III., "Degrees of Freedom and the Case Study." *Comparative Political Studies* 8 (July):178–193, 1975.

Campbell, Donald T., and Julian C. Stanley, *Experimental and QuasiExperimental Designs for Research*. Chicago: Rand McNally College Publishing Co., 1963.

Chatov, Robert, *Corporate Financial Reporting*. New York: The Free Press, 1975.

Churchman, C. West, *The Design of Inquiring Systems*. New York: Basic Books, Inc., 1971.

Dickie, Robert B., "MNC Responses to Equity-Sharing Policies: The Indonesian Experience." In Lee E. Preston (ed.), *Research in Corporate Social Performance and Policy*, vol. 3. Greenwich, CT: JAI Press, Inc., 1981, pp. 203–228.

Dierkes, Meinolf, "Corporate Social Reporting and Performance in Germany." In Lee E. Preston (ed.), *Research in Corporate Social Performance and Policy*, vol. 2. Greenwich, CT: JAI Press, Inc., 1979, pp. 251–290.

Duncan, Robert B., "Qualitative Research Methods in Strategic Management." In Dan E. Schendel and Charles W. Hofer (ed.), *Strategic Management: A New View of Business Policy and Planning*, Boston: Little Brown and Co., 1979.

Epstein, Edwin M., "Business Political Activity: Research Approaches and Analytical Issues." In Lee E. Preston (ed.), *Research in Corporate Social Performance and Policy*, vol. 2. Greenwich, CT: JAI Press, Inc., 1980, pp. 123–138.

Epstein, Edwin M., *The Corporation in American Politics*. Englewood Cliffs, NJ: Prentice-Hall, Inc., 1969.

Epstein, Edwin M., "The Emergence of Political Action Committees." *Political Finance: Sage Electoral Studies Yearbook*, Beverly Hills: Sage Publications, Inc., 5(1979):159–197.

First National Bank of Boston vs. Bellotti. 98 S Ct. 1407, 1978.

Frederick, William C., "Auditing Corporate Social Performance: The Anatomy of a Social Research Project." In Lee E. Preston (ed.), *Research in Corporate Social Performance and Policy*, vol. . Greenwich, CT: JAI Press, Inc., 1978, pp. 123–138.

Friedman, Milton with the assistance of Rose D. Friedman, *Capitalism and Freedom*. Chicago: The University of Chicago Press, 1962.

Galbraith, J. K., *The New Industrial State*. Boston: Houghton-Mifflin, paperback edition, Signet Books, 1967.

Gerlach, Luther P., "Milk, Movements and Multinationals: Complex Interactions and Social Responsibilities." In *Responsibilities of Multinational Corporations to Society*, vol. III. Proceedings of the Fifth Panel Discussion, Council of Better Business Bureaus, Washington, D.C.: (June 1–2) 1978.

Glaser, Barney G., and Anselm L. Strauss, *The Discovery of Grounded Theory: Strategies for Qualitative Research*. Observation Series (ed.), Howard S. Becker. New York: Aldine Publishing Co., 1967.

Hanson, Kirk, "Corporate Strategy and Public Policy." Paper presented at the Academy of Management Meetings, Atlanta, August, 1979.

Herman, Edward S., *Corporate Control, Corporate Power*. New York: Cambridge University Press, 1981.

Horwitch, Mel, "Uncontrolled and Unfocussed Growth: The U.S. Supersonic Transport, SST, and the Attempt to Synthesize Fuels from Coal." *Interdisciplinary Science Reviews* 5 (3):231–244, 1980.

————, *Clipped Wings: The American SST Conflict*. Cambridge, MA: MIT Press, 1982.

Isaac, S., and W. B. Michael, *Handbook in Research and Evaluation*. San Diego, CA: Edits Publishers, 1971.

Jesaitis, Patrick T., "Corporate Strategies and the Urban Crisis: A Study of Business Response to a Social Problem." Unpublished doctoral dissertation. Harvard University, 1969.

Kelly, Donald W., "Canadian Corporate Social Responsibility Survey." In Lee E. Preston (ed.), *Research in Corporate Social Performance and Policy*, vol. 1. Greenwich, CT: JAI Press, Inc., 1978, pp. 279–286.

Kuhn, Thomas S., *The Structure of Scientific Revolutions*. International Encyclopedia of Unified Science, Chicago: University of Chicago Press, 1962 (1970, 2nd ed.).

Lijphart, Arend, "Comparative Politics and the Comparative Method." *American Political Science Review* (65):682–693, 1971.

Lindblom, Charles E., *Politics and Markets: The World's Political-Economic Systems*. New York: Basic Books, Inc., 1977.

Lodge, George, *The New American Ideology*. New York: Alfred Knopp, 1975.

Logsdon, Jeanne M., "Organizational Responses to Environmental Regulation: Oil Refining Companies and Air Pollution." Unpublished paper, 1981.

Mahon, John F., "The Corporate Public Affairs Office: Structure, Process, and Impact." Unpublished doctoral dissertation. Boston University, 1982.

Marris, Robin, ed., *The Corporate Society*. London: Macmillan Press, 1974.

Merenda, Michael J., "The Process of Corporate Social Involvement: Five Case Studies." In Lee E. Preston (ed.), *Research in Corporate Social Performance and Policy*, vol. 3. Greenwich, CT: JAI Press Inc., 1981, p. 3.

Miles, R. E., and C. Snow, *Organizational Strategy, Structure and Process*. New York: McGraw Hill, 1978.

Mintzberg, Henry, "Process as a Field of Management Theory." *Academy of Management Review* (January):88–103, 1977.

Monsen, R. Joseph, and Kenneth D. Walters, "State Owned Firms: A Review of the Data and Issues." In Lee E. Preston (ed.), *Research in Corporate Social Performance and Policy*, vol. 2. Greenwich, CT: JAI Press, Inc., 1980, pp. 125–156.

Murray, Edwin A., Jr., "The Implementation of Social Policies in Commercial Banks." Unpublished doctoral dissertation. Harvard University, 1974.

Murray, Edwin A., Jr., "The Social Response Process in Commercial Banks: An Empirical Investigation." *Academy of Management Review* (July):1976.

Nozick, Robert, *Anarchy, State, and Utopia*. New York: Basic Books, 1974.

Orren, Karen, *Corporate Power and Social Change*. Baltimore: John Hopkins, 1974.

Page, Robert R., "Organizational Response to Social Challenge: Theory and Evidence for Two Industries." Unpublished doctoral dissertation. Indiana University, 1972.

Post, James E., *Corporate Behavior and Social Change*. Reston, VA: Reston Publishing Co., Inc., Prentice-Hall, 1978.

———, *Risk and Response: Management and Social Change in American Insurance Industry*. Lexington, MA: D. C. Heath, 1976.

Post, James E., and Edward Baer, "The International Code of Marketing for Breast-milk Substitutes: Consensus, Compromise, and Conflict in the Infant Formula Controversy." *International Commission of Jurists Review* 25(December):52–61, 1980.

———, "Demarketing Infant Formula: Consumer Products in the Developing World." *Journal of Contemporary Business* 7(1979):17–35.

Post, James E., and John Mahon, "Articulated Turbulence: The Impact of Regulatory Agencies on Corporate Responses to Social Change." *Academy of Management Review*, 1980.

Preston, Lee E., "Corporation and Society: The Search for a Paradigm." *Journal of Economic Literature* 13(June 1975): 434–453.

Preston, Lee E., "Corporate Social Responsibility Accounting: A Proposal for a Format and an Example of the State of the Art." *Journal of Contemporary Business* 7(Winter):1978.

Preston, Lee E. and James E. Post, *Private Management and Public Policy*, Engelwood Cliffs, N.J.: Prentice-Hall, Inc., 1975.

Purcell, T. V., "Management and the 'Ethical' Investors." *Harvard Business Review* 57 5(September-October):24–62 plus, 1979.

Randall, Frederic Dunn, "Corporate Strategies in the Drug Industry." Ph.D. dissertation, Harvard University Graduate School of Business Administration, 1972.

Rawls, John, *Theory of Justice*. Cambridge: Harvard University Press, 1971.

Redman, Eric, *The Dance of Legislation*. New York: Simon and Schuster, 1973.

Rey, Francoise, "Corporate Social Performance and Reporting in France." In Lee E. Preston (ed.), *Research in Corporate Social Performance and Policy*, vol. 2. Greenwich, CT: JAI Press, Inc., 1980, pp. 291–325.

Scott, Bruce R., "Stages of Corporate Development-Parts I and II." Boston Intercollegiate Case Clearing House, 9-371-294/BP998, 1971.

Selznick, Phillip, *TVA and the Grass Roots*. New York: Harper and Row, Inc., 1965.

Sethi, S. Prakash, *Advocacy Advertising and Large Corporations*. Lexington, MA: Lexington Books, 1977.

————, "An Analytical Framework for Making Cross-Cultural Comparisons of Business Responses to Social Pressures: The Case of the United States and Japan." In Lee E. Preston (ed.), *Research in Corporate Social Performance and Policy,* vol. 1. Greenwich, CT: JAI Press, Inc., 1978, pp. 201–221.

————, "Corporate Law Violations and Executive Liability." In Lee E. Preston (ed.), *Research in Corporate Social Performance and Policy,* vol. 3. Greenwich, CT: JAI Press, Inc., 1981, pp. 71–104.

————, "Dimensions of Corporate Social Performance: An Analytical Framework." *California Management Review* 17(1975):58–64.

Sonnenfeld, Jeffrey, *Corporate Views of the Public Interest: Perceptions of the Forest Products Industry.* Boston: Auburn House, 1981.

Stone, Christopher D., *Where the Law Ends: The Social Control of Corporate Behavior.* New York: Harper Colophon Books, Harper and Row, 1975.

Taylor, Marilyn L., "Implementing Affirmative Action: Impetus and Enabling Factors in Five Organizations." In Lee E. Preston (ed.), *Research in Corporate Social Performance and Policy,* vol. 3. Greenwich, CT: JAI Press, Inc., 1981, pp. 43–70.

————, "The Role of the Staff Specialist in the Public Implementation Process." Unpublished doctoral dissertation. Harvard University, 1979.

Thompson, James, *Organizations in Action.* New York: McGraw-Hill Book Company, 1967.

Unterman, Israel, "A Comparative Study of the Strategies of New Life Insurance Companies in New York State." Unpublished doctoral dissertation. Harvard University, 1968.

Vogel, David, *Lobbying the Corporation.* New York: Basic Books, 1978.

Weber, Max, *The Theory of Social and Economic Organization.* A.M. Henderson and T. Parsons (trans. and eds.), New York: Oxford University Press, Inc., 1947.

Zeitlin, Maurice, "Managerial Theory vs. Class Theory of Corporate Capitalism." In Lee E. Preston (ed.), vol. 1. Greenwich, CT: JAI Press, Inc., 1978, pp. 255–264.

# AN EMPIRICAL MEASURE OF CORPORATE SOCIAL ORIENTATION

## Kenneth E. Aupperle

Empirical work in the area of corporate social responsibility (CSR) has been gaining momentum, but much of it remains limited and often simplistic in terms of methodology. Abbott and Monsen (1979, p. 501) have noted that "the empirical study of corporate social involvement is in an undeveloped state." Perhaps the overriding research constraint has been the difficulty of developing valid measures of CSR. The study of CSR is relatively new, and the subject is value laden and susceptible to ideological interpretations. Thus, it is not surprising to find research efforts having an ideological basis.

One of the areas that has been examined fairly extensively over the past few years is the question of whether socially responsible firms are more profitable or better investments than those less socially responsible. While assessing profitability is a relatively well-established process, this is not the case with the assessment of CSR. Arlow and Gannon's recent review (1982) of studies concerning the profitability-CSR relationship observed that all the studies relied upon questionable indexes of social responsibility. Parket and Eilbirt (1975, p. 6) earlier remarked that:

> To be sure, the scope of endeavor categorized by the term social responsibility cannot be analyzed on the order of a balance sheet or profit and loss statement. There are as yet, no accounting techniques, analytical tools, or statistical methods which will objectively differentiate companies that are socially responsible from those that are not. To measure degrees of social responsibility would be an even more ethereal task

The whole process of the social audit is so vague that Robert Jensen, perhaps the leading researcher in the social accounting arena, has commented that "in most instances we are still groping in the dark concerning what to disclose, how to disclose it, and how to compare and evaluate business enterprises" (1976, p. 2). Jensen also observes that:

> Social accounting, and especially corporate social accounting, is in some instances an attempt to conjure up an image or representation of the institution constituting the "real object." The image created may range from hideous to angelic depending on who is conjuring up the image. Social accounting is like a kaleidoscope in that the same pieces turned a little differently form a whole new pattern. (p. 1)

Compounding the difficulties in the CSR arena has been the lack of effort to empirically test definitions, propositions and concepts. Instead, there has been a tendency for researchers to create their own measures of CSR rather than to use one of the many existing definitions in the literature. Not only has this hindered interstudy comparisons and analyses, but has limited the development of a research base in the social issues area.

The initial purpose of this study was to develop a social responsibility measurement instrument based upon a definitional model of CSR that has appeared in the literature. The definition of CSR used here for instrument development is that developed by Carroll (1979) as a part of his larger model of corporate social performance. Although no single definitional construct has universal acceptance, this conceptualization has multiple components that make it conducive to operationalization and testing.

A second objective of the study was to deploy the instrument in order to assess how chief executive officers (CEO's) viewed their firm's social responsibilities. Finally, the ultimate concern of this inquiry was to investigate the relationship between CSR as measured here and profitability.

## THE CARROLL CONSTRUCT

The definitional construct offered by Carroll is comprehensive. As portrayed in Figure 1, the four components which comprise the definition include dimensions

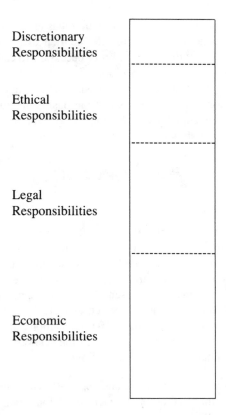

*Figure 1.* A Corporation's Total Social Responsibilities

*Source:* Carroll, 1979, p. 499.

that are economic, legal, ethical, and discretionary in nature. The four components are defined as follows: Economic responsibilities of business arise from the fact that business has an obligation to be productive and profitable and to meet the consuming needs of society. Legal responsibilities of business suggest a need for economic responsibilities to be approached within the confines of written law. The ethical responsibilities of business reflect the unwritten codes, norms, and values implicitly derived from society and as such, go beyond the mere legal frameworks and are capable of being strongly held as well as being nebulous and ambiguously stated. The discretionary (voluntary) responsibilities of business are volitional or philanthropic in nature and as such are also difficult to judge and ascertain.

The model in Figure 1 suggests not only four general CSR categories, but also implicitly proposes different relative weights for each. The relative weight of each category indicates, in a general sense, how CSR is defined at a given point in time. Since the major objective of this study was to develop an instrument for determining how business organizations define their own social responsibilities, the Carroll construct provided the flexibility necessary to capture empirically the CSR orientations of business organizations.

By using the Carroll construct, it was possible both to assess the CSR perspectives of major corporations as well as test the basic construct to see if, in fact, four CSR components actually existed and, if so, whether the actual weighted proportions were those shown in Figure 1.

# METHODOLOGY

## Questionnaire Construction

Operationalizing the definitional model in Figure 1 required developing an instrument that assessed each of the four CSR components. Because of the potential problem of social desirability bias resulting by simply asking respondents to rate (e.g., on a Likert Scale) the importance of each CSR component, a forced-choice format was chosen. The questionnaire contained 20 items, each comprised of four statements reflecting Carroll's four components. By instructing respondents to allocate up to 10 points among the four statements, the relative importance of each CSR statement in the set was assessed. Instructions on the final questionnaire form were as follows:

> Based on their relative importance and application to your firm, allocate up to, but not more than, 10 points to each set of four statements. For example, you might allocate points to a set of statements as follows:

| | | | | | |
|---|---|---|---|---|---|
| A = 4 | | A = 1 | | A = 0 | |
| B = 3 | | B = 2 | | B = 4 | |
| C = 2 | or | C = 0 | or | C = 3 | etc. |
| D = 1 | | D = 7 | | D = 0 | |
| Total = 10 points | | Total = 10 points | | Total = 7 points | |

## Item Development

Both validity and reliability were considered in item development. First, an exhaustive list of statements representing the three non-economic components was drawn from five recent studies (Eilbirt and Parket, 1973; Corson and Steiner, 1974; Paluszek, 1976; Holmes, 1977; and Ostlund, 1977). Only items or statements rated as important by respondents were taken from these studies. Also, industry specific items were omitted. While numerous opportunities for industry specific CSR research clearly exist, the objective was to develop items that would facilitate meaningful ratings from respondents regardless of their industry association. Items selected to represent the economic performance component were drawn from performance measures typically found in corporate scoreboard sections of *Business Week* and *Forbes* and commonly referred to in well-established managerial finance texts. A total of 117 statements comprised the initial set of items.

A blind panel of judges was used to reduce the number of items from the initial list and to further ensure content validity. The panel consisted of six faculty members and Ph.D. students from a large southeastern university, each with demonstrated expertise and interest in CSR or strategic management. Judges independently classified each of the 117 CSR statements into one of Carroll's four CSR components. The degree of consensus among judges is shown in Table 1. High Congruence was deemed to exist when five of the six judges classified a statement into the same component. The Table 1 data show that high congruence existed for 78 of the original 117 statements. The panel also classified the original statements into two broader categories: "concern for society," consisting of the three non-economic components (legal, ethical, discretionary), and "concern for economic performance," representing the economic component. Panel members had little difficulty discriminating between these two dimensions.

From the pool of 78 high congruence statements and from two statements where only four of the six judges showed congruence, a 20-item instrument consisting of four CSR statements per item was constructed. Because of the paucity of high congruence discretionary and ethical statements, several of them were used in more than one item. As statements were assigned to items, three panel members reviewed them to help ensure that statements had relatively equal levels of social desirability. Statements were also randomly ordered within items to reduce response bias. Table 2 contains three of the final instrument items. Each item consists of four statements corresponding to the four CSR components. As indicated earlier, respondents were instructed to distribute up to ten points among the four statements in each item.

A preliminary reliability assessment was conducted by administering the instrument to 158 undergraduate business students enrolled in a senior level busi-

*Table 1.* Panel's Degree of Consensus
for the 117 CSR Statements

| CSR Components | Number of Initial Statements | Consensus | |
|---|---|---|---|
| | | *Five or Six Panel Members* | *Four or More Panel Members* |
| Economic | 27 | 26 | 26 |
| Legal | 27 | 20 | 22 |
| Ethical | 31 | 15 | 29 |
| Discretionary | 32 | 17 | 25 |
| Total | 117 | 78 | 102 |

*Table 2.*    Sample Items from the Main Instrument

| *CSR Classifications* | | *Sample Sets* |
|---|---|---|
| | 6. | It is important to ensure long-term survival by being a: |
| (discretionary) | ____ | A. charitable corporate citizen |
| (economic) | ____ | B. profitable corporate citizen |
| (ethical) | ____ | C. morally and ethically responsible corporate citizen |
| (legal) | ____ | D. law-abiding corporate citizen |
| | 8. | It is important to: |
| (economic) | ____ | A. examine regularly new product-market opportunities |
| (legal) | ____ | B. comply promptly with new laws and court rulings |
| (discretionary) | ____ | C. examine regularly new opportunities and programs which can improve urban and community life |
| (ethical) | ____ | D. recognize and respect new or evolving ethical/moral norms adopted by society |
| | 14. | It is important to monitor new opportunities which can enhance the organization's: |
| (ethical) | _____ | A. moral and ethical image in society |
| (legal) | _____ | B. compliance with local, state, and federal statutes |
| (economic) | _____ | C. profitability |
| (discretionary) | _____ | D. ability to help solve social problems |

ness policy course. Respondents completed the instrument by placing themselves in the role of a corporate CEO. Coefficients of internal consistency (Cronbach's alpha) for each of the CSR components were as follows: Economic (.93), Legal (.84), Ethical (.84), and Discretionary (.87). It was concluded that the four components demonstrated satisfactory internal consistency.

## Procedure

The final instrument, containing the 20 CSR items and other questions pertaining to both CSR and strategic management, was sent to the 818 chief executive officers (CEO's) listed in Forbes 1981 Annual Directory. A first mailing and two follow-up mailings generated 241 (30%) usable responses.

# RESULTS

To test the discriminant validity of the instrument as reflecting Carroll's four-part CSR model, factor analyses were performed on the 80 statements allocated to the 20 CSR items. An N-factor, principal factor analysis with varimax rotation identified twenty-two factors with eigen values greater than 1.0. Because a scree test pointed to clear breaks between factors three and four and between factors four and five, two further rotations were performed—one a three-factor; the other, a four-factor.

The four-factor rotation produced no clear results. Only four of the eighty statements had primary (greater than .40) loadings on the fourth factor. Factor 1 contained statements representing both the economic and ethical CSR components. The three factor rotation accounted for 40 percent of the total variance and produced clearer results, which are presented in Table 3. Statements were considered representative of a factor if they had a single primary loading above .40. The Table 3 data show that fifty-nine statements (boldface numbers) met this criterion. In only nine of these fifty-five cases were secondary loadings greater than .30. Factors 1 and 2 clearly reflected the discretionary and legal components, respectively, while Factor 3 contained both the economic (all negative loadings) and ethical (all positive loadings) statements. This not only provided empirical support for the existence of the four-part CSR construct within the three factors, but produced an unanticipated revelation. There clearly existed a strong inverse relationship between the economic and ethical dimensions which suggested a natural conflict of strategic choices.

Unweighted scale scores were computed for each of the four components from the fifty-nine items identified in Table 3. Coefficients of internal consistency for each component were: Economic (11 items) = .90, Legal (15 items) = .86, Ethical (17 items) = .87, and Discretionary (16 items) = .84. It was again concluded that the categories demonstrated satisfactory internal consistency. Table 4 contains the zero order correlations among the four component scores. As would be expected from the factor structure, the strongest correlation ($r = -.71$, $p < .001$) is between the economic and ethical components. In fact, the economic component correlates negatively with all three of its non-economic counterparts. Generally, then, the analysis supports the existence of four clear, but related CSR components.

As indicated earlier, Carroll (1979) assigned relative (but nonnumeric) weights to each of the four CSR components, reflecting their relative magnitude as aspects of corporate social responsibilities. To provide a rather crude test of Carroll's weightings, mean scores for each of the four components were computed. Figure 2 contains these means. Their relative sizes reflect Carroll's weightings fairly accurately, being comparable in magnitude and declining from economic to discretionary. Also, six paired comparison t-tests showed significant differences ($p = .001$) among these means, with t-values ranging from 6.37 to 25.30.

The mean percentages depicted in Figure 2 reflect to a certain extent how the corporate community perceives or interprets its social contract with society. It is interesting to observe that while the economic component received the greatest emphasis (35.0%), the non-economic components collectively accounted for more than 60 percent of the weighting.[1] This is a particularly profound result given a forced-choice and bias reducing instrument used to obtain the data.

*Table 3.*   Three-Factor Factor Analysis (Rotation Method: Varimax)

| Item | | Factor 1 | Factor 2 | Factor 3 | Item | | Factor 1 | Factor 2 | Factor 3 |
|---|---|---|---|---|---|---|---|---|---|
| 1 | (econ) | −.25 | −.35 | −.29 | 41 | (econ) | −.31 | −.36 | −.58 |
| 2 | (legal) | −.01 | .52 | −.04 | 42 | (legal) | .07 | .59 | −.14 |
| 3 | (discr) | .45 | .04 | −.13 | 43 | (ethical) | .26 | .16 | .34 |
| 4 | (ethical) | .03 | −.08 | .45 | 44 | (discr) | .09 | −.07 | .38 |
| 5 | (econ) | −.39 | −.22 | −.42 | 45 | (discr) | .63 | −.03 | −.11 |
| 6 | (legal) | .32 | .25 | .10 | 46 | (ethical) | .21 | .08 | .66 |
| 7 | (discr) | .54 | .01 | .16 | 47 | (legal) | −.10 | .68 | −.06 |
| 8 | (ethical) | −.03 | .09 | .44 | 48 | (econ) | −.44 | −.45 | −.34 |
| 9 | (legal) | −.21 | .11 | −.11 | 49 | (discr) | .66 | −.03 | −.03 |
| 10 | (econ) | −.16 | −.22 | −.25 | 50 | (econ) | −.43 | −.43 | −.49 |
| 11 | (discr) | .49 | −.00 | .21 | 51 | (legal) | −.07 | .59 | .17 |
| 12 | (ethical) | .13 | .19 | .30 | 52 | (ethical) | .13 | −.00 | .56 |
| 13 | (econ) | −.17 | −.45 | −.56 | 53 | (ethical) | .31 | .06 | .47 |
| 14 | (discr) | .50 | −.05 | .09 | 54 | (legal) | −.02 | .55 | .00 |
| 15 | (legal) | .04 | .64 | .03 | 55 | (econ) | −.48 | −.41 | −.48 |
| 16 | (ethical) | −.12 | .04 | .67 | 56 | (discr) | .47 | −.03 | .25 |
| 17 | (ethical) | .01 | −.01 | .53 | 57 | (legal) | −.07 | .50 | −.04 |
| 18 | (legal) | .08 | .66 | −.00 | 58 | (discr) | .48 | .03 | −.03 |
| 19 | (discr) | .55 | −.14 | .08 | 59 | (ethical) | −.10 | −.08 | .55 |
| 20 | (econ) | −.26 | −.43 | −.42 | 60 | (econ) | −.18 | −.27 | −.44 |
| 21 | (discr) | .57 | −.08 | −.04 | 61 | (legal) | −.14 | .31 | .17 |
| 22 | (econ) | −.36 | −.45 | −.43 | 62 | (ethical) | .27 | .06 | .50 |
| 23 | (ethical) | .11 | .14 | .62 | 63 | (econ) | −.31 | −.40 | −.57 |
| 24 | (legal) | −.00 | .63 | .12 | 64 | (discr) | .32 | .15 | .17 |
| 25 | (legal) | −.11 | .27 | .06 | 65 | (discr) | .56 | .00 | .21 |
| 26 | (econ) | −.21 | −.27 | −.52 | 66 | (legal) | −.14 | .41 | .07 |
| 27 | (discr) | .58 | −.02 | .13 | 67 | (ethical) | .01 | −.04 | .35 |
| 28 | (ethical) | −.06 | .03 | .46 | 68 | (econ) | −.29 | −.31 | −.46 |
| 29 | (econ) | −.31 | −.44 | −.41 | 69 | (econ) | −.28 | −.28 | −.56 |
| 30 | (legal) | −.08 | .61 | −.04 | 70 | (discr) | .28 | .01 | .20 |
| 31 | (discr) | .50 | −.16 | .26 | 71 | (legal) | −.02 | .51 | .14 |
| 32 | (ethical) | .11 | .09 | .41 | 72 | (ethical) | .13 | −.04 | .53 |
| 33 | (discr) | .47 | −.07 | −.02 | 73 | (ethical) | −.03 | −.12 | .48 |
| 34 | (econ) | −.36 | −.23 | −.37 | 74 | (legal) | .07 | .50 | −.23 |
| 35 | (legal) | −.05 | .31 | .16 | 75 | (econ) | −.25 | −.33 | −.49 |
| 36 | (ethical) | .12 | .10 | .45 | 76 | (discr) | .23 | −.03 | .38 |
| 37 | (econ) | −.37 | −.31 | −.63 | 77 | (discr) | .59 | −.13 | .12 |
| 38 | (legal) | .23 | .39 | .28 | 78 | (legal) | −.14 | .40 | .22 |
| 39 | (discr) | .45 | .06 | .19 | 79 | (econ) | −.32 | −.35 | −.55 |
| 40 | (ethical) | .04 | .08 | .61 | 80 | (ethical) | −.01 | .04 | .42 |

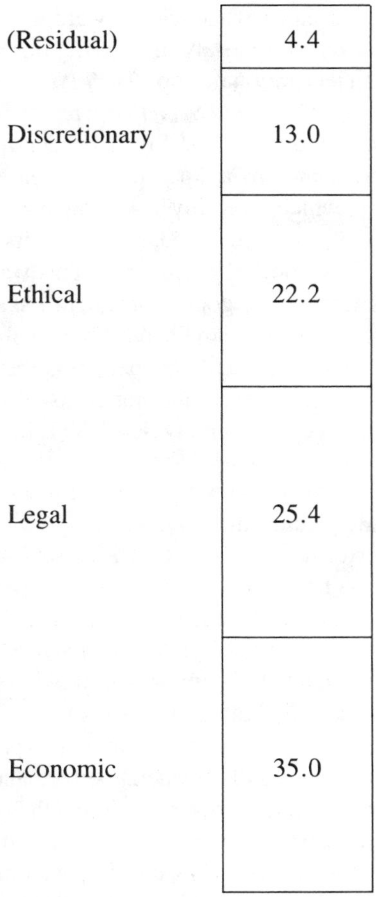

| | |
|---|---|
| (Residual) | 4.4 |
| Discretionary | 13.0 |
| Ethical | 22.2 |
| Legal | 25.4 |
| Economic | 35.0 |

*Figure 2.*   Relative CSR Weights on a Percentage Basis (N = 241)

*Note:* A residual exists because respondents were not required to allocate all ten points to the four statement CSR sets.

## CSR AND PROFITABILITY: LITERATURE REVIEW

Interest in the relationship between CSR and profitability dates back at least to the first issue of the *Business and Society Review* (Spring, 1972), where Milton Moskowitz suggested that socially responsible firms are good investment risks even though "there is at this point no real evidence that capital markets will be materially affected by social performance." He recommended 14 firms as potential investments because of their social performance: "the securities are being suggested here on the basis of corporate behavior that can be considered socially responsive.'' It is never revealed what criteria were used in selecting these 14 firms although his "four years of closely monitoring businesses' social environment" is perhaps a sufficient rationale (pp. 71–72).

In the next issue of the *Business and Society Review* (where Moskowitz served as an editor), it was observed that the 14 CSR firms identified by Moskowitz had registered over the past six months a stock price increase of 7.28%. This is in contrast to the Dow-Jones which rose only 4.4%, the New York Stock Exchange which increased but 5.1%, and the Standard and Poors Industrials which increased 6.4% ("So Far So Good," 1972, p. 88). This was presented as support for the notion that CSR firms were good investment risks.

However, this 14 firm sample was small and subjectively selected. The performance time period was too short and the performance criteria based on the increase in stock price was inadequate and not adjusted for risk. An investor's yield includes not only capital gains but dividends and, in turn, an adjustment for risk is absent. Not all stocks gave the same degree of risk.

The findings and claims of Moskowitz and the *Business and Society Review* were challenged by Stanley Vance in a 1975 *Management Review* article. Vance examined the market performance of the 14 CSR firms from 1972 to 1975 and found that all the firms had declined in price and had performed far below the Dow-Jones, the New York Stock Exchange Index, and the Standard and Poors Industrial. To support his tentative conclusion that CSR firms are not good investment risks, Vance extended his analysis to looking at the performance of high and low CSR firms identified in other surveys reported by the *Business and Society Review*.[2] The reliability of these reputational type surveys did not concern Vance. Instead, he compared the financial performance of the highest rated CSR firms with the lowest rated CSR firms and found the latter to outperform the former. While no statistical test was performed to determine whether differences were significant, Vance did correlate CSR and financial performance and found that there is a negative relationship. He concluded that CSR firms are not good investments.

*Table 4.*   Intercorrelations
Among the Four CSR Components
$(N = 241)$

|                    | 1        | 2      | 3      |
|--------------------|----------|--------|--------|
| 1.  Economic       |          |        |        |
| 2.  Legal          | $-.48^{***}$ |        |        |
| 3.  Ethical        | $-.71^{***}$ | $.13^*$  |        |
| 4.  Discretionary  | $-.47^{***}$ | $.04$    | $.25^{**}$ |

*Notes:*   $^*p < .05$
$^{**}p < .01$
$^{***}p < .001$

Vance's research possesses many of the same methodological problems as the Moskowitz study. The most important are a questionable sample, an inadequate measure of performance, and no adjustment for risk.

Table 5 provides a chronological review of the major research efforts in this area, some of which will now be briefly examined. As important study that followed up on the efforts of Moskowitz and Vance was done by Alexander and Buchholz (1978). The major methodological difference between the Vance study and that of Alexander and Buchholz involves risk adjustment. The latter study utilized the betas of each firm to adjust performance. The use of this measure to adjust for risk enabled Alexander and Buchholz to conclude that "there seems to be no significant relationship between stock risk levels and degree of social responsibility. These findings suggest that the interpretations of both Moskowitz and Vance are invalid" (p. 485).

Since the data was derived from both three-year and five-year assessment periods and was adjusted for risk, this study reflected major methodological improvements. However, the sample of firms remains questionable as does the performance criterion of stock prices.

A study which used a different approach in investigating the CSR-profitability issue was performed by Bowman and Haire (1975). In this study firms were identified as low or high in CSR based on the number of lines devoted to the topic of CSR in their annual report. The researchers point out that:

> In searching for a readily available surrogate measure for actual activities in the area of corporate citizenship, we chose to measure the proportion of lines of prose in the annual report devoted to social responsibility. The annual report is a kind of projective test that allows a firm to express its goals and motives in much the same way that a Rorschach or TAT does for an individual. . . . A critic could immediately scoff at this measure. It is at least a popular belief that "everybody that talks about heaven ain't going there," that talk is cheap, and that talk about socially desirable behavior is not necessarily a predictor of such behavior (pp. 49–50).

To validate this CSR line count method the researchers compared it with Moskowitz' list and found that his 14 CSR firms devoted much more line space to the topic of CSR than did 14 other randomly chosen firms.

Through the use of this line count procedure, 82 firms were classified into high, medium, and low CSR categories. Each category was then evaluated on the basis of five-year ROE. The researchers discovered that firms with a medium CSR rating performed the worst. Thus a U-shaped relationship was found to exist.

Numerous methodological problems can be identified in this study. First, what is or is not a CSR sentence or comment can be difficult to ascertain and this was demonstrated by two examples provided by the researchers. Second, the issue of validity also arises when CSR is simply based on quantitative line count and cross referenced by 14 other CSR firms which are also of dubious value as was

*Table 5.* Studies Examining the CSR and Corporate Profitability Relationship

| Study | Methodology | Performance Criteria | Findings/Implications | Limitations |
|---|---|---|---|---|
| Moskowitz, 72: *Business and Society Review* | Simplistic comparison of stock price increases in Moskowitz' 14 perceived high CSR firms with the average increase in the Dow-Jones Index. | Stock price increases over time | CSR firms outperform the Dow-Jones Industrials | No adjustment for risk; small sample; sample is not necessarily representative of high CSR firms; study was done over a short time interval; performance criteria is questionable. |
| Bragdon and Martin, 72: *Risk Management* | Seventeen firms in the paper and pulp industry were rated on a pollution index developed by the Council of Economic Priorities. Each firm's index was compared to its ROE. | Return on Equity (ROE) | The better the pollution index, the higher the ROE | No adjustment for risk; findings limited to one industry; limited definition of CSR; small sample; performance criteria of ROE is questionable. |
| Bowman and Haire, 75: *California Management Review* | Eighty-two food processing firms classified into low, medium, and high CSR categories based on the number of lines devoted to the topic of CSR in corporate annual reports. The CSR categories are compared on the basis of their ROE. | Five year Return on Equity | Existence of a U-shaped performance curve; the highest performing firms being those found in the middle range of CSR. | No adjustment for risk; lopsided sample; simple statistics; reliance on annual reports and on the CSR firms of Moskowitz; performance criteria of ROE is questionable. |
| Parker and Eilbirt, 75: *Business Horizons* | It is assumed that 96 firms that responded to the researcher's previous CSR survey can be assumed as CSR firms. Eighty of these firms have their profitability compared to that of the Fortune 500. | Absolute Net Income, Profit Margin, ROE, and EPS | On all four measures, the 80 CSR firms proved to be more profitable. | No adjustment for risk; simple statistics; questionable sample; short-term measurement (12 months). |

| Study | Methodology | Measure | Findings | Critique |
|---|---|---|---|---|
| Vance, 75: *Management Review* | Two-fold:<br>1. Replicating Moskowitz<br>2. Correlating CSR firms derived from two *Business and Society Review* surveys with stock price changes over time. | Stock price increases over time | CSR firms are determined not to be good investments; negative correlation between CSR and stock price increases. | No adjustment for risk; questionable samples; limited time focus (12 months); regression line does not fit the data; performance criteria is questionable. |
| Heinz, 76: *Akron Business and Economic Review* | Correlating CSR ratings of 29 firms from a *Business and Society Review* survey with ROE. | Several measures such as ROA, ROE, and profit margins | A significantly positive correlation between CSR and ROE | No adjustment for risk; small sample; questionable sample; reliance on reputational rating system for determining CSR. |
| Sturdivant and Ginter, 77: *California Management Review* | A population of 67 high CSR firms as identified by Moskowitz in the *Business and Society Review* are used in a CSR survey. Twenty-three firms returned 130 questionnaires. The 67 firm population is also reduced down to 28 firms and reclassified into four industrial groupings. CSR and the 10-year growth in EPS is examined. | 10 year EPS growth | High CSR firms (Best and Honorable Mention) outperform low CSR firms. Honorable mention CSR firms have the best performance and supports findings of Bowman and Haire and to some extent that of Bragdon and Martin. Researchers fail to focus on this development. | No adjustment for risk; employed T-test with very small sample; industrial categories are inconsistent. Many low CSR firms outperform high CSR firms in the same industry group; questionable sample; removal of outliers reduces greatly the differences between high and low CSR firms; performance measure is questionable. |
| Alexander and Buchholz, 78: *Academy of Management Journal* | Replicating efforts of Vance by using reputational ratings derived from *Business and Society Review* surveys. CSR ratings are correlated with stock price increases over time and adjusted for risk. | Stock price increases over 2 years and 5 years | CSR has no effect on stock market performance; repudiates both Moskowitz and Vance | Reliance on a questionable sample; performance measure is inadequate. |

*(continued)*

Table 5.  (Continued)

| Study | Methodology | Performance Criteria | Findings/Implications | Limitations |
|-------|-------------|----------------------|------------------------|-------------|
| Abbott and Monsen, 79: *Academy of Management Journal* | Development of a Social In-volvement Disclosure (SID) Scale from a content analysis of *Fortune* 500 firms. The SID is used to determine CSR firms which are then compared on the basis of their investment yield. | 10 year yield | CSR has no effect on the total return to investors. | No adjustment for risk; the SID does not reflect the true level of CSR; the content analysis used is superior to that of Bowman and Haire but is still question-able; performance measure is inadequate. |

earlier observed. Third, many more non-CSR Firms (51) were used in contrast to the moderate CSR firms (18) or the high CSR firms (13). Fourth, the reliance on ROE as a measure is debatable considering it is a function not only of profitability but also of a firm's financial leverage. Finally, no T-tests were performed on the data, nor was performance adjusted for risk.

A subsequent study by Abbott and Monsen (1979) employs a similar but more sophisticated methodology. The researchers utilized a content analysis of *Fortune* 500 annual reports which is done annually by the accounting firm of Ernst and Ernst. This content analysis involves 28 items which are monitored in the annual reports. The content analysis is then used to construct a Social Involvement Disclosure (SID) scale. Abbott and Monsen use SID as a surrogate for CSR. Four hundred and fifty firms from the *Fortune* 500 were divided into high and low SID firms and then examined for profitability. The profitability measure found that there was little difference in yield for the two groups even when accounting for size. Abbott and Monsen comment that "Being socially involved does not appear to increase investor's total rate of return. Nor does it appear that being socially involved is dysfunctional for the investor" (pp. 514–515).

Some methodological problems do exist with this study. The annual report method used here to assess CSR may be superior to that used by Bowman and Haire but it is still subject to validity problems. In addition, there was no adjustment for risk and the performance criteria of investor's yield is not necessarily an adequate surrogate for profitability; yield is a function of both capital gains and dividends, neither of which need be tied directly to profitability.

Parket and Eilbirt (1975) conducted a study which utilized still another approach. In a previous CSR study the researchers were able to get 96 firms from the *Forbes* 500 to respond. Since these firms had responded it was assumed that they must then be more CSR oriented. They point out that:

> The fact that all ninety-six of the replying firms identified themselves as engaged in endeavors associated with social responsibility suggests that firms not actively undertaking such work are more heavily represented among our nonrespondents (p. 6).

Eighty of these so called CSR firms were then compared to the *Fortune* 500 and the *Fortune* 500 minus these 80 firms. The performance criteria that were utilized were dollar net income, profit margin, ROE, and EPS. The researchers conclude that "By all four measures, the 80 respondents who were considered to be the most socially active show up as more profitable" (p. 8).

However, no t-test was performed and it appears that the differences in ROE and EPS are insignificant. Other methodological problems abound. The assumption that the 80 firm sample is representative of CSR is very questionable. Again, there is no risk adjustment and the profitability measures employed are not adequate and are used but for a single year. Finally, the statistical methods are far too simplistic.

Another major research effort in this area was again based on the judgment of Moskowitz, who had over time classified 67 firms as essentially high, moderate, and low in CSR (Sturdivant and Ginter, 1977). The researchers note that:

> The study was based on the sixty-seven corporations that had been cited by business journalist Milton Moskowitz as exhibiting exceptional social responsiveness or lack thereof. While no claim can be made about the accuracy of these ratings, they had the advantage of consistency in that they came from a single source (p. 30).

While such procedures facilitate consistency, they are insufficient in regard to validity. Sturdivant and Ginter use this sample to derive yet a smaller 28 firm sample which is sub-divided into four industrial groupings. The high, moderate, and low CSR firms in each grouping are compared on the basis of ten-year EPS growth. Each firm is then normalized by dividing this growth by the industry average. It is observed that the high and moderate CSR firms outperform the low CSR firms. Unaccountably, no real mention is made of the fact that the moderate CSR firms were the best performers and that this was similar to what was discovered in the Bowman and Haire study. Perhaps such a finding was felt to conflict with a fundamental premise of the authors that "executives can recognize and act on the broader social dimensions of managing an enterprise without losing sight of their basic economic mission" (p. 38).

A number of methodological problems exist in this study beginning with the sample selection. The four industrial groupings are very odd. For instance, Weyerhaeuser is matched with U.S. Steel, Giant Food is matched with S.S. Kresge Company, and Ralston Purina is matched with Campbell Soup. In addition, the sample is very small and unbalanced (12 low CSR firms are matched up with 6 high CSR firms). There is also no adjustment for risk and the performance measure of EPS growth is of questionable value.

It is not surprising to find the various studies flawed. They involve very different degrees of methodological rigor. The two studies employing the most rigor (Abbott and Monsen, and Alexander and Buchholz) found no relationship between CSR and financial performance. However, two studies employing contrasting methodologies found a curvilinear relationship between CSR and financial performance with moderate CSR firms being the best performers. Two additional observations should be made: First, none of the studies elected to use the most definitive and credible financial performance measures—the Return on Assets (ROA or ROI); Second, only one study recognized the critical importance of adjusting performance on the basis of risk.

# CSR AND PROFITABILITY: NEW RESEARCH

In order to examine empirically the relationship between CSR and profitability, the survey data generated through the Carroll Construct required partitioning.

The four CSR Components were rearranged into two categories. The first category was denoted as "a concern for society" (CS) and consisted of the three non-economic components (legal, ethical, discretionary). The remaining economic component was labeled as a "concern for economic performance" (CEP).

This dichotomy is not uncommon since social responsibility is often viewed from the collective vantage point of the legal, ethical, and philanthropic. The social orientation of an organization is appropriately observed through the importance placed on the three non-economic components relative to the economic, and higher CS scores for an organization were considered to demonstrate a stronger social orientation. The development of CS scores for each firm—derived through this study's instrument—is believed to be a substantial improvement over previous methods used to classify a firm as low or high in social responsibility.

Another improvement was the use of return on assets (ROA) as the profitability indicator. ROA is generally considered to be one of the best performance measures; both the short-term (one year) and long-term ROA (five year) were employed. However, in order to rely on the ROA for the performance criteria, it was necessary that it be adjusted for the risk propensities representative of various firms and industries. The adjustments used were taken from *Value Line*—which publishes betas and safety measures for most large corporations. While these measures pertain directly to risk in regard to a firm's stock, they also reflect the firm's general risk characteristics. The safety index is perhaps the most comprehensive measure of total risk confronting a firm since it incorporates the beta and many other factors as well. *Value Line* (1981) observes that the safety index is:

> a measure of potential risk associated with individual common stocks rather than large diversified portfolios (for which the Beta is a good risk measurement). Safety is based on the stability of price (which includes sensitivity to the market—i.e., Beta—as well as the stock's inherent volatility) adjusted for trend and other factors—including company size, the penetration of its markets, product market volatility, the degree of financial leverage, the earnings quality, and the overall condition of the balance sheet. Safety Ranks range from 1 (highest) to 5 (lowest). (Part IV, p. 7)

When computing the long-term safety index, a five year period was used and then averaged. This measure was then divided by three in order to accommodate the need for directly adjusting the long-term ROA. This result was then used to divide into the ROA. That approach was used to standardize the ROAs of all firms. For instance, if a firm's safety index over five years was 3, 4, 3, 4, and 3, it would average out to a 3.4. Since 3 was an average for Value Line, it was divided into 3.4 to produce 1.1. Because 3.4 for a firm would be slightly above the risk norm and since greater levels of risk require greater compensating payouts, such a firm's ROA of (say) 20 percent would be adjusted downward by dividing it by 1.1, bringing the risk-adjusted ROA down to 19 percent. An average safety index of 1 would also need to be divided by 3, yielding an adjustment factor of .333; this in turn would be divided into an ROA of (say) 7 percent. By adjusting ROA for risk it would be found that the latter firm would have the higher performance: 21 versus 19 percent risk-adjusted ROA. This method, while uncommon, serves the purpose of standardizing the ROA in order that the firms can be compared with one another.

## Results

It can be seen in Table 6 that no statistically significant relationships were found between social responsibility (CS) and financial performance. It did not matter whether the short-term or long-term ROA was used. Nor did it matter whether the ROA was adjusted or unadjusted. No relationships could be found to exist. It was concluded that it was not possible to support the notion of a positive or negative relationship between profitability and social responsibility. However, a statistically significant, but very modest and negative, relationship was found to exist between social responsibility (CS) and total risk. These results are basically consistent with what Arlow and Gannon (1982) conclude in their review where they point out that research studies have not provided strong support for a positive association between profitability and CSR. The study here apparently suggests that it is neither beneficial nor harmful for a firm to be socially motivated in fulfilling its social contract.

The results displayed in Table 6 parallel other empirical findings derived with the research instrument. For instance, the instrument examined two issues related to the social orientation of an organization. One question regarding organizational policy involved determining whether social forecasting was employed. Another question addressed whether a CSR Committee was utilized on the board of directors.

*Table 6.*   Relationship of CS
with Financial Performance and Risk

| Predictors | N | r | p |
|---|---|---|---|
| LTROA | 174 | .00 | .99 |
| ALTROA | 166 | .11 | .16 |
| STROA | 228 | .10 | .15 |
| ASTROA | 192 | .13 | .08 |
| SINAVG | 189 | −.17 | .02 |
| LTBETA | 189 | −.08 | .25 |

    LTROA = Long-term ROA
  ALTROA = Risk Adjusted, Long-term ROA
    STROA = Short-term ROA
  ASTROA = Risk Adjusted Short-term ROA
  SINAVG = Five-year Total Risk
  LTBETA = Long-term Beta

*Table 7.* Social Forecasting and Profitability

| Firms | N | Mean | t | p |
|-------|---|------|---|---|
| Social Forecasting Firms | 69 | 10.83 (LTROA) | −.59 | .550 |
| Remaining Firms | 111 | 11.27 (LTROA) | | |
| Social Forecasting Firms | 68 | 15.56 (ALTROA) | 1.16 | .250 |
| Remaining Firms | 103 | 13.40 (ALTROA) | | |

The t-tests results in Table 7 clearly suggest that social forecasting firms are not statistically different from nonsocial forecasting firms in regard to long-term profitability, with or without an adjustment for risk. The same results also appear to be true for the sister category concerning CSR committees on corporate board. The t-test results found in Table 8 reveal no statistically significant differences in regard to adjusted or unadjusted profitability. As a result, it was concluded that firms with a CSR board committee were not any different in profitability than other firms.

# RESEARCH INTO OTHER CSR ISSUES

A number of additional CSR issues were also examined in this study. There was a concern whether any relationship could be ascertained between CSR and such characteristics as industrial classification, respondent type, firm visibility and firm size. Another area of interest was the relative importance firms placed on integrating social issues into their strategic planning.

## Firm Type

Are there significant CSR differences between various firm types? Do firms in different industries display varying social orientations? Eight firm types were considered: conglomerate, financial, industrial, utility, retail/consumer, transportation, energy related, and other. In order to analyze whether differences existed between firm types on the basis of their concern for society (CS), a one-way analysis of variance procedure was used, as was Duncan's multiple range test. The overall F value was 2.60 (df = 6,207; p = .02).

*Table 8.* CSR Board Firms and Profitability

| Firms | N | Mean | t | p |
|-------|---|------|---|---|
| CSR Board Firms | 53 | 10.43 (LTROA) | 1.18 | .24 |
| Remaining Firms | 127 | 11.39 (LTROA) | | |
| CSR Board Firms | 53 | 14.60 (ALTROA) | −.02 | .98 |
| Remaining Firms | 118 | 14.63 (ALTROA) | | |

The results of Duncan's multiple range test indicated that there were CS differences between the various firm types. Utilities displayed the highest mean in social orientation score, and were statistically different from financial, retail, and transportation firms. Retail firms demonstrated the lowest mean score in social orientation and were statistically different from utilities, conglomerates, and industrial firms.

### Respondent Type

Respondents to the survey included the following: CEO, senior line officer, senior staff officer, aide to CEO, corporate planning officer, public officer, executive secretary and other. While public affairs officers as a group had the highest social orientation score and senior line officers had the lowest, a one-way analysis of variance on CS by respondent's position produced no statistically significant differences. The overall F value was 1.66 (df = 5,207; p = .14). Consequently, it was impossible to conclude that organizational role was important in influencing one's social orientation.

### Degree of Visibility

Another research issue believed to merit attention was whether high visibility firms were more or less concerned about CS. It was hypothesized that greater visibility would enhance their dependence on the external environment and, accordingly, require a more socially responsive attitude.

Determining who was or was not visible proved to be a difficult task and eventually required a somewhat subjective determination. The researcher and an outside expert classified firms as highly visible if they fell into one of three criteria by being: among the top 100 advertisers (in dollars spent), an international oil firm, or having received heavy general media coverage. From the responding firms, there were 24 which met one of these criteria.

From this limited framework, it was found that highly visible firms were more CS oriented than the other firms. A t-test gave significant differences (p < .02) between the two groups (see Table 9).

### Firm Size

The relationship between firm size and CS was assessed in zero order correlations. In addition, a number of other criterion variables were also selected when

*Table 9.* T-Test of Visibility and Social Orientation (CS)

| Firms | N | Mean | t | p |
|-------|---|------|---|---|
| Highly visible firms | 24 | 2.15 | 2.26 | .0249 |
| Remaining firms | 204 | 1.98 | | |

*Table 10.* Relationship of Asset Size
to Other Dependent Variables

| | Dependent Variables | N | r | p |
|---|---|---|---|---|
| CS | (Concern for Society) | 226 | .14 | .04 |
| LTROA | (Long-term ROA) | 180 | −.03 | .65 |
| STROA | (Short-term ROA) | 237 | −.13 | .04 |
| ALTROA | (Adjusted Long-term ROA) | 171 | .21 | .01 |
| ASTROA | (Adjusted Short-term ROA) | 200 | −.01 | .91 |
| LTBETA | (Long-term Beta)* | 197 | −.06 | .42 |
| SINAVG | (5-year Safety Index Average)* | 197 | −.29 | .0001 |
| STBETA | (Current Beta)* | 199 | −.11 | .11 |
| SFTYIN | (Current Safety Index)* | 200 | −.25 | .0005 |
| CEP | (Concern for Economic Performance) | 237 | −.14 | .04 |
| ISPASI | (Importance of Social Issues) | 237 | .14 | .03 |
| STRIMP | (Strategic Planning Importance) | 236 | .04 | .53 |

*Note:*
*Calculated from *Value Line*

using size as the predictor. Table 10 indicates that a number of statistically significant relationships were discovered, but the correlations were rather small.

Of particular importance is the finding that firm size (assets) had little relationship with social orientation. A stronger and more significant relationship was found with risk propensities as measured by *Value Line's* safety index. Size and risk were, to some extent, inversely related, which is what would be predicted. The relationship between assets and financial performance was also interesting. Only when the long-term ROA was adjusted for risk was a significant but weak relationship found.

## Social Issues and Strategic Planning

The importance corporations placed on integrating social issues into their strategic planning was measured on a five-point Likert scale (with 1 very unimportant and 5 very important). The resulting variable was labeled ISPASI. Despite the potential social desirability bias likely to affect such responses, it was surprising that nearly 13 percent of the firms admitted placing little importance on the integration of social issues with strategic issues. In addition, another 38.5 percent of the firms viewed such integration as only mildly important. Still, 49 percent of the firms thought such integration was important and the overall mean scale score was 3.5. However, the question that emerged was what is the relationship between ISPASI and other variables such as a concern for society (CS), a concern for economic performance (CEP), and profitability (ALTROA)?

A significant but moderately weak relationship exists between ISPASI and CS and ISPASI and CEP (Table 11). As would be expected, the relationship with the

*Table 11.*   Correlation of ISPASI
with CS, CEP, and ALTROA

| Variables | N | r | p |
|-----------|-----|------|-------|
| CS | 228 | .25 | .0002 |
| CEP | 239 | −.24 | .0002 |
| ALTROA | 171 | .14 | .07 |

latter is negative. No significant relationship existed between ISPASI and the adjusted long-term ROA. These findings suggest that firms which attempt to integrate social issues into their strategic planning are not necessarily more profitable or more socially oriented.

## DISCUSSION

The primary concern of this study was to develop an instrument to assess a corporation's social orientation and use it to study the relationship between CSR and profitability. However, since the instrument itself was embedded in Carroll's (1979) four-part CSR definitional model, it was imperative that this construct's validity be examined as well.

The results appear to support both the model and the instrument. First, it was concluded from the factor analyses performed that there are four empirically interrelated, but conceptually independent, components of CSR. The content validity studies reported here show that "experts" have little difficulty distinguishing among the four components when sorting written statements reflecting each component. A test of discriminant validity for an instrument developed to reflect the components clearly identified those components for 59 of the 80 statements used in the study. Two separate studies verified the internal consistency of each component as a reflection of CSR responsibilities.

Second, the results give tentative support to the relative weightings Carroll earlier assigned to each of the four CSR components. The relative weight the corporate community placed on each component percentage wise was: economic = 35.0, legal = 25.4, ethical = 22.2, discretionary = 13.0. Although the mean scores used to determine these weightings are rather crude indicators, their relative magnitude and order confirm that, at least for 241 active CEO's or their designated associate, Carroll's weightings are close approximations. Interestingly, while the respondents clearly placed more emphasis on the economic component, the non-economic components taken together are of much greater weight than the economic component alone. Perhaps this suggests the corporate community is more responsive to social issues that has been suspected.

The research inquiry also produced an unanticipated finding. Apparently, there is a strong inverse relationship between the economic and ethical components. This was made clear in the factor analyses when the economic component loaded *positively* on one factor and the ethical component loaded *negatively* on the same factor. In addition, there are strong negative correlations between the economic and each of the three non-economic components which suggests that the more economically motivated a firm is, the less emphasis it places on ethical, legal, and discretionary issues. This was particularly interesting given the fact that the three non-economic components had modest or insignificant correlations among themselvs. The correlations among the non-economic components show little substantive relationships from the emphasis respondents placed on them. Consequently, the results point to fairly unambiguous negative associations CEO's apparently draw between economic and non-economic components as a group, but little association among the non-economic components themselves.

A related purpose of this study concerned the use of the instrument to facilitate additional inquiries into the CSR area. While this survey instrument was directed primarily at relatively large, prominent firms, other population targets could and should be surveyed. In the business community, it would be useful to survey smaller scale firms as well as entrepreneurial businesses. Perhaps their CSR orientation would be considerably different from what was found in this study. Perhaps small, developing firms will have different priorities. Survival may or may not be the primary concern. It would be interesting to discern whether CSR is a luxury or a necessity for a developing company.

By modifying the initial set of directions, the questionnaire could have greater application. For instance, the directions could be changed to elicit responses from population groups outside of the business community. This would then make it possible to compare and contrast the CSR orientation of the corporate business community with that of the general public as well as more narrowly defined population targets. It is likely that other population targets would have a different notion of what the social contract should be between business and society. Perhaps the weightings found in this study would contrast sharply with societal expectations.

Since CSR means something different to various individuals, it could be useful to identify these differences. This study's instrument provides the means by which to document the CSR orientations of numerous constituencies or population targets. Consequently, this instrument could be valuable for the firm which wishes to understand the terms of its "social contract" in order to have an appropriate CSR response strategy. The revised and validated instrument can be seen in the appendix.

This study has made an attempt to avoid some of the problems which persisted in earlier studies by using a more objective social orientation measurement technique and more representative profitability criteria. Many of the earlier studies relied upon profitability measures of dubious value when performing inter-company comparisons. The ROA used in this study was thought to be a more universally acceptable profitability instrument. It was used on both a short-term (one year) and long-term basis and was adjusted for risk. The ROA represents a standardized approach in that profitability is converted to a relative basis by looking at net income as a percent of assets. While ROE is also a relative measure using net income, it also is influenced or manipulated by the organization's degree of financial leverage, and as a result can be misleading.

When correlating social orientation with profitability, no statistically significant relationships were observed. Much the same was also discovered when surrogate measures for social orientation were used. The profitability of social forecasting firms was not found to be statistically different from non-social forecasting firms. This was also the case with those firms using a CSR committee on their corporate boards. It seems that there is insufficient evidence to support the claim that socially responsible firms are more profitable.

It would appear that this study has not been able to corroborate the claims of either the advocates or critics concerning the corporate value of CSR. Perhaps the merits of CSR simply do not show up in the "bottom line." It could very well be that the intangible benefits of CSR tend to be evasive of scientific inquiry. Investigating the area of social responsibility has been, and will likely remain, a delicate, difficult and frustrating endeavor. Rodgers and Hammerstein once asked, "how do you hold a moonbeam in your hand?"

# APPENDIX

## Revised CSR Research Instrument

Based on their relative importance and application to your firm, allocate up to, but not more than, 10 points to each set of four statements. For example, you might allocate points to a set of statements as follows:

| A = 4 | | A = 1 | | A = 0 | |
|-------|----|-------|----|-------|------|
| B = 3 | | B = 2 | | B = 4 | |
| C = 2 | or | C = 0 | or | C = 3 | etc. |
| D = 1 | | D = 7 | | D = 0 | |
| Total = 10 points | | Total = 10 points | | Total = 7 points | |

1. It is important to perform in a manner consistent with:
   _____ A.   expectations of maximizing earnings per share.
   _____ B.   expectations of government and the law.
   _____ C.   the philanthropic and charitable expectations of society.
   _____ D.   expectations of societal mores and ethical norms.

2. It is important to be committed to:
   _____ A.   being as profitable as possible.
   _____ B.   voluntary and charitable activities.

       \_\_\_\_ C.   abiding by laws and regulations.

       \_\_\_\_ D.   moral and ethical behavior.

3.  It is important to:

       \_\_\_\_ A.   recognize that the ends do not always justify the means.

       \_\_\_\_ B.   comply with various federal regulations.

       \_\_\_\_ C.   assist the fine and performing arts.

       \_\_\_\_ D.   maintain a strong competitive position.

4.  It is important that:

       \_\_\_\_ A.   legal responsibilities be seriously fulfilled.

       \_\_\_\_ B.   long-term return on investment is maximized.

       \_\_\_\_ C.   managers and employees participate in voluntary and charitable activities within their local communities.

       \_\_\_\_ D.   when securing new business, promises are not made which are not intended to be fulfilled.

5.  It is important to:

       \_\_\_\_ A.   allocate resources on their ability to improve long-term profitability.

       \_\_\_\_ B.   comply promptly with new laws and court rulings.

       \_\_\_\_ C.   examine regularly new opportunities and programs which can improve urban and community life.

       \_\_\_\_ D.   recognize and respect new or evolving ethical/moral norms adopted by society.

6.  It is important to:

       \_\_\_\_ A.   provide assistance to private and public educational institutions.

       \_\_\_\_ B.   ensure a high level of operating efficiency is maintained.

       \_\_\_\_ C.   be a law-abiding corporate citizen.

       \_\_\_\_ D.   advertise goods and services in an ethically fair and responsible manner.

7.  It is important to:

       \_\_\_\_ A.   pursue those opportunities which will enhance earnings per share.

       \_\_\_\_ B.   avoid discriminating against women and minorities.

       \_\_\_\_ C.   support, assist, and work with minority-owned businesses.

       \_\_\_\_ D.   prevent social norms from being compromised in order to achieve corporate goals.

8.  It is important that a successful firm be defined as one which:

       \_\_\_\_ A.   is consistently profitable.

       \_\_\_\_ B.   fulfills its legal obligations.

       \_\_\_\_ C.   fulfills its eithical and moral responsibilities.

       \_\_\_\_ D.   fulfills its philanthropic and charitable responsibilities.

9.  It is important to monitor new opportunities which can enhance the organization's:
    ____ A.  moral and ethical image in society.
    ____ B.  compliance with local, state, and federal statutes.
    ____ C.  financial health.
    ____ D.  ability to help solve social problems.

10. It is important that good corporate citizenship be defined as:
    ____ A.  doing what the law expects.
    ____ B.  providing voluntary assistance to charities and community organizations.
    ____ C.  doing what is expected morally and ethically.
    ____ D.  being as profitable as possible.

11. It is important to view:
    ____ A.  philanthropic behavior as a useful measure of corporate performance.
    ____ B.  consistent profitability as a useful measure of corporate performance.
    ____ C.  compliance with the law as a useful measure of corporate performance.
    ____ D.  compliance with the norms, mores, and unwritten laws of society as useful measures of corporate performance.

12. It is important to:
    ____ A.  recognize that corporate integrity and ethical behavior go beyond mere compliance with laws and regulations.
    ____ B.  fulfill all corporate tax obligations.
    ____ C.  maintain a high level of operating efficiency.
    ____ D.  maintain a policy of increasing charitable and voluntary efforts over time.

13. It is important to:
    ____ A.  assist voluntarily those projects which enhance a community's 'quality of life.'
    ____ B.  provide goods and services which at least meet minimal legal requirements.
    ____ C.  avoid compromising societal norms and ethics in order to achieve goals.
    ____ D.  allocate organizational resources as efficiently as possible.

14. It is important to:
    ____ A.  pursue only those opportunities which provide the best rate of return.

      \_\_\_\_ B.  provide employment opportunities to the hard-core un-employed.

      \_\_\_\_ C.  comply fully and honestly with enacted laws, regulations, and court rulings.

      \_\_\_\_ D.  recognize that society's unwritten laws and codes can often be as important as the written.

15.  It is important that:

      \_\_\_\_ A.  philanthropic and voluntary efforts continue to be expanded consistently over time.

      \_\_\_\_ B.  contract and safety violations are not ignored in order to complete or expedite a project.

      \_\_\_\_ C.  profit margins remain strong relative to major competitors.

      \_\_\_\_ D.  'whistle blowing' not be discouraged at any corporate level.

## NOTES

1.  For ease of interpretation the 10 point scale was converted to a percentage basis.

2.  These reputational surveys reflect a response rate of only 11%. In addition, the typical responder rated only 20 to 45 firms.

## REFERENCES

Abbott, Walter F., and Monsen, Joseph R. "On the Measurement of Corporate Social Responsibility." *Academy of Management Journal* (September 1979) 22, (3):501–515.

Alexander, Gordon J., and Buchholz, Rogene A. "Corporate Social Responsibility and Stock Market Performance." *Academy of Management Journal* (September 1978) 21, (3):479–486.

Arlow, Peter, and Gannon, Martin J. "Social Responsiveness, Corporate Structure, and Economic Performance." *Academy of Management Review* April, 1982) 7, (2):235–241.

Aupperle, Kenneth E. *An Empirical Inquiry Into the Social Responsibilities as Defined by Corporations.* Doctoral Dissertation, University of Georgia, 1981.

Bowman, Edward H., and Haire, Mason. "A Strategic Posture Toward Corporate Social Responsibility." *California Management Review* (Winter 1975) 18, (2):49–58.

Bragdon, J. H., and Marlin, J. T. "Is Pollution Profitable?" *Risk Management* (April 1972) 19, (4):9–18.

Carroll, Archie B. "A Three Dimensional Conceptual Model of Corporate Social Performance." *Academy of Management Review* (October 1979) 4, (4):497–505.

Corson, John J., and Steiner, George A., *Measuring Business' Social Performance: The Corporate Social Audit.* New York: Committee for Economic Development, 1974.

Eilbirt, Henry, and Parket, Robert I. "The Practice of Business: The Current Status of Corporate Social Responsibility." *Business Horizons* (August 1973) 16, (4) 5–14.

Heinz, D. C. "Financial Correlates of a Social Measure," *Akron Business and Economic Review* 1976, 7, (1):48–51.

Holmes, Sandra L. "Corporate Social Performance: Past and Present Areas of Commitment." *Academy of Management Journal* (September 1, 1977) 20, (3):433–538.(a)

Jensen, Robert E. *Phantasmagoric Accounting: Research and Analysis of Economic, Social, and*

*Environmental Impact of Corporate Business*. Sarasota, Florida: American Accounting Association, 1976.

Moskowitz, Milton. "Choosing Socially Responsible Stocks." *Business and Society Review/ Innovation* (Spring 1972) (1):71–75.

Ostlund, Lyman E. "Attitudes of Managers Toward Corporate Social Policy." *California Management Review* (Summer 1977) 19, (4):35–49.

Parket, Robert and Eilbirt, Henry. "Social Responsibility: The Underlying Factors." *Business Horizons* (August 1975):5–10

Paluszek, John L. *Business and Society: 1976–2000, an AMA Report,* New York: AMACOM, 1976.

"So Far So Good." *Business and Society Review,* Summer, 1972, No. 2, 88.

Sturdivant, Frederick D. *Business and Society.* (Rev. ed.), Homewood, Illinois: Richard D. Irwin, Inc., 1981.

Sturdivant, Frederick D. and Ginter, James L. "Corporate Social Responsiveness." *California Management Review* (Spring 1977) 19, (3):30–39.

*Value Line Investment Survey* (Part IV, Glossary), October 2, 1981, 37, No. 1.

Vance, Stanley C. "Are Socially Responsible Corporations Good Investment Risks?" *Management Review,* 1975, 64, No. 8, 19–24.

# THE IMPACT OF CORPORATE SOCIAL RESPONSIVENESS ON SHAREHOLDER WEALTH

Walter R. Holman, J. Randolph New and
Daniel Singer

It is generally conceded that corporations have responsibilities to a variety of stakeholders, and most large firms have taken some steps to respond to at least some of their various constituencies. Given limited resources, however, it is necessary to make trade-offs among the needs of various stakeholder groups (Sethi, 1984); and it apparently remains true that management considers the economic wealth of stockholders to be their top priority concern (Drucker, 1984). Therefore, the question arises: What is the impact of socially responsive behavior toward other constituencies on the economic well-being of stockholders?

This question is of interest to corporate management in their calculation of trade-offs and also to external analysts and agencies. Federal policy makers at the Securities and Exchange Commission (SEC) have recently devoted considerable attention to the question of whether investors would use information on corporate social responsiveness. Since 1979, the SEC has substantially increased the disclosure requirements for publicly-held corporations in the area of environmental pollution control. In an interpretive release, the SEC required firms to disclose additional information on pollution abatement activities including estimated capital expenditures on pollution abatement for a two-year period beyond the issuance date of their 10K reports (Jaggi and Freedman, 1982). The SEC has also entertained the idea of expanding the reporting requirements to other areas of social responsibility.

The purpose of this study is to provide additional information relevant to two questions:

1.  What information do investors consider, if any, regarding a corporation's socially responsive activities;
2.  What impact does investors' evaluation of this information have on shareholder wealth?

## MEASURING CORPORATE SOCIAL RESPONSIVENESS

Measurement of corporate social responsiveness is undeveloped compared with measurement in other areas. A primary reason is the unavailability of detailed quantitative data regarding socially relevant activities (Abbott and Monsen, 1979). This creates difficulties for both researchers and investors who are interested in this information. Despite the inherent difficulties, researchers in the area of social responsiveness have attempted to develop usable measures. A review of the published research indicates that at least three different measures of social responsiveness have been used: (1) reputational scales, (2) content analysis of corporate documents, and (3) indices of the degree and/or cost of regulatory compliance.

Reputational scales measure the perceptions of a sample population regarding the degree of social responsibility of an individual corporation or group of corporations. This method has been used with samples of graduate students (Heinze, 1976), corporate staff (Vance, 1975), businessmen and students (Alexander and Buchholz, 1978), and a variety of "critical stakeholders," including investment analysts, trade union leaders, federal regulators, and industry CEOs (Makin, 1983; Sonnenfeld, 1982).

The second approach, content analysis, involves analyzing corporate communications in a systematic and objective manner to create measures representing the quantification of qualitative data (Kerlinger, 1973, p. 525). In its simplest form, content analysis uses a dichotomous classification: the communication contains a particular type of information or it does not. Other measures include amount of communication, frequency, word usage, etc. Content analysis has been used to assess corporate social responsiveness through the examination of speeches of top executives (Hull and Bunting as reported in Abbott and Monsen, 1979), annual reports (Abbott and Monsen, 1979; Belkaoui, 1976; Beresford, 1978; Bowman and Haire, 1975), and SEC 10K reports (Jaggi and Freedman, 1982).

The third kind of measures used by researchers are indices of the degree of regulatory compliance and/or the monetary cost of such compliance. Regulatory compliance indices assess the extent to which corporations comply with mandatory or suggested federal, state, and local governmental regulations. Noncompliance or a low degree of compliance is viewed as evidence of lack of social responsiveness. Indices focused on the cost implications of regulatory compliance have been used along with these degree-of-compliance indices to provide a more specific measure of the relationship between compliance levels and costs across different industries. Compliance level and cost of compliance indices have been used in studies of social responsiveness by Spicer (1978) and Holman, Martinelli and Chamberlain (1982).

Although investors undoubtedly do not assess a firm's social responsiveness as systematically as do academic researchers, they must nonetheless utilize some type of measurement if activity in this area is used as a criterion in their investment decisions. The push by accounting professionals and federal policymakers for both disclosure and measurement standards indicates that they believe investors do (or would) use this information. The measurement approaches used by researchers may provide useful starting points for identifying the information investors might employ in making their judgments. At the same time, it should be noted that investors do not necessarily adhere to the rigorous standards applied to measurements used for purposes of research. Also, investors have access to information which is not generally available to researchers, such as brokerage firm proprietary research, conversations with key corporate executives, and insider trading data.

Content analysis and construction of regulatory compliance and cost indices are the two measurement approaches expected to most closely model the subjective assessment process used by investors. The underlying assumption is that to the extent investors assess corporate social responsiveness, they would utilize such publicly-available information in their analysis. Three studies previously cited provide support for this contention. Spicer (1978) and Holman et al. (1982) analyzed data which suggested that the compliance degree and compliance cost indices which they developed were useful in explaining investor-perceived differences in the level of expected return and risk inherent in corporate common stocks. Jaggi and Freedman (1982) concluded that estimated capital expenditures on pollution abatement in a corporation's annual report or SEC 10K was information used by investors in their portfolio decisions. In essence, these studies support the hypothesis that information concerning corporate social responsiveness does influence shareholder wealth or firm value.

## SOCIAL RESPONSIVENESS AND STOCK PRICES

If investors do utilize publicly available information to assess corporate social responsiveness, the question emerges as to whether they respond positively or negatively to evidence of favorable social performance. Theory and research exist that support a prediction of either a positive or a negative investor response.

A positive impact could be anticipated given either of two logics. One, as the American Accounting Association 1966–68 Committee on External Reporting (1969) pointed out, public disclosure of social involvement may be useful to some investors because they "wish to avoid some investments entirely for ethical reasons or because of personal biases" (p. 18). Rudd (1981, 1979) discusses the exercise of investor's ethical concern through the employment of portfolio selection rules based in part on information concerning social responsiveness.

Direct evidence that some investors prefer so-called "clean investment" is provided by the existence of institutions specializing in these investments. Independent Pax World Fund, Eaton and Howard's Foursquare Fund, and Dreyfus' Third Century Fund are current examples of institutional portfolios constructed in part on the basis of various social concerns (Terpstra and Olsen, 1982). Some researchers have concluded that this expressed preference for socially responsive corporations has a positive impact on firm value (e.g., Belkaoui, 1976; Jaggi and Freedman, 1982).

A second basis for predicting a positive financial impact from disclosure of social involvement is provided by Narver (1971). His thesis is that for corporate managers to maximize the present market value of the firm, it is necessary that investors have confidence that the firm will not be subjected in the future to government sanctions as a result of violations regarding pollution and other social involvement matters. Thus, the firm must at times forego short-term profits in order to ensure its long-run welfare. Other authors (e.g., Bragdon and Martin, 1972) have argued along similar lines that certain socially responsive activities, such as modernization of plant and equipment for purposes of pollution abatement, will be conducive to higher productivity and will result in better profitability in the long run. Bowman and Haire (1975), for example, reported that food-processing firms providing some discussion of corporate social involvement in their annual reports had a significantly higher mean return on investment than firms with no discussion. Terpstra and Olsen (1982) found for a sample of Fortune 500 companies that the more socially responsive firms (based upon publicly disclosed information from a variety of sources) generated superior economic performance both in terms of the profitability of their sales and the rates of return on their shareholders' equity in comparison to the less socially responsive firms. It should be noted that when a positive relationship is found between measures of social responsiveness and stock market performance, it is difficult to determine whether the relationship is the result of ethical investment choices, or simply of rational financial investment decisions oriented to the long run, or a combination of the two.

Conversely, the prediction can be made that investors will react negatively to disclosure of corporate social involvement. Some economists, most notably Milton Friedman (1970), have argued that when firms use their resources to discharge social responsibilities, they are likely to experience reduced profitability. Investors are likely to react negatively to such firms if they anticipate reduced profitability and lower cash flows with no corresponding reduction in risk. Vance (1975), for example, analyzed the relation between reputational indices of corporate social responsiveness and percent change in price per share and found an inverse relationship.

From an investment portfolio perspective, Rudd (1981) argued that the application of noneconomic criteria (e.g., degree of social responsibility) to the selection of investments could result in inferior portfolio performance. Terpstra and Olsen (1982) found that excessive investment (more than 12 percent of a large portfolio) in common stocks of Fortune 500 companies with a high level of social performance resulted in inferior portfolio performance.

The mixed views evident in academic theory and research also appear among business practitioners. Holmes (1976) asked top executives in 560 major firms in a variety of industries to indicate possible positive and negative outcomes of a firm performing social responsibility activities. Of the respondents, 36.6 percent indicated the positive outcome of "investors prefer socially responsible firms," while 24.1 percent expected the negative outcome of "disaffection of stockholders."

## STRUCTURE OF THE STUDY

This study examines, at least indirectly, the extent to which investors utilize information on corporate social responsiveness and the impact, if any, of this evaluation on shareholder wealth. Two sources of publicly available information were considered to accomplish this purpose: (1) the corporate annual report; and (2) federal government regulatory analysis documents estimating the degree and potential costs of corporate regulatory compliance.

Prior research on public disclosure of corporate socially responsive activities has focused on the corporate annual report and, to a lesser extent, on its more comprehensive counterpart, the SEC 10K report. These sources have been content analyzed in a very basic manner: the reports did or did not contain information on corporate social responsiveness. Typically, these documents contain little or no comprehensive data on regulatory compliance levels or potential versus actual compliance costs. The second source (federal documents) contains comprehensive data on regulatory compliance levels and anticipated compliance costs which federal policymakers employ in the assessment of the potential effects of regulation on corporate financial positions. Securities analysts during the 1970s made frequent reference to these cost estimates in their assessments of corporate common stocks and bonds. Thus, one anticipates that investors would directly or indirectly (through investment advisors) have access to, and utilize, these data in their evaluation of the consequences of corporate social performance.

## Measurement of Independent Variables

Measures of socially responsive activities were developed for both the annual report information and the federal regulatory report information. The information contained in annual reports was measured using the approach developed by the national accounting firm of Ernst & Whinney (formerly Ernst & Ernst) under the direction of partner Dennis R. Beresford (1973, 1978). This method was also used in published research by Abbott and Monsen (1979), Beresford and Feldman (1976), and Beresford (1974). The method involves a content analysis of corporate annual reports and results in a measure of corporate social responsiveness identified in this study as the Social Responsibility Disclosure (SRD) scale. From 1971 to 1978, Beresford conducted an annual survey of social responsibility disclosure in the annual reports of the Fortune 500 Industrials, and classified each disclosure by topic into 27 specific categories (this number varied slightly from year to year) grouped into seven general categories. These were: environment, energy, fair business practices, human resources, community involvement, products, and other disclosures. A disclosure consisted of any mention of a firm's activity within one of the 27 categories. Disclosure could take place in monetary form—e.g., the firm made grants totalling $1,391,000 to health care institutions, civic associations, and various charitable organizations—or in nonmonetary form—e.g., in the professional ranks there was a 32.5 percent growth in women and a 14.3 percent growth in minorities (Beresford, 1974, p. 31). Each disclosure of an activity is counted as a single item, and the SRD score is the total number of items in each of the 7 categories mentioned by each firm.

The information contained in the federal regulatory analysis reports relating to corporate socially responsive activity was measured using a Regulatory Compliance Capital Expenditure Index (RCCEI) developed by Holman (Holman et al., 1982). This index is the ratio of the estimated capital expenditures necessary to comply with specific federal "social responsibility" regulations to the cumulative capital expenditures (excluding the mandated expenditures) over the mandated period for compliance. The index attempts to measure the importance of specific federal regulations to each corporation in terms of the increased burden of capital investment in ''nonproductive'' assets. Each additional dollar of investment in nonproductive assets puts increased pressure on short-term corporate profit margins and cost of capital. The index also represents the most important of the three primary indices employed by federal agencies (most notably, the U.S. Environmental Protection Agency) to assess the potential effects of proposed regulations on firm and industry performance and financial health.

## Measurement of Shareholder Wealth (Firm Value)

In order to assess the effects of investor evaluation of publicly disclosed corporate social responsiveness on shareholder wealth or firm value, it was necessary to adopt a measure of shareholder wealth. The generally-accepted measure for the past several decades has been the total rate of return (TRR) on a firm's common stock. The total rate of return on a common stock for any given period is the ratio of the sum of the price change and cash dividend for the period to the beginning price for the period. (Weston and Brigham (1981), Van Horne (1982), and Johnson and Melicher (1981) present detailed discussions of shareholder wealth measurement.)

In addition to the selection of TRR as the measure of stockholder wealth or firm value, it was also necessary to employ a common stock price valuation model which met two important criteria:

1. It contains a high level of explanatory power concerning common stock prices;
2. It allows direct testing of the potential impact of new information (in this case, public information concerning corporate social responsiveness) on common stock prices over the longer run.

Since the mid-1960s, the Capital Asset Pricing Model (CAPM) developed by Markowitz (1959), Sharpe (1963), and Lintner (1965), has been employed extensively to assess the impact of a wide variety of different types of information on common stock prices. Applications have included: (1) earnings and dividends announcements (e.g., Charest, 1978; Pettit, 1972); (2) changes in bond ratings (e.g., Grier and Katz, 1976); (3) changes in accounting procedures (e.g., Kaplan and Roll, 1972); (4) product recall announcements (e.g., Simpson and Mowen, 1982); (5) labor strikes, acquisitions (Morse, 1982); and (6) public announcements concerning research, development and strategic planning activities (Kudla, 1980). Applications more directly related to this study have been the assessment of investor reaction to corporate announcements concerning pollution control expenditures (Belkaoui, 1976; Holman et al., 1982; Jaggi and Freedman, 1982; Spicer, 1978) and corporate social responsibility (Rudd, 1979, 1981; Terpstra and Olsen, 1982).

This study uses the CAPM to explain variance in TRR that is associated with different levels of publically disclosed information for the firms under consideration.

*Sample Selection and Timeframe*

Selecting the sample for this study was difficult for two reasons: first, SRD scores were only available for the Fortune 500 industrial corporations; and second, comprehensive and reliable firm-specific compliance cost information was only available in the area of environmental pollution control. The available sample was 49 Fortune 500 industrial corporations (see Table 1) in four pollution prone industries: (1) steel, (2) pulp and paper, (3) textile manufacturing, and (4) rubber manufacturing.

Our focus on this sample of data is appropriate because of the aggregate size and importance of these firms, and the current interest in environmental issues. The Ernst & Whinney *1978 Survey of Social Responsibility Disclosure* identified environmental issues as the area of greatest concern to corporations during the 1970s. In 1974 for example, 50.4 percent of annual reports of the Standard &

*Table 1.*   Firms Included in the Study Sample

| Industry | Firms | |
| --- | --- | --- |
| Pulp and Paper | Boise Cascade | Kimberly Clark |
| | Champion International | Mead |
| | Crown Zellerback | Potlach |
| | Diamond International | St. Regis Paper |
| | Georgia Pacific | Scott Paper |
| | Great Northern Nekossa | Union Camp |
| | Hammermill | Westvaco |
| | International Paper | Weyerhauser |
| Steel | Alleghany Steel | LTV |
| | Armco | McLouth Steel |
| | Bethlehem Steel | National Steel |
| | Cyclops | Republic |
| | Inland Steel | U.S. Steel |
| | Interlake | Wheeling-Pittsburgh |
| | Kaiser | |
| Rubber | Armstrong | General Tire |
| | Cooper Tire | Goodrich |
| | Dayco | Goodyear |
| | Firestone Tire | Uniroyal |
| Textiles | Burlington Industries | Lowenstein |
| | Cannon Mills | Mohasco |
| | Collins & Alkman | Spring Mills |
| | Core Mills | Stevens (J.P.) |
| | Dan River | United Merchants |
| | Fieldcrest | West-Point-Pepp |

Poors industrial corporations cited concerns over environmental matters. Environmental pollution control has also received significant attention by the SEC, culminating in 1979 in substantially more stringent public disclosure requirements. Moreover, air and water pollution control was believed to be the major issue of social concern for firms in the four selected industries. Over 50 percent of the Fortune 500 corporations in these industries cited concerns over air and water pollution control in their annual reports.

The 1973–1977 period was selected for study for several reasons. It encompassed the period immediately following the enactment of a number of important pieces of federal environmental legislation (Federal Clean Air Act, 1970; Federal Water Pollution Control Act Amendments, 1972; Resource Recovery Act, 1970; National Environmental Policy Act, 1969). During this period the EPA, other federal agencies, and the affected industries developed their estimates of mandated pollution control costs and conducted their assessments of the potential impacts on industry/firm performance and financial health. In addition, the 1973–1977 period encompassed the mandatory compliance deadlines for most industries with respect to both Federal and State air and water pollution control standards (initial phases). Finally, it was during this time period that significant volumes of information began to reach investors concerning the magnitude and potential impacts of mandated pollution control expenditures.

## Capital Asset Pricing Model

The CAPM was employed to assess the impact of publicly-disclosed social responsibility activities on shareholder wealth, as measured by the TRR. According to CAPM, investors evaluate common stocks and other financial assets in terms of the level of return (measured by the expected value) and the level of risk (measured in terms of the variability of return). A basic tenet of CAPM is the linear relationship between expected return and risk when markets are in equilibrium. Consequently, expected return and risk can be used interchangeably in the testing of investor reaction to information relating to firm value. In addition, according to CAPM, investors focus on two related measures of common stock risk: (1) total risk, and (2) market-related risk. Total risk, measured by the standard deviation of common stock returns, represents the total variability in returns over time. Market-related risk, as measured by the CAPM $\beta$ (beta) coefficient, represents the component of total risk which cannot be eliminated or reduced through portfolio diversification.

Mathematically, CAPM is usually specified:

$$R_i = \alpha_i + \beta_i R_m + \epsilon_i.$$

Where: $R_i$ is the total rate of return on the "ith" common stock, $\alpha_i$ represents the component of total return related to non-market or firm-specific factors, and $\epsilon_i$ is the stochastic error term. The $\beta_i R_m$ term is the market-related component of total return—that component of total return resulting from the influence of the returns on common stocks in general. The $\beta_i$ term measures the relationship between the total rate of return on common stock $i$ and the total rate of return on the population of common stocks ($R_m$). The variance of the CAPM equation is:

$$\sigma^2_i = \sigma^2_{\alpha i} + \beta_i^2 \sigma^2_{R_m}.$$

Again, $\sigma^2_i$ is the total risk in stock $i$; $\beta_i^2 \sigma^2_{R_m}$ is the level of market-related risk; and $\sigma_{\alpha i}^2$ is the level of nonmarket or firm-specific risk.

*Analysis*

The general forms of the accounting-based models utilized in this study were as follows:

Model I:          $\sigma = f$   (financial leverage, payout ratio, acid-test ratio, industry category)

Model II:         $\beta = f$   (firm size, growth rate, industry category)

In these models:

- $\sigma$ is the total risk inherent in a common stock
- $\beta$ is the measure of market-related risk
- financial leverage is measured as the average of the annual ratios (1973–1977) of long-term debt to total assets
- payout ratio is measured as the sum of cash dividends paid to common stockholders to the sum of net income available for common stockholders for the 1973–1977 period
- acid-test ratio is measured as the average of the annual ratios (1973–1977) of current assets minus inventory to current liabilities
- industry category is measured in terms of a set of dummy variables which differentiate among the four sampled industries
- firm size is measured as the average of the natural logarithms of annual total assets for the 1973–1977 period
- growth rate is measured as the annual growth in total assets over the 1973–1977 period

Multiple regression analysis was used to assess the effects of social responsiveness disclosures on both the total and market-related risk inherent in the common stocks of the 49 sampled corporations. The SRD and the RCCEI variables were added separately to existing models which attempt to explain cross-sectional differences in $\sigma$ and $\beta$ among common stocks in terms of firm-specific, accounting-based variables. The contributions of these two variables were assessed in terms of their effect on the corrected $R^2$ for each regression model. This approach has been used by other researchers (e.g., Beaver, Ketler, and Scholes, 1970; Lev and Kunitzky, 1974) to measure the association between common stock risk and both accounting-based and nonaccounting based variables. Spicer (1978) and Holman et al. (1982) used this approach to measure the effect of public disclosure of regulatory compliance levels on both total and market-related risk.

## RESULTS OF THE STUDY

The results of the regression analyses are given in Tables 2 and 3. For the dependent variable total risk ($\sigma$), shown in Table 2, the RCCEI variable enters the regression equation with a positive sign and shows a statistically significant coefficient. This finding suggests that a larger value for the RCCEI (representing greater proportionate capital expenditures mandated, but not yet incurred) is perceived by investors as threatening the firm's deployment of productive capital in the future and thus increases the risk associated with the TRR. Thus, the effect of the market is to "punish" firms with proportionately higher outstanding social capital investment requirements by reducing shareholder wealth through lower stock prices.

The addition of the RCCEI to the CAPM results in an increase in the adjusted $R^2$ from 0.2110 to 0.4277, which represents a substantial increase in the explanatory power of the model. Spicer (1978), for example, achieved only a 7.5 percent

*Table 2.* Total Risk ($\sigma$) Regressed on Accounting-Based Variables and the RCCEI

| Variables | Regression Equation with only the Accounting-Based Variables<br>Coefficient[1] | Regression Equation with Addition of the RCCEI Variable<br>Coefficient[1] | Regression Equation with Addition of the SRD Scale Variable<br>Coefficient[1] |
|---|---|---|---|
| Constant | 0.1743* | 0.111* | 0.1747** |
| Leverage | 0.1616* | 0.1686** | 0.1608* |
| Industry Dummy (Textiles) | 0.0355* | 0.0480** | 0.0354* |
| Payout Ratio | −0.0504* | | −0.0500* |
| Acid-Test Ratio | −0.0429** | −0.0364** | −0.0428** |
| Added Variables: | | | |
| RCCEI | | 0.1939** | |
| SRD | | | |
| Summary Statistics: | | | |
| Corrected $R^2$ | 0.2110 | 0.4277 | 0.1904 |

*Notes:* [1]Coefficients omitted where $p \geq .05$.
    *p < .05
    **p < .01

*Table 3.* Systematic Risk ($\beta$) Regressed on Accounting-Based Variables and the RCCEI

| Variables | Coefficient[1] | Coefficient[1] | Coefficient[1] |
|---|---|---|---|
| Constant | 7.4034** | 7.4560** | 7.3281** |
| Industry Dummy (Steel) | −0.4845** | −0.4903** | −0.4851** |
| Size | −0.4652* | −0.4561* | −0.4613* |
| Growth Rate | −0.9638* | −0.9582* | −0.9607* |
| Added Variables: | | | |
|   RCCEI | | | |
|   SRD | | | |
| Summary Statistics: | | | |
| Corrected $R^2$ | 0.2035 | 0.1854 | 0.1871 |

*Notes:* [1]Coefficients omitted where $p \geq .05$.
    *p < .05
    **p < .01

increase in explained variation as a result of the addition of a compliance rate variable to an accounting-based CAPM equation.

In contrast, the addition of the SRD variable to the CAPM did not yield a statistically significant relationship between total risk and the SRD variable. There are a number of possible explanations for this result. First, investors may have previously adjusted stock prices based upon their perceptions (present and prospective) of corporate social responsiveness during the period just preceding the 1973–1977 timeframe. Thus, they did not find the information contained in annual reports over the 1973–1977 period to be useful. Second, investors find information relating to the cost aspect of disclosures more useful than the disclosures alone. Comparison of the results for the RCCEI versus the SRD variable suggests that disclosure of socially responsive activity alone does not provide sufficient information for assessing the scope and quality of social responsiveness activities, or their effect on corporate financial health and performance. An examination of the sample of corporate social responsiveness disclosures presented in the Ernst & Whinney document supports this view. Steel companies, for example, frequently reported the level and nature of specific pollution control expenditures. Investors during the 1973–1977 period, however, were also aware from information in the financial and news media that many steel companies faced potential litigation and substantial required capital expeditures as a result of their lack of compliance with the Federal Clean Air and Clean Water Acts.

Although the results in Table 2 suggest that the SRD variable is not useful in explaining the observed cross-sectional differences in firm's,it is possible that both the SRD and RCCEI variables have significant explanatory power with respect to changes in individual firm total risk over time. A comparison of the $\alpha$ values for the sampled firms for 1968–1972, versus 1973–1977, revealed that only 3 firms had values significantly different at the 95 percent confidence level. Hence there was no intertemporal variation to explain, and the question remains open.

The results in Table 3 are for market-related risk as measured in terms of $\beta$. The addition of neither the SRD or RCCEI variable improved the corrected $R^2$ for $\beta$. Testing for changes in firm $\beta$ values for the 1968–1972 versus 1973–1977 period resulted in statistically significant changes in only two instances; thus, inter-temporal effects cannot be investigated.

A possible explanation of the significant impact of the RCCEI variable on $\sigma$ and its lack of significance on $\beta$ is found in capital market theory. Market-related risk ($\beta$) is believed to be the only relevant measure of risk (or conversely, return—$\beta R_m$) for common stocks held in well-diversified (e.g., institutional) portfolios. On the other hand, total risk ($\sigma$) is believed to be relevant to investors and smaller institutions whose limited capital resources preclude the establishment of well-diversified portfolios in which all nonmarket related risk has been eliminated. Therefore, the results in Tables 2 and 3 suggest that well-diversified portfolios do not use (or have already incorporated in their portfolio selection processes) publicly disclosed information on corporate social responsiveness. However, investors without well-diversified portfolios find useful the public disclosures on the potential costs of social responsive activities which are contained in the federal regulatory analysis documents. These investors could reduce their overall portfolio risk by differentiating among firms in pollution prone industries on the basis of the type of information captured by the RCCEI.

## SUMMARY AND IMPLICATIONS

This research examined the effects of firm value of publicly-disclosed information on corporate social responsiveness contained in corporate annual reports and federal regulatory analysis documents. The results suggest that general disclosures (SRD index) have little impact on perceived risk, whereas more specific information (RCCEI) is found to be important. Disclosure of high environmental cost requirements has an adverse impact on shareholder wealth or firm value. Investors find the total risk of the common stocks of companies with higher RCCEI values to be significantly greater than the total risk for their counterparts with low potential compliance costs.

Through the use of shareholder wealth measure and the CAPM, the study attempted to overcome a major weakness of many of the previous studies of this subject. A general equilibrium model such as CAPM isolates the effects of specific disclosures by controlling other extraneous, independent variables that may influence economic performance. Further, by focusing on shareholder wealth as opposed to profitability, return on assets, net profits, or some other less appropriate measure, one uses a measure of economic performance which adjusts for risk in measuring shareholder or investor returns and which represents an important goal toward which much of financial management is directed (Kudla, 1980).

The findings of this study support the thrust of recent attempts by the SEC to expand the mandatory corporate disclosure requirements in the area of pollution control activities. The 1979 SEC interpretive release requiring firms to disclose additional information on the estimated level of future capital expenditures for pollution abatement reaffirmed the agency's belief that stockholders and prospective investors would use additional cost information which would facilitate an assessment of the potential effects of such costs on financial performance. The finding in this study of a significantly positive relationship between total risk and the RCCEI variable adds empirical support to this contention.

The findings also suggest to SEC policymakers that further expansion of mandatory corporate disclosure requirements in other areas of social performance should be focused on the potential costs of such activities and their potential effects on corporate financial performance. Since 1980, the SEC has been considering an expansion of the disclosures requirements for mandated activities to include not only an estimate of future compliance costs but, in addition, to include an assessment of the impact of such costs on future corporate earnings.

Finally, the findings in this study also have significant implications for corporate managers. In order to avoid adverse effects on firm value or shareholder wealth, managers need to anticipate where the government will regulate and develop strategies for reporting and compliance focused on the long-run. Corporations that fail to do so will be subjected by investors to penalties in the capital market.

# REFERENCES

Abbott, W. F., and Monsen, R. J. On the measurement of corporate social responsibility: self-reported disclosures as a method of measuring corporate social involvement. *Academy of Management Journal* 22 (1979):501–515.

Alexander, G. J., and Buchholz, R. A. Corporate social responsibility and stock market performance. *Academy of Management Journal* 21 (1978):479–486.

American Accounting Association 1966–68 Committee on External Reporting. *The Accounting Review* (Supplement to Vol. XLIV) 1969:23–41.

Beaver, W., Ketler, P., and Scholes, M. The association between market determined and accounting determined risk measures. *Accounting Review* 45 (1970):1015–1026.

Belkaoui, A. The impact of the disclosure of the environmental effects of organizational behavior on the market. *Financial Management* 21 (4) (1976):26–31.

Beresford, D. R. *Compilation of social measurement disclosures in Fortune 500 annual report-1973.* Cleveland: Ernst & Ernst, 1973.

Beresford, D. R. How companies are reporting social performance. *Management Accounting* 56(2) (1974):41–44.

Beresford, D. R. *Social responsibility disclosure: 1978 survey.* Cleveland: Ernst & Ernst, 1978.

Beresford, D. R., and Feldman, S. A. Companies increase social responsibility disclosure. *Management Accounting* 59 (1976):51–55.

Bowman, E. H., and Haire, M. A strategic posture toward corporate social responsibility. *California Management Review* 18 (1975):49–58.

Bragdon, J., and Martin, J. Is pollution profitable? *Risk Management* 19 (1972):9–18.

Charest, G. Dividend information, stock returns and market efficiency. *Journal of Financial Economics* 6 (June–Sept. 1978):265–330.

Davis, K. Five propositions for social responsibility. *Business Horizons* 18(3) (1975):19–24.

Davis, K., and Blomstrom, R. L. *Business and society: Environment and responsibility.* New York: McGraw-Hill, 1975.

Drucker, Peter. The New Meaning of Corporate Social Responsibility. *California Management Review* 26(2) (1984):53–63.

Friedman, M. The social responsibility of business is to increase profits. *The New York Times Magazine* (September 13, 1970):33 ff.

Grier, P., and Katz, S. The differential effects of bond rating changes among industrial and public utility bonds by maturity. *Journal of Business* 49 (1976):226–239.

Heinze, D. C. Financial correlates of a social involvement measure. *Akron Business and Economic Review* 7 (1976):48–51.

Holman, W. R., Martinelli, P., and Chamberlain, K. Pollution control, disclosure and market risk. Paper presented at the Annual Meeting of the Southwestern Finance Association, 1982.

Holmes, S. L. Executive perceptions of corporation social responsibility. *Business Horizons* 19(3) (1976):34–40.

Jaggi, B., and Freedman, M. An analysis of the informational content of pollution disclosures. *The Financial Review* 17 (1982):142–152.

Johnson, R., and Melicher, R. *Financial management.* Allyn & Bacon, 1981.

Kaplan, R., and Roll, R. Investor evaluation of accounting information: Some empirical evidence. *Journal of Business* 45 (1972):226–257.

Kerlinger, F. N. *Foundations of behavioral research.* New York: Holt, Rinehart and Winston, 1973.

Kudla, R. J. The effects of strategic planning on common stock returns. *Academy of Management Journal* 23 (1980):5–20.

Lev, B., and Kunitzky, S. On the association between smoothing measures and the risk of common stocks. *Accounting Review* 49 1974:259–270.

Lintner, J. D. Security prices, risk, and maximal gains from diversification. *Journal of Finance* 20 (1965):587–616.

Makin, C. Ranking corporate reputations. *Fortune* (January 1983):34–43.

Markowitz, H. *Portfolio selection: Efficient diversification of investments.* New York: J. Wiley and Sons, 1959.

Morse, D. Wall Street Journal announcements and the securities markets. *Financial Analysts Journal* April (1982):51–60.

Narver, J. C. Rational management responses to external effects. *Academy of Management Journal* 14 (1971):99–115.

Pettit, R. Dividend announcements, security performance, and capital market efficiency. *Journal of Finance* 27 (1972):993–1007.

Rudd, A. Divestment of south african equities: How risky? *Journal of Portfolio Management* 17(3) (1979):5–10.

Rudd, A. Social responsibility and portfolio performance. *California Management Review* 24 (1981):55–61.

Sethi, S. P. Dimensions of corporate social performance: An analytical framework. *California Management Review* 18 (1975):58–64.

Sethi, S. P. Ethical Boundaries. *Business and Society Review* 48 (1984):10.

Sharpe, W. F. A simplified model for portfolio analysis. *Management Science* 9 (1963):227–293.

Simpson, W., and Mowen, J. The reaction of stock prices to information on product recall. Paper presented at the Annual meeting of Southwest Finance Association, March, 1982.

Sonnenfeld, J. Measuring corporate social performance. *Proceedings of the Academy of Management* (1982):371–375.

Spicer, B. H. Market risk, accounting data and companies' pollution control records. *Journal of Business Finance and Accounting* 5(1) (1978):67–81.

Steiner, G. A. *Business and society.* New York: Random House, 1975.

Terpstra, R. H., and Olsen, R. A. Investor social responsibility and portfolio performance. Paper presented at the Annual Meeting of the Eastern Finance Association, April. 1982.

Van Horne, J. C. *Financial management and policy.* Prentice-Hall, 1982.

Vance, S. C. Are socially responsible corporations good investment risks? *Management Review* 64(8) (1975):18–24.

Weston, J. F., and Brigham, E. *Managerial finance.* Dryden Press, 1981.

# CORPORATE SOCIAL PERFORMANCE IN CANADA, 1976-86

Max B.E. Clarkson

---

This paper describes a research project, begun in 1983, the purpose of which was to develop a methodology for the evaluation of corporate social performance (CSP) which could be used by MBA students and applied by them to corporations. Prior to that date, there had been only one significant empirical study of CSP in Canada and the situation in the United States was very much the same: "actual empirical research designed to test the multitude of definitions, propositions, concepts, and theories that have been advanced has been scarce" (Aupperle, Carroll, Hatfield, 1985).

## ORIGIN OF THE STUDY

A Canadian research project had been undertaken in 1976 on behalf of the Royal Commission on Corporate Concentration (RCCC), a major inquiry ordered by the Government of Canada, as a result of a series of major takeovers and attempted takeovers which had aroused considerable public concern about concentration of corporate power in fewer hands in Canada. The terms of reference of the Commission included "the economic and social implications for the public interest in such concentrations." In its final report the Commission admitted that "We found the social area the most difficult part of our mandate" (RCCC, 16). The Royal Commission contracted for separate research studies of several large corporations, both Canadian and foreign-controlled, which provided data relevant to the subject of corporate concentration. Several of these studies incuded sections about social involvement and performance.

The Commission also engaged researchers for a series of special studies, one of which was "Corporate Social Performance in Canada" (RCCC Study 21, 1977). Conducted by the Niagara Institute for the commission, this represented the first serious study in Canada of the attitudes, policies and actions of a wide range of corporations in regard to the then ill-defined area called 'Corporate Social Responsibility.' The researchers used a mail survey directed towards 1083 companies with sales in excess of $10,000,000, in order to ascertain the current state of awareness, analysis and response to social issues. The 284 usable responses yielded a significant amount of valuable data. Case studies were also commissioned for nine large companies, who undertook to respond in depth to questions about social responsiveness and the management of social issues.

These self-studies, which had been included in the final report on "Corporate Social Performance in Canada" (Study 21), formed the basis for a research project initiated in 1983 for MBA students in the second year elective course on "Corporate Social Responsibilities" at the University of Toronto. The first objective of this project was to evaluate what changes, if any, had taken place in the strategies, policy-making and actions of the companies involved in the original studies in terms of their social performance. Small groups of students were formed, classroom discussion of Study 21 and its methodologies were held, and the field studies began.

The analytic framework used was the Corproate Social Response Matrix, developed by Preston, academic consultant for the Niagara Institute study (Study 21), and implemented using survey instruments and guidelines developed by Kelly and McTaggart (1979). It was based on defined stages of the process of social involvement and the management of social issues:

1.  awareness or recognition of an issue
2.  analysis and planning
3.  response in terms of policy development
4.  implementation

Classroom discussion of Daniel Bell's essay on the post-industrial society (1970) led to conceptualisation of a scale between the "economizing" and "sociologizing" modes of management. Some student groups found this approach helpful and evaluated the subject company's position on such a scale, both in 1976 and currently. Hay and Gray's (1974) typology of management styles was also found to be useful in analysis and evaluation. A scale was conceptualised for identifying the management styles and values classified by Hay and Gray as profit maximisation, trusteeship and quality of life. The companies' positions on this scale were evaluated in terms of various issues.

Following the publication of Wartick and Cochran's (1985) Corporate Social Performance Model, the decision was made to use this model as the framework for further analysis and evlauation. This model, first presented by Carroll (1979), is described by Wartick and Cochran as follows:

> This integrative nature of CSP is what makes it unique. Instead of arguing that economic responsibility and public policy responsibility are inconsistent with social responsibility (Buchholz, 1977; Friedman, 1962; Heyne, 1968; Preston and Post, 1975), the CSP model integrates economic responsibility and public policy responsibility into its definition of social responsibility. Instead of viewing responsibility, responsiveness and issues as separate, alternative corporate concerns (Ackerman and Bauer, 1976; Frederick, 1978; Murphy, 1978; Sethi, 1979), the CSP model reflects an underlying interaction among the principles of social responsibility, the processes of social responsiveness, and the policies developed to address social issues. The CSP model relies on this expanded version of social responsibility and this principle/process/policy approach in order to provide a distinctive view of a corporation's overall efforts toward satisfying its obligations to society.

The framework of the model is shown in Exhibit 1.

*Exhibit 1.* The Corporate Social Performance Model

| *Principles* | *Processes* | *Policies* |
|---|---|---|
| Corporate Social Responsibilities | Corporate Social Responsiveness | Social Issues Management |
| (1) Economic | (1) Reactive | (1) Issues Identification |
| (2) Legal | (2) Defensive | (2) Issue Analysis |
| (3) Ethical | (3) Accommodative | (3) Response Development |
| (4) Discretionary | (4) Proactive | (4) Implementation |
| Directed at: | Directed at: | Directed at: |
| (1) The Social Contract of Business | (1) The Capacity to Respond to Changing Social Societal Conditions | (1) Minimizing "Surprises" |
| (2) Business as a Moral Agent | (2) Managerial Approaches to Developing Responses | (2) Determining Effective Corporate Social Policies |

*Source:* Wartick and Cochran (1985), with 'Implementation' added by the author as the fourth stage of Social Issues Management.

The single most important feature of this model is that it recognizes and incorporates economic performance as the first among the principles of social responsibility, without excluding the other and necessary legal, ethical and discretionary responsibilities. Once this conceptual step, and it is a major one, has been taken, there is no need to engage in the fruitless and sterile debates which have been the result of the separation of economic from social responsibilities. "The distinction between the 'economic' and 'social' roles of a business organization is mostly a false one" (The Royal Bank, 1985). As soon as this distinction can be seen for what it is, theoretically convenient but realistically false, we can revise a well-known dictum by stating that "the business of business is business in society," and proceed about our business. If the firm cannot fulfill its economic responsibilities, clearly it cannot fulfill any social responsibilities, no matter how these are defined.

A business organization fulfills its social contract by being profitable over an extended period of time and by responding to changing values, conditions and expectations in society by implementing effective policies, both in the markets in which it is competing and in the society of which those markets are a part.

## THE FIELD STUDIES

One does not need to be unnecessarily sceptical in order to raise questions about the ability of organizations to mislead student researchers. Students themselves tend to be sceptical, however, when studying corporate social performance. The media expose assiduously most cases of misbehavior, perceived or actual, and the natural bias against business and its social performance, as shown by many polls and opinion surveys, is certainly evident in the classroom. The students are strongly urged to seek data and opinions from outside the corporation, using such sources as unions, government departments and data bases, and municipalities in company towns. Finally the completed studies themselves are presented in class and discussed, with representatives of the companies present if they choose to attend.

Reliability and replicability of evaluations is clearly a matter of concern in empirical studies. The difficulties inherent in even defining corporate social responsibility and performance have acted as a major constraint for researchers in this area. The research project under discussion provided the means by which the value and usefulness of the conceptual model developed by Carroll, Wartick and Cochran could be tested in the field.

As the project progressed and the reports were studied and discussed, it was clear that certain characteristics of corporate behavior and performance could be identified, described and evaluated, that evaluations could be made about the social orientation of particular organizations, and that these evaluations could be objectively examined and questioned.

These characteristics of corporate behavior and performance have now been organized to conform with the components and classifications of the CSP model, Exhibit 1: Principles, Processes, Policies. The field studies provide relevant data on these characteristics which can then be evaluated.

# THE PRINCIPLES OF CORPORATE SOCIAL RESPONSIBILITIES

## Economic Responsibilities

"Economic responsibilities of business reflect the belief that business has an obligation to be productive and profitable and to meet the consumer needs of society" (Carroll, 1979).

In fulfilling its economic responsibilities, a corporation must be evaluated primarily by comparison with its own industry. A bank's economic performance cannot reasonably be compared with that of an integrated energy company or a manufacturer of chemicals. The criteria of economic performance should be those appropriate to that industry. Thus the researcher avoids the trap of so many studies examining CSR and profitability. The shortcomings of all these approaches were demonstrated by Aupperle, Carroll, Hatfield (1985) and need no further elaboration here, except to point out that their own use of adjusted Return on Assets (ROA) provided little additional illumination on this hitherto dark subject. Economic performance must be evaluated on a disaggregated, industry-specific basis, over a reasonably long period of time. When we are dealing with the creation of wealth, profitability, return on assets, return on shareholder's equity, financial soundness or long-term investment value, the results of last year or the last quarter provide an inadequate basis for evaluation.

In our studies a company's economic performance, within its industry's competitive context during the last five years, was measured and then classified as: loss, below average, average, or above average.

## Legal Responsibilities

"Legal responsibilities of business indicate a concern that economic responsibilities are approached within the confines of written law" (Carroll, 1979).

The students search appropriate information data bases for evidence of past legal actions concerning alleged kickbacks, wrongful dismissals, unfair labor practices, discrimination, environmental pollution and so on, which may reveal a pattern of legal problems sufficient to justify comment and evaluation in the report. Checks are also made with appropriate government departments to determine whether there have been serious problems or complaints in terms of laws concerning the environment, safety, health, labor, consumer protection, etc.

### Ethical Responsibilities

"Ethical responsibilities of business reflect unwritten codes, norms, and values implicitly derived from society; ethical responsibilities go beyond mere legal frameworks and can be both strenuously undertaken and nebulously and ambiguously ignored" (Carroll, 1979).

Student searches of information data bases usually reveal major problems that could be considered ethical in nature. These may involve, besides those described above under legal responsibilities, such additional matters as sudden large lay-offs; plant, mine or head office closings without adequate preparation or notice; false advertising; inadequate disclosure, etc.

### Discretionary Responsibilities

"Discretionary responsibilities of business are volitional or philanthropic in nature, and, as such, also difficult to ascertain and evaluate" (Carroll, 1979).

The data in the reports relate to the record of the company in terms of donations and of support for community activities. The focus of this element of the research is the question: What is the corporation putting back into the communities from which it is deriving its revenues and profits?

## THE PROCESSES OF CORPORATE SOCIAL RESPONSIVENESS

In evaluating corporate social responsiveness, the research is focused on finding out how an organization responds to changing values, issues and conditions in the society of which it is a part. What are the processes by means of which corporations identify social and public policy issues as distinct from market issues? What is the corporation's stance or posture with reference to social and public policy issues?

Wartick and Cochran's model identifies four categories of social responsiveness: (1) reactive, (2) defensive, (3) accommodative, and (4) proactive. The research objective in this context is to obtain sufficient relevant data to form the basis for evaluation. In order to provide guidance in this area, completed reports were analyzed in order to identify those characteristics which were examples of "best practice." Companies that were clearly high performers in terms of social performance were analyzed and the characteristics which follow were derived from those studies.

1. Clear, explicit, widely-circulated statements of mission, strategic goals or purpose, which include references to social and ethical, as well as to economic or competitive, goals.

2. The existence of scanning systems which extend beyond the core economic and market activities of the company to social and political trends and issues.

3. The integration of the output of such extended scanning systems with the processes of corporate strategic planning and goal setting.

4. Linkages between statements of mission, strategic goals or purpose and the processes of policy formulation, operational planning, budgeting, performance appraisal and compensation/reward systems.

5. Meaningful involvement in public policy issues.

In order to evaluate a corporation's processes of social responsiveness as proactive, the students search for evidence of these characteristics. When there is little or no evidence of their presence, an evaluation will be made that the responsiveness processes of the company in question are at best accommodative or else defensive or reactive.

## THE MANAGEMENT OF SPECIFIC SOCIAL ISSUES

In all cases the research objective is to find out how the subject company has actually responded to social and public policy issues, how current policies in these areas are developed and implemented, and how the company analyzes and develops responses to new issues. Questionnaires are developed for each company and hard data are sought. Researchers know that there can be a gap between words and action, between policy development and actual implementation, between what Argyris has called "espoused theory" and "theory in action."

Four principal areas are selected for detailed analysis:

1. *Human Resource Issues.* Communication with employees, training and development, career-planning, retirement and termination counselling, lay-offs, redundancies and plant closing, stress and mental health, absenteeism and turnover, health and safety, employment equity and discrimination, women in management, performance appraisal, day care, etc. Are these issues being actively managed? Are relevant data on these issues available and used?

2. *Environmental Issues.* Responses to legal requirements; evidence that compliance is managed and that, for example, incidents of spills, emissions,

and pollution infractions are promptly reported to the appropriate authorities; reponses to issues relating to the internal environment, such as noise, smoking, VDTs etc. Are relevant environmental assessments an integral part of the system for capital expenditure proposals and budgeting? Are policies related to energy conservation in effect where relevant?

   3.   *Community Relations.*   Have enternal stakeholder and interest groups been identified? Are contributions policies defined and managed? Is employee involvement in community activities encouraged?

   4.   *Ethics.*   Is there evidence of an enviroment or culture in which the ethical values of the corporation are clear or explicit, whether or not in the form of a code? Is there careful consideration of the effects of actions taken, contemplated or planned on all important stakeholders?

## EVALUATING CORPORATE SOCIAL PERFORMANCE

Each case study evaluated the performance of the subject company based on the data obtained and on analysis using current methodologies. As the studies completed by each class were analyzed, additional learning took place the following year. The characteristics of high performing companies were identified in terms of the processes of Corporate Social Responsiveness for use by the student researchers in their projects. The identification of current social and public policy issues was also derived from analyzing the studies. Key questions were developed and difficulties and problem areas were identified in order to assist students in distinguishing between "what they say" and "what they do," between stated values and policies and actual behavior. In some organizations, it was not easy to get access to those who could or would provide hard answers to hard questions. In others, access to several levels of the organization was facilitated, and in one case the student researchers were allowed to send-out their own confidential questionnaire to employees, using company facilities.

   One major difficulty, as this project grew in scope, was to provide access to the ever larger body of data represented by the field studies. After reproducing for three years key extracts from the studies in order to serve as a "case book," and making all the studies available in the library, it became clear that another approach was needed. Consequently, in order to be prepared for the course in the fall term of 1987, an index to 32 of the studies was prepared. Exhibit 2 shows the outline of this index, which reflects the CSP model in Exhibit 1. (Not all studies covered every outlined point, of course.) All 32 original studies were then made accessible through data storage in the school's computer system, which is available to all students. Floppy discs were also made available, at cost, for those students who preferred to use their own personal computers. The discs are available for most word-processing

*Exhibit 2.*   Index for CSP Studies in Computer Database

| | | | |
|---|---|---|---|
| 1 | **Company Name** | 23 | Health & Safety Policy |
| 2 | Year of Study | 24 | Stress & Mental Health |
| 3 | Contents or Index | 25 | Employment Equity, Discrimination |
| 4 | Introduction | 26 | Women in Management |
| 5 | Recommendations | 27 | Performance Appraisal |
| 6 | **Social Responsibilities** | 28 | Daycare |
| 7 | Economic Performance | 29 | Other HR Issues |
| 8 | Legal Responsibilities | 30 | *Environmental Issues* |
| 9 | Ethical Responsibilities | 31 | External Environment Policies |
| 10 | Discretionary Responsibilities | 32 | Energy Conservation |
| 11 | **Social Responsiveness** | 33 | Internal Environment Policies |
| 12 | Mission Statement | 34 | *Community Relations* |
| 13 | Scanning Systems | 35 | Donations Record |
| 14 | Internal Linkages | 36 | Contributions Policy |
| 15 | Public Policy Involvement | 37 | Employee Involvement |
| 16 | **Management of Social Issues** | 38 | Community Relations |
| 17 | *Human Resource Issues* | 39 | *Ethics* |
| 18 | Training & Development | 40 | Codes of Conduct/Ethics |
| 19 | Career Planning | 41 | *Customer Relations* |
| 20 | Retirement & Termination Counseling | 42 | *Other Items* |
| 21 | Layoff & Redundancy Policy | 43 | *Other Items* |
| 22 | Employee Communication | | |

*Exhibit 3.*   Case Studies in C.S.P. Database

| | |
|---|---|
| Abitibi Price (R) | Manufacturers Life Insurance |
| Bank of Montreal | McDonald's Canada |
| Bell Canada | Molson (R) |
| Canada Trust | Moore Business Forms |
| Canada Wire and Cable | Noranda |
| Canadian National (R) | Northern Telecom |
| Carling O'Keefe | Ontario Hydro |
| CIL | Petrocan |
| Esso Petroleum | Royal Bank (R) |
| Gulf Canada | Shoppers Drug Mart |
| Hudson's Bay Co. (R) | Stelco |
| IBM Canada (R) | Suncor |
| Inco (R) | Toronto Dominion Bank |
| Labatt (R) | Wardair |
| Maclean Hunter | Westinghouse Canada |
| Magna International | Xerox Canada (R) |

packages, such as Wordperfect, Multimate, Wordstar, MacWrite, Microsoft Works, etc. for use with either Macintosh or IBM type systems. Hard copy printouts of each report are also available in the library. Data accessibility has been achieved.

Exhibit 3 identifies the 32 companies in the computerized data base. Three studies were omitted because the companies had requested confidentiality. Two were omitted for reasons of quality. Eleven new studies will be added to the data base in early 1988. Ten studies of government departments, agencies, and nonprofit organizations were also excluded. Exhibit 3 also identifies with (R) nine companies originally studied in 1975/76 for RCCC.

Another problem was presented as a result of the changing methodologies that the students had been using as the project progressed from year to year. In the case studies of 1975/76, mostly self-studies, the use of "methodology" is clearly inappropriate. It was necessary, therefore, to construct a revised and uniform system of evaluation, which could be applied to all existing case studies, using data and the preliminary evaluations of the student researchers as guidance for the senior researchers. The system of evaluation which has been developed is based on the Wartick and Cochran model shown in Exhibit 1, and makes use of the evaluation ystem that is an implicit part of this model. The system is explained in the balance of this section. The output of this approach is shown in Exhibit 4. The companies selected for display are the nine companies studied in 1975/76 for RCCC. In order to avoid presenting an excess of data in Exhibit 4, the evaluations of the 1975/76 data are not shown, but comments on the comparisons with the earlier data follow in a later section.

*Types of Responsibilities*

The first and most important social responsibility is *economic performance* (line 3), which is also, of course, the easiest to measure, for individual companies and their industry group. The evaluation scale is:

1. loss or negative results;
2. below average for the industry group;
3. average for the industry group;
4. above average for the industry group.

*Legal* and *ethical* responsibilities (line 28) are evaluated in terms only of significant legal or ethical problems in the recent history of the corporation. If no problems have been identified, there is no entry. An 'X' indicates that the reader must refer to the relevant study in order to determine its nature. Codes of Conduct/Ethics are evaluated on line 29. This evaluation is based on the values explained below in the section on Evaluating the Management of Social Issues. *Discretionary* responsibilities are evaluated under the heading of 'Community Relations' which includes data about donations records, contribution policies, and policies about employee involvement and community relations (lines 23-26).

## Evaluating Social Responsiveness

The evaluations in this section (lines 5-8) are based on the data about the presence or absence of the characteristics identified and defined in the section above on social responsiveness. Conforming with the model in Exhibit 1, an evaluation is made whether the subject corporation's processes are:

1. reactive;
2. defensive;
3. accommodative;
4. proactive.

If there is no evidence of the existence of the characteristics of Social Responsiveness, this absence is indicated by '0'; 'N' signifies that there were no data in the report.

## Evaluating Management of Social Issues

The evaluations in this section (lines 10-26) are based on the stage of development of responses to a wide range of current social issues. The stages are defined again to conform with the model in Exhibit 1:

1. issue awareness and identification;
2. issue analysis;
3. response and policy development;
4. implementation.

An entry of (4) indicates that the stage of implementation has been reached,but does not necessarily imply that the quality of implementation is similar to that of other companies. If the issue has not been identified, or there is no evidence of awareness, the evaluation cell will show "0"; 'N' signifies that there were no data in the report to indicate that this issue had been explored by the researchers.

It should be noted here that it is important to recognize that the value '4' in this section connotes 'implementation of policy,' whereas the value '4' in terms of Social Responsiveness connotes 'Proactive.' The value '4' under economic performance connotes 'above average' performance when compared with the industry group.

*Exhibit 4.*  Evaluations of Corporate Social Performance

| | Name | Abitibi | CN | Hudson Bay | Inco | IBM | Labatt | Molson | Royal Bank | Xerox |
|---|---|---|---|---|---|---|---|---|---|---|
| 1 | Name | | | | | | | | | |
| 2 | Year of Study | 83 | 84 | 83 | 85 | 85 | 83 | 84 | 84 | 83 |
| 3 | Economic Performance | 3 | 2 | 1 | 1 | 4 | 4 | 3 | 3 | 4 |
| 4 | **Social Responsiveness** | | | | | | | | | |
| 5 | Mission Statement | 4 | 0 | 0 | 4 | 4 | 4 | 4 | 4 | 4 |
| 6 | Scanning Systems | 1 | 1 | 1 | 3 | 4 | 4 | 4 | 4 | 4 |
| 7 | Internal Linkages | 2 | 1 | 1 | 0 | 4 | 4 | 4 | 4 | 4 |
| 8 | Public Policy Involvement | 4 | 1 | 1 | 4 | 4 | 4 | 4 | 4 | 4 |
| 9 | **Mgm't Social Issues** | | | | | | | | | |
| 10 | *Human Resource Issues* | | | | | | | | | |
| 11 | Traning & Development | 4 | 4 | 4 | 4 | 4 | 4 | 4 | 4 | 4 |
| 12 | Career Planning | 4 | N | N | 3 | 4 | 4 | 4 | 4 | 4 |
| 13 | Ret. & Termination Couns. | N | N | N | 4 | 4 | 4 | N | N | N |
| 14 | Employee Communication | 3 | 1 | N | 4 | 4 | 4 | N | N | N |
| 15 | Health & Safety Policies | 4 | 4 | 4 | 4 | 4 | 4 | 4 | N | 4 |
| 16 | Stress & Mental Health | N | 0 | 0 | 4 | 4 | 4 | 4 | N | N |
| 17 | Employ Equity/Discrim. | 2 | 2/3 | 4 | 4 | 4 | 2 | 3 | 4 | 4 |
| 18 | Women in Management | 1 | 1 | 3 | 1 | 4 | 2 | 1 | 4 | 4 |
| 19 | *Environmental Issues* | | | | | | | | | |
| 20 | External Env. Policies | 4 | 4 | 4 | 4 | 4 | 4 | 4 | N | 4 |

| | | | | | | | | | |
|---|---|---|---|---|---|---|---|---|---|
| 21 | Energy Conservation | 4 | 4 | N- | 4 | 4 | 4 | 4 | N | N |
| 22 | *Community Relations* | | | | | | | | | |
| 23 | Donations Record | 4 | 4 | 4 | 4 | 4 | 4 | 4 | 4 | 4 |
| 24 | Contributions Policy | 2 | 4 | 4 | 4 | 4 | 4 | 4 | 4 | 4 |
| 25 | Employee Involvement | 4 | 4 | 4 | 4 | 4 | 4 | 4 | 4 | 4 |
| 26 | Community Relations | 4 | 4 | 4 | 4 | 4 | 4 | 4 | 4 | 4 |
| 27 | *Ethics* | | | | | | | | | |
| 28 | Legal/Ethical Problems | X | | | | | | | | |
| 29 | Code of Conduct/Ethics | 0 | 0 | 0 | 0 | 4 | N | 4 | 4 | 4 |
| 30 | | | | | | | | | | |
| 31 | | | | | | | | | | |
| 32 | **Summary** | | | | | | | | | |
| 33 | Economic Performance | 3 | 2 | 1 | 1 | 4 | 4 | 3 | 3 | 4 |
| 34 | Economic Orientation | 4 | 3 | 4 | 4 | 4 | 4 | 4 | 4 | 4 |
| 35 | Social Orientation | 3 | 3 | 3 | 3 | 4 | 4 | 4 | 4 | 4 |
| 36 | Visibility | 2 | 4 | 4 | 3 | 4 | 4 | 4 | 4 | 4 |
| 37 | | | | | | | | | | |
| 38 | Ownership | C | G | C | F (60%) | F (100%) | C | C | C | F(79%) |
| 39 | Sales/Revenue-$B | 2.8 | 5.0 | 5.7 | 2.0 | 2.9 | 3.17 | 1.7 | 9.8 | 0.865 |
| 40 | Assets-$B | 2.2 | 8.1 | 4.3 | 4.1 | 1.9 | 1.8 | 1.1 | 100 | 1.3 |
| 41 | Employees-M | 16.2 | 61 | 41 | 20 | 12 | 15.5 | 11 | 38 | 4.2 |

*Summary*

The Summary section (lines 33-41) in Exhibit 4 has several components. The objective of this section is to fulfill two principal functions: first, to provide values that summarize both economic and social performance data, and, secondly, to display data about size and ownership.

Economic Performance (line 33) simply repeats the entry shown in line 3. Economic Orientation (line 34) represents an evaluation of the "orientation" of the organization towards economic performance, as this concept was developed by Aupperle (1984), based on the original Carroll construct (1979). The distinction between economic and social orientations provided the conceptual framework for the integration of economic performance into the definitional model of social responsibilities, along with legal, ethical and discretionary responsibilities. Inherent in this construct were different weightings, or values, for each of these components. Aupperle's empirical test of the construct supported its validity and also determined that "there are four empirically interrelated, but conceptually independent, components of CSR." He further concluded that while corporations

clearly placed more emphasis on the economic component, the noneconomic components taken together are of much greater weight than the economic component alone . . . . In addition, there are strong negative correlations between the economic and each of the three noneconomic components which suggests that the more economically motivated a firm is, the less emphasis it places on ethical, legal and discretionary issues.

Since the data in the case studies supported Aupperle's findings, it was clear that the evaluation of economic and social orientation was a worthwhile objective. The following proposition, based on completed studies, was developed: There is, in the high performing company, a balance between its economic orientation and its social orientation; the presence of this balance does not inhibit emphasis on economic performance, but this emphasis is not at the expense of its social performance; when this balance is not present, economic performance, as Aupperle wrote, will be at the expense of social performance.

It should be noted here that in nonprofit and governmental organizations, economic responsibilities will not be considered as the most important. Legal responsibilities will usually be the focus of attention, with economic performance being evaluated on a basis appropriate to the organization, that is in terms of the effectiveness with which funds provided are administered and spent. The point is that the Wartick and Cochran model is applicable to organizations other than profit-oriented corporations. For this latter group, their economic orientation will normally be very important.

It seems wise to avoid the trap of over-precision in these matters, although it is clearly possible, given the body of data available in this project, to discriminate between 'average' and 'above-average' economic performance, between 'reactive' and 'proactive' processes, between 'important' and 'very important' orientations. Economic orientation (line 34) therefore has been evaluated on the following scale:

1. absent
2. not important
3. important
4. very important

With one exception, all of the market-oriented corporations in the sample to date have been evaluated as having a 'very important' orientation (4) towards economic performance. This evaluation does not apply, however, to all the government and nonprofit organizations which have also been studied, including CN (the exception referred to above), owned 100% by the government of Canada, whose economic orientation is evaluated as 'important' (3), but not 'very important' (4).

In evaluating the social orientation of a company, it is helpful to recall Frederick's description of social responsiveness, as quoted by Carroll (1979, p. 501).

> Corporate social responsiveness refers to the capacity of a corporation to respond to social pressures. The literal act of responding, or of achieving a generally responsive posture, to society is the focus. . . . One searches the organization for mechanisms, procedures, arrangements and behavioral patterns that, taken collectively, would mark the organization as more or less capable of responding to social pressures.

Principal objectives of the studies in this project have been to identify and describe (1) these "mechanisms (and) procedures," the characteristics of which were described above as the Processes of Social Responsiveness, and (2) the "arrangements and behavioral patterns" described above as the Management of Social Issues. Since the awareness and identification of social issues requiring managerial attention are an outcome of the processes of social responsiveness, the evaluation of a company's social orientation is based on the same scale as that used for social responsiveness:

1. reactive
2. defensive
3. accommodative
4. proactive

The evaluations of the company's management of social issues must also be reviewed, together with relevant data and observations in the case studies, in order to arrive at an objective assessment of the company's philosophy, posture, or orientation. This managerial approach can also be expressed in the terms used by McAdam (1973) and quoted by Carroll (1979, p.502):

1. Fight all the way (reactive)
2. Do only what is required (defensive)
3. Be progressive (accommodative)
4. Lead the industry (proactive)

Visibility is another concept explored by Aupperle (1984) in order to determine whether high visibility firms were more or less concerned about CSP. Visibility is evaluated (line 36) using the following scale of values:

1. very low
2. low
3. average
4. high

This evaluation is somewhat impressionistic since data on advertising expenditures and media coverages, as used by Aupperle, were not available. The market orientation of the firm was used as a surrogate, using 'industrial orientation' and 'consumer orientation' as opposite ends of the scale. Clearly companies like Abitibi and Inco have high visibility in company towns, but, given their orientation towards industrial markets, their overall visibility is 'low' (2) and 'average' (3), respectively.

Ownership or control of a controlling block of voting shares (line 38) is identified as Canadian (C), Government (G) or Foreign (F). This information is included in order to explore, as the number of studies increases, whether there are any correlations betwen ownership and social performance.

The last three lines of the Summary section contain data about sales, assets, and number of employees (lines 39-41).

## ANALYSIS OF THE DATA

*Social Orientation and Economic Performance*

The three firms in Exhibit 4 with profit levels above average for their respective groups are evaluated as having Social Orientation of level 4-proactive. The five companies with proactive Social Orientation are shown to have profits of at least average levels. These results are consistent with the observation of RCCC Study 21 that superior profits and social responsiveness tend to be associated. Further confirmation is found by examining the data for the 32 companies in the computerized data base, 17 of which show social orientation as proactive and have above average economic performance. Exhibit 5 summarizes the results.

No company whose social orientation was evaluated as proactive (4) had economic performance below average or at a loss. No company in the sample showed economic performance above average unless its social orientation was evaluated as proactive.

*Exhibit 5.*   Social Orientation and Economic Performance

| | Economic Performance | | |
| Social Orientation | Above Average (4) | Average (3) | Below Average (2) or Loss (1) |
| --- | --- | --- | --- |
| Proactive (4) | 17 | 6 | — |
| Accommodative (3) | — | 1 | 8 |

*Comparisons between 1976 and 1986*

Exhibit 4 shows that the Social Responsiveness of IBM, Labatt, Molson, Royal Bank and Xerox is evaluated as 'proactive' (4).

The criteria that provide the basis of these evluations were described above. The essence of these criteria is the integration by the company of data about values, social and public policy trends and issues, derived from the external environment, with strategic and operational planning, and the linkage of this planning with the day-to-day management of the company.

The data for these five companies on the Management of Social Issues in Exhibit 4 (lines 10-29) show that they were at the implementation stage (4) in most cases. Four of the five companies had widely-circulated codes of conduct or ethics (line 29). All had high visibility (line 36). These companies are very diverse. Three were Canadian-owned and two were foreign-controlled. Assets ranged from 1-100 billion, and employees from 4-38,000 (lines 38-41). Three of the five companies had above average economic performance (4), and two were average (3) (line 33). But since 1976 the social orientation of these five companies has remained proactive (4). Despite the difficult economic and turbulent social environment of the last decade, the data show a continuing proactive stance towards social responsiveness and continuing attention to the management of social issues. Policies had been developed and implementation was under way about such issues as employment equity, women in management and stress and mental health.

The social orientation of Abitibi-Price, CN, Hudson's Bay and Inco is evaluated as 'accommodative' (3) (line 35). In 1976 the evaluation of social orientation was 'defensive' (2) for Abitibi-Price, CN and Inco and accommodative (3) for Hudson's Bay. Exhibit 4 shows that the evaluation of Social Responsiveness is reactive (1) for CN and Hudson's Bay, whereas with Abitibi-Price and Inco the trend is towards a proactive (4) position (lines 5-8). This trend, or movement, towards a proactive stance is made clearer by referring to the 1976 studies, when the social responsiveness of these two firms was evaluated as defensive (2) or reactive (1). In terms of Social Responsivenes both Abitibi-Price and Inco have made significant progress since 1976.

None of the four companies had widely circulated codes of conduct or ethics, so that the evaluation of Codes of Conduct or Ethics (line 29) is zero for all but Abitibi-Price, which was at the policy development (3) stage. In 1986 CN published a code of conduct covering Conflicts of Interest. CN has encountered serious legal and ethical problems concerning discrimination against women, a situation not without irony for a crown corporation, controlled 100% by the Federal government since its founding over 60 years ago. Hudson's Bay has encountered severe losses and major reorganisation since the study in 1983.

Since 1976 more attention has been paid to the elements of social responsiveness (lines 5-8) at Abitibi-Price aend Inco. An increasing number of social and public policy issues have been identified and analyzed at all four companies, and policy development and implementation have taken place on such issues as employee communication, retirement and termination, health and safety, stress and mental health and employment equity (lines 11-29). Awareness of the issue of women in management has not yet, however, been developed into policies or implementation at these companies (line 18).

Ten years ago, in the group of companies that were studied, Labatt and Xerox were both identified as "the only two companies which appear to have consciously attempted to weave social concerns into their long-term, strategic planning cycle." These two companies provided:

the most evidence of what has been described as 'institutionalisation.' In other words, there has been a conscious and careful attempt to ensure that social performance is built into the whole organisation, its policies and day-to-day practices, rather than restricted to the Chief Executive Officer, a small circle of senior managers, or a specific department of public affairs. . . . Both companies appear to have adopted a 'philosophy' of corporate responsibility which enjoys the approval and support of the management group as a whole, and both firms have clearly identified the key issues they feel obligated to act upon. These include employee relations, environmental protection, corporate philanthropy and community involvement (RCCC, Study 21, p.79, 1977).

These conclusions are corroborated by the data in Exhibit 4, which confirm the proactive stance of these two companies in terms of Social Responsiveness and the Management of Social Issues.

By 1986, however, the data now show that many other companies can also be described in similar terms. In 1976 the summary of Study 21 (p.87) stated that:

> we find an evolutionary process underway in Canada, particularly among large corporations. This evolution embraces a number of critical factors including the recognition of social impacts caused by the basic economic activities of the firm, the assumption by management of at least some responsibility to deal with these impacts and the development of approaches and tools which make this management task more realizable.

It is clear from the data in the research project that this evolutionary process has indeed been underway and was not wishful thinking. The data also confirm another important conclusion in study 21 (p.44) from the survey data of ten years ago that "higher levels of corporate social involvement activity among the respondent companies appear to be generally associated with above-average levels of corporate profits." It can now be stated unequivocally that this is so. 17 companies, out of a total of 32 in the sample, with proactive social orientation showed above-average profits (Exhibit 5). This may be the most important finding in the research project. Substantiation of this finding is shown by comparisons within the same industry, in the section which follows.

## Comparisons within Industry Groups

Evaluations for the three largest brewery conglomerates in Canada are shown in Exhibit 6, as well as for three of the five largest banks.

Social orientation (line 35) is evaluated as accommodative (3) for Carling O'Keefe, but not proactive (4) as it is for Labatt and Molson. Carling O'Keefe's economic performance is below average, while the other two are average or above. In terms of Social Responsivenes (lines 5-8), Carling O'Keefe is at the reactive stage (1), while Labatt and Molson are evaluated as proactive (4). In the management of social issues Carling O'Keefe is at a lower level of awareness, identification and policy development on a wide range of issues. It is a company with a strong economic orientation (line 34) and "the bottom line" is stressed at the expense of what are perceived to be extraneous social responsibilities. The company was recently taken over by Elders of Australia.

Of the five largest banks in Canada, the Bank of Montreal has had the lowest return on assets and net margin over the last five years. It ranked fourth in return on equity. The Toronto Dominion Bank has ranked first by these measures. The Royal Bank has an average ranking, slightly above the mid-point. (Exhibit 6). Social orientation (line 35) for the Toronto Dominion and

*Exhibit 6.*  Evaluations of Corporate Social Performance

|  | Name | Brewery conglomerates | | | Banks | | |
|---|---|---|---|---|---|---|---|
|  |  | Carling O'Keefe | Labatt | Molson | Bank of Montreal | Royal Bank | Toronto Dominion |
| 1 | **Name** |  |  |  |  |  |  |
| 2 | Year of Study | 84 | 83 | 84 | 86 | 84 | 84 |
| 3 | Economic Performance | 2 | 4 | 3 | 2 | 3 | 4 |
| 4 | **Social Responsiveness** |  |  |  |  |  |  |
| 5 | Mission Statement | 0 | 4 | 4 | 0 | 4 | 4 |
| 6 | Scanning Systems | 1 | 4 | 4 | 3 | 4 | 4 |
| 7 | Internal Linkages | 0 | 4 | 4 | 3 | 4 | 4 |
| 8 | Public Policy Involvement | 0 | 4 | 4 | 4 | 4 | 4 |
| 9 | **Mgm't Social Issues** |  |  |  |  |  |  |
| 10 | *Human Resource Issues* |  |  |  |  |  |  |
| 11 | Training & Development | 3 | 4 | 4 | 4 | 4 | 4 |
| 12 | Career Planning | 0 | 4 | 4 | 4 | 4 | 4 |
| 13 | Ret. & Termination Couns. | 0 | 4 | N | 0 | N | 4 |
| 14 | Employee Communication | 2 | 4 | 4 | 3 | 4 | 4 |
| 15 | Health & Safety Policies | 4 | 4 | 4 | N | N | 4 |
| 16 | Stress & Mental Health | 2 | 4 | 4 | 4 | N | 4 |
| 17 | Employee Equity/Discrim. | 0 | 2 | 3 | 3 | 4 | 4 |
| 18 | Women in Management | 0 | 2 | 1 | 4 | 4 | 4 |
| 19 | *Environmental Issues* |  |  |  |  |  |  |
| 20 | External Env. Policies | 4 | 4 | 4 | N | N | N |

| | | | | | | |
|---|---|---|---|---|---|---|
| 21 Energy Conservation | 4 | 4 | 4 | 4 | 4 | 4 |
| 22 *Community Relations* | | | | | | |
| 23 Donations Record | 4 | 4 | 4 | 4 | 4 | 4 |
| 24 Contributions Policy | 2 | 4 | 4 | 4 | 4 | 4 |
| 25 Employee Involvement | 1 | 4 | 4 | 4 | 4 | 4 |
| 26 Community Relations | 4 | 4 | 4 | 4 | 4 | 4 |
| 27 *Ethics* | | | | | | |
| 28 Legal/Ethical Problems | | | | | | |
| 29 Code of Conduct/Ethics | N | N | 4 | 3 | 4 | 4 |
| 30 | | | | | | |
| 31 | | | | | | |
| 32 **Summary** | | | | | | |
| 33 Economic Performance | 2 | 4 | 3 | 2 | 3 | 4 |
| 34 Economic Orientation | 4 | 4 | 4 | 4 | 4 | 4 |
| 35 Social Orientation | 3 | 4 | 4 | 3 | 4 | 4 |
| 36 Visibility | 4 | 4 | 4 | 4 | 4 | 4 |
| 37 | | | | | | |
| 38 Ownership | C | C | C | C | C | C |
| 39 Sales/Revenue-$B | 0.6 | 3.17 | 1.7 | 8.3 | 9.8 | 5.2 |
| 40 Assets-$B | 0.6 | 1.8 | 1.1 | 87 | 100 | 51 |
| 41 Employees-M | 4.8 | 15.5 | 11 | 33 | 38 | 20 |

Royal is proactive (4). For the Bank of Montreal it is evaluated as accommodative (3). Like other companies whose economic performance is below
average, its processes of social responsiveness are not evaluated as proactive
(4), but as accommodative (3), and in its management of social issues it is not
as far along in its progress towards implementation as the other two higher
performing banks (lines 11-29). Its "bottom-line" orientation has been more
important than its social orientation. In 1986 the Bank of Montreal published
a statement of commitment or purpose, and devoted substantial coverage in
its annual report to it. It appears that the bank is moving from an
accommodative towards a more proactive stance in terms of its social
responsiveness.

## CONCLUSIONS

The data from the studies supports the following concluding observations:

- The social performance of the 17 companies, with above average
  economic performance and a social orientation which is proactive can
  be described as 'satisfactory.'
- The social performance of the 7 companies, with average economic
  performance and a social orientation which is proactive or accommodative can also be described as 'satisfactory.'
- The social performance of the remaining 8 companies, whose economic
  performance was below average and whose social orientation was
  accommodative can be described as 'unsatisfactory.'
- Firms with 'satisfactory' social performance are, by definition, profitable
  at average or above-average levels of their industry. Firms with
  'unsatisfactory' social performance are less profitable, or below average
  for their industry.
- In the less-profitable firms, with 'unsatisfactory' social performance, the
  economic orientation of the company outweighs the social orientation.
  In these less-profitable firms there exists an imbalance between economic
  and social orientation, which is accompanied by reactive or
  accommodative (but not proactive) social responsiveness. This means
  that, to repeat the words of Study 21, there has not been a conscious
  attempt "to weave social concerns into their long-term, strategic planning
  . . . (or) to ensure that social performance is built into the whole
  organisation, its policies and day-to-day practices." There is, in these less-
  profitable companies, a lower level of awareness and analysis of social
  and public policy issues, and consequently of policy development and
  implementation. Emphasis on the bottom-line (economic orientation) at

the expense of social orientation is shown to be related to economic performance which is below-average within an industry group.

- The findings of this research study confirm Aupperle's statement that "there are strong negative correlations between the economic and each of the three noneconomic components which suggests that the more economically-motivated a firm is, the less emphasis it places on ethical, legal and discretionary issues." (Aupperle, 1984, p.49). Not only is less emphasis placed on ethical, legal and discretionary issues, but economic performance itself is below average, resulting in unsatisfactory social performance. The economic component of corporate strategy and action, in these companies, has not been integrated with social and ethical goals and issues from either strategic or operational viewpoints. Examination and analysis of past performance, of the processes of social responsiveness and the management of social issues, show clearly that the economic component is the responsibility on which these companies have placed so much emphasis that there is little evidence of concern for the ethical and discretionary components. Their orientation is economic, not social, and they have not integrated economic issues with social and ethical issues in their processes or their policies.

- The Wartick and Cochran model, based on Carroll's construct, provides a useable and relevant framework for analyzing and evaluating CSP. As a result of this approach, economic responsibility and public policy responsibility are integrated into the defintion of social responsibility. No longer is it possible to view economic responsibility as being inconsistent with, or in opposition to, social responsibility. Economic responsibility is complementary to, and also the first and most important, social responsibility, but it is not the only one. Business does not carry on its affairs in a compartment labelled "economic," separate from the society of which it is a part. Average or above-average economic performance, in an industry group over several years, is related to the integration of social, ethical and discretionary responsibilities and goals with the strategic planning of the company, which is, in turn, linked wth management performance and decision-making at the operating level. To be socially responsible is to be ethically responsible and profitable.

- Empirical case studies of social performance are time-consuming, but can be undertaken successfully by students who have received adequate classroom exposure to the theories underlying the evaluation of CSP, CSR, Social Issues Management and ethical analysis.

- Additional research is necessary in the United States and Canada to validate the initial conclusion of this project. Since the case studies provide an excellent means for 'action learning' on the part of students, the adoption by other business schools of this approach to learning about CSP would generate significant volumes of data in a relatively short period of time. Computerisation of such data with consequent accessibility does not represent a major problem.

- Refinement and reassessment of the systems of evaluation used in this project are necessary. A means by which the quality of social issues management can be evaluated is also necessary. At this stage, evaluation is basically limited to levels of awareness and implementation.

- The focus of additonal research should not be restricted only to the market-oriented, profit-making sector. The Wartick Cochran model can be applied to government departments and agencies, to non-profit organisations, and to voluntary associations. Eleven such case studies have been completed to date. Legal responsibilities replace economic responsibilities as the most important for these organisations. When the component of legal responsibility, however, is emphasized at the expense of economic, ethical and discretionary responsibilities, social performance is less than satisfactory. When legal orientation outweighs social orientation, there is a lack of concern for ethical issues and for public policy issues outside or beyond the legal mandate, the processes of social responsiveness are reactive or defensive, and the management of social issues is at a low level of awareness.

## ACKNOWLEDGEMENTS

I am indebted to my colleague A. Isenman, PhD. for his constructive advice and for teaching the course and supervising the case studies in 1985.

This project would not have been possible without the willing, and often enthusiastic, co-operation, diligence and skills of so many students who have written the case studies. Lloyd Smith, B.Com. PhD. provided invaluable assistance in developing the index to the case studies, in evaluating independently all numerical values, and in conceptualising the computerised data base. Ray Lum, B.Com. assumed total responsibility for the organisation, input and verification of all data to the data base and delivered on budget and on time.

## REFERENCES

Aupperle, K.E. "An Empirical Measure of Corporate Social Orientation." *Research in Corporate Social Performance and Policy,* Vol. 6. 1984: 27-54. JAI Press.

Aupperle, K.E., Carroll, A.B., Hatfield, J.D. "An Empirical Examination of the Relationship between Corporate Social Responsibility and Profitability." *Academy of Management Journal* 28 (2) (1985):446-463.

Bell, D. "The corporation and society in the 1970s." *The Public Interest* (Fall 1970):5-32.

Carroll, A.B. "A Three-Dimensional Conceptual Model of Corporate Performance," *Academy of Management Review* (4) (1970):497-505.

Hay, R., Gray, E. "Social Responsibilities of Business Managers," *Academy of Management Journal* (March 1974).

Kelly, D., McTaggart, T., *Research in Corporate Social Performance and Policy,* Vol.1, 1979. JAI Press.

McAdam, T.W., "How to put corporate responsibility into practice." *Business and Society Review/ Innovation* 6 (1973):8-16.

The Royal Bank of Canada, "Banking . . . and More." 1985.

The Royal Commission on Corporate Concentration, *Report,* 1978. *Corporate Social Performance in Canada, Study No.21,* 1977. Ministry of Supply and Services, Ottawa.

Wartick, S.L., Cochran, P.L. "The Evolution of the Corporate Social Performance Model," *Academy of Management Review* (4) (1985):758-769.